William Gaddis, "The Last of Something"

William Gaddis, "The Last of Something"

Critical Essays

edited by Crystal Alberts,
Christopher Leise *and*
Birger Vanwesenbeeck

McFarland & Company, Inc., Publishers
Jefferson, North Carolina, and London

Excerpts from *Agapē Agape* by William Gaddis, copyright 2002 by the Estate of William Gaddis. Used by permission of Viking Penguin, a division of Penguin Group (USA) Inc.

Excerpts from *Carpenter's Gothic* by William Gaddis, copyright 1985 by William Gaddis. Used by permission of Viking Penguin, a division of Penguin Group (USA) Inc.

Excerpts reprinted with the permission of Simon & Schuster, Inc. from *A Frolic of His Own* by William Gaddis. Copyright 1994 by William Gaddis. All rights reserved.

The Recognitions copyright 1952, 1955 by William Gaddis. Copyright renewed 1983 by William Gaddis. *J R* copyright 1971, 1974, 1975 by William Gaddis. Both titles reprinted by permission of The Wylie Agency LLC.

Excerpts from *The Rush for Second Place: Essays and Occasional Writings* by William Gaddis, edited by Joseph Tabbi, copyright 2002 by the Estate of William Gaddis. Used by permission of Penguin, a division of Penguin Group (USA) Inc.

LIBRARY OF CONGRESS CATALOGUING-IN-PUBLICATION DATA

William Gaddis, "the last of something" : critical essays / edited by Crystal Alberts, Christopher Leise and Birger Vanwesenbeeck.
   p.   cm.
Includes bibliographical references and index.

ISBN 978-0-7864-4309-3
softcover : 50# alkaline paper

1. Gaddis, William, 1922–1998 — Criticism and interpretation.
2. Literature and society — United States — History — 20th century.   I. Alberts, Crystal.   II. Leise, Christopher, 1978–
III. Vanwesenbeeck, Birger.
PS3557.A28Z95   2010
813'.54 — dc22   2009034520

British Library cataloguing data are available

©2010 Crystal Alberts, Christopher Leise and Birger Vanwesenbeeck. All rights reserved

No part of this book may be reproduced or transmitted in any form or by any means, electronic or mechanical, including photocopying or recording, or by any information storage and retrieval system, without permission in writing from the publisher.

Cover image: ©2010 Shutterstock

Manufactured in the United States of America

McFarland & Company, Inc., Publishers
  Box 611, Jefferson, North Carolina 28640
    www.mcfarlandpub.com

Acknowledgments

We would like to give special thanks to the William Gaddis Estate, Washington University Libraries, and the University of Texas at Austin's Harry Ransom Center for granting us permission to use various previously unpublished materials. We would like to acknowledge the support of the Department of English and the dean of the College of Arts and Sciences at the University of Buffalo for funding "William Gaddis: Fifty Years *The Recognitions*," SUNY Fredonia English Department's Mary Louise White Fund, as well as the University of North Dakota for its assistance in bringing this collection to fruition. Finally, we would like to express our gratitude to Brock Berglund, Rebekah Billings, Meghan Brown, Erin Carr, Alex Cavanaugh, Laura Cory, Douglass Haugan, Debrah Iverson, and Jennifer Steele for their editorial assistance.

Contents

Acknowledgments	v
Introduction	1
1. Mapping William Gaddis: The Man, *The Recognitions*, and His Time (CRYSTAL ALBERTS)	9
2. The Kvetch, the Rant, and the Bitch (WILLIAM H. GASS)	27
3. The Power of Babel: Art, Entropy, and Aporia in the Novels (CHRISTOPHER LEISE)	35
4. Trying to Make Negative Things Do the Work of Positive Ones: Gaddis and Apophaticism (CHRISTOPHER J. KNIGHT)	51
5. Failing Criticism: *The Recognitions* (JOSEPH CONWAY)	69
6. *Agapē Agape*: The Last Christian Novel(s) (BIRGER VANWESENBEECK)	86
7. "A disciplined nostalgia": Gaddis and the Modern Art Object (LISA SIRAGANIAN)	101
8. *The Recognitions* and *Carpenter's Gothic*: Gaddis's Anti-Pauline Novels (JOHN SOUTTER)	115
9. This Little Prodigy Went to Market: The Education of J R (TIM CONLEY)	126
10. Fields Ripe for Harvest: *Carpenter's Gothic*, Africa, and Avatars of Biopolitical Control (MATHIEU DUPLAY)	143
11. After Gaddis: Data Storage and the Novel (STEPHEN J. BURN)	160
Chapter Notes	171
Bibliography	193
About the Contributors	199
Index	201

Introduction

The unsettling global economic situation that began in the United States in 2008 led to some events that would be more believable as fiction. Under house arrest in his $7 million New York apartment for allegedly masterminding a $50 billion Ponzi scheme, Bernard Madoff mailed millions of dollars' worth of assets to friends and family. Meanwhile, seventy-five-year-old hedge-fund operator Arthur G. Nadel fled Florida with an estimated $350 million, destination unknown. Not to be out done, Marcus Schrenker, a financial manager from Indiana, faked a suicide by crashing his private plane only to be captured at a Florida campground. Apparently, we have not learned from our past. After the Icarusian fall of Enron in 2001, a team of documentarians sifted through the wax-molten remains of the brief but mighty energy empire, trying to understand — and, seemingly a more difficult task, explain — exactly how the entire financial world had been duped into helping a very few rich men extract real wealth for real people from an intricately complex fiction, and how then real people of very little wealth were left paying the price. Some were left without their jobs and their pensions, as well as without "savings" that were tied up in Enron stock and, therefore, rendered worthless. Others were left to pay staggering electricity bills, the product of counterfeited shortages of supply and thus an inflated perceived demand. In the course of their investigation, the filmmakers managed to uncover the phone conversations between some of the company's ground-level traders, men who knew they were needlessly taxing the poor and the elderly — victims that were reified in the form of the helpless "Grandma Millie [...] the one who couldn't figure out how to fuckin' vote on the butterfly ballot" — needing electricity to live, but powerless to control the skyrocketing prices that the suppliers, in the words of traders/traitors in question, "jammed right up her ass."[1]

For these traders, if there was any kind of ethical crisis, it was quickly put aside in the whirlwind of profiteering. To quote one of them: "It's kinda hard to say we shouldn't do this even though it's allowed because, you know, I mean, that's what we do."[2] Tellingly, the syntax and message of that statement echoes the choral motif of the character J R Vansant in William Gaddis's 1975 breakthrough novel *J R*, a 12-year-old self-made and equally ruthless entrepreneur who learns early on (in an executive's toilet) that "that's just what you do." The practice of carrying out actions "because that's what you do," or, as

Stanley Fish might put it, of "doing what comes naturally," may seem a rather unexpected link between the acts of a puberal (hence amoral) fictional Long Island schoolboy, and those of a group of opportunistic adults bent on swift company promotion, but it illustrates very well one particular characteristic of capitalism that Gaddis's fiction was perhaps the first to recognize: its fundamentally infantile character. Not only has the story of the teenaged trader J R Vansant in the meantime begotten at least one real-life adolescent equivalent,[3] but the story of Enron, as displayed in the documentary *Enron: The Smartest Guys in the Room* (2005), also aptly indicates that for those involved the process of trading and buying comes perhaps closest to being a quick-paced and endlessly flashing video game where one is merely applying the rules prescribed in the game's user's manual. It is that game, and its rules, that Gaddis, throughout his literary career, tirelessly analyzed, satirized, and mimicked up to the point that the novel *J R* (1975), with its sudden chapter breaks and babbling protagonists, comes in fact closest to being a video game itself, one where successful readerly navigation largely depends, as in *Super Mario Bros.* or *Halo 3*, on multiple extended sittings.

With the benefit of retrospect, and the now-complete oeuvre of a writer whose true mastery is yet to be fully comprehended, it is indeed easy to divine the remarkably contemporary quality of Gaddis's fiction: one need merely look around. His is the language of high-school classrooms and executive boardrooms (and bathrooms); his is the world of art critics disputing the provenance of a possible Pollock, purchased for five bucks in the back of a junk-shop; his preachers and politicians are our preachers and politicians, polarizing everyone and politicizing everything and working for no one's interest but their own; his suggested dust jacket for *Carpenter's Gothic* (1985), a novel concerned with evangelism and mineral rights in Africa, depicted an airplane crashing into the New York skyline and strikes a little too close to home post–September 11. Even the whimsical fiction of a man suing himself for a self-inflicted car accident in *A Frolic of His Own* (1994) now reads less as a hyperbolic dystopia than as an only slightly exaggerated picture of the legalomaniac society of twenty-first-century America.

The prophetic qualities of Gaddis's fiction, like those of his friend and admirer Don DeLillo, have long constituted one of the main interests of Gaddis criticism, from John Johnston's early categorization of *The Recognitions* (1955) as a precursor to the postmodern fictions of the 1960s and '70s (a claim now tacitly admitted by most scholars) to Joseph Tabbi and Rone Shavers' most recent essay collection on Gaddis and globalism. This collection of essays continues to draw out some of these pioneering, forward-looking qualities of Gaddis's fiction, yet it also wishes to *look back*: back into the traditions out of which Gaddis's novels emerged—into the history of art, into philosophy and Christianity, and (perhaps most importantly) into the history of literature. Gaddis, after all, in addition to being a masterful and perhaps unparalleled stylistic innovator, also thought of himself "as the rear guard, as the last of something,"[4] and as a writer whose "influences are more likely to be found going from Eliot back rather than forward to [his] contemporaries."[5]

While making use of the rigorous criticism before us — to whom, if even in departure, all the contributors herein owe a great debt — the present collection therefore looks to update the body of thought on Gaddis's fiction by emphasizing its traditional and innovative aspects. The various, sometimes competing perspectives that thus emerge are at the very foundation of Gaddis's writing. For, as Gaddis noted in his manuscripts for *The Recognitions*, "The instant a thing happens it has happened, and when it has happened it has happened in a thousand ways none of which alone is true though Flaubert could make it seem so."[6] Although numbering far less than a thousand, the contributors to this volume return time and again to this notion of opposition. This dialectical interplay between the contradictory facts, feelings, and opinions that appear within Gaddis's texts reflect the breadth and depth of the tensions that, like the bridges that the forger Wyatt Gwyon designs in *The Recognitions*, mark the beauty and complexity of the intellectual tradition of the West: a tradition, like a bridge, that binds us together and yet also marks our separation. Indeed, it is precisely the hybrid nature of the bridge, a restless being pulled in two directions at the same time, which accounts for the discomfort that Gaddis's name still evokes in many literary and academic circles. This is also how *The Recognitions* describes the structure of the bridge — or better, the arch. Looking over a recently finished bridge design, Wyatt muses over "that sense of movement in stillness, that ... tension at rest and still ... do you know that Arab saying, 'the arch never sleeps'?"[7] The proverb in question, as Steven Moore has indicated,[8] refers to the Hindus' preference for straight lines over the arch structures of Arab architecture because with the latter "there is pressure in two directions, downwards and upwards."[9] In adopting the arch as a metaphor for literary criticism — as we intend it here — we hope to do justice to the hybrid and restless nature of Gaddis's fiction, at once one of the most innovative corpora of twentieth-century literature and one of its most traditionally integrated ones. Rather than privileging tradition over innovation or vice versa, this collection therefore seeks to place the two approaches next to each other in order to emphasize the "arch-writing" (to reappropriate a well-known term from Derrida) that is a hallmark of Gaddis's fiction as a whole.

Crystal Alberts begins this willfully deviant journey into the landscape of Gaddis's fictions by literally mapping geographical references found in passports and "messy notes taken on the spot in Real Life"[10] among the William Gaddis Papers as well as those discovered within the text of *The Recognitions* to argue that geography, particularly that of Spain, plays an essential structural and metaphorical role in Gaddis's first novel in her essay "Mapping William Gaddis: The Man, *The Recognitions*, and His Time." Alberts questions the role of the (auto)biographical in *The Recognitions* based on her years of research in the William Gaddis Papers. She further illustrates the symbolic use of autobiographical materials within *The Recognitions* by revealing portions of Gaddis's travel notebooks that have been transcribed word-for-word repeatedly within the text, thereby challenging previous critical assertions that Gaddis's words "[bear] no relationship to any reality."[11]

William H. Gass, who once called his longtime friend Gaddis a "creative complainer,"[12] charts his characters' many and varied invectives into a taxonomy of complaint. Focusing primarily on *Carpenter's Gothic*, Gass dissects the writing of Gaddis thirty years after the latter claimed to have written "the last Christian novel" at a time when "the only thing that rouse[d Gaddis] these days all these god damned born-agains & evangelicals."[13] In his first critical essay on Gaddis, Gass investigates the "outrage" that inspired the author of *Carpenter's Gothic* to write his romance. Gass elaborates upon his description of Gaddis, defining the differences between "The Kvetch, the Rant, and the Bitch" in Gaddis's fiction and explaining the various motivations for each of these forms of complaint, and positions these forms within the history of rhetoric.

If Gaddis's characters are consistently frustrated, Christopher Leise argues that the prose itself frustrates in an instructive and productive manner. "The Power of Babel: Art, Entropy, and Aporia in the Novels" situates first- and second-order cybernetic theories, and therefore the discourses of science and communications theory, within Gaddis's much longer, historical view of discourse. Suggesting that Gaddis's language is playfully serious and seriously playful in its delivery of information, Leise asserts that Gaddis's texts criticize America's shortcomings, specifically its inherent desire to simplify the complex in an effort to apprehend what is inherently elusive, while constructing potential pathways (through the world of art) towards its improvement. He contends that Gaddis's fiction points to a better way by inviting readers to join the Greek parlor game of aporia, where the point is to ask questions for which there are no answers. Because there are no absolute solutions to the problems presented in and by Gaddis's work, Leise asserts that readers of Gaddis will be moved to think for themselves, rather than in cliché or vacuous idiom, and thereby be prevented from succumbing to thoughtless homogeneity.

Moving from aporia to apophaticism, Christopher J. Knight contends that Gaddis's method is one of indirection and hints that leaves the reader guessing. "Trying to Make Negative Things Do the Work of Positive Ones: Gaddis and Apophaticism" points out that poets both before and after Robert Frost don't say what they mean; rather, they speak in parables, having placed their faith not necessarily in Jesus Christ, but in literature. In light of this poetic faith, based firmly on the willful suspension of disbelief, Knight considers the ambiguous answers Gaddis gives to questions raised throughout his work, particularly in relation to music, religion, and the role of the author. Knight not only discusses Gaddis's individual talent, but he also situates Gaddis in the larger literary traditions of New Englanders (from Emerson to Eliot), as well as European authors (from Coleridge to Waugh), arguing that Gaddis esteems the values of belief/disbelief and satire in his fiction. As such, Knight asserts that Gaddis's fiction is "difficult," not because Jonathan Franzen called it that once, but because that is how all serious artists, especially those of the twentieth century, must write.

Frustrated with the previous critical views of Gaddis, Joseph Conway in "Failing Criticism: *The Recognitions*" argues that too many scholars have taken Gaddis's texts at face value, thereby disfiguring it to accommodate a single reader's linear perspective. By examining the tradition of Gaddis criticism within the immediate aesthetic tradition Gaddis encountered in the literary world, Conway points out that, like the Flemish masters that Wyatt copies in *The Recognitions*, "[t]here isn't any single perspective, like the camera eye, the one we all look at now and call it realism."[14] Conway elaborates upon this idea by embracing Gaddis's claim that, in Spain, "Everything [he has] observed has been only for its symbolical (simile) value: anything is met with [his] frame of references: exact opp[osite] Hemingway." By comparing the writing styles of Gaddis and Hemingway, Conway demonstrates that unlike Hemingway's plain prose, which presents "reality" in what Gaddis called a "single light," the seeming excesses in Gaddis's style are what really matter. In other words, the reader must go beyond the surface, follow Gaddis's nearly encyclopedic allusions, and be willing to fail creatively when found in a new critical position.

Birger Vanwesenbeeck analyzes the presence of Christianity in Gaddis's fiction. In "*Agapē Agape*: The Last Christian Novel(s)," he argues that Gaddis's well-known but hitherto unexamined self-categorization of *The Recognitions* as "the last Christian novel" is an epithet that can in fact be applied to each one of his novels, including the posthumuously published *Agapē Agape* (2002). The latter novel, so Vanwesenbeeck contends, continues Gaddis's lifelong interest in the relationship between art and community and, more specifically, his attempt to move beyond the traditional Western identification of community with communion, that is, with the sacrament of the Christian Eucharist. Vanwesenbeeck thus reads *Agapē Agape* "as an extended '*hoc est corpus meum*' by which the dying narrator offers up his narrative — in the manner of the Christian host — for it to be internalized by the reader," and argues that "with the narrator's prednisone-affected skin already eerily reduced to 'parchment' not to mention the wafer-like thinness of the novella itself, such a eucharistic reading of the text — literature as the transubstantiated body of the author — seems naturally implied." Yet Gaddis is far from endorsing this Eucharistic model (to which the titular term *agapē* refers) but instead reinscribes and supersedes it through the novella's simultaneous emphasis on artistic individuality.

In "'A disciplined nostalgia': Gaddis and the Modern Art Object," Lisa Siraganian also contemplates the collaborative nature of art. Siraganian reveals how Gaddis's theory of art and the art object's relation to the viewer or reader occupy a key position in the genealogy of modernism and cultural theory. The aesthetic history Siraganian sketches investigates authors, artists, and critics ranging from Wyndham Lewis, Marcel Duchamp, Jackson Pollock, and Arshile Gorky to, more recently, Richard Powers, Colson Whitehead, and Gaddis. According to her genealogy, twentieth-century writers were interested in the status of the art object in its particular, phenomenological relation to the beholder. Siraganian shows how Gaddis's impact can be observed theoretically (and not just stylistically) on contemporary American novelists who have altogether different cultural interests and concerns.

In "*The Recognitions* and *Carpenter's Gothic:* Gaddis's Anti-Pauline Novels," John Soutter locates Gaddis's work within the Christian tradition it inherits and contests. Arguing that Gaddis's major preoccupation is with fictions that are assumed as reality, Soutter asserts that Hans Vaihinger's *The Philosophy of 'As if': A System of the Theoretical, Practical and Religious Fictions of Mankind* (1911) is a major influence from his first novel, *The Recognitions*, and onward. Using Vaihinger's investigation of how the original teachings of a founder of a religion — in this case, one Jesus Christ — were transformed by his disciples (especially Paul) into a dogma, Soutter argues that the "as-if" function of a hypothetical fiction becomes, in Gaddis's words, "a 'that' and 'because.'" As such, he demonstrates how *The Recognitions* illustrates a modern-day secular society in which people suppress their own first-hand experience in order to conform more easily to the demands put on them by other people.

How one can learn from social and corporate pressures is central to "This Little Prodigy Went to Market: The Education of *J R*." In this essay, Tim Conley reads *J R* as a philosophical treatise in the tradition of Jean-Jacques Rousseau's *Emile* (1762). He contends that by considering *J R* in this light the novel's implicit understandings of human nature are revealed. Conley asserts that despite Gaddis's statements to the contrary, the text confirms that children are "gay and innocent and heartless." As such, Conley argues that while the text attacks hypocrisy, sloth, and stupidity, simple, cheerful greed is not one of its vices. He concludes that in a work dominated by market capitalism and games, there is one essential lesson — "play to win" — which J R has learned by heart. Yet, Conley contemplates the ambiguous stance that Gaddis takes towards J R, who, like Rousseau, was "awfully fond of" his invented child, but remained anxious that the articulated doctrine, which "promote[s] the meanest possibilities of human nature," might be "the most workable system we've produced."

Mathieu Duplay considers the corruption of religion by and through colonial impulses in the works of Gaddis, particularly in *Carpenter's Gothic*. In "Fields Ripe for Harvest: *Carpenter's Gothic*, Africa, and Avatars of Biopolitical Control," Duplay looks at Gaddis's use of the "Dark Continent" through the postcolonial lens. Demonstrating the parallels between the character Elizabeth and Africa, he claims that Gaddis draws a sharp distinction between *bios*, intelligent life as lived by "civilized" members of the *polis*, and *zōē*, or mere survival. Duplay asserts that by "othering" both Elizabeth and Africa, the acts of those in power, particularly the privileged American missionaries and businessmen of *Carpenter's Gothic*, are justified. Yet, for Duplay, Gaddis is not merely venting his "outrage" at the "god damned born-agains" and capitalists, who so often sparked his ire; rather, Gaddis problematizes the language of fiction and the fictions of language in what might be deemed a post-human world.

In the final essay, "After Gaddis: Data Storage and the Novel," Stephen J. Burn considers the role of the "encyclopedic" knowledge contained within the works of Gaddis. Burn argues that Gaddis's use of data goes beyond merely using the novel as a storage device and provides a careful critique of the role of facts and data in American life. He further asserts that Gaddis's use of this information has influenced a number of more recent American authors, including Richard Powers and David Foster Wallace. Burn also addresses Jonathan Franzen's claim that this abundance of data makes Gaddis "Mr. Difficult" by demonstrating how Franzen's own work manifests the same "encyclopedic" tendencies as Gaddis.

These essays consider Gaddis's oeuvre in various contexts, including philosophy, literature, geography, art, economics, politics, and theology. Rather than presenting the work of Gaddis in a "single light," they illustrate some of the multiple perspectives from which Gaddis may be viewed. They also demonstrate that even within a single volume there can be conflict between interpretations. Yet, this tension, what Wyatt called "movement in stillness," creates a foundation upon which scholars can build an innovative critical and artistic tradition. This collection intends to be one such base from which readers of Gaddis can develop and design their own interpretations. Most importantly, it invites the audience to keep in mind that, like the colossal night-lit monument hovering over Saint Louis, Missouri, visible from the Washington University campus, where the William Gaddis Papers are now housed, when engaging the writings of William Gaddis, "the arch never sleeps."

1

Mapping William Gaddis:
The Man, The Recognitions, *and His Time*

CRYSTAL ALBERTS

> *I think that this book will have to be on voyaging, all the myth & metaphor of that in modern times. (&so mobile, not static)*
> —William Gaddis Papers

> *Here Spain: Everything I have observed has been only for its symbolical (simile) value: anything is met with my frame of references: exact opp[osite] Hemingway. Finding the situation &c. as simile, phrasing so, noting it down here so, knowing that later I shall have the requisite actuality to fill out. Backwards. Style[....] Nothing in actuality is valid; (circumstances) exist only for their symbolic usage.*
> —William Gaddis Papers

> *The human bodies which carry the meanings die, but either the lasting monument, or the inherited and traditional artistic skills, embodied in the making of certain images, patterns, rhythms, survive to continue the process of organization.*
> —Raymond Williams, *The Long Revolution*

Those familiar with William Gaddis's first novel, *The Recognitions*, know a number of locations in Spain appear and reappear in the text.[1] However, many readers are unaware that shortly after World War II, from 1947 to 1951, William Gaddis began an extensive period of travel that took him to Mexico, Central America, Western Europe, and Northern Africa. Even fewer scholars realize that during his time abroad, Gaddis called Spain home for approximately twenty-two months.[2] Past essays on *The Recognitions* have attempted to draw connections between biographical fact and fiction. But Gaddis did not want to have his work turned "into a cartoon," or himself, "the creative artist [turned] into a performer, into a celebrity like Byron,"[3] and he held a deep suspicion against those who attempted to discover his "sources." In his 1982 *Review of Contemporary Fiction* interview, Gaddis explained, "The question of autobiographical sources in fiction has always seemed to me one of the more tiresome going, usually what simply amounts to gossip and about as reliable, not that we don't all relish gossip."[4] However, Gaddis's primary complaint was that those who pursue this type of reading suffer from the "urge to scrimp and ice the creative act, the creative personality [....] Because finally the work itself is going to stand or fall uniquely on its own."[5] Educated in the heyday of New Criticism and confident in the careful construction of his writing, Gaddis thought everything that one needed to understand the text was contained within it. As Frederick Karl, literary critic and friend of William Gaddis, once declared: Gaddis was an "icon to serious writing."[6] Gaddis's belief in his finished piece is echoed by yet another of his friends, William H. Gass, who asserts in *Finding a Form*, "[t]he poet, every artist, is a maker, a maker whose aim is to make something supremely worthwhile, to make something inherently valuable in itself."[7] The ability "to make something inherently valuable in itself" is the result of the creative act, which is defined by Raymond Williams, contemporary of Gaddis and Gass, in *The Long Revolution*: "The 'creative' act, of any artist, is in any case the process of making a meaning active, by communicating an organized experience to others."[8] All of this is summarized by Gaddis in his 1987 *Paris Review* interview:

> Wyatt asks what people want from the man they didn't get from his work, because presumably that's where he's tried to distill this "life and personality and views" that you speak of. What's any artist but the dregs of his work: I gave that line to Wyatt thirty odd years ago and as far as I'm concerned it's still valid.[9]

Simply put, Gaddis did not want hunters of sources and personal information to kill the text and make the author its trophy. He hoped his readers would understand that his text had integrated life and art for a particular creative purpose.

Because critics pursuing autobiographical interpretations often lacked biographical information and because they stopped at a simple one-to-one comparison, essays of this type have left much to the imagination.[10] In the first part of this essay, based on geographical references found in passports and manuscripts among the William Gaddis Papers, I map the travels of William Gaddis using Geographic Information Systems (GIS).[11] I then plot the physical locations alluded to in *The Recognitions* using the same technology. When the results are overlaid, one discovers that there is an undeniable correspondence in coordinates: Gaddis incorporated his actual travel experiences into his novel. Yet, he did not consider this method autobiographical. As he told his friend John Napper, "All I know of it [his daughter Sarah's first novel] is that it's somewhat 'autobiographical' (as all first novels are but mine?)."[12] Instead, he thought of himself as recording life as it really was. Again, as he closes a letter to Napper, "I have a lot of messy notes taken on the spot in Real Life, to go through before the ten-o'clock shout from Isabelle."[13] His design was to encompass "on the spot [...] Real Life," specific geographical locations and local details for a particular "symbolical (simile) value."

Gaddis began writing *The Recognitions* in 1948, continued to work on it throughout his aforementioned travels, and completed it in the winter of 1953 while staying at Alan Ansen's farmhouse in Woodmere, New York. The novel has been described as encyclopedic and includes discussions of art, history, religion, and alchemy, among other topics. Consequently, it has spawned a reader's guide that is nearly as long as the novel itself to explain these allusions. As one might expect, the novel contains dozens of characters, each with their own interwoven stories and neuroses; however, at the most reductive level, it follows the life of Wyatt, a young artist of Calvinist New England background who forges a living by creating original counterfeits. The reader meets Wyatt at the age of four immediately after his father, Reverend Gwyon, returns from Spain without his mother, Camilla, who was killed by a counterfeiter posing as the ship's doctor on the initial voyage. Caught between his zealous Aunt May and his increasingly insane father, all the while being haunted by the image of his mother in white, Wyatt turns to art. However, his Aunt May rails against him, convinced his drawings are an attempt to usurp the power of God. Wyatt learns that any further art must be created in private and not aspire to originality. Eventually, Aunt May allows Wyatt to make copies of pictures, as long as they are of a religious topic. Wyatt obeys May for the short remainder of her life; while he begins original paintings, most importantly one of his mother, he only completes copies. Wyatt takes this incomplete image of his mother, as well as her Byzantine gold hoop earrings, with him when he leaves for Divinity School. However, theological training is not what Wyatt seeks and he withdraws after only a year. He sets out for Europe, where he receives instruction from Herr Koppel in Germany, who tells Wyatt:

> That romantic disease, originality, all around we see originality of incompetent idiots, they could draw nothing, paint nothing, just so the mess they make is original [....] When you paint you do not try to be original, only you think about your work, how to make it better, so you copy masters, only masters, for with each copy of a copy the form degenerates ... you do not invent shapes, you know them, auswendig wissen Sie, by heart.[14]

Reinforcing the lesson of Aunt May and introducing the main preoccupation of the novel, Koppel (albeit inadvertently) sets Wyatt on the counterfeiting path, where he will contemplate the relationship between art, imitation, and creative originality.

From Germany, Wyatt travels to Paris, then to the United States. He enters the art scene in New York's Greenwich Village, where he eventually finds himself in the clutches of the devilish Recktall Brown who sells Wyatt's forgeries as originals. After a failed marriage, Wyatt journeys to Spain where his mother is buried, enters a monastery to restore the paintings of masters to their original blank canvases, and finally disappears into the countryside with a prostitute named Pastora and their child.

Given its content, form, length, and publication date, *The Recognitions* defies simple classification. Is it an example of (high) modernism? Postmodernism? Or does it bridge the two movements? Perhaps it is a proto-Beat novel? Convincing arguments can be and have been made that establish *The Recognitions* as each of these.[15] Critical works on *The Recognitions* that read the text in light of postmodernism, such as that by John Johnston, have analyzed counterfeiting in the text. Johnston pursues the idea of "copies of copies," concluding that "the central 'event' pervading *The Recognitions* must be envisioned as a reversal from the Platonic paradigm of model and copy (or original and imitation) to the Deleuzian (or Nietzschean) one of the simulacrum and phantasm."[16]

Johnston, using Mikhail Bakhtin's ideas of the dialogic or polyphonic novel, investigates Gaddis's use of language in *Carnival of Repetition: Gaddis's "The Recognitions" and Postmodern Theory* (1990). As his title implies, Johnston argues *The Recognitions* should be read as a "contemporary Menippean satire or carnivalesque fiction"[17] in which "characters, situations, catch phrases, and allusions—everything occurs and recurs in some grosser or more refined version, in both serious and parodied formulations."[18] Following the thread of certain phrases, Johnston attempts to demonstrate how language either "is degraded in use from context to context until it finally reaches the point of being virtually meaningless" or "having no past or earlier and more meaningful use, its precise reference floats in an eternal and reiterated present."[19] In other words, these terms "[bear] no relation to any reality."[20] They are examples of simulacra, which "are ground*less*."[21]

Just as language cannot be fixed, according to Johnston, people and places suffer from similar slippage. He argues that "no coherent and unified subject"[22] exists within the text and that "what we find are characters who are delineated in terms of multiple identities, who occupy one or more places—even if only briefly—in a symbolic system (i.e., they are identified with mythic, historical, or literary figures) or in terms of a single and overriding obsessions."[23] Johnston further asserts that while certain representations of place, such as the Real Monasterio de Nuestra Señora de la Otra Vez may have "enough physical and historical detail [...] to produce what Barthes calls *l'effet du reel*,"[24] ultimately, "Gaddis's depiction of the monastery [...] treads a thin line between a credible representation of an actual place and an elaborate joke."[25] Johnston dismisses much of Gaddis's "citable" instances of actual events within *The Recognitions* as examples of Gaddis's use of "'double-voicing' as a constant fictional strategy."[26] Because Gaddis's allusions to literature, art, history, popular culture, music, science, and religion form simulacra that "insure that the 'real' and 'fictional' never harden into an antithetical opposition," Johnston claims the text remains open with all of its multiplicities.[27]

Allison Russell extends Johnston's interpretation of Gaddis's use of place in her chapter "Baedeker's Babel: William Gaddis's *The Recognitions*" from *Crossing Boundaries: Postmodern Travel Literature* (2000). Russell asserts, "Gaddis's novel explores the similarity of traveling through language to traveling through the world and experiments with narrative form and structure in ways that reflect the changing conditions of travel in the "'real' world."²⁸ For Russell, *The Recognitions* is a satire of tourism — travel that has become "too safe, too predictable, and too fast."²⁹ Tracing the various transportation methods (nautical, rail, and air), geographical descriptions (Paris, Spain, and Central America), and allusions to famous landmarks (Sacré Coeur), Russell claims that the travel represented in Gaddis's novel is "inherently artificial."³⁰ According to Russell, "The sights and scenes of Paris unfold amid cynical narrative observations of the city's 'infinite vulgarity,' parodic variations of Baedecker's historical commentaries,"³¹ which leads Russell to declare that *The Recognitions* is not only a critique of travel, but also a critique of realism.³² For Russell, "Places become mere locations, interchangeable landscapes that serve as the backdrop for recycled dramas."³³ Russell argues that the type of travel represented by Gaddis becomes a "metaphor for the state, or status, of language," as such "*The Recognitions* moves into the problematic territory of postmodernism, spaces dominated by dislocation, disorientation, and distortion."³⁴ She continues, asserting that among "the consequences of shifting or lost foundations" are "the number of suicide attempts in the novel that involve jumping out of windows; these people literally discover firm ground."³⁵ Russell interprets the representations of these characters as a criticism of contemporary life and as Gaddis echoing Thoreau's thoughts in *Walden*. She claims, "*Walden*, then, becomes the only reliable 'guidebook' in *The Recognitions*" and goes so far as to draw a connection between Thoreau's retirement to Walden Pond with Gaddis's "retreat to a farmhouse, to write what is, in many ways, a book about journeys that should never have been taken."³⁶ She concludes her essay by asserting "Baedeker's books are survival manuals: they offer maps, note places to eat and sleep, provide useful information on local customs, currency, and transportation. Unfamiliar territory is mapped out in advance so the traveler is always on 'firm ground.' *The Recognitions* does not offer these kinds of reassurances to its travelers."³⁷ As such, "[r]eading *The Recognitions* is like traveling without a map; the novel allows us to experience the kind of journey Gaddis values. It is a long, difficult, unguided trip (thus, heroic, as the Town Carpenter would say) that requires a willingness to get lost."³⁸

Although she raises the issue of geography in *The Recognitions*, Russell makes a number of assertions that are not supported by or are completely contradicted by the William Gaddis Papers. To be fair, the literary archive was not available to Russell at the time of publication; however, she also fails to recognize patterns within Gaddis's novel and its historical context, which complicates her argument. Russell seems to have forgotten that *The Recognitions* is written in the late 1940s to early 1950s and set in post–World War II Europe. She uses *The Recognitions* as an example of "literary experimentation,"³⁹ something that Gaddis did not believe he was doing.⁴⁰ More importantly, Russell reads the text as postmodern, when even she admits it merely "*anticipates* the postmodern condition of language and travel."⁴¹ The text was written before or in the midst of the rise and realization of multinational capital. Hence, while analyzing *The Recognitions* in postmodernist terms can be very insightful, one cannot allow its modernist foundations to go unrecognized. Likewise, one must acknowledge its historical context. Given the, perhaps, "too safe, too predictable, and too fast" of airplanes of today, one doubts the same could be said of crossing the Atlantic via ship, essentially the only mode of transportation used by people wishing to make this journey from 1492 into the 1960s.[42] As for travel by rail to and through Paris and Rome, Russell overlooks the fact that large portions of these cities (and countries for that matter) were virtually leveled by World War II and that, even by 1955, reconstruction was not complete.[43] Moreover, travel in Central America during the late 1940s, when Gaddis was there, was not "too safe, too predictable, and too fast," especially in Costa Rica where Gaddis participated in the 1948 Civil War. During this time, Spain was also not a land easily traversed, having just survived not only World War II, but also a Civil War of its own. Most glaringly, even today, crossing Northern Africa does not evoke the adjectives safe, predictable, or fast.

As for *Walden* being the only "reliable guidebook in *The Recognitions*" or, as Russell implies, the inspiration for the writing of it, scrawled within Gaddis's notes on *The Recognitions* is "left Harvard without knowing whether it was Walden's *Thoreau* or Thoreau's *Walden*."[44] This is not to say Gaddis was unfamiliar with the text, but suggests that perhaps he was not as intimately connected to *Walden* as Russell seems to believe. In addition, although Russell does not list Baedecker's travel guides in her bibliography or footnotes, she alludes to them in her argument. Gaddis's working library does not contain a Baedecker's guide for any country, suggesting that he did not use Baedecker for any commentary on Paris as Russell claims.[45] However, based on materials found within the manuscripts, it does appear that Gaddis was at one time in possession of *Baedecker's Spain and Portugal*. Moreover, as Gaddis asserts on a page dated "El Escorial 25 December, 48," "The Monastery my first taste of Spanish magnificence, too much for any but the factual account, & brilliant, of Baedecker." The rest of the page and others within the William Gaddis Papers go on to describe El Escorial, implying that Baedecker's accounts were insufficient.

Finally, evidence found within the William Gaddis Papers and *The Recognitions* proves *The Recognitions* does "offer maps, note places to eat and sleep, provide useful information on local customs, currency, and transportation," which counters Russell's assertion that the text lacks the "kinds of reassurances" that are found in a guidebook like Baedeker's. Equally flawed is Johnston's conclusion that there is no stability of language within Gaddis's text. While some terms might become "copies of copies," there is "firm ground" within *The Recognitions*; it is geography, which is described using consistent language and creates a map of the novel's structure.

. . .

Gaddis's movements upon his arrival in Spain are quite easy to plot on a map. According to his "Statement of Personal History," William Gaddis left New York (he had been living alternately in Massapequa and Greenwich Village) on December 9, 1948, and arrived in Gibraltar on December 15; he entered Spain at Algeciras the following day.[46] From Algeciras, Gaddis traveled by rail to Madrid, most likely via Granada.[47] Less than two weeks after establishing himself at Pension Filo in Madrid, he took a short Christmas excursion to El Escorial, a sixteenth-century monastery just outside the city. Although his "Statement of Personal History" claims he resided in Madrid from December 1948 to August 1949, evidence in the manuscripts and passport stamps reveal he continued to travel and was in Sevilla in March 1949, as well as on May 11, 1949. While residing in Madrid, Gaddis also visited the Real Monasterio de Guadalupe in the village of Guadalupe in the province of Extremadura. After Madrid, he traveled to Paris, via train, receiving an exit stamp from the Policia de [E] Norte Zona Occidental on June 10, 1949. In all likelihood, this passport stamp refers to Irun, just across the border from Hendaye, France; this route would have taken him through Burgos, Spain.[48] After nearly a year, Gaddis left France and returned to Spain in June 1950 and would remain there until April 1951.[49]

During this time, Gaddis also toured North Africa for a little over a month; he departed from Algeciras and entered Tangier on February 24, 1951. Gaddis's passports and "Statement of Personal History" reveal that, while in Africa, he also visited Morocco, Algeria, Tunisia, and Libya before returning to Spain on March 31. However, a letter written to John Napper upon returning from Africa discloses more details of his travel:

> The truth is, we have just escaped from Africa. Or, to go further back, he [David Tudor-Pole] showed up here one day in late february [sic] bound for Libya in an Austin, and two hours later I had assembled what there was of myself at hand and we were gone. Unfortunately I can't immediately give you my picture of Africa, still trying, here now, to sort it out for myself [...] the girl with the safety-pin in her ear in Bous Saada, the broken truck spring and tea in the Zintan pharmacy, the sick arab in the back seat and Saturday night in Sfax, the subterranean lunch with the sheik of Nalut, the Sundanes who served cognac as a beveridge [sic] with supper, and the Berber friend in Fes who shared his highly suspicious pipe, the Foreign Legion at Sidi-Bel-Abbes, the bacarrat table in the casino at Algiers, and Easter in the Casbah, the expensive beer-drinking party in Biskra, and twenty-some seat gentlemen's lavatory at Leptis Manga..all this, and so much more.[50]

Shortly thereafter, April 24, 1951, Gaddis would leave Spain to return to New York.

From part I, chapter one—"The First Turn of the Screw"—readers of *The Recognitions* are given geographical references that mimic Gaddis's actual movements. Specifically, Reverend Gwyon traces Gaddis's travels almost exactly. On the first page, we are told that Gwyon and Camilla set out from America to Spain via ship from Boston harbor, presumably to Gibraltar or Algeciras, Spain.⁵¹ On board, Camilla has a deadly encounter with a counterfeit surgeon, Sinisterra, leaving Gwyon with the task of locating a proper burial site for his wife. After paying extensive fines and fees, Gwyon "[enters] the port of Spain"⁵² and quickly finds himself "on the rise behind the village of San Zwingli overlooking the rock-strewn plain of New Castile,"⁵³ which Gaddis considered to be "an open parody on Escorial?"⁵⁴ Because a limited number of railroad routes would permit travel from Gibraltar or Algeciras to El Escorial at the time, one can deduce that Gwyon took a train through Granada or Córdoba to Madrid and then continued on to San Zwingli/El Escorial.

After burying Camilla, but not before removing her Byzantine hoops,⁵⁵ Gwyon wanders Spain:

> In the next few months, various reports were received at home concerning the pastor's sabbatical: rococo tales, adorned with every element but truth. It was not true that, to exercise the humility struck through him by this act of God (in later years he was heard to refer to the "unswerving punctuality of chance") he had dressed himself in rags, rented three pitiful children, and was to be encountered daily by footloose tourists in a state of mendicant collapse before the Ritz hotel in Madrid; it was not true that he had stood the entire population of Málaga to drinks for three days and then conducted them on an experimental hike across the sea toward Africa, intending that the One he sought should manage it dryshod; it was not true that he had married a hoary crone with bangles in her ears, proclaimed himself rightful heir to the throne of Abd-er-Rahman, and led an insurrection of the Moors on Córdoba.⁵⁶

In a passage such as this one, questions of how reports made their way back home to America come to the surface, along with inquiries concerning the veracity of the statement "it was not true that." Given the geographical locations of Madrid, Córdoba, and Málaga in relation to Gwyon's route to San Zwingli/El Escorial, it is likely that he found himself in each of these cities with little deviation off the course. Moreover, "an experimental hike across the sea toward Africa" would involve merely a short ferry ride from Gibraltar to Tangier and then onto Fes, Morocco, onetime home of the sultan Abd-er-Rahman.⁵⁷

After his purported wanderings, Gwyon "enter[s] a Franciscan monastery" named The Real Monasterio de Nuestra Señora de la Otra Vez "as a guest."⁵⁸ Upon falling ill, Gwyon is taken to Madrid. He spends time in Retiro Park, views the Sierra de Guadarrama, and returns to Camilla's grave at San Zwingli/El Escorial.⁵⁹ Before returning home, we are told:

> He visited cathedrals, the disemboweled mosque at Córdoba, the mighty pile at Granada, and that frantic Gothic demonstration at Burgos where Christ shown firmly nailed was once said to be fashioned from stuffed human skin, but since had been passed as buffalo hide[....] He collected things, each of a holy intention in isolation, but pagan in the variety of his choice. He even got to a bullfight when the season opened.⁶⁰

Finally, Gwyon returns to New England, presumably from Gibraltar, as, when we leave him, he is awaiting the arrival of his "Barbary ape from Gibraltar, being held in quarantine."[61]

Gaddis's movements through Spain are repeated again *The Recognitions* in "The Last Turn of the Screw," part III, chapter three. Wyatt (soon to be known as Stephen) arrives in Algeciras, Spain, from New York City, where he had been living in Greenwich Village, and views Gibraltar across the bay.[62] From Algeciras, like his father and Gaddis before him, Wyatt travels to Madrid via train. From Madrid's Estación del Norte, Wyatt sets out on a train towards Segovia, "along whose route his destination lay not far distant."[63] San Zwingli/El Escorial is located along this route. Taking note of the Sierra de Guadarrama, Wyatt meets Mr. Yak (Sinisterra), who tells him he would "make a good Swiss."[64] For the rest of the chapter, Wyatt moves back and forth between San Zwingli and Madrid.[65] We next find Wyatt in part III, chapter five, where he has taken up residence at The Real Monasterio de Nuestra Señora de la Otra Vez. While staying at the monastery to work on his latest text, Ludy, "the distinguished novelist,"[66] encounters Wyatt. In this chapter, we learn that Wyatt killed Han, "in Africa, Algeria, the bullet went right through and broke his neck, in Sidi-bel-Abbès."[67] Other geographical references in Northern Africa appear before Wyatt wanders away from the monastery never to be heard from again, including Djelfa, Biskra, Sfax, Bou-Saâda, and Nalut.[68]

While a comparison of these mapped movements is interesting, it reduces *The Recognitions* to a simple autobiographical source reading of the type that Gaddis feared and loathed: evidence exists that Gaddis visited the aforementioned places in Spain and Northern Africa; therefore, his work is autobiographical because Gwyon and Wyatt also travel to or through these locations. Until now, scholars have been content to stop here, but, when one scours the manuscripts of *The Recognitions*, occasionally, buried amongst the pages or wedged between thoughts on various novel characters, one unearths passages apparently transferred from the notebook entries.[69] These hidden passages record Gaddis's observations while traveling and, intermittently, provide a date, as well as a place of composition. Initially, their placement betwixt and between materials of *The Recognitions* might seem rather odd. However, when one takes the name of the place mentioned by Gaddis in an entry and finds a corresponding reference to that geographical location within *The Recognitions*, one makes yet another discovery — Gaddis's personal observations are frequently transcribed word for word within the text and are a part of Gaddis's fiction, dispelling Russell's assertions that descriptions of travel and locations within *The Recognitions* are "inherently artificial." Moreover, further mapping of the novel reveals, as Johnston suggested, these places repeatedly appear in "both serious and parodied formulations." But contrary to Johnston, the language used to describe these geographical locations neither "degrade[s] in use from context to context until it finally reaches the point of being virtually meaningless" nor lacks a "past or earlier and more meaningful use."[70] The linguistic representations of historical locations remain absolutely consistent. Moreover, these descriptions are not "ground*less*,"[71] but taken from the notes of Gaddis's "Real Life" experience and must be read as creating an underlying stable structure of the novel.

But, the question once again becomes, beyond the autobiographical, what is the significance of incorporating personal observations? What is its "symbolical (simile) value"? It is a question Gaddis answered himself in his manuscripts and demonstrated in his text:

> IT is the *sensed* reaffirmations (not that I remember this on page 72) that give the sense of unity, the pat[t]ern, the movement in stillness. The whole point is that whether we like it or not we live in a whole & so limited world of symbolism, a framework which has been passed on to us and which bounds every hope thought intention: though the characters in a Creative work must be shown to ([succeed] to their own thinking, & the reader's interest) act freely; it is only when the whole pattern is exhibited that we have it as a limited piece bound by itself; this is the point of the reaffirmations felt but unlettered unless by a knife as TSE's [sic] repetition of rhyme&metre at the beginning of each verse in DS [sic], sensed (though really calculatedly there for the analyst) & reversal of the same idea (line) upon itself which validates the idea advanced as self-contained.[72]

In this passage, Gaddis refers to T.S. Eliot's "The Dry Salvages," number three of the "Four Quartets." At one point in time, Gaddis considered parodying the entire "Four Quartets" in *The Recognitions*.[73] "The Dry Salvages" presumably meditates on a geographical location and geological formation off the coast of Cape Ann, Massachusetts. Through repetition of rhyme and meter, which might also be called rhythm, Eliot creates the "sense of unity, the pat[t]ern, the movement in stillness." This pattern is not explicitly mapped out; however, the analyst will *sense* that it is calculated and understand that, among other things, in this poem Eliot communicates the stability and endurance of the geographical structure (or one might add monument) in comparison to the ebb and flow of human life.

In this way Gaddis anticipates what Raymond Williams articulates in *The Long Revolution*:

> Rhythm is a way of transmitting a description of an experience, in such a way that the experience is re-created in the person receiving it, not merely as an "abstraction" or an "emotion" but as a physical effect on the organism[....] We use rhythm for many ordinary purposes, but the arts [...] comprise highly developed and exceptionally powerful rhythmic means, by which the communication of experience is actually achieved[....] The dance of the body, the movement of the voice, the sounds of instruments are, like colours, forms, patterns, means of transmitting his experience in so powerful a way that the experience can be literally lived by others.[74]

Through rhythm, artists stimulate affects in their readers; the readers sense the pattern on physical, intellectual, and emotional levels. For Williams, this communication of actual experience while reading, what one might be tempted to call movement in stillness, is key to the creative act and the success of art. Communication, as one might expect, involves transmission of experience from one person to another or others, meaning one must have knowledge of the experience to transmit. Simply put, the artist must live the experience. According to Williams, "By living the experience we mean that, whether or not it has been previously recorded, the artist has literally made it part of himself, so deeply that his whole energy is available to describe it and transmit it to others."[75] Given Gaddis's own observations of Eliot and Williams's later, similar articulations on art in general, the reason Gaddis incorporated personal experience into his novel become clear.

The "symbolical (simile) value" of incorporating "Real Life" into Gaddis's novel is the recognition of the pattern that emerges in "the life of significant soil."[76] When William Gaddis wrote *The Recognitions*, he believed that it would be "the last Christian novel."[77] He thought it was about "'the massive character of the dissolution and corruption of authority, in belief, in ritual and in temporal order...,' about our histories and traditions as 'both bonds and barriers among us,' and our art which 'brings us together and sets us apart.'"[78] Gaddis also described the purpose of his work another way. Found in what was perhaps meant as prefatory notes to *The Recognitions*, discussing in particular the form and length of the novel, Gaddis writes:

> [t]his is all in opposition I guess to what we've learned from our American and any-country recent writers who teach us to tell precisely what <u>happened</u>. Well it is opposition then, because things don't happen, or if they do they don't happen in a single light, that single light which is very effective in Hemingway for instance, and so damned boring in those who "derive" from him[....] Because the instant a thing happens it has happened, and when it has happened it has happened in a thousand ways none of which alone is true though Flaubert could make it seem so. Well, that was the age when reason and causality worked hand in hand; now even science, from Einstein to evolution, is up against the blank wall of Indetermination; and though I want this book to have very much a thread of inevitability, it is that Indetermination that I am writing about.[79]

Given its historical context, it is not surprising that these issues would weigh heavily upon Gaddis's mind. Nietzsche had already declared God dead in *The Gay Science* (1882). In light of Hiroshima and Nagasaki, T.S. Eliot's assertion the world would end not with a bang but with a whimper seemed unlikely. Millions were dead, displaced, and/or disfigured. Belief and knowledge were threatened with meaninglessness in the face of concentration camps, ruined buildings, and nuclear bombs. Gaddis, traveling through much of the Western European and North African military arenas, witnessed some of the aftermath of the war; however, his novel is conspicuously void of such descriptions. Rather, his text focuses on structures left standing, particularly Spanish monasteries, which implies a mnemonic purpose similar to that suggested by "The Dry Salvages." The reader is lead to acknowledge that repetition of people, places, and symbols will inevitably occur in our limited world; such repetitions create a sense of unity in the novel (and elsewhere), illustrating that certain geographical features or historical places, in spite of present events, will survive.

Gaddis recognized both the chaotic continuing repercussions of World War II on society and the contemporary need to turn to the historical past, especially in tangible forms, to combat them. The most cursory glance at *The Recognitions* illustrates that he captured the chaos of the post-war period within the pages of his text, although, unlike Edna St. Vincent Millay, he chose to use more than fourteen lines to order it. However, what has not been obvious is the significance of the contemporary need for the historical. Gaddis writes in Sevilla, 1949: "The US myth(lessness) leaves no place for going backwards; unlike such a country, which has taken refuge in its (RCCH [Roman Catholic Church]) myth & myth-history (Philip II y antes), has no forward-looking; US still trying to prove its legitimacy; here dead past is lived in as valid."[80] Put another way elsewhere in *The Recognitions* manuscripts: "A town being enamoured [sic] of its Foreign past: v Granada & the Moors: produces a parody of anomalies. But what with the weight of monuments apparently everywhere today the present is thoroughly unsatisfactory: has any rising civilisation spent so much time preserving & exhibiting things from the past, testimony to its legitimacy?"[81] Plotting Gaddis's movements, the geography of the novel, and the topologies of the manuscripts begin to answer this question posed by Gaddis and reveals a symbolically significant map of the text.

According to Steven Moore, Gwyon derives from "'guyon' meaning 'guide' in Old French." [82] As his name suggests, Gwyon's movements throughout Spain and Northern Africa guide Wyatt's subsequent travels through the same areas. With few exceptions, the descriptions of landscape found within "The First Turn of the Screw" are minimal, leading the reader to focus on the places that are represented in greater detail and nearly overlook those that are merely mentioned.[83] As with nearly everything in Gaddis's texts, nothing is accidental, and this reaction would have been anticipated by Gaddis. The detailed depictions of San Zwingli/El Escorial and Real Monasterio de Nuestra Señora de la Otra Vez recreates a lived experience that forms an impression on the reader making the monasteries stable structures that the text returns to again and again with uncanny similarity.

In post–World War II Spain, only one railroad line takes people from Madrid to El Escorial, meaning anyone traveling this route by rail must follow the same path. As Gwyon approaches the monastery, he views the village: "San Zwingli appeared suddenly, at a curve in the railway, a town built of rocks against rock, streets pouring down between houses like beds of unused rivers, with the houses littered like boulders carelessly against each other along a mountain stream."[84] His son shares the same experience thirty years and 660 pages later: "San Zwingli appeared suddenly, at a curve in the railway, a town built of rocks against rock, streets pouring down between houses like beds of unused rivers, and the houses littered one against another like boulders along mountain streams."[85] Gaddis, also, presumably had the same experience as his train came around the bend, although the words used to describe the appearance of the village appear in his notebook entries in association with Guadalupe: "The village is heaped up around its walls, streets wander down mountainside like creeks, & surfaced like creekbeds, stones placed; //// on edge; houses too in corresponding natural order, like boulders beside a mtn stream."[86] The similarities between the various experiences and the underlying pattern of the novel have only begun to emerge.

From the train, Gwyon observes his surroundings and begins to walk.

> Swallows dove and swept with appalling certainty at the tower of the church, and the air was filled with their morning cries, with the sound of water running and the braying of burros, and the distant voices of people. Gwyon had climbed to the pines behind town, pausing to breathe and smell the delicious freshness of manure, to realize how his senses had fallen into disuse under the abuses of cities. The day deepened weightlessly, a feast day, crowds wandering through the streets, groups singing and playing, in one a boy with half an arm supporting a broken anis bottled played scratching accompaniment on that corrugated glass surface.[87]

Following in his father's footsteps, Wyatt

> was soon up behind the town, where the sound of running water nearby, the braying of burros and the desultory tinkling of bells, and the distant voices of people below reached him where he paused to sniff, and then stood still inhaling the pines above him and the delicious freshness of cow manure, like a man rediscovering senses long forgotten under the abuses of cities. Then he was off again, and when he reached the road bounded by cypress trees, he hardly paused to cross himself at the first station he encountered as he hurried up the hill toward the white walls of the cemetery.[88]

The road to the cemetery where Camillia is buried: water, burros, people, pine trees, and manure. In spite of all that has happened in the time between Gwyon's arrival and that of Wyatt, essentially, the sights, smells, sounds, and physical geography has not changed. Nor was the experience for Gaddis any different, as he writes in a notebook entry titled "El Escorial December 25, 1948":

> It was arriving at El Escorial early this morning, walking up the mile to the town & the Royal Monastery of Philip II: suddenly to be Out again — the air, the birds around the towers making such a wondrous morning noise around the great weight of that building. The Monastery my first taste of Spanish magnificence, too much for any but the factual account, & brilliant, of Baedeker. But being on that rocky hillside of a town: to the left, east, mountains capped with snow, and before, the rocky plain toward Madrid. A good meal & a cigar — such Christmas comfort! — and walking, endless walking & I find myself untired now, alive instead. Climbing: the purgative effect of that. & the town, in no way special perhaps, but often as I imagine the Tyrol. Then the road to the cemetery, interrupted regularly by the 14 stations of the cross. The sound of water running, of burros braying, in that air! One suddenly realises [sic] his senses have fallen into disuse under the abuses of the city, and must pause to breathe & smell — the delicious freshness of cow manure — and climb again, up to the pines above the town, &

look, only look. Such harsh land, how one admires the people who live from it. & today festively groups wandering through the streets singing & playing, even to one which included a boy with one arm which played the scratching accompaniment on a broken anis bottle supported by a stump."[89]

One author and two of his creations cover the same ground, in reality and in fiction, with little to no deviation of initial experience. People may come and go, but historic events—whether genocide, world upheaval, demolished cities, death of God, social chaos, personal loss, or whatever has come since the monastery's construction in the sixteenth century—alter neither San Zwingli/El Escorial nor its description. This is "movement in stillness,"[90] which leads the reader to believe that if she were to climb the road to El Escorial's cemetery, she would also smell cow manure.

Yet another monastery, fictional and factual, experiences this stability. That Gaddis modeled Real Monasterio de Nuestra Señora de la Otra Vez on the Real Monasterio de Guadalupe in Extremadura has become common knowledge among Gaddis scholars; however, the extent to which he borrowed from reality for fiction is not. Found among his reading notes for *The Recognitions* is a page marked "Real Monasterio de Guadalupe Estremadura March 49." It is a full page, single-spaced, describing the actual appearance of the monastery, the day and nighttime activities, as well as exact details of the contents of the room Gaddis stayed in while there.

In this notebook entry Gaddis writes: "On approach, like mediaeval castle; embattled walls, towers crenelated, spired; machicolated; with spired bartizan; almost romanesque dome on church; gothic traceries; round arching with almost Moorish extension of imposts; [gothic traceries] in spandrels; ch[urch] doors trefoil arch w[ith] traceries." Looking around, he comments: "Central plaza is at foot of steps to wide church porch, there the fountain where all day women fill copper & stone jugs, at eve apparently unattended horses, illustriously horned, oxen, mules, & burros come to drink, like respectable citizens stopping at pub on way home; sow & 3littles go up st like respectable family, in at doorway; goats leave pebble-droppings on ch steps, butt each other off, thought balustrade..(streets clamber up the hill, & the houses are littered like the factors upon the scene of some natural prodigy)." Moving beyond the walls of the monastery, Gaddis states, "Mountains steeped in clouds (it had been raining), grey-green of olive trees tempers heavy green, blue of mtns; smoke rising on a mtnside at evening; smoke from villages tile-pitch-topped chimneys, the far-off racket of voices, bells of cattle goats sheep rises peacefully with smoke, peace of eve with work done; quiet freshness of air."[91]

Taking in the monastery from a different point of view over the course of a few days, specifically from his room, Gaddis remarks:

> This evening, to step out onto the balcony, on the façade of the church overlooking the fountain where the fountain splashes, voices rise in a clear & undistinguishable language, the sky clear & starred and the light of a full moon [...] on

the roofs, on the black mountains which are ragged & appear 2-dimensional, smelling the smoke out of the chimneys which lies heavy in the valley. In the room behind me the electric light in the room dims where the organ below commences, barely heard through the corridors; — then out through the doors below figures which become a procession, led by the white surplice of an altarboy two lines of women in black adjusting their veiling, there lines enclosing two boys who carry candles on [e]ither side of the tall white-figured priest in the centre — down the steps, past the fountain, carrying the Eucharist to someone lying near death, down a street whence their singing, too soft to echo against the walls slip back through the night air, and lights appear at windows on their way as they carry innocence in their song, in the candles, in the cold white light and into the shadows without faltering..to step out against the five centuries of the face of the church into the moon's light (risking enchantment)[....] Lunch with padre J., he in brown Franciscan robes, sitting vis-a-vis at octagonal table with brazier underneath & floor-length cloth hiding the heat around our legs from the cold of the room, which decorated w beautiful antique Sp ceramic, plates patterned against white walls.[92] My room hard to find in corridors; large, brick-floored, bed in clandestine alcove sug. Worldly not ascetic fantasies; good bed, woollenness of blankets; décor: a Raphaelite virgin & opposite the morena Our Lady. sign: Se ruega, por lo tanto, a neustros visitants la mas estricta moralidad y compostura en todos sus actos y conversaciones, y se recomienda a las Sras. que en el vestido se atengan (no wd) a las prescriptions de la modestia cristiana.[93]

Those familiar with Gaddis's novel undoubtedly recognize a number of images and sentences from this notebook entry, as nearly every sentence of it appears within the text of *The Recognitions,* often more than once.

In *The Recognitions,* three characters stay at the Real Monasterio de Nuestra Señora de la Otra Vez: Gwyon (the father), Wyatt (the son), and Ludy ("the distinguished novelist").[94] As the first member of this trinity arrives at the monastery, we are told that when it "was finished [in the fourteenth century] with turreted walls, parapets, crenelations, machicolations, bartizans, a harrowing variety of domes and spires in staggering Romanesque, Byzantine effulgence, and Gothic run riot in mullioned windows, window tracings, and an immense rose window whose foliations were so elaborate that it was never furnished with glass, the brothers were brought forth and tried for heresy,"[95] which echoes Gaddis's initial reaction on approach exactly. Because Gwyon arrives in winter, we learn that the monastery has no heat, as such, "the good Brothers were immobilized, stagnating round heavily clothed tables with braziers underneath which toasted their sandled feet, warmed them to their privities,"[96] which alludes to Gaddis's experience with Padre Julio. Furthermore, we discover that Gwyon, like Gaddis before him, stays "in a small room whose window lay in the countenance of the church façade overlooking the town's muddy central plaza."[97] At night, while he has hallucinations, "he struggled up from the alcoved bed, across the room to the window where a cold light silently echoed passage. There was the moon, reaching a still arm behind him, to the bed where he had lain."[98] Later in the dark, just before Gwyon is sent to Madrid by the monks who can no longer care for his delusions, the "clouds blew low over the town, shreds of dirty gray, threatening, like evil assembled in a hurry, disdained by the moon they could not obliterate."[99] As such, the reader is left with a sentence whose phrases have a staccato feel, like something "assembled in a hurry," which describes the atmosphere surrounding the Real Monasterio de Nuestra Señora de la Otra Vez: low-hanging, dirty gray clouds that portend evil while they simultaneously experience the moon's scorn.

Eight hundred forty-four pages later, the reader encounters "the sound of the bells sank on the air and was gone, while clouds in shreds of dirty gray, threatening like evil recalled and assembled hurriedly, blew low over the town clinging for refuge to the embattled walls of the Real Monasterio de Nuestra Señora de la Otra Vez."[100] Although the sentence invokes the phrase "assembled hurriedly," it no longer holds implications for the sentence itself, as the structure has been transformed from phrases *papier collé* to a mature work of art. This change, perhaps, has been wrought by the modification to evil, which is now being "recalled," rather than experienced for the first time. Of course, the reader too is recalling: the monastery, the sentence, and the evil clouds described.

In case the reader failed to recognize the repetition in atmospheric description, the novel provides yet another textual echo. Immediately following the sentence quoted above is this one: "In the muddy plaza open beneath the wide porch of the monastery church, whose gothic façade and unfinished rose window overlooked it, the village fountain spouted, and women with stone and copper jugs came to fill them."[101] Once again, the description of the church alludes to that provided when Gwyon visited, as well as incorporates Gaddis's own observations.

Adding to the pattern, as Ludy settles into his room, we are told that "there was a narrow balcony before him, and the window itself was set in the façade of the church through it was the guest room."[102] Further details of Ludy's room emerge, it

> was large and, in spite of not being especially warm, a comfortable one. On a white wall to his left hung a color print of a Raphaelite Madonna; on the wall to his right, a picture of his hostess in still dark effigy, Nuestra Señora de la Otra Vez[....] The bed was set in an alcove. It was one of the softest he would find in the country, made up with a blanket of rich wool, and in this clandestine arrangement highly suggestive of pleasures beyond the walls, reminiscent of illustrations in Boccaccio, stimulating to every sense but the aesthetic.[103]

Moreover, one night Ludy awakes in his room, pulls open the windows, and sees the moon, "a sharp shape in the clear sky waiting in continent ambush. Then he made out the jagged black rim of the mountains, and he smelled the smoke loitering in the valley."[104] Again there is no doubt that Ludy is staying in the room that Gwyon occupied approximately thirty years before or that the fictional room represented in *The Recognitions* and the actual room in which Gaddis resided are virtually identical. Further adding credence to this assertion, the Spanish message mentioned in the notebook entry is transcribed word for word on page 861.

Only two members of the father, son, and distinguished novelist trinity are associated with descriptions of the monastery. This seeming omission of Wyatt increases the symbolic value of the pattern that is emerging. Wyatt, who is busy restoring paintings, has already (mistakenly) consumed the ashes of his father, as such, he literally embodies Gwyon. Ludy, who shares not only Gaddis's profession but also his tendency to spread manuscript pages all over the room wherever he goes, has incorporated Gaddis's observations and made them his own. As such, it seems appropriate that only the novelist would be able to articulate such a complex situation. The distinction between these characters, as well as the separation between them and the author, have symbolically collapsed, leaving the geographical location as one of the only stable structures in this portion of the text. Put another way, the inclusion of the Real Monasterio, the presence of Gwyon and Stephen/Wyatt at the monastery, the mention of Friar Eulalio, the elder, and Friar Eulalio, the younger, at the beginning and the end of the novel, as well as the repetition of Gaddis's own geographical descriptions allows the text, like the orobouros that appears on the title page, to come full circle.

In *The Road to Botany Bay: An Exploration of Landscape and History*, Paul Carter states: "A place, a historical fact, detached from its travelers; static, at anchor, as if it was always there, bland, visible."[105] Although all of the geographical locations mapped within *The Recognitions* embody Carter's assertion that physical location is "always there," the representations of San Zwingli/El Escorial and The Real Monasterio de Nuestra Señora de la Otra Vez are the static anchors of *The Recognitions*. These two monasteries incorporate Gaddis's historic observations into the fictional text with little to no variation of the factual language. However, far from being simple, bland, autobiographical instances, like Eliot, Gaddis repeats places and descriptions with a particular purpose in mind. As Gaddis notes, "The recognitions is a title I like perfectly because it implies the impossibility of escape from a (the) pattern."[106] In other words, he forces readers to recognize when they have seen the geographical location before, who was there, and what, if anything, has changed. Once these recurrences are mapped, they create an underlying, stable structure that, until now, has been ignored or, in the case of Russell and Johnston, misread.

At the heart of *The Recognitions*' pattern is Spain. In a notebook entry dated Sevilla March 49, Gaddis writes: "(Op. f. ch. On S) S—is not a country one travels in: it is a land one flees across. Whether God designed the people for earth, or the earth for the people, or inflicted them one on the other, is for the Pope to say..The harsh earth & the Sky. The object being, as in any respectable metaphysic, to get from one place to another..The trains do not depart: they set out."[107] This sentiment does, in fact, appear in variation as the opening for the final chapter on Spain:

> Spain is a land to flee across[....] Trains do not depart; they set out, and move at a pace to enhance the landscape, and aggrandize the land they traverse, laboring

their courses with the effort of journeys never before made, straining the attention on sufferance of minutes passed separately until concentration is exhausted, and no other pace conceivable. The very distances become greater, through landscape irreplaceable by the exhausted fancy, unaltered by the most resourceful imagination.[108]

Unlike the manuscript description, the passage found in *The Recognitions* has the "requisite actuality" and has been "fill[ed] out [...] for [its] symbolic usage." Spain becomes "landscape irreplaceable by the exhausted fancy, unaltered by the most resourceful imagination." No matter what happens in the mind, in the text, or in the world, historic Spain remains virtually unchanged. More specifically, regardless of the destruction of belief, the destabilization of language, the demolition of cities, the decimation of a group of people, the monasteries remain standing.

2

The Kvetch, the Rant, and the Bitch

WILLIAM H. GASS

Do you think that's why people write it? fiction I mean?
— From outrage[1]

they cleaned that up in Tennessee sixty years ago, all your ranting about Genesis and evolution[2]

The rant is perhaps William Gaddis's most frequently employed rhetorical form. *Carpenter's Gothic*, for instance, is a festival of rant and rodomontade. Another name for the rant is the tirade. It is angry in tone, blasphemous in expression, pell-mell in delivery, built of associations rather than with logical connections, although it makes a show of inference and argument, attribution and citation, data and demonstration. It tends to be fueled by its own heat, beginning with annoyance and ending in a fury of exasperation. The errors of others ignite it, so it is fault finding and warns of sin and error; it is based on an astonished disbelief at what others believe or do. It finds itself aghast at the lengths the human race will go to prove its incompetence; and the jeremiad itself is irritated by the fact that no one heeds its message or shows the least regard for its good intentions. Some masters of the form adopt an ironic tone, as Erasmus does, some are boisterous and hyperbolic like Rabelais, some are full of fiery condemnation and fatherly disappointment as one finds in Jonathan Edwards; but above all the rant is driven by despair, because nothing can really be done to change demented minds or alter ill-advised behavior, or stay the lemmings from their appointment with the cliff.

Ranters need not wait for the occurrence of some serious event or the expression of an outrageous belief to rouse them into song. Like nitro, a cocktail shaker will set them off. Cassandras all, they warn of disastrous choices and dire consequences, but when what has been foretold comes to pass no one notices how bad it is or even remembers what was predicted. That is why the rant so often begins with a desperate plea: wait ... the ranter says. Listen....

The kvetch is hinged to the rant like a door to a door frame: the kvetch is particular, the rant general; the kvetch intimate, the rant impersonal; the kvetch is about injuries done to the speaker by family and fate, the rant about injuries others do to themselves, the race, and mother nature. The kvetch is raspy like a rant, and equally tiresome to listen to, but it is always specific and weighed down by detail, although habitual as a door chime—complaints about wife, or mother, children or job, car or car payments—when the button is pushed they ring; moreover it strikes a different set of notes than the rant regularly does, notes of self-pity principally, such as "o woe is me!" "how I suffer!" "no one cares!" "what will become of me!" and so on.

Those of us who care about the niceties of meaning and try now and then to scrub a little careless usage from a few commonly used words, will appreciate the difference between the bitch and the kvetch, though they are allies, as their spelling suggests, with shared companions like "botch," "itch," "retch," and other bad stuff such as "ditch," "glitch," "hitch," and "snitch." A bitch sounds like this:

> —Anyplace he goes, somebody cleaning up after him every God damn place he goes. You clean up, Adolph cleans up that's all Adolph's ever done is clean up after him. That car wreck in Encino? and Yale? He's kicked out of every school he gets near so they buy his way into Yale, you know what he told me once? that they'd held him back in eighth grade because he was such a great hockey player?[3]

And a kvetch like this:

> —Does this coffee table have to be right in the middle of the God damn room here? [So far a simple complaint that could be a bitch.] Bang my leg every time I walk past it. [Now it is a kvetch.][4]

Bitching is low toned, in contrast to the kvetch which can resemble the wail of paid mourners. You can bitch about your boss and be bitching for an entire office, representing complaints held in common, as soldiers bitch, but a purely egocentric complaint has to be called a kvetch — why am I always sent out to forage for weedy greens? why must I bear the burden of your lazy nephews?— whereas if the entire household has to get up at dawn to do in the dandelions, it is bitching. However, if it is your neighbor who annoys you by weeding his own yard at such an ungodly hour; if it is just someone who is always on time, or looks happy at funerals, who "gets your goat"— then that is someone who may provoke a rant. Perhaps it begins with an observation:

> On the corner opposite, the old man from the house above bent sweeping leaves into a dustpan, straightened up carrying the thing level before him like an offering, each movement, each shuffled step reckoned anxiously toward an open garbage can where he emptied it with ceremonial concern, balanced the broom upright like a crosier getting his footing, wiping a dry forehead, perching his glasses square and lifting his bald gaze on high to branches yellow-blown with benisons yet to fall.[5]

Many pages later the old man turns up again, timed by a jacket that's fallen as firmly as a leaf.

> He had no jacket on, it was still where he'd dropped it on a chair in the living

room and from behind his shoulders appeared to fall, to turn in, to shed substance, standing there watching the morning arrival of the old man out on the corner, broom in one hand and the flattened dustpan in the other as though reporting for duty.[6]

As exasperation, for other reasons, mounts, the old leaf sweeper becomes a catalyst.

> I laid out the whole floor in here, end up staring out the window at that old man out there with his damned recessional toward the garbage can trying to look useful till I, till he finally drove me out of the house.
> — But he, that old man? I mean do you know him?
> — Know him! A cloud of smoke billowed at the windows, and he leaned down to stamp out the cigarette — every time I'd look up, see him out there every time I looked up pretending he's doing something worth doing look at him, ten dead leaves in his damned dustpan he's still trying to prove he was put here for some purpose? Swing low sweet chariot, staring up there at that string of toilet paper coming for to carry him home good God, you talk about bare ruined choirs? Gaping up there as if he hears their gentle voices calling, that's when I started pouring a drink in the morning.[7]

The religious lingo enters early: "from the house above" "like an offering" "ceremonial concern" "upright like a crosier" "gaze on high" "benisons." A military tinge is added: "reporting for duty." Finally, at the very edge of the rant, the real subject surfaces: "damned recessional" "put here for some purpose" "swing low sweet chariot" "comin for to carry him home" "good God" "bare ruined choirs." Shakespeare amid spirituals. And a T-Peed tree.

The clouds are forming for the on-coming storm. Our speaker has been making a little change by writing text books, stuff on Darwin, evolution, origins, and of course these texts were censored by people resembling (so he thinks) the dustpan man. The tirade breaks. Quarter-sized hail rains down.

> — Because it's the same damned thing! here... — a high school encyclopaedia entry on Darwin, see all this blue penciling? They cut it from sixteen thousand to a hundred and ten the next edition it won't be there at all.
> Origins of life get twenty eight, twenty eight mealy mouthed words, listen....[8]

We start in the gear called "high dudgeon" because we have been held in neutral for a long time when we want to roar, gun the engine, drive off in a shower of gravel, sparks, and exhaust. The rant likes to assume a moral tone appropriate to an ignored prophet, but there is always in the background a personal complaint, a festering sore, an injury as local as a toothache. It was not just the emasculation of Darwin's text that was annoying, it was the ranter's own textbook account that was cut. (It is Gaddis's own hand that we see in the spelling of encyclopedia though, like an initialed ok, because his encyclopaedia is undeniably Greek and its spelling untouched by contemporary practice).

> — here's what they want now, listen. Some people believe that evolution explains the diversity of organisms on earth. Some people do not believe organisms were

created as they appear. No one knows for sure how the many different kinds of living things came to be. No one knows for sure how many smug illiterate idiots are out there peddling this kind of drivel here's another one, listen to this.[9]

The rant, as you hear it, is built on repetition. Its sentences love to return to their beginnings. "Some people believe...." "Some people do not believe...." Not only does the return allow a balance between positive and negative assertions of formally equal weight, but it also permits nice small alterations of placement and meaning. "No one knows for sure how the many...." "No one knows for sure how many smug...."

Will Rogers used to read the papers to us, and Karl Kraus captured lies as Nabokov did butterflies and showed them to the Viennese, *wort für wort*, as they spoke them, as if they were convicted by their own mouths and had paraded their foolishness down the public streets. His audiences laughed; they felt entertained; they experienced some satisfactory superiority as this pomposity passed; and then they went home and slipped into a healthy sleep as easily as they did into their slippers. Gaddis clipped too. He had pockets full of imbecilities, and books like *J R* are made of newspapers and magazines laid out like drying noodles. What generates the steam of the rant is its futility.

> Another hypothesis about the creation of the universe with all its life forms is special creation. In some school systems, it is mandated that the evolution and special creation theories be taught side by side. That seems a healthy attitude in view of the tenuous nature of hypothesis. A healthy attitude! [...] find their biology textbook, you look up geologic eras? fossil remains? Nothing. Paleontology? The word itself is gone, it's just disappeared.[10]

The suspicion strengthens that these censorious people (that this rant is censorious about) cannot be as stupid as they sound; that they know they stand on nothing but weakness; therefore they must have a profit or a power motive, since this would account for their dissembling. And the contradictions in their behavior are another indication of hypocrisy. For instance, they — and now it's "they" — pretend to oppose abortion at the same time they oppose sex education and contraception, and refuse to support healthy social reforms that might solidify families, alter macho attitudes in order to lessen peer pressure on women to yield to men. In short, they want to increase the need for abortion while denouncing it. The ranter contemplates the numbers of his enemies, their organization, its zealotry, its wealth, and he feels alone, unheard, and impotent.

Gaddis works with fragments: bit of news, scraps of speech, pieces of information, dollops of data. His rants are broken and scattered too, popping up in the text here and there like distant echoes. He has been reading H.L. Mencken's *The American Language* (1919) where he found a name that had been in the news:

> Few persons would recognize Smackover, the name of a small town in Arkansas, as French, and yet in its original form it was Chemin Couvert. Schele de Vere, in 1871, recorded the degeneration of the name to Smack Cover; the Postoffice,

always eager to shorten and simplify names, has since made one word of it and got rid of the redundant c.[11]

The rant rises like the mistral from moan to howl.

> Think I made it up? like the name on that book there? You think ignorance isn't dead serious? Red Dirt, rolling hills, a rail line, trickle of a stream and a town grows up there, great trees meeting overhead down the main street and some civilized person names the place Chemin-couvert. A generation or two of ignorance settles in and you've got Smackover, a hundred years of it and you've got a trial like that one, defending the Bible against the powers of darkness they're doing more to degrade it taking every damned word in it literally than any militant atheist could ever hope to. Foolishness found in the heart of a child but the rod of correction shall drive it out so they whale the daylights out of their kids with sticks. And they take up serpents so they get liquored up and see how many rattlesnakes they can get into a burlap bag, talk about homo habilis in East Africa two million years ago, homo sapiens homo anything they know what a homo is don't they? the men of Sodom telling Lot to bring out his two visiting angels for a little buggery? back in Deuteronomy breaking down the houses of the sodomites? and abomination in Leviticus? these vile affections in Saint Paul burning in their lust to one another?[12]

Incoherent sputter is the consequence of a mind driven to exasperation.

So another occupation of the ranter is his habit of reading a lot from newspapers, magazines, and whatnot outrageous statements, claims, and predictions made by the mad members of the opposition, putting it into the speech stream à la Karl Kraus in the same way other missteps were scissored from some offending periodical. This is best done while enjoying a breakfast coffee. It begins the damnable day.

> —No no here it is, here it is listen. You think that circus in Tennessee straightened things out? Here's a judge in Georgia right now, listen to him.[13]

Now we arrive at a more complex distinction than heretofore has been necessary, but its occurrence is common enough. The ranter reads the rant of another ranter, sometimes one of whom he approves, although more often it is that of an opponent. Unlike metaphysics or metalanguage, the metarant does not pretend to furnish its object basic principles or justifications of any kind, or even talk about the rant the way I'm doing, but instead rants about their ranting and its specific occurrences. He mocks his adversary's style by entering into it, complains of this imposture's place in Hyde Park, sneers at the printing of his handouts, and wants to slam shut every opening of his present speciman's mouth with a passion born of alliteration and allusion.

> This monkey mythology of Darwin is the cause of abortions, permissiveness, promiscuity, pollution, poisoning, and proliferation of crimes of all types what happened to pederasty, penis envy, peeping Toms, do you think he's got business with the Bible? those bums in Samuel that pisseth against the wall by the morning light?[14]

You can be certain that the ranter is reading from his source correctly because he has his source in the witness box, accuracy is essential to the case; but Gaddis may have made his own arrangement of the material so that the o sounds are in the first series and the e sounds in the second. It is not that rephrasing is not permitted, but usually it is confined to sarcastic summaries of the opponent's point of view, during which the proper disdain may be displayed.

> Two versions right there in the first two pages, have your choice. You get the animals first and then man around the sixth day, male and female created he them, or you get man from the dust and then the animals show up lined up like kids at summer camp to get their names and finally Miss America made from a spare rib.[15]

The ranter likes to be a table-turner. If his enemy likes to quote scripture, he's ready and has a line up of contradictions, confusions, shocking admissions, and other signs of malfeasance to refer to. The thumper bellows a citation, the debunker thunders back another — better than a snowball fight. Very recently I received in the mail a message from Tony Alamo Christian Ministries that would have delighted Gaddis. Included was a leaflet warning the reader about the dangers of being blessed by the Pope. "In 1912, the Pope blessed the Titanic," and look what happened to it, "it sank on the maiden voyage." Being cursed by the Pope, on the other hand, is a stroke of luck. "Garibaldi was excommunicated" and look was happened to him, "he became Italy's hero." Arguments with Marxists were a lot like this when we had them. But if holy books are not involved it can be data and testimonials about global warming from this scientific authority or that government agency. These are not rational disagreements, of course; these are not debates but pissing contests and spews of hate. And the people who attend these brawls are usually so suspicious they will believe anything.

So, in the face of so much fearful stupid stubbornness, what's the real effect of the anti-rant rant? I ask the question of Gaddis because I share his feelings: why the bother? when it is so useless? when every day people carry their shit to the midden? If one is sitting on the hill of righteousness beyond the smell of such error, misinformation, ignorance, and bad logic, should we not settle down to a nice wedge of brie and a bottle of cab beneath the bough? Every year we can read with smug satisfaction about how many were trampled to death this time in Mecca, and how the bullets from celebrant rifles rained down on some unhappy town. Is it really because one day they will piss lead on us? Let the baby washers save the little children from the fires of hell. Let the Jews line up against one wall to pray and another to be shot. Let the rapture threaten to pull up everything by its roots. Can't we wash these hands of ours at least; that can't do any decent surgery anyhow? hands we can only throw in the air in despair. The human race desires to be benighted, desires to be deceived, has loved its myths and superstitions since those first dawns when we stood as if noble on our own two feet and found our thumbs were so opposed we cut them off.

2—The Kvetch, the Rant, and the Bitch *(William H. Gass)*

We love all the implements of death we've made since we found a rock with a real edge to cut our meat, or to remove the hearts of maidens from their otherwise unfondled breasts. We have scarified ourselves, circumcised one another, and vowed to mingle our blood in the brotherhood of HIV. Death indeed is our destination, and our one real god. Not money. Not duncery. Not even a saving membership in some rigmarole society. So what is the point of ranting and raving? Ah, yes, we enjoy it. And I have a rant I can lend you that will raise you right off the ground on jets of orgasmic steam.

> The new generation blames the old one for the mess it inherits and they lump us all together because all they see is what we've become, lying in wait for you out there one misstep and they pounce, grab one straw of expediency and they're on to you for betraying yourself, betraying them, selling out like the ones writing bad books and bad everything who are doing the best they can.[16]

But this is a bitch not a rant.

It is ironic to turn one's rant against the religious, because they practically invented the form. The ranter was not just a noisy talker or a merry jovial fellow deep in his cups, although the tongue that likker likes to loosen leads to ranting so regularly that the word slid over from the sot's slurs to the toss pot himself. He was a mad Methodist contaminating street corners and haranguing passersby in 1810 or thereabouts. Earlier, the Ranters were associated by the careless mind with other off-beats who occupied the seventeenth century in irregularity: Levellers, Quakers, Muggletonians, Fifth Monarchists, Behmenists, Diggers, and ill-assorted hermeticists. Protestant fusillades were met by Catholic flurries, from pamphlet to tome and back again bounced bad-tempered missiles, and expressions of tolerance could be best summed up in a joke: as the modern clergyman said to the dissenting minister: "After all, we both serve the same Master, you in your way and I in His."[17] "The first commission given by God to John Reeve and Ludowick Muggleton was to visit the Ranting prophets, John Robins and Thomas Tany, and pronounce upon them a sentence of eternal damnation."[18] Some of these belligerent volumes sound more interesting than others however. I especially admire (without ever having seen them) *The Back-Parts of Jehovah* (1608) and *Bowels Opened* (1639).

With Gaddis's rants there is intermixed a curiously morose lyricism. It appears without warning, and often occupies a chapter's concluding moment. There are instances of sensuality too, but these are often diabolically undercut, as if the prose understood the price that must be paid for a pleasant sensation. Liz, the unfortunate lady of *Carpenter's Gothic*'s house, lies back on an adulterous bed and makes a gesture that is rendered thus:

> Feet curled close in the frolic of sunlight through the trees outside and her nipples drawn up hard with a hand passing down her breast, out to the knee flexing up for its reach, gliding down slowly on a hard edge of nails to the rising fall and the warmth of breath lingering in the villous suspense of her legs fallen wide open.[19]

The knee that rises to meet its caress is cat-like as are the claws that follow. The unfamiliar word appears to create a bit of villous suspense. They — these villi — are fine light hairs that create a velvety surface — especially that on the mucous membrane of the small intestine. In a subsequent grooming gesture, as her lover nuzzles her breast, a blackhead is removed from the blockhead's face.

The lyricism is undercut too, because the good things of life live a perilous existence, moving in and out among evils like imprisoned fish dart about in their plastic grottos and palaces of painted plaster. A male character (in Gaddis you learn the actor's names only when one of them refers to another in that way), McCandless, sits in front of a fire where he's burned more than wood, sits and settles to read a passage from V.S. Naipaul's *The Mimic Men* (1967), a book he has selected from packed shelves, and one that will be introduced with a series of rhymes loud as trumpets.

> Taking one down, and another, running through them to stop at pages checked in the margins, to stare at those passages perplexed as though someone else must have marked them, must have found some stinging revelation in this inconsequential line, or that one, jamming them back till he came on one with a narrow orange spine as if it were what he'd been after all this time.[20]

The passage McCandless reads is quoted, a rare act, so we recognize this as an important moment. Meanwhile, "from the kitchen, the chords of Bach's D major concerto heaved into the room around him and settled like furniture."[21]

The great heavy music has arrived as he has, at home in his old house as he is, yet most uncomfortable there as he is, reading a novel about cultural disjunction and alienation on a Caribbean island where the natives mimic the colonial culture they believe to be superior to their own while trying to discard the ways that they were given when they were born. But if a people lose faith in their customs and callings, what about their rejected clothing, cuisine, their arts of writing, music, and the dance? Like all those gods now disbelieved in, they wander about looking for a job, for love and devotion, appreciation and security.

The music issues from the kitchen? heaves itself as though thrown? everywhere in this house, amid the bickering, petty thievery, and betrayal, there is a sadness too sad for rant.

3

The Power of Babel: Art, Entropy, and Aporia in the Novels

CHRISTOPHER LEISE

> *Once again the Roman qualities of America overwhelm one: everything based on power, on mean gold rather than the golden mean. America is in a way the inability to think of gold metaphorically.*
> —John Fowles, *The Journals*, Vol. 2

> *[M]oney's just a yardstick, isn't it. It's the only common reference people have for making other people take them as seriously as they take themselves, I mean that's all they're really asking for, isn't it?*
> —William Gaddis, *A Frolic of His Own*

INTRODUCTION

Near the middle of *The Recognitions*, a very drunk Otto Pivner stumbles into the Viareggio, a favorite Italian restaurant of the New York intellectual/art scene that populates Gaddis's first novel. As the jukebox ceaselessly pumps out the strains of *Return to Sorrento*, Otto attempts to persuade his social network that he has just sold his play, while he is himself convinced that he has just met his father for the first time, who gifted the struggling playwright five thousand dollars in cash.[1] Otto is in large part ignored: only Stanley exhibits interest.

As is so often the case in Gaddis's novels, Otto's attempted conversation with the composer and Catholic acolyte is continually interrupted. One of its greatest antagonists is the poet Anselm, who constantly interjects with insults, commentary on Otto's comments, and occasional readings from the texts that he is carrying. The frustrating sequence begins with a kind of monologue:

—"The whole gripping story is grounded on fact. Look at the beautiful girl shown in the accompanying cut...." Anselm read aloud.—Are you listening? "Note the cruel marks cut in her tender body by the lash of the cat-o'-nine tails wielded by the hands of a heartless and Christless Mother Superior in whose heart all human sympathy had been assassinated by the papal system...." He lowered *The Moan of the Tiber* to look up at Stanley.[2]

Perhaps one of the reasons that the source for this quote has remained hitherto elusive to Gaddis critics is due to the fact that Gaddis is not quoting Guy Fitch Phelps's 1917 narrative of a Protestant girl lured into a Catholic convent, *The Moan of the Tiber,* but something only close.³ That *The Recognitions* would cite a tale of suspicion regarding the treacherous influence of "popery," a kind of convent captivity, is not surprising: in the fifth chapter of part III, Esme is found reading a number of similar editions. She asks, with Rebecca Reed's *Six Months in a Convent* (1835) in hand, apparently in preparation for joining a convent herself: "—But isn't that how it's going to be?...[.]"⁴ Anselm's quote is actually culled from an advertisement for *Moan of the Tiber,* which specific copy is really describing a woodcut that serves as *cover art* on the edition described, not the narrative itself.⁵

Notably, the entire chaotic encounter concludes, after Anselm has quoted variously from a magazine, as "his elbow rest[ed] on *The Moan of the Tiber.*" In a maneuver that is characteristically Gaddis, it would seem (mostly from the italics, suggesting a full work, and most probably a book) that Anselm's elbow is resting upon a book, a volume independent of the magazine from which he also reads. But it is equally possible the narrative is indicating Anslem's elbow rests upon the advertisement for that book, contained within his magazine. What remains unclear is exactly which discourse to which the narrative is appealing: the book, a description of the book, or a wood-carving that serves as emblematic for the content that is to be contained within the book.

This collapse of advertisement, cover art, and primary text as given in the example of *The Moan of the Tiber* is an exemplar of Gaddis's method. Evidencing numerous playful challenges to his reader's intelligence, Gaddis's novels are often as patient and accommodating as one needs be to read them, simultaneously providing his own best artistic accomplishments along with a methodology by which they can be understood.⁶ Beginning with *Agapē Agape,* this essay will show that Gaddis's fictions theorize themselves by developing a hermeneutic based upon the assumption that his reader is listening closely, and that one can learn both from Gaddis's own prose and the numerous texts he brings to his aid. Moving into the larger novels— *The Recognitions, J R,* and *A Frolic of his Own*— an exegetical practice most clearly laid out in his final work will reveal a complex but coherent idea of what a successful work of art is and does. Like Fowles, as quoted above in this essay's epigraph, Gaddis's novels bemoan the fact that "America is in a way the inability to think of gold metaphorically"; instead, his writing congratulates art-works that expose America's thinking of gold *synecdochically,* as one kind of discourse that serves in place of the full set of numerous, competing discourses which compose contemporary life.

In working to rethink America's reliance on a kind of "gold standard" that tends to reduce all meaning to a pragmatist's cash value, Gaddis's novels invite their reader to play an ancient game: the Greek parlor game of aporia,⁷ wherein the point is to ask questions for which there are no answers. In playing this game, Gaddis effectively rewrites the biblical story of the Tower of Babel in moments like Anselm's tirade by creating sites where absolute interpretation is obviated through the collision of discourses. Rather than misunderstandings between languages, his game plays out in irresolvable ambiguities that require his reader to assent to multiple conclusions and thus no single interpretation. These collisions serve to contest the claims to determinacy asserted by society's most powerful institutions through the opening of these various discourses to their environments, thereby preventing the entropic decline of clichéd and idiomatic language that constantly moves towards the meaninglessness of homogeneity.

ENTROPY AND APORIA

As in the majority of his novels, it seems that most of the characters in *J R* are artists, who profess a highly developed set of expectations for what artifacts can and should do. But Stephen Schryer illustrates that these characters' impulses to create "an object that is purposive without a purpose, giving disinterested pleasure but irreducible to immediate gratification" are countermanded by the representation of these same characters within the novel itself.[8] In fact, Schryer's argument holds with most of Gaddis's would-be artists: almost to the last, they not only fail to achieve their stated goals, but they also rarely ever actually *complete* anything. While characters like Jack Gibbs (*J R*'s would-be playwright who instead only succeeds at amassing massive quantities of source materials in disorganized boxes), Edward Bast (a second-generation composer whose grandiose dreams of an elaborate opera are consistently scaled down to a final expression of a solo cello piece scrawled in crayon), and Oscar Crease[9] (*Frolic's* failed playwright) endlessly seek to keep the outside world out of their compositions, Schryer contends that the era of commercialization continually recontexualizes all art within a corporate/consumerist paradigm. The ostensibly "closed," autotelic works that Bast or Gibbs (named after the seminal systems theorist, Josiah Willard Gibbs) would produce are opened to their environments and are thus manipulated and interpreted for and by their audiences to serve ends unintended at the time of their composition. Hence, though Jack Gibbs often refers to the first-order cybernetics of Willard Gibbs and Norbert Wiener as a method of critiquing his own situation, Schryer shows that the works Gaddis produces more fully exemplify, and are better explicated through, the ideas promoted by second-order cybernetics.

According to Schryer, "*J R*'s second-order perspectivalism turns the novel into a theatrical work, one that solicits the reader's participation in the creation of its meaning"[10]; and he distills the evolution of first-order cybernetic theory into second-order as follows:

> The purpose of cybernetics, for Norbert Wiener and most other first-order cyberneticists, was to reduce phenomena to information patterns, which could then be discussed in terms of the order (information) and disorder (entropy) found within them. Most first-order cyberneticists assumed that the systems being described could be observed from an outsider's point of objective point of view; cybernetics allowed scientists to describe real features of the world.[11]

The problem with this type of observation, Schryer continues, is something of a standard postmodern critique of scientific principles, which is that true objectivity is ultimately impossible. From this shortcoming, a productive difficulty emerges: all observers have blind spots of which they are unaware. With observation, the system observed is made into a new system, which then must be observed — in the process creating yet another system, and so on.[12] In effect, the object of study is always the product of its observer's epistemic framework, and so the system being observed has no inherent meaning as such.

The impossibility of self-contained meaning problematizes any concept of the art-object as self-sufficient inasmuch as the discrete art entity cannot be perfect in and of itself. Hence Gaddis's fictions, Schryer points out, discount this modernist ideal by opening themselves to every possible distraction and influence presented by the world in everyday life. Conversations are continually interrupted, as often by radio, television, and print as they are by the numerous self-interested characters that populate his worlds. *J R*, like *Carpenter's Gothic* and *A Frolic of His Own*, constantly present systems at the brink of chaos, all requiring an ordering observer, which produces its meaning.[13] By their almost total suppression of the narrative voice, Schryer concludes "the reader becomes a second-order observer, able to look at the characters' blindspots but unable to achieve a total understanding of their world. At times in his novel, Gaddis thus juxtaposes different characters' points of view, forcing the reader to decide between them."[14] While a compelling suggestion, I contend that this apparent irresolvability, rather than "forcing the reader to decide," seizes upon a productive ambiguity that is the key to Gaddis's own theory of art. For, while he criticizes most of his own characters' attempts to produce the autonomous, sublime object, Gaddis is also highly suspicious, appealing to scientific discourse to explain away art's most affective instances, even if — or, as I will explain, precisely *because* — they defy explication.

Throughout *J R*, Jack Gibbs's language and environment consistently indicate the near-constant presence of entropy — that is, the measure of the tendency within closed systems to reach a state of maximum chaos or disorder. Within mechanical systems, forces like friction are in large part responsible: within communications, the entropic agent is noise. Norbert Wiener clarifies his belief in the relationship between entropy and communication systems in the unfortunately titled *The Human Use of Human Beings* (1954), a book that Gaddis's Gibbs identifies as essential to understanding successful communication. Recognizing that entropy is the most likely condition in a system, Wiener examines the successful message in relation to disorder:

> Messages are themselves a form of pattern and organization. Indeed, it is possible to treat sets of messages as having entropy like sets of states of the external world. Just as entropy is a measure of disorganization, the information carried by a set of messages is a measure of organization. In fact, it is possible to interpret the information carried by a message as essentially the negative of its entropy, and the negative logarithm of its probability. That is, the more probable the message, the less information it gives. Clichés, for example, are less illuminating than great poems.[15]

Yet with entropy threatening at every turn, one must expend a good deal of energy in an attempt to overcome it. Thus, Wiener identifies two solutions — keep the message simple, and repeat it often. By referring us to the primary texts that inform his creative process, Gaddis is in fact teaching his readership how to decode his messages: repetition, first-order cybernetics illustrates, clues us in to the novels' greatest concerns. Second-order cybernetics reminds us that our understanding will always be incomplete: an incompleteness that, after reexamining the novels' *successful* artworks (as well as the artistry of the novels themselves), is productive rather than prohibitive.

But if science provides a useful metaphor for making sense of the kind of work Gaddis aims for in his fictions, ultimately what one takes away from the experience cannot be fully shared. As Wyatt explains, taken too far, scientism can shine so bright a light as to make the art itself invisible:

> — Science explains it to us now. The man who painted [the *Mona Lisa*] couldn't see what he was doing. She didn't really have an enigmatic smile, that woman. But he couldn't see what he was doing. Leonardo had eye trouble.[...] — Art couldn't explain it [....] — But now we're safe, since science can explain it.[16]

Science, Wyatt continues, goes so far into reducing the world, and the art in the world into its constituent parts, that the whole is no longer recoverable.[17] But Gaddis does not leave us foundering in the wake of science entirely problematized: through his prose, he demonstrates the method he advocates.

It is the reading lesson inherent that makes Gaddis's final novel first in approachability, and it is for this reason that the following examination begins with *Agapē Agape*. Unlike the two most critically successful novels — the winners of the 1975 (*J R*) and 1994 (*Frolic*) National Book Award for fiction — which both begin with *questions,* *Agapē Agape* begins with a declaration of purpose: "No but you see I've got to explain all this because I don't, we don't know how much time there is left and I have to work on the, finish this work of mine."[18] Like the details of his estate, the narrator wants desperately to "sort out" his work, to

> get it cleared up and settled before everything collapses and it's all swallowed up by lawyers and taxes like everything else because that's what it's all about, that is what my work is about, the collapse of everything, of meaning, of language, of values, of art, disorder and dislocation wherever you look, entropy drowning everything in sight.[19]

In large part, his "work" is directly related to "sorting out" the problems facing the art world. In effect, the world of art, artists, collectors, and "appreciators" presented in *Agapē Agape* is a mess. Rather than succumb to the fear of failure even though "we've always hated failure in America like some great character flaw,"[20] this novel seeks to pose a question that cannot be answered. Its discourse comprises a series of contradictions and irresolvable questions: the ranting *Agapē Agape* is like the Greek parlor game aporia, which Gaddis defines as:

> [the] game you couldn't win, nobody could win, a parlour game proposing questions there was no clear answer to so winning wasn't the point of it no, no that's ours isn't it, *right on the money* because that's what the game is, the only game in town because that's what America's.[21]

So maybe Sven Birkerts is right, as he insists in his introduction, that "Gaddis has never been what we would call 'reader-friendly.'"[22] But he's in our neighborhood, and he's willing to play a little game. Though unable to win, we also cannot lose; and all along, he's teaching us the strategy: one that only reveals itself while we play, instructing not only how to live with uncertainty, but also to embrace and exalt the positive aspects of confusion. Unconcerned with getting it exactly right or merely avoiding failure, Gaddis's final novel is one that ultimately answers its own question about evaluating art with "this swamp of ambiguity, paradox, anarchy they're calling aporia" to seize upon the positive potential of confusion, to invoke the power of Babel as productive and creative, rather than the biblical punishment for creative hubris.[23]

Aporia and Art/Criticism

That discord and disagreement can be a positive element of understanding art has been noted by other critics of Gaddis's writing: in his introduction to *The Rush for Second Place*, Joseph Tabbi argues that "[t]he novel as a generic form was all things for Gaddis; not least, it was a medium for criticism" that "widened the boundaries of fiction to include [a] criticism" in which he "redefined the creative artist as a performer."[24] Despite their self-consciously critical elements, however, we must also be careful to retain the sense that, above and beyond the works' critical aspects, the novels are themselves creative works, and Gaddis himself a major artist. At once critical and artistic, contestant and creative, his fictions have a unique quality of the metafictional that branches beyond commentary on fiction and into the whole of the artistic proper. They present a theory of art that positions the artwork and its creator within the system of capital that problematizes the conditions of creative production, but ultimately allows for resistance against the system's totalizing efforts by effecting the examination of a society too wholly reliant upon exchange value as a definitional principle.

One of the clearest examples of Gaddis's meta-artistic commentary appears in a characteristically intertextual moment that unifies the action of *J R* and *Frolic*. In the former, we learn that a young boy finds himself entrapped in the Long Island instantiation of the sculpture series *Cyclone Seven*; Gaddis's readers would have to wait nineteen years to learn of the resolution of the crisis, wherein Judge Crease reports that "a proffered ten dollar bill brought [the boy] forth little for the worse."[25] While Gaddis makes it clear through this fictional example that the lure of the dollar may serve to distract, or even save (in a militantly capitalist manner of speaking) a curious mind from the danger that art poses, the rest of his works serve the purpose of disproving the possibility for the inverse: that exchange value can neither serve to represent art, nor can it fully bring art under control, coax it into arm's length where a relieved parental figure can wrap a blanket around its shoulders and bring it safely back to the familiar.

But the expectation for art that his corpus presents goes much further than the difficulty of articulating the impact of the artwork: many aestheticians have noted the ineffable quality inherent in great art objects. Surely any attempt to arrive at a dollar figure as representative of a work's true worth is ultimately arbitrary; though it may represent something of the collector's desire for it, such a figure says nothing of the work's inherent value.[26] The failure of the discourse of commodity capitalism to adequately represent such value provides a key for unlocking the potential for a successful artwork in Gaddis's novels. By both depicting and creating works of art that force disparate discourses into competition for the accurate expression of the place that art holds in society, these texts clearly bring forth America's (extraordinarily flawed) tendency to rely upon the terms of commodity capitalism — namely, the dollar — to function as the stable signifier to and on which all meaning production relies and abides.

Tabbi argues that "[Gaddis's] fiction is not *opposed* to religion or the state," as in the sense of dialectics, "[r]ather, his work tries to discover what individual life can and should be in the midst of collective life."[27] To this, I would add that it is fiction that attempts to acknowledge the inevitability of the resistant voice to be co-opted into the dominant discourse(s) of American society. Gaddis's theory of art does not mandate that the artist reach some point "outside" the system as much as it recognizes a fundamental inability to do so: second-order cybernetics has shown that such an outside position always finds itself on the inside of a new system produced at the site of contact between the observer and the system being viewed. Indeed, so many of his characters' projects, as well as many of Gaddis's own writings, rely upon funding from the centers of political and economic power (in the form of institutional grants or, when necessary, actual *jobs* undertaken by the artists outside the sphere of purely artistic work) to provide the support for their creation. Rather, Gaddis's fictions (as well as his characters' successful art-works) utilize their position *within* an imperfect society to develop the conditions wherein meaningful and productive conversations about the failures of that system are addressed. In its being co-opted by systemic forces that endeavor to totalize, Gaddis shows the artwork can have a unique type of efficacy that gets to the very center of discursive systems and exposes their edges, their failure to account for everything, their limited and restrictive terms.

Yet the ubiquitous attempts to resolve questions of meaning into the terms of capital permeate all of the novels. *A Frolic of his Own* repeatedly asserts the complaint that "money is the only language they speak," a use of "they" that seems to refer to absolutely everyone, perhaps none more so than those voicing that criticism. Similarly, the title character in *J R* practices the uncompassionate, unrelenting exploitation and exhaustion of an institution's or individual's commodity value for as much personal gain as possible because "That's just what you do." Gaddis is acutely aware of the capitalistic obsession with the primacy exchange value, and particularly concerned with the deleterious effect that such a drive can have on art, and on human behavior in general.[28] Sven Birkerts, in his introduction to *Agapē Agape,* notes Gaddis's concerns "about the growth of binary thinking and what he saw as the epochal shift from artistic to entertainment values[....] The questioning of the authenticity and authority of the artistic work (*The Recognitions*) and the warping force of capitalism (*J R*), especially in the cultural arena."[29] Similarly, Gaddis himself expressed a wariness of the types of capitalist reductions that stemmed from the legacy of pragmatism and the Protestant ethic:

> In his lecture "What Pragmatism Means," the pragmatist, said James, "turns away from abstraction and insufficiency, from verbal solutions, from bad *a priori* reasons, from fixed principles, closed systems, and pretended absolutes and origins. He turns towards concreteness and adequacy, towards facts, towards actions and towards power.... You must," he insisted — bypassing "God" as a verbal solution — "bring out of each word its practical cash-value, set it at work within the stream of your experience."
>
> Pragmatism, says Hofstadter, "was absorbed into the national culture when men were thinking of manipulation and control." [...] In a nation ravenous for progress in the shape of material goods, the logical outcome was the concept of mass production.[30]

From this skepticism towards pragmatism, by extension, one can see the decline in the ability of the artistic public to appreciate great art on the grounds of pure aesthetic appreciation alone. If the masses demand widely intellectually unchallenging works that Valentine characterizes as "soul-seeking abominations"[31] for base pleasure or personal affirmation, the elitists demand only that which has been sanctioned by tradition and validated at the auction block. In either case, artistic production and aesthetic value are corrupted by a desire for the simple experience of pleasure or the collection of more and more wealth. The impulse of art for art's sake, if it ever existed, is surely now extinct.

IN THE SHADOW OF BABEL

Being more than a critic, however, Gaddis provides us with writings that successfully challenge the oppressive forces they face, both within his fictions and the world into which they are published. The manner in which he enacts his theory is particularly evident at several points in *A Frolic of His Own*, by producing the type of art that can contest the systemic reduction, or reification of abstracts, to a quantitative figure in the form of a dollar value. A particularly revelatory passage occurs at a rare moment when Gaddis gives one of the oblique narrative markers that signify a passage of time or a scene shift: here, we learn that Oscar Crease, the adjunct history professor and aspiring playwright, recently parted company with his much younger lover, Lily. He has slept, woken, and is at breakfast reading a newspaper when a surfeit of details overwhelms reader and character alike. Oscar slams the paper down to voice his disgust and frustration about the *Cyclone Seven* lawsuit, over which Oscar's father is presiding. To this outburst, his sister Christina responds:

> —The confusion of tongues was the way Harry [Christina's husband] put it, simply another language, art theory referring only to itself "stripping the forms of art to the bone, shaking off the emotional excesses of abstract expressionism" reducing art itself to theory with no more substance than that swarm of flies the Judge stepped on in his Szyrk opinion while Szyrk himself is out there somewhere right now hearing it exalted in terms of death and transfiguration, of the sacred seizing the profane in an embrace seething with sexual ferment saying it all "makes him puke" with these "hints of Christian sacrifice and suffering, its suggestions of journeys without end as the sculptor seems to turn away, smitten to the point where its beams buckle in shyness yet remain as firm and vigilant as a dog who has cornered its prey"—to coin a phrase, as Christina broke off.[32]

The nature of the referential quality of this passage is extraordinarily difficult to determine. Whether certain elements are either direct or indirect discourse, and what sources are cited in the formulation of Szyrk's reactions to the controversy, are left entirely unclear—are, in a word, aporetic. Careful attention to the development of Christina's voice throughout the novel shows that there is a significant deviation from her usual manner of speaking ("seething with sexual ferment" departs significantly from her established parlance), suggesting the intrusion of the narrative voice. Similarly, the comma after "the way Harry put it" and the subsequent hyphen preceding "to coin a phrase" is consistent with the types of signification used to indicate the cessation and resumption of direct discourse. This difficulty of determination creates frustrating conditions for a reader interested in an exact knowledge of what she is being presented. Birkerts says of Gaddis's prose, "I was told by one Gaddis-adept that reading [*J R*] was a swim or drown proposition, that to strive for exact coordinates was to court madness; that the only way to hold the sense was by moving forward in great gulps."[33] In fact, this instilled frustration is a crucial element in Gaddis's presentation of the possibility for politically or critically efficacious artworks.

Gaddis's gesture to the Tower of Babel reveals another facet of the possibilities available to the artist interested in the production of a work for some other purpose than monetary compensation. Recalling how the tower produced in the biblical allegory created confusion within the spoken languages of its maker (though, in this instance, the ensuing frustration is detrimental to society), we can see how both *Cyclone Seven* and the novel in which it is created produces a similar "confusion of tongues."[34] Gaddis's enacted critique of the tendency of American discursive practices to rely upon capitalist valuation as a stabilizing signifier is manifest precisely in this notion of a confusion of tongues. By producing a novel of frustration, Gaddis creates a field into which many different systems of representation are thrown into contact, each wrestling to arrive at an understanding of things in the human experience — human life, aesthetic appreciation, youthful sentiment towards a mixed-breed pound pup, etc. — that are utterly un-exchangeable, and thus un-representable in monetary terms. For Gaddis, then, it is the job of the artist to create the spaces where different discourses collide, demonstrating their inability to represent values that exist outside the sphere of monetary figuration. The reader's frustration follows, who might then recognize the shortcomings of the tendencies of capitalist discourses to treat commodity value as a fixed and fixing center of meaning. We are frustrated, Gaddis shows us, precisely because the discursive systems available are frustrated in their attempts to adequately deal with these problems with which they are confronted.

The game of aporia continues when the narrative follows Christina's intrusion into an intimate interaction between Oscar and Lily in *Frolic*. As Lily attempts to get at Oscar's wallet (although via the *front* of his pants), Oscar "retreats" from the awkward situation by himself referring to an historical retreat:

> —I told you. I have to get together my notes for this talk on Shiloh, the battle at Shiloh, it was the second great battle of the of the war he went on, covering his wavering retreat from this hostile incursion with the haphazard deployment of Grant's forces in the face of the surprise Confederate advance on Pittsburgh Landing in an April dawn near Shiloh church till he gained the redoubt of cardboard cartons still stacked there in the hall where he pawed through folders, loose notes, exam books, raw troops on both sides fueled by the exuberance of battle as disorder mounted.[35]

Again, attempts to determine what exactly is being presented in these lines are extraordinarily frustrating. Whose "wavering retreat" is being described is not clearly articulated: it is either Oscar's retreat from his awkward situation, Grant's retreat from the Confederate onslaught, or, most likely, both.[36] The passage nearly demands rereading, but ultimately defies an absolute interpretation: the reader cannot win, but can continue to play Gaddis's parlor game.

As Schryer has shown, any sense of "winning" would be illusory: something will always escape the permanent fixing of meaning. Instead, the nature of the reader's responsibility in meaning production plays a significant role in the type of critique the novels enact. Struggling to sort the information provided into meaningful structures (and, as we know from Thomas Pynchon, sorting most certainly *is* work[37]), the reader discovers other artworks that demonstrate the inability for discursive systems to impose order on significant cites of chaos. The most obvious case in point involves the *Cyclone Seven* sculptures and their tendency to incite nationwide controversy. In a 1994 review of *Frolic*, Jonathan Raban points out: "Gaddis sees entropy: the world is not so much going to hell as suffering from the inevitable degradation of a closed system, its language wearing out from overuse."[38] The atrophying of language has been a concern of Gaddis's fictions from the start. Treating Esme's poetics in *The Recognitions*, the narrator explains:

> The sole way, it seemed to her often enough when she was working at writing a poem, to use words with meaning, would be to choose words for themselves, and invest them with her own meaning: not her own, perhaps, but meaning which was implicit in their shape, too frequently nothing to do with dictionary definition. The words which the tradition of her art offered her were by now in chaos, coerced through the context of a million inanities [...] and when they reached her hands they were brittle, straining and cracking [...].[39]

Recalling Wiener's critique of cliché, Esme notes that overuse by conventional poetic language has strained language to the point of breaking. In *Frolic*, we see that the closed system of legal discourse has homogenized the meaning of language to a single signifier: $. The successful artist, Gaddis shows us, opens up these closed systems and provides an outside source of energy that disrupts the homogeneity of meaning and revitalizes the language. Thus, his prose itself stands in opposition to legal discourse: while the language of law reluctantly opens itself to outside influence (after all, *stare decisis*, the principle that precedent should be observed in all but the most extreme of cases, is the rule), Gaddis's novels prevent any discourse from "referring only to itself," creating aperatures to their environments and allowing the feedback that slows entropic decline.

Uncharacteristically, Gaddis concedes one significant point of orientation to his reader very early on in *A Frolic of His Own*, stating:

> And so we may as well begin this sad story with the document that has set things off or, better, that merely paced the events that follow, spattered as it was all over the newspapers, since it had nothing directly to do with them, much less its remote participants, distant in every way but the historic embrace of civil law in its majestic effort to impose order upon? or is it rather rescue order from the demeaning chaos of everyday life in this abrupt opportunity, as Christina has it, to be taken seriously before the world, in an almost inverse proportion to their place in it.[40]

The document that follows is Oscar's father's (Judge Crease) circuit court decision in the lawsuit between the young owner of a puppy trapped beneath a sculpture and the artist suing to keep the statue intact. In arranging the development of Oscar's own series of lawsuits against the backdrop of the Tatamount controversy, the novel invites a comparitist reading of the various texts, events, conversations, and decisions that are rendered throughout. As the courts, media, politicians, and public wrangle with issues that seem to defy satisfactory representation, we are shown several instances where art and artist become embroiled in the very discourses that often seek to contain and constrain art in simple, familiar expressions—most often, monetary terms.

Cyclone Seven oscillates wildly in the appreciation of the residents of Tatamount: initially celebrated for the Szyrk's "moral" and "spiritual" concerns, it is sharply derided when these same residents realize that Szyrk was commenting on the present state of "moral torpor" and "spiritual vacuity," particularly when they learn what "torpor" and "vacuity" actually mean. As a result, they sue for its destruction; but when the controversy surrounding it yields significant tourism revenues, they drop the suit and seek the sculpture's institution as a national landmark.

It is important to recognize the broad range of discourses that take up the task of representing and adjudicating the developing situation in the small Virginia town. More than just the courts—televisual and print media; art criticism; religious and political rhetoric, and public demonstrations—all are given voice in an effort to, at base, attempt to discern whether the life of a young boy's dog or the integrity of a publicly owned and displayed artwork is of greater value. In this way, the systems of representation reach the peak of frustration: critics theorize art in a language "serving only a corresponding self referential confrontation of language with language and thereby, in reducing language itself to theory, rendering it a mere plaything," the very same civil court that concedes an inability to evaluate a given entity's worth in anything but a specific dollar amount.[41] Justice, it admits, can only be administered by arriving at an exchange value: loss, or damage, must be quantified by a seemingly arbitrary assignation that then must be paid by the offender to the claimant.[42]

Within *Frolic*, these aporetic conflations and reductions of discourses dominate. Protesting one of Judge Crease's decisions regarding *Cyclone Seven*, a Senator from Virginia remarks on his inability to discern modern art from pornography, using the controversy as a soapbox from which to discuss issues as widely reaching as agriculture subsidies to abortion to states' rights, all of which is heavily laden with religious rhetoric.

> And that's where this government interference with our sacred state's rights so many died for is leading us, sending in these Federal judges that take our great American language and twist the words around to mean whatever they want, calls God no better than a cat's shinbone, calls this beautiful land of ours a botched Creation and throws God right out of the courtroom[...]. They pay him with your good U.S. tax dollars and I'm going to tell them to take a look at one, take a

good look at a U.S. dollar bill where it says In God We Trust and that U.S. dollar's gospel enough for me.[43]

Because *Cyclone Seven* "became the lightning rod for the passions of this once sleepy community,"[44] it became a new Tower. This time, rather than prompting the division of language into many languages, it brought various autonomous discourses into a competitive field. The sculpture helped awaken a once-dormant community to political discourse, while showing the gilded grounds upon which much of this discourse is founded. Additionally, hidden behind a rhetoric that seems to call upon a Judeo-Christian god's authority, it becomes clear that religious authority is ultimately backed by that which is "gospel enough," the almighty dollar. As in *Agapē Agape* where "the only game in town" is "right on the money," *Frolic* plays its game of aporia, refusing to let the dollar define all meaning.

The dangers of such a reduction of experience to money, Gaddis illustrates, can lead to serious existential and legal complications. What seems a minor element to *Frolic's* plot actually expresses the potential ramifications of this practice of reifying abstract but essential elements of the human experience in terms of something that is itself abstract;[45] in its effort to fix meaning, capitalist discursive practices of the nature William James advocates merely defer the attempt to stabilize meaning to an equally volatile abstract. A minor character, the gaudily wealthy Trish, attempts to understand her daughter's attempted suicide. She explains to Christina, "Jerry says money means entirely different things to different people but it doesn't mean anything to her at all."[46] Raised in a society where the impetus to action is the acquisition of material comfort, a child born into excessive wealth has already arrived at America's *telos*. Trish's daughter's social life is already at its end before it has begun—since she need not attain to it, money has no meaning to her. Thus, life itself has no meaning, and her only recourse is an attempt at taking her own life. In *The Recognitions,* Mr. Pivner (father to yet another would-be playwright, Otto) faces a similar crisis nearing the end of his working life:

> Here in the foremost shambles of time Mr. Pivner stood, heir to that colossus of self-justification, Reason, one of whose first accomplishments was to effectively sever itself from the absurd, irrational, contaminating chaos of the past. Obtruding over centuries of gestation appeared this triumphal abortion: Reason supplied means, and eliminated ends.
> What followed was entirely reasonable: the means, so abruptly brought within reach, became ends in themselves. And to substitute the growth of one's bank account for the growth of one's self worked out very well. It had worked out almost until it reached Mr. Pivner, for so long as the means had remained possible of endless expansion, those ends of other ages (which had never shown themselves to be very stable) were shelved as abstractions to justify the means[...].
> Retirement? the word shook him hollow, left him in a void where nothing remained to be done.[47]

For Gaddis, there is a solution to this problem, a solution that exists in the art world. Life has an extremely poignant meaning, though such meaning may never be fully captured or pinned down in such terms as money, the law, or any other over-determining representative structure can articulate. It is a meaning that is present, but linguistically unrepresentable. It is that experience which art can produce but language cannot express. It is, as teacher Amy Joubert tries desperately to communicate to the capital-obsessed J R Vansant, the beauty of the sky without a millionaire profiteer behind it to serve as evidence to its value. Gaddis illustrates that it is incumbent upon the artist to be content with creating the possibility for such an experience without a palpable reward, as too many of his artists fall into the trap of a desire for recognition, for tangible recompense. Gaddis's successful artists—most notably Szyrk—are visual artists whose works stymie efforts to understand them more than they assist their audiences in understanding some concrete meaning behind subjective experience. So, too, with Gaddis's fictions, although they represent human speech in all its complexities in a superbly "realistic" manner, they more successfully communicate frustration than something that can be agreed upon as "meaning." But most artists in Gaddis's novels fail to find the productive elements in "meaninglessness:" Edward Bast particularly suffers the results of such a condition, a situation evidenced by his insistence that J R represent his aesthetic experience in linguistic terms. Granted, J R may not be listening closely, but Bast's adamancy forces the eleven-year-old into an appalling reduction of an aesthetically powerful cantata:[48]

> [J R speaking]—No wait hey I mean holy shit I don't mean where everybody's crazy about us and all, see goodwill that means the excess of purchase price over the value of these net tangible assets where they really screwed us on that Endo deal see so ouch!
> [Bast replies]—That's not what it means! That's what I'm trying to, listen all I want you to do take your mind off these nickel deductions these net tangible assets for a minute and listen to a great piece of music [...] damn it JR can't you understand what I'm trying to, to show you there's such a thing as as, as intangible assets? what I was trying to tell you that night the sky do you remember it? walking back from the rehearsal that whole sense of, of sheer wonder in the Rhinegold you remember it?
> —Well I, sure I mean we're still having it Mrs di...
> —How it can lift you right out of yourself make you feel things that, do you know what I'm talking about at all?

Breaking off, Bast's inability to vocalize his sense of the power of music fails mid-metaphor: even comparison fails at this point. Yet J R is not quite able to grasp his meaning, and replies:

> —Well sure I, I mean when like where there's this storm so Mrs diCephalis gets the art class to cut out these here big clouds which they pull them over you on this clothesline and like somebody's rolling these marbles around in this here piepan and you get this here real feeling.

Bast's frustration grows, dissatisfied with the school's performance's analogical representation of the music representing a mounting storm. For him, the music transcends such attempts at narrativizing an aesthetic encounter:

—It doesn't have to be like that's what I mean! Music's a, it's not just sound effects there are things only music can say, things that can't be written down or hung on a clothesline.

Bast's effort to define music in positive terms fails, and he can only make an effort to try and discourage J R's tendency to simplify the affect through a familiar experience. Yet he asks the boy to try again, describing the cantata as "sort of a dialogue between the soul and Jes[us]." So even though music can say things that cannot be written down, Bast still resorts to the trope of a dialogue, and thus discourse, however unreachable.

Forcing a linguistic response from his listener, he is unsatisfied with J R's simple assertion, "Okay I heard them!" He resumes his prodding of J R's reaction, asking the youth to explain the experience of his perception. Seeking to resolve the conversation by repeating Bast's own articulation of his experience J R replies, "What like it lifted me out of myself..." to which Bast snaps back "Not what I said no you! what you heard!"

Unable to accept that J R's own encounter might well have been ineffable (as his own seems to be), Bast demands that the child rely upon an inadequate lexicon, and leads to the ultimate degradation of the Wagner opera's impact on the older, better educated teacher.

J R begins:

—[...] I mean what I heard first there's all this high music right? So then this here lady starts singing up yours up yours so then this man starts singing up mine, then there's some words so she starts singing up mine up mine so he starts singing up yours so they go back and forth like that up mine up yours up mine up yours that's what I heard! I mean you want me to hear it again! [...]
—Never want you to hear it again I never want to hear it again myself! you, everything you ruin everything you touch[....] Think I could ever hear it again without hearing your, everything everybody! you destroy whatever you....

Recalling how King Midas ruined his most treasured object by turning his daughter into gold due to his base greed, J R's childish mind can only ape the "experts" without really understanding or appreciating the meaning behind the things he sees, says, and does. It is the same behavior he demonstrates through his experience in the world of capital investment. Like Bast, Gaddis's novels also suggest that, perhaps, all lexica will be inadequate to express the aesthetic experience; perhaps, the game of aporia reminds us, it is the very nature of this inadequacy that makes art not only effective (because affective), but necessary.

However ineffable, Gaddis recognizes and portrays the unswerving ambition to represent, and thus contain, artistic existence. Both the marketplace and the courtroom attempt to reduce art to terms they think they understand, which *can* lead to its corruption. His artist (perhaps the most commendable of all being Szyrk who, upon realizing that his work is being exploited for purely economic gain by the Tatamount tourist element, sues to have his work destroyed) can find ways to enter into these reductive discourses and demonstrate their inability to perform in the totalizing manner in which they purport to function. By getting to the very center of the system, rather than being subsumed into it, the artwork can expose the system's limits. In *Frolic, Cyclone Seven* becomes a physical center of public outcry with everyone from animal rights to anti-abortion activists grasping to the sculpture for some purchase. And Gaddis's own works become a site of a whole range of emotional responses from contempt to pity, from humor to frustration.

Unwilling to pursue the routes Bast travels with J R, works like *The Recognitions, J R,* and *Frolic* are instead, in significant ways, the kind of artwork that performs the critical function that his fiction advocates. Satire is his vehicle and doubtless best suited to his ends: through the mocking presentation of his subjects—subjects that cut across all designations of race, class, gender, and ethnicity—the novels effectively produce an ironic, critical presentation of the whole of American society. They are works that frustrate, confuse, and mobilize a readership into an active engagement with works that themselves demonstrate the collision of discourses in their desperate, necessarily inadequate attempts to represent what is present, but ultimately unrepresentable. In this way, then, Gaddis's works of art expose the dangerous tendency of capitalist-influenced discourse to reduce, debase, and destroy the work's aesthetic impact.

Rather than perspicuity, his art plays at aporia and coloring the fissures created by the series of blind spots in our feedback loops. Finding productivity in failure emphasizes the positive nature opened up in the absence of absolute answers; refusing to allow capital to reduce art to mere capital itself, Gaddis at once criticizes one of America's inherent desire to simplify the complex, to apprehend what is inherently elusive, while constructing potential pathways (through the world of art) towards its improvement.

Yes, Gaddis's are not reader-friendly novels. They are confusing and discomforting, constantly contesting very basic assumptions about art, law, and everyday life, and all while posing questions that actively defy authoritative responses. But they *are* playful novels, and everyone's welcome to join the game.

4

Trying to Make Negative Things Do the Work of Positive Ones: Gaddis and Apophaticism

CHRISTOPHER J. KNIGHT

> *Poetry provides the one permissible way of saying one thing and meaning another. People say, "Why don't you say what you mean?" We never do that, do we, being all of us too much poets. We like to talk in parables and in hints and in indirections — whether from diffidence or some other instinct.*
>
> — Robert Frost[1]
>
> *It is no longer possible for people to believe something because a lot of other people do. To believe something is not now a naïve act.*
>
> — W. H. Auden[2]

"The man is elusive — one might almost say, systematically elusive. There is something eerie about a figure that can write so much and give away so little," so writes A. D. Nuttall about William Shakespeare, noting that compared to John Milton, "we have no idea what Shakespeare thought, finally, about any major question."[3] With the publication of William Gaddis's *The Rush for Second Place: Essays and Occasional Writings* (2002),[4] we cannot quite say that we do not know where Gaddis stood on several major questions. Yet even when we think we know, we do well to proceed cautiously, for Gaddis's method is one of indirection, of apophaticism. Here, among twentieth-century artists, he is not alone, for apophaticism presents the artist with a way of dealing with, of expressing, those sorts of questions (themselves major) that the recent history of art, so ensnared in the net of irony, has forced underground. "We'd kept everything witty and cool, until the air between us was so ironized that to say anything in earnest would have been a breach of manners, even of trust," writes Tobias Wolff, in *Old School* (2003).[5] Wolff is recalling a mid-twentieth century schoolboy's experience with irony, but he is not unmindful of how reflective this ethos was of the cultural moment, and he also knows its limitations. "Irony [can be] a way of not talking about the unspeakable," he writes in the introduction to *Matters of Life and Death* (1983). "It can be used to deflect or even to deny what is difficult, painful, dangerous — that is, consequential."[6] He admits that he needs irony — "I can't live without it" — but he is also quite wary of it: "I do think it has its temptations, and one of them of course is to make flippant what is not to be taken flippantly."[7]

Of course, Shakespeare — to return briefly to the dramatist — had his own reasons for embracing apophaticism. There is ample suggestion that his father was a recusant and at a time when the Protestant monarchy stood always under threat, it did not make sense for the nation's leading playwright to identify himself too publicly with one religious practice or another. The situation in the late twentieth century, when Gaddis practiced his art, was naturally rather different. In the United States, there existed no state religion, though the prevalence of a host of prominent religious practices and cultural ideologies did make it less easy for an artist to identify himself, in too pronounced a manner, with any particular one less he should alienate all those — often the majority — who did not share his more particular beliefs.[8] To this difficulty might be added the matter of difficulty itself, the growing sense that things are frequently not what they seem. Shakespeare's Hamlet might postulate a reality more real than apparent — "Seems, madam? nay, it is, I know not seems"[9] — and we, in turn, might believe him, if only for another act or two. But the conviction has become more difficult to maintain. Thus, the Irish poet Paul Muldoon notes,

> It's hard to make a poem these days that is absolutely clear and direct — if the poem is really to be equal to its era. This is not an era in which clarity and directness, however much we hope for them, are entirely justifiable, because so much is unclear and indirect. I'm not just talking about *willed* obfuscation and crookedness, though, God knows, there's plenty of that. I'm just talking about a realization that very little is as it seems, that everything has within it massive complexities — maybe even the inappropriateness of being certain about things. A proper awareness that things are just not at all as they seem — one would wish for more of that[...].[10]

Here, Muldoon, who first began writing poetry "under the spell of T. S. Eliot,"[11] again echoes Eliot, who in his 1921 essay "The Metaphysical Poets" wrote:

> It is not a permanent necessity that poets should be interested in philosophy, or in any other subject. We can only say that it appears likely that poets in our civilization, as it exists at present, must be *difficult*. Our civilization comprehends great variety and complexity, and this variety and complexity, playing upon a refined sensibility, must produce various and complex results. The poet must become more and more comprehensive, more allusive, more indirect, in order to force, to dislocate if necessary, language into his meaning.[12]

Like Muldoon, Gaddis learned something about complexity, allusiveness, and indirection from Eliot — as well as from Shakespeare — and displays his own "proper awareness" throughout his writings, as for instance in *The Recog-

nitions, when Wyatt Gwyon, addressing his wife Esther, comments on the pitiful consequences that ensue when writing makes material transparency its desideratum:

> That's why most writing now, if you read it they go on one two three four and tell you what happened like newspaper accounts, no adjectives, no long sentences, no tricks they pretend, and they finally believe that they really believe that the way they saw it is the way it is, when really ... why, what happened when they opened Mary Stuart's coffin? They found she'd taken two strokes of the blade, one slashed the nape of her neck and the second one took the head. But did any of eye-witness accounts mention two strokes? No ... it never takes your breath away, telling you things you already know, laying everything out flat, as though the terms and the time, and the nature and the movement of everything were secrets of the same magnitude.[13]

In fact, if there should be one creed that Gaddis seemed to follow throughout his career it would be that articulated by Samuel Taylor Coleridge when, in *Biographia Literaria* (1817), he identifies "poetic faith" with the "willing suspension of disbelief."[14] "What one is asking for," said Gaddis in his 1990 New York State Writers Institute reading, "is the 'willing suspension of disbelief,'"[15] a request made so poignantly necessary by the Reign of Disbelief's late twentieth-century triumphalism. This triumphalism was especially evident in the form of managerial science with its conviction, grounded in its own circumscribed rationality, that any truth claim that did not manacle itself to material evidence was unworthy of consideration. So it was that in Gaddis's very last fiction, *Agapē Agape*,[16] he again came back to this question of disbelief — or of belief seeking solace in the maw of disbelief — as it found itself embodied in the history of the player piano, a late nineteenth-, early twentieth-century mechanical invention that was, as I have written elsewhere, "to music what the computer had been to thinking — something that reduced the intangible to the tangible, that reduced the mystery of meaning into a host of binaries. Music, real music, reached up to the heavens; it was humankind's most noble effort to fight back the tide of entropy. It challenged, at once, both disbelief and belief."[17] In *Agapē Agape*, this is the challenge alluded to in the dying narrator's words, his protest:

> Finally I really don't believe any of it. You see? I don't really believe you can take ninety-six people, that's almost two hundred hands, take out some of them like sleigh bells there's still more than a hundred-odd hands doing entirely different things, guiding bows across strings pressing the neck so fast it's dizzying, fingers pushing, plunging valves, keys opening holes and closing them, the clarinet changing whole registers translating every jot and title on the score into a stab, a wail, a delicate lonely suspense, a blast to wake the dead, sforzando, piano God knows what all it going on at once but not exactly all at once because what's coming out of all this is a Pastoral Symphony, what's rising to the heavens is Bruckner's Eighth or Mozart's D Minor Piano Concerto, what overwhelms the senses is Eliot's "music heard so deeply That it is not heard at all, but you are the music While the music lasts" but isn't that then, isn't that then the hallucination? Trans-

forming this chaos of hands guiding bows, fingers plunging valves resolving this clutter of physical, you see? I can't think about it, I can't not think about it but when I try not to think about it I go absolutely crazy but that's, no. Can you hear me? Listen.[18]

When asked to "[l]isten," when asked to practice a "willing suspension of disbelief," we are mindful that "the poetic faith" that the Romantic poet had in mind "excite[d] a feeling analogous to the supernatural, by awakening the mind's attention from the lethargy of custom and directing it to the loveliness and the wonders of the world before us; an inexhaustible treasure, but for which, in consequence of the film of familiarity and selfish solicitude, we have eyes yet see not, ears that hear not, and hearts that neither feel nor understand."[19] And it was a faith — with its very clear allusions to Isaiah 6:9–10; Mark 4:4–12; and Matthew 13:13 — steeped in Biblical understanding (Matthew: "This is why I speak to them in parables, because seeing they do not see, and hearing they do not hear, nor do they understand."), a faith that in literature would carry forward into the next century for the likes of Joseph Conrad (Preface to *The Nigger of the Narcissus*: "to make you hear, to make you feel — it is, before all, to make you *see*. That — and no more, and it is everything!"[20]). It continues in Gaddis's *J R*, wherein the admirable Edward Bast flummoxed by the schoolboy J R's intransigence still strives to awaken him to the beauty of the night sky, the harmonies of a Bach cantata: "— To make you hear! to make you, to make you feel to try to...."[21] There is here then a faith, which is more than poetic, that "[i]n every being that is real there is something external to, and sacred from, the grasp of every other." A faith, to continue the William James quotation, that "God's being is sacred from ours," and that "[t]o co-operate with his creation seems all he wants for us[...]. In the silence of our theories we then seem *to listen*, and *to hear* something like the pulse of Being beat; and it is borne in upon us that the mere turning of the character, the dumb willingness to suffer and serve this universe, is more than all theories about it put together."[22]

When Gaddis himself began publishing in the 1950s, he was of the mind that the intellectual climate was less conducive to acts of faith, poetic faith included, than of reaction. "Faith is not a mood but an act," said Hilaire Belloc, "a matter of the will."[23] But action appeared to be giving way to something less positive. "People react," says *The Recognitions*'s Wyatt Gwyon, "That's all they do now, react, they've reacted until it's the only thing they can do, and it's ... finally there's no room for anyone to do anything but react."[24] Of course, Gwyon, unlike Gaddis, is a failed artist, and one needs to place his words in this context, among others. Still, the conditions of which he speaks were analogous to Gaddis's own understanding of them, even as he was, in time, able to triumph over them. But the point is that the century was experienced, by many a talented artist, as frustrating to those who would have preferred to work according to a positive, rather than a negative, blueprint. As Franz Kafka noted, "The positive has already been given: it is up to us to achieve the negative."²⁵ Why so? Well, in part, there was a predominating mood of historical belatedness, along with the self-consciousness that attended to the expression of past pieties. In 1980, Gaddis would say that in *The Recognitions* "there is still hope that there are 'origins of design.' There is a nostalgia for order in both *The Recognitions* and *J R*, but more the first novel."²⁶ And so when comparing the two novels, Gaddis spoke of the first, published in 1955, as more allusive to, and reflective of, a cultural grand narrative than the latter, published in 1975:

> It [*The Recognitions*] was heavily allusive, but one of the points of *J R* is the transiency of the atmosphere, its instantaneousness, its happening right when you read it. Allusions would have been antithetical to the style and intention of *J R*. *The Recognitions* was an attempt to set the then current life in a larger perspective. In *J R*, characters can occasionally say wistfully, "I do like Mozart," but I have included as few allusions as possible. That world of order is no longer around.²⁷

In another interview, Gaddis would speak of *The Recognitions* as "the last Christian novel."²⁸ By this, he appeared to mean something akin to Giles Gunn's conviction that

> it is as misguided to suppose that one can understand, say, the literary heritage of the West dissociated from the variety of religious assumptions, doubts, and aspirations that underlie it as it is to presume that one can comprehend the manifold complexity of Western religious experience without examining the literary as well as liturgical, doctrinal, and ecclesiastical forms in which that experience has been refracted.²⁹

The novel, whatever the author's religious beliefs, makes, as Gaddis says, too many allusions to a religious "world of order" to be imagined as existing entirely outside the frame of this order. So it is that Gaddis found himself envying the character Stanley, whose religious faith "allowed him to bring his work to completion": "Twenty-five years ago I both envied him and despised him for this framework. But there are alternative frameworks."³⁰ Developing this notion of "alternative frameworks," Gaddis, rather contradictorily, says,

> The tangible framework of forgery presents Wyatt a context for accomplishment, a tradition of delimited and delineated perfection in painting. Forgery makes him feel safe, and confident, and able to accomplish his work. The difference is that Stanley is not taking a risk. With the writer Gibbs in *J R*, there's no framework whatsoever. He takes the risks, but is destroyed because he has not pursued his work to the end. He is not able to sustain his belief that what he wants to do — his book — is worth doing. Once he saw solutions, the accomplishment didn't interest him. He was just too bored. That, if you like, is tragedy. Mrs. Joubert's love for him is not quite enough to get him through, as Esme's love was not enough in *The Recognitions*.³¹

I say "contradictorily" for the reason that the alternatives given — including that of one person's love for another³² — prove, by Gaddis's own admission, insufficient. And while it would appear — given Gaddis's own lifelong commitment to his artistry — that art itself might be imagined as a viable alternative here, we can't quite overlook the fact that the three artists mentioned here — Wyatt, Stanley, and Gibbs — are, their initial promise notwithstanding, conjoined by their failure. Still, there does remain the sense that for Gaddis, artistry, especially that identifiable with the achievements of classical music, proves the most viable alternative to a religious order that in the author's mind appears linked to the past. In fact, as much as Gaddis detested George Steiner, the consequence of the latter's dismissive *New Yorker* review of *J R*, the novelist's repeated allusions (as in the earlier quoted passage from *Agapē Agape*) to classical music as a repository of meaningfulness recalls an analogous sentiment expressed by the critic in *Real Presences* (1989):

> In ways so obvious as to make any statement a tired cliché, yet of an undefinable and tremendous nature, music puts our being as men and women in touch with that which transcends the sayable, which outstrips the analysable. Music is plainly uncircumscribed by the world as the latter is an object of scientific determination and practical harnessing. The meanings of the meaning of music transcend. It has long been, it continues to be, the unwritten theology of those who lack or reject any formal creed. Or to put it reciprocally: for many human beings, religion has been the music which they believe in.[33]

There is a difference, however, between Steiner's and Gaddis's reverence for classical music. While both men conceive of a connection between classical music and the unsayable, the sublime, Steiner is able to close himself off to the quotidian world's increasing indifference to this music's authority, while Gaddis is not. Like Edward Rothstein who, in "Classical Music Imperiled: Can You Hear the Shrug?," is painfully alive to the fact that "traditions do come to an end," and that, as far as classical music is concerned, "[w]hat has changed is not how much the tradition means to its devotees, but how little it means to everyone else,"[34] Gaddis, in the pages of *J R*, offers one of the most poignant testimonies of a people — caught up, drowning even, in their own quotidian preoccupations — turning their back upon a tradition that deserved better. Here, music finds itself displaced by noise with all its entropic energies. Or as the downtrodden Gibbs says to Bast, aspiring to compose music in the space of the Ninety-Sixth street tenement apartment's havoc,

> —Problem Bast there's too God damned much leakage around here, can't compose anything with all this energy spilling you've got entropy going everywhere. Radio leaking under there hot water pouring out so God damned much entropy going on think you can hold all these notes together know what it sounds like? Bast?[35]

Or as Bast himself, seeking to introduce J R, society's child, to Johann Sebastian Bach's cantata number 21 ("Ich hatte viel Bekümmerniss" ["I Had Much Sorrow"]), finds his efforts rebuffed with all the vulgarity that passes, in American society, for a healthy rejection of intellectual pretension:

> —That's what I've been trying to tell....
> —What tell me what! I mean you're telling me how neat the sky looks you're telling me listen to this here music you even get pissed off when I....

—I asked you what you heard! that's all, I....
—What like it lifted me out of mysel....
—Not what I said to you! what you heard!
—What was I suppose to hear!
—You weren't! you weren't supposed to hear anything that's what I'm....
—Then how come you made me lis....
—To make you hear! to make you, to make you feel to try to....
—Okay okay! I mean what I heard first there's all this high music right? So then this here lady starts singing up yours up yours so then this man starts singing up mine, then there's some words so she starts singing up mine up mine so he starts singing up yours so then they go back and forth like that up mine up yours up mine up yours that's what I heard! I mean you want me to hear it again?
—No!
—See I knew you'd....
—Never want you to hear it again I never want to hear it again myself! you, everything you ruin everything you touch![36]

Here, we find evidence, too palpable, that, in Rothstein's words, "[t]he sounds of a dying tradition are painful, particularly if the tradition's value is still so apparent, at least to the mourners, and still so vibrant to a wide number of sympathizers."[37] And while Gaddis may, with Alfred Tennyson, hold to the view that "There lives more faith in honest doubt, / Believe me than in half the creeds," one can't help but wonder whether the eclipse of one tradition (religious) is not to be followed on the heel by another.[38] One also wonders whether there is not a connection, especially if the latter tradition — musical and artistic — has been conceived as a substitute for the former because it was also derived from it, as in the instance of Bach's cantata. That is, might the turn to art be likened to Irving Babbitt's turn to Humanism at least as represented by Eliot:

> Is it, a view of life that will work by itself, or is it a derivative of religion which will work only for a short time in history, and only for a few highly cultivated persons like Mr. Babbitt — whose ancestral traditions, furthermore, are Christian, and who is, like many people, at the distance of a generation or so from definite Christian belief? Is it, in other words, durable beyond two generations?[39]

This question, as it is raised by Eliot, also raises the question of how far did Gaddis seek to emulate Eliot. From the work and from Gaddis himself, we know that the novelist felt an extraordinary debt to Eliot. The poet's lines are quoted, without acknowledgment, repeatedly in Gaddis's fiction, as in *Carpenter's Gothic* wherein the narrator's phrase "to recover what had been lost and found and found and lost again and again"[40] alludes to the following passage from "East Coker": "There is only the fight to recover what has been lost / And found and lost again and again: and now, under conditions / That seem unpropitious."[41] And in *The Recognitions*, wherein the narrator's phrase "if present and past are both present in time future, and that future contained in time past, there is no redemption but one"[42] alludes to the opening lines of "Burnt Norton": "Time present and time past / Are both perhaps present in time future, / And time future contained in time past. / If all time is eternally present / All time is unredeemable."[43] And then we hear Gaddis say of Eliot's *The Waste Land* in the LeClair interview, "Very few [of *The Recognitions*'s first critics] mentioned *The Waste Land*. I read that in college and it has never left me. Keats talks about poetry as being the finest wording of one's highest feelings. But to find in a poem perfectly articulated your vision of the world is remarkable. I was just beginning to draw together my own view of the world and here it was."[44] And in the Logan and Mirkowicz interview, he says that Eliot "was very formative in my life and thinking when I was in college and even later, when *Four Quartets* came out. I even wanted to include the whole of it in *The Recognitions*. I think Eliot still has very much to do with my thinking, with my attempts to use language, and so forth."[45]

The "so forth" is intriguing. It could be read as an instance of apophatic omission, as an acknowledgment that Gaddis's respect for Eliot went so far as to include the poet's more conservative cultural views, including perhaps his religious views. (LeClair, in his preface to the interview, writes that Gaddis "seemed to be quite pleased to be speaking about his work, particularly the influence of T. S. Eliot, which he felt was unrecognized. That's when I realized that interviewing this patrician-dressed novelist was probably like interviewing the old banker-poet."[46]) Or it could be an invitation to us to see where Eliot and Gaddis pursued separate paths, for Eliot's conversion to Anglicanism, followed by his open and serious attachments to its dogmas, was not a path that Gaddis chose to take. Rather, it is easier seeing Gaddis as more responsive to the side of Eliot that spoke of "[r]eal irony" as "an expression of suffering," where it is understood that "the greatest ironist was the one who suffered the most,"[47] who spoke of "my fatal disposition toward skepticism."[48] The side that spoke, in response to I. A. Richards's representation of *The Waste Land* as effecting "a complete severance between poetry and *all* beliefs," of the intimacy between belief and disbelief: "A 'sense of desolation,' etc. (if it is there) is not a separation from belief; it is nothing so pleasant. In fact, doubt, uncertainty, futility, etc. would seem to me to prove anything except this agreeable partition; for doubt and uncertainty are merely a variety of belief."[49] Take this side of Eliot and combine it with Evelyn Waugh's lacerating satire and perhaps a pinch of Henry Adams (he, who wrote about seeking to find consolation in the aftermath of his sister Louisa's death by tetanus, "The usual anodynes of social medicine became evident artifice. Stoicism was perhaps the best; religion was the most human; but the idea that any personal deity could find pleasure or profit in torturing a poor woman, by accident, with a fiendish cruelty known to man only in perverted and insane temperaments, could not be held for a moment. For pure blasphemy, it made pure atheism a comfort. God might be, as the Church said, a Substance, but he could not be a Person"[50]) and one finds oneself in an approximate relation to Gaddis. Or so I contend.

It is not uncommon to seek to locate Gaddis within the ambit of a particular tradition, be it that of modernism, postmodernism or, as Joseph Tabbi in the Introduction to *Paper Empire* (2007), recently argues, "network aesthetic":

What's called for is not a change in attitude or a modernization of content, but a far-reaching network aesthetic that has, uniquely in American world literature, models going back to Melville, Emerson, Crane and Dos Passos. It is to this tradition that Gaddis rightly belongs, not literary modernism, not the literary avant-garde although elements of both can also be identified in Gaddis's work.[51]

Here, I am prepared to trust Tabbi that something called a "network aesthetic" exists, though his confidence that Gaddis's work "rightly belongs" within it seems a tad overconfident, much like Gregory Comnes's earlier judgment that "[a]s postmodern texts, Gaddis's novels are ideologically sound."[52] In any event, my own inclination is, as suggested, to see Gaddis's work as especially identifiable with a literary tradition that esteems the values of (1) belief/disbelief as they find themselves in a continual tussle; and (2) satire. And what conjoins these two—to make more explicit the theme of this essay—is their apophatic character, the way in which, for Gaddis, they tend to approach the positive via the avenue of the negative via Eliotian indirection and Waughian satire.

But to return to the question of Eliot and Gaddis, of how far the latter follows in the footsteps of the former, I would like to point to the fact that both poet and novelist thought of themselves as New England writers. In a 1933 address at the University of Virginia, for instance, Eliot told his audience, "I speak as a New Englander,"[53] recalling the fact that though he grew up in St. Louis, he was descended from a long line of New England forebears, in addition to the fact that his family summered on Cape Ann, and he attended the Milton Academy and Harvard College. Gaddis, alluding to his time at a Connecticut Congregationalist boarding school and attendance at Harvard, told Lloyd Grove, "I was brought up pretty much in New England,"[54] despite being born in New York City and raised on Long Island. Coincidently, on these two occasions, both writers make connections between a place, New England, and a religious tradition, Protestantism, colored either by Calvinism or a sense of obligation its equal. In Eliot's lecture, later published as the infamous *After Strange Gods* (1934), he invoked the concepts of "heresy," "Original Sin," and the "diabolic."[55] Gaddis, meanwhile, spoke of how "the entire Protestant Ethic has been very much in me from my boarding school days on. My mother's family was Quaker. I was brought up pretty much in New England and I was taught that 'This is what you do and you do it right. These are the rules.'"[56] And though it might strike some that both Eliot and Gaddis were stretching the notions of regional affiliation by speaking of themselves as New England authors—"Nobody tells fibs in Boston," observes Mrs. Luna in James's *The Bostonians* (1886)—to this reader, the self-descriptions appears helpful and accurate.[57] Gaddis might have grown up but a few miles from where Walt Whitman was born, yet his work appears more indebted to the tradition that begins with the Puritans and reaches us through Ralph Waldo Emerson, Henry David Thoreau, Nathaniel Hawthorne, Emily Dickinson, and Henry Adams. And as with three other New York born authors—Herman

Melville, William James and Henry James—what is shared with this tradition appears more significant than what might be gained by thinking of them as strictly New York writers (their appreciation of the marketplace notwithstanding).

This said, it should also be noted that Eliot was something of an exception regarding this literary tradition, for if it was characteristic of its practitioners that they would place themselves in a vexed relation to organized religion, following his 1927 conversion to Anglicanism, Eliot embraced the Church as an institution, submitting to its dogmas and expressing skepticism for the New England brand of religious individualism. In *The Idea of a Christian Society* (1939), he writes, "The Liberal notion that religion was a matter of private belief and of conduct in private life, and that there is no reason why Christians should not be able to accommodate themselves to any world which treats them good-naturedly, is becoming less and less tenable."[58] More characteristic of this tradition, so indebted to the Emerson of "The Divinity School Address" (1838)—"The idioms of his [Jesus's] language and the figures of his rhetoric have usurped the place of his truth, and churches are not built on his principles, but on his tropes. Christianity became a Mythus, as the poetic teaching of Greece and of Egypt, before"[59]—was William James's warning, issued in *The Varieties of Religious Experience* (1902), against the spirit of religious corporation:

> The basenesses so commonly charged to religion's account are thus, almost all of them, not chargeable at all to religion proper, but rather to religion's wicked practical partner, the spirit of corporate dominion. And the bigotries are most of them in their turn chargeable to religion's wicked intellectual partner, the spirit of corporate dominion, the passion for laying down the law in the form of an absolutely closed-in theoretic system. The ecclesiastical spirit in general is the sum of these two spirits of dominion; and I beseech you never to confound the phenomena of mere tribal or corporate psychology which it presents with those manifestations of the purely interior life.[60]

To this reader, Eliot is a more subtle thinker than James—in this brief passage, James is repeatedly found employing weasel words (e.g., "wicked," "absolutely," "mere," "purely," etc.)—but James's concern regarding the baleful consequences of Christian institutionalization remains pressing. In his 2005 book *Faith in Honesty: The Essential Nature of Theology*, the respected Anglican theologian Andrew Shanks offers a very acute examination of the unhappy consequences of this "Constantinianism," writing,

> The conceit of Christian moral consensualism turns a blind eye to forms of dishonesty operative under cover of upholding some already established social order. Such conceit comes in many different guises, depending on the particular demands of its context: conservative or liberal; hierarchical or egalitarian; nationalist or cosmopolitan. But its defining feature, in every instance, is its ultimate complicity with some ideology of rule, designed to smooth away moral conflict between the church and the surrounding world. Theologically, therefore, the result is to reduce Christian discipleship, in effect, to the role of a mere back-up

to common-sense morality—interpreting faith not as a continual calling into question of moral prejudice but, on the contrary, merely as an energizing principle, inspiring us to pursue our given moral ideals in ever more strenuous fashion, that is, with ever greater sincerity. And talk of heaven and hell is understood here as a straightforward incentive to such strenuousness.[61]

In his 1994 essay "Old Foes with New Faces," Gaddis offers his own spirited response to "Christian moral consensualism," beginning with the fifth-century story of Hypatia, as retold by the nineteenth-century Anglican minister and "muscular Christian" Charles Kingsley in his novel *Hypatia, or New Foes with Old Faces* (1851).[62] In retelling the story, Gaddis gives point to the readiness of the Church to ignore Jesus's instruction to keep the realms of God and the state separate,[63] noting how the Church moved to fill the vacuum created by the eclipse of the Roman state:

> Her [Hypatia's] leanings, however, were toward the intellectual rather than the mystical side of Neoplatonic thought, and we are told that when she pushed things too far by taking the pagan prefect of the city for her lover she was torn from her chariot and dragged to the Caesarium, lately become a Christian church, where she was stripped naked, done to death with oyster shells, and burnt by a fanatical Christian mob. Her writings have not survived.
>
> And so the task before us is scarcely a new one. We may think of it as nearer, in the words of T. S. Eliot, to the "fight to recover what has been lost / And found and lost again and again: and now, under conditions / That seem unpropitious."[64]

With the quotation from Eliot, Gaddis would remind us of just how difficult it is—and has always been—to keep the two realms separate, not to be tempted by desire to reconcile one form of happiness—immediate, sexual and material—with another, by its nature spiritual. Not surprisingly, Gaddis reserves his most excoriating critique, in "Old Foes with New Faces," for "the popular apologist Reverend Andrew M. Greeley," who comes to symbolize Janus-faced compromise:

> "The argument is not whether Catholics should leave their tradition or whether they stay for the right reasons," counters the popular apologist Reverend Andrew M. Greeley, relishing the fact that Catholicism "is not a democracy." Extolling the church as "resolutely authoritarian," Father Greeley blithely offers us such glaring instances as its discrimination against women and homosexuals, its intrusions on behavior in the marital bedroom, its anti-abortion stance everywhere and proscription of birth control even where famine, disease, and overpopulation reign, its repression of disagreement and dissent, and its having, looked quietly the other way for decades in the face of sexual abuses by its priests. "But let the charges stand for the sake of argument," he concludes, handily ducking the entire issue by default, finding refuge in the make-believe monumental mischief perpetuated by David Hume two centuries ago. "How can 85 percent of those who are born Catholic remain, one way or another, in the church?" Greeley asks.
> "Catholics like their heritage because it has great stories," and there is no shortage of those spawned along the way, some dating back six centuries to the *Decameron*, the work of one of Italy's greatest poets, Giovanni Boccaccio.
> "Catholics have sex more often than other Americans," Father Greeley persists, ever divisive, and "are more playful in their erotic amusements than others." The

Decameron bears him out in many of its tales: a woman is tricked by an imposter priest into believing that he is the angel Gabriel and has fallen in love with her; after solacing himself with her, he escapes in a cloud of feathers, leaving his wings behind; elsewhere, an abbess surprised *in delicto* pulls the errant priest's pants over her head, mistaking them in the dark for her cowl. Then there is the story of the nuns who coax a youth feigning mutism to service the entire convent — till one hot day the abbess finds him stretched out, apparently asleep. But "the wind lifting the forepart of his clothes," she discovers his attraction and seizes upon him for herself.[65]

Is the representation fair? Obviously not; it is satire, the tone caustic and unforgiving, reflecting the disappointment of one who, by his own admission, has "barked my shin against [Christianity] for over half a century in one form or another of its avatars,"[66] and who therefore spares neither Catholicism nor Protestantism, the latter spoken of as a "movement throughout the Western world, a movement of such wide appeal that it now appears in the pied garb of some four hundred denominations asserting their liberation from the papal yoke by bickering among themselves at every opportunity."[67] Not surprisingly, here, late Gaddis solicits late Mark Twain as his ally, quoting generously from the latter's splenetic *Letters from the Earth* (1909):

> "Life was not a valuable gift," in Mark Twain's view, but "death was man's best friend; when man could endure life no longer, death came and set him free. In time, the Deity perceived that death was a mistake," for "while it was an admirable agent for the inflicting of misery upon the survivor, it allowed the dead person to escape from all further persecution in the blessed refuge of the grave. This was not satisfactory. A way must be contrived to pursue the dead beyond the tomb. The Deity pondered this matter during four thousand years unsuccessfully, but as soon as he came down to earth and became a Christian his mind cleared and he knew what to do. He invented hell, and proclaimed it."[68]

Paradoxically, Twain writes that "[l]ife is not a valuable gift" precisely because it had — in the form of his wife Livy and children Langdon, Susy, Clara, and Jean — so proven to be, before illness and death (three times prematurely) had transformed happiness into loss. But, as the poet wrote, "Prosperity's the very bond of love, / Whose fresh complexion and whose heart together / Affliction alters."[69] Twain endured, sadly, more affliction than most; and Gaddis also experienced his share, though certainly in smaller dollops. Meanwhile, in Twain's blasphemous *Letters* or Gaddis's essay, we find confirmation of Gaddis's earlier contention that "[o]nly a religious person can perpetrate sacrelige [*sic*]: and if its blasphemy reaches the heart of the question; if it investigates deeply enough to unfold, not the pattern, but the materials of the pattern, and the necessity of a pattern; if it questions so deeply that the doubt it arouses is frightening and cannot be dismissed; then it has done its true sacreligious [*sic*] work, in the service of its adversary: the only service that nihilism can ever perform."[70] Or as Paul Ricoeur eloquently states the matter:

> Whoever accuses God is far less godless than the one who does not care at all about God. Such accusation, perhaps, expresses in its own way the impatience of

hope, the prototype of which may be found in the cry of the Psalmist: "How long, O Lord?" Second, should we not go so far as to say that unjust suffering is a scandal only for those who expect from God that God be only the source of all good? In this sense, it is the very faith in God that generates indignation. Consequently, it is in spite of evil that we believe in God, rather than what we believe in God in order to explain evil.[71]

Replete with its own indignation, "Old Foes with New Faces" is not, in fact, an easy piece to like. Akin to Twain's later writings, the target of which is the "damned human race," or to Gaddis's own spite-inflected novel *Carpenter's Gothic* (1985), the essay presumes to take up, in Jung's words, "'the eternal problem of religion,'"[72] with the emphasis on the notion of "problem," as in Alfred North Whitehead's conviction (also quoted) that "[r]eligion is the last refuge of human savagery."[73] Gaddis begins the essay (first read as a conference paper), after the allusion to the story of Hypatia, with a mock gesture "of fellowship," taking note of the dependence of both religious believers and fiction writers to practice a "'willing suspension of disbelief'":

> Rather than initiating our undertaking with a confrontation—I am sure we will see plenty of that—I propose to extend the hand of fellowship from the criterion central to both: that which constitutes poetic faith for the writer in Coleridge's familiar "willing suspension of disbelief," and for the religionist the leap of faith enshrined in Augustine's misquotation of Tertullian, "Credo quia absurdum."
> In other words, we are all in the same line of business: that of concocting, arranging and peddling fictions to get us safely through the night.[74]

As noted earlier, Gaddis had a career-long fondness for the Coleridgian admonition, and he was certainly not wrong to draw a parallel here between poetic and religious faith,[75] or even to link them by reference to the imagination to fiction. As Ricoeur writes, "Through fiction and poetry new possibilities of being-in-the-world are opened up within everyday reality. Fiction and poetry intend being, but not through the modality of givenness, but rather through the modality of possibility. And in this way everyday reality is metamorphosed by means of what we would call the imaginative variations that literature works on the real." To which he adds, "Religious texts are kinds of poetic texts: they offer modes of redescribing life, but in such a way that they are differentiated from other forms of poetic texts."[76] Of course, they are most significantly differentiated from poetic texts by the claim of revelation. But revelation here need not be understood either as opposed to the poetic or to reason, unless such are understood in terms unnecessarily circumscriptive. Or as Shanks writes,

> Far better, I think, would be to speak of two basic different levels of divine revelation: one the implicit revelation of God to us in and through every experience of serious conversation that we ever have, as we come to appreciate what makes for good communication and good listening in general, the essential qualities of Honesty[....]
> But then, at the second level, we also need the richest possible shared poetic resources for actually articulating that implicit awareness. And, I would argue, the

authority of the Bible, as of any sacred scripture, essentially derives from its efficacy in this. Of course, not everything in any scripture serves the purposes of revelation, understood along such lines. What counts as revelation, in scripture, is what helps challenge conventional sympathy-inhibiting gut reactions, not what confirms them; what helps make us more open and attentive to unfamiliar voices, not what reinforces closedness. I do not see how there could be anything revelatory in texts that merely reproduce conventional homophobia, for instance, or conventional patriarchy.[77]

So, like Ricoeur, Shanks can say, "Cannot fiction, after all, also be a valid medium for divine revelation, just as much as factual reportage?"[78]; and Ricoeur, like Shanks, can say, "Revelation [...] designates the emergence of another concept of truth than truth as adequation, regulated by the criteria of verification and falsification: a concept of truth as manifestation, in the sense of letting be what shows itself. What shows itself is each time the proposing of a world, a world wherein I can project my own most possibilities."[79]

The young Gaddis—or a Gaddis more himself, as in *Agapē Agape*—might have well have taken solace in such representations as Shanks's and Ricoeur's, but the Gaddis of "Old Foes with New Faces" almost drives himself to the point of self-rejection (or, as he puts it, "round the bend"[80]), granting a little too much countenance to the notion of fiction—poetic and religious—as a testimony of delusion:

> Certainly an enhanced capacity for self-delusion is a valuable attribute for the writer in nurturing both his fictional characters and, often enough, his own. Thus it is hardly surprising to find this capacity to be fueled by an equally large appetite for strong drink: the majority of America's native-born winners of the Nobel Prize in literature have been confirmed alcoholics. We may even go so far as to find their counterparts in Alfred North Whitehead's remark that "a relic of the religious awe at intoxication is the use of wine in the Communion service"—at all odds a relic of the drunken license turned loose at pagan saturnalias of a still earlier time where, habit breeding expectation, promiscuous intercourse provided plentiful material for the marvels of virgin birth that followed. "Speaking for instance of the motive of the virgin birth," Jung cautions us again that he is "only concerned with the fact that there is such an idea" but not "whether such an idea is true or false in any other sense."
>
> The priest is the guardian of mysteries, the artist is driven to expose them. The manifest difference between them is that the writer is a teller of secrets who grapples with his audience one reader, one page at a time; where the priest engages the collective delusion of his entire congregation all at once.[81]

Gaddis immediately follows this with a litany of evidence in support of the notion that his "countrymen" are mired in the most gross form of self-delusion ("our ubiquitous polls count nine in ten of our countrymen saying they have never doubted God's existence, eight in ten expecting to be called before him on judgment day, seven in ten planning on life after death, and more than half believing in angels"[82]) and later in the essay will vituperate against those countrymen conceived to be the most benighted, Mormons and Fundamentalists:

open the barn door for each individual Christian to have a direct relationship to God and experience the descent of the Holy Ghost and perhaps be born again as a Pentecostal-charismatic, an Evangelical, a Moonie, indeed any of the fifty million Fundamentalists who range across the country today, each — like Stephen Leacock's Lord Ronald, flinging himself upon his horse and riding madly off in all directions — proclaiming the inerrancy of the Bible, laying on hands, speaking in tongues, handling snakes, and converting Jews to speed up the Second Coming.[83]

This vituperation is not entirely without interest, as it returns us to a key concern of Gaddis's, the Socratic distinction between stupidity and ignorance, but I would rather, in what space remains, address the prior distinction made, between the priest and the artist vis-à-vis notions of mystery and secrecy.

Ostensibly, of course, Gaddis, in the space of his vituperations, comes across as the artist exposing mysteries, but at the same time he is found propounding mysteries, adding to our stock of secrets. His notion of the author might, in fact, be likened to that of Søren Kierkegaard when the latter makes a distinction between the man who writes and the true author, the distinction grounded in each's respect for what cannot be said, for the world's mystery:

He [the ordinary man] may have extraordinary talents and remarkable learning, but an author he is not, in spite of the fact that he produces books.... No, in spite of the fact that the man writes, he is not essentially an author; he will be capable of writing the first ... and also the second part, but he cannot write the third part — the last part he cannot write. If he goes ahead naïvely (led astray by the reflection that every book must have a last part) and so writes the last part, he will make it thoroughly clear by writing the last part that he makes a written renunciation to all claim to be an author. For though it is indeed by writing that one justifies the claim to be an author, it is also, strangely enough, by writing that one virtually renounces this claim. If he had been thoroughly aware of the inappropriateness of the third part — well, one may say, *si tacuisset, philosophus mansisset* [if he had kept quiet he would have remained a philosopher].[84]

For Gaddis, both the priest and the artist involve themselves with secret knowledge, but the priest, who "engages the collective delusion of his entire congregation all at once,"[85] is of necessity bound by a systematic, or institutional, understanding of such, whereas the writer, "a teller of secrets who grapples with his audience one reader, one page at a time,"[86] is not and, moreover, "is driven to expose" those mysteries that are less mysteries than institutional bulwarks.[87] As such, Gaddis's relation to secrecy and story-telling is analogous to the barefoot ("that desert where the truth still walks barefoot"[88]) Jesus's when explaining to the disciples why he spoke in parables: "To you has been given the secret of the kingdom of God, but for those outside everything is in parables; so that they may indeed see but not perceive, and may indeed hear but not understand; lest they should turn again, and be forgiven."[89] My point is that Gaddis, as fiction writer, has long practiced a "careful obscurity," a phrase borrowed from Iris Murdoch's *Metaphysics as a Guide to Morals* (1992), wherein she astutely writes, "The written word can fall into the hands of any knave or fool. Only in certain kinds of personal converse can we thoroughly clarify each other's understanding. The thinker's defence against this may be, like that of Socrates or Christ, not to write. Or it may be, like that of (for instance) Kierkegaard, Wittgenstein, Derrida, to employ a careful obscurity."[90]

Of course, some might object that the direction of "Old Foes with New Faces" doesn't appear especially obscure. And while I don't think this is the case, I do think that in this essay Gaddis's faith in the need for a "willing suspension of disbelief" finds itself teetering above a precipice. He has pursued the connection between fiction and delusion a little too far, to the point that, at the very end, he comes close to trapping himself in that Platonic corner wherein fiction and deception are said to be conjoined:

> Once upon a time, fiction was a way of getting at some kind of truth: we concocted fictions to get us through the night or, nostalgic for absolutes, we embraced revelation as ultimate Truth. Now fiction is used to bring on the darkest night of all, in which historical reality in its most monstrous epiphany is dismissed as a mischievous, fictive concoction by the so-called Holocaust revisionists, a deceptively mild label for those bent on giving substance to Hitler's maxim that any lie will pass muster provided it is big enough. This denial, made in the face of all the tangible evidence and all the witnesses, living and dead, of the systematic murder of six million human beings of different race and religion, is a lie of such enormous proportions that it will live on and reemerge to taint history forever. It offers the worst-case scenario of the willing suspension of disbelief.
> In short, "Who do you believe?" Groucho Marx asked. "Me? Or your own eyes?"[91]

With the final joke, courtesy of Marx, Gaddis seeks to rescue the essay from succumbing to unmitigated despair. Throughout his career, he has relied upon irony and satire to get him "through the night" with the understanding that they implied something more, something positive. In *The Recognitions*, Wyatt gives expression to this "something missing" in conversation with his wife Esther:

> —There's always the sense, he went on, — the sense of recalling something, of almost reaching it, and holding it.... She leaned over to him, her hand caught his wrist and the coal of tobacco glowed, burning his fingers. In the darkness she did not notice.— And then it's ... escaped again. It's escaped again, and there's only a sense of disappointment, of something irretrievably lost.[92]

The Recognitions does not itself give confirmation of this something being "irretrievably lost"; it keeps the question open, the conversation going, in the spirit of Hans-George Gadamer's sense that "the purpose of the Socratic art of conversing was to avoid being talked out of the fact that there is such a thing as the Just, the Beautiful, and the Good."[93] And the novel's putative hero, Wyatt Gwyon, also recalls to us the New Critical claim that "[t]he literary work comes closest to religion [...] in formal terms, by reenacting the Christian model of the Incarnation through the artist's sacrifice of him- or herself to the materials of his art or her craft,"[94] a claim that should have seemed as applicable to the novel's author as to its hero. Or as Gaddis himself so often claimed,

> In the past I've resisted [interviews] partly because of the tendency I've observed of putting the man in the place of his work, and that goes back more than thirty years; it comes up in a conversation early in *The Recognitions*. That, and the conviction that the work has got to stand on its own — when ambiguities appear they are deliberate and I've no intention of running after them with explanations.[95]

Again, the "careful obscurity," the "ambiguities," have always been a crucial dimension of Gaddis's work, from beginning to end, and I don't mean to suggest that Gaddis's work ever became vulgarly transparent. For him, there is the value of Eliot's notion of the vague ("When a subject matter is in its nature vague, clarity should consist, not in making it so clear as to be unrecognisible, but in recognizing the vagueness, where it begins and ends and the cause of its necessity, and in checking analysis and division at the prudent point"[96]); of Martin Heidegger's "haziness"[97]; and Wallace Stevens's notion of the indefinite: "That a man's work should remain indefinite is often intentional. For instance, in projecting a supreme fiction, I cannot imagine anything more fatal than to state it definitely and incautiously."[98] And yet there remains the question, raised itself in *The Recognitions* and here borrowed for a title, of whether the author, like so many of his contemporaries, did not in time find himself "[t]rying to make negative things do the work of positive ones"?[99] Belief, in Gaddis's time, was not what it was, say, in Emerson's, a fact poignantly expressed by Gaddis's friend and fellow author William Gass:

> "The universal impulse to believe," as Emerson both manifested and expressed it, was as positive in his time as it is negative in ours, because beliefs are our pestilence. Skepticism, these days, is the only intelligence. The vow of a fool — never to be led astray or again made a fool of — is our commonest resolution. Doubt, disbelief, detachment, irony, scorn, measure our disappointment, since mankind has proved even a poorer god than those which did not exist.[100]

Gass's is the sophisticated intelligence of his time, and though Gaddis lived by the ethos encapsulated in Coleridge's "willing suspension of disbelief," the negation of disbelief never quite amounted to a clear belief, at least not if such is understood in the terms set by Kierkegaard: "To comprehend is the range of man's relation to the human, but to believe is man's relation to the divine."[101] Gaddis seemed to miss such, and desire such, and he — like Robert Penn Warren's Eliot —"had the charisma of any man who is struggling for reality."[102] Yet in the end, *agapē*, or Christian love, was found agape, and like the older Gaddis, who, as mentioned, thought that even *The Recognitions*' "world of order is no longer around"[103] and who, when asked by Tom LeClair whether he might share "Stanley's framework of faith," replied quite absolutely, "Good heavens, no."[104]

In the end, then — in the very end, which is to say the last words of *Agapē Agape*— the author's final note is both elegiac and apophatic, entailing an envious looking back to the thirty-three-year-old man who not only believed in something "worth doing"[105] but who also, in the brilliant form of *The Recognitions*, did it; and a sense of meaning expressive of the conviction — belief even — that "[a]ll of our highest goals are inhuman"[106] without quite naming them:

> Age withering arrogant youth and worse, the works of arrogant youth and the book I wrote then, my first book, it's become my enemy, o Dio, odium, the rage and energy and boundless excitement the only reality where the work that's become my enemy got done and the only refuge from the hallucination that's everything out there is the greater one that transforms you good God, Pozdnyshev, those words that Levochka gave you to transform the whole thing when "music carries you off into another state of being that's not your own, of feeling things you don't really feel, of understanding things you don't really understand, of being able to do things you aren't able to do" yes, that transforms that transfigures you yourself into the self who can do more! That was Youth with its reckless exuberance when all things were possible pursued by Age where we are now, looking back at what we destroyed, what we tore away from that self who could do more, and its work that's become my enemy because that's what I can tell you about, that Youth who could do anything.[107]

5

Failing Criticism: The Recognitions

Joseph Conway

In his much-discussed 2002 *New Yorker* essay, "Mr. Difficult," Jonathan Franzen recounts how a year of dead-end screenplay work made him "far too sick of audience-friendly narrative."[1] Thus, in search of intellectual stimulation, he runs out of his loft into the New York City night "in a state of grim distraction, like somebody going out to score some hard drugs." Eventually he gets his fix from a Sixth Avenue bookstore where he "bought *The Recognitions* in a beautiful, newly reissued Penguin edition."[2] No small aspect of the beauty of the 1993 edition of William Gaddis's 1955 novel derives from the front cover's striking portrait of a gaping man glassily staring into the distance somewhere beyond the beholder's own gaze. Starkly isolated, this mysterious face appears in close-up like a captured film still, allowing the observer to minutely analyze each disembodied feature. One's interested gaze can drift across the man's dirty teeth, his irregularly groomed beard, shaggy eyebrows, and uncombed hair. The unrestricted intimacy one's eye has with this face provokes an appreciation for its representation of unvarnished earthiness. Yet the gleaming intensity of the man's stare also invites one's gaze to focus on the man's eyes which, in their reflecting of some unseen light, radiate a brilliant shine missing from the face's otherwise coarse surface. Perhaps the oddness of one's experience with this image derives from the cross-purposes at which subjective observer and objectified observed intersect: I wish to linger on the material details of the face, but the face itself is far more interested in focusing its gaze away from me, toward something outside my own line of vision.

The irony of allowing oneself to be absorbed by this one face is that it is but merely one in over thirty others to be found in Hugo van der Goes's monumental *Portinari Altarpiece* (1475–6), a triptych commissioned by Tommaso Portinari to appear inside of his family's chapel. The process by which this particular face, a center panel detail, is extracted from the whole painting, which has itself been extracted from Portinari's personal chapel and repackaged as an "object of art" in the Galleria degli Uffizi at Florence, might be used as a Benjaminian parable about the way in which the "aura," or ritual meaning, of a work of art is destroyed through the desacralizing processes of mechanical reproduction inside of a ubiquitous commodity marketplace. Of course this is an obvious critical lens for reading *The Recognitions* as well. Yet, rather than address the cover's image in a theoretical way, I'd like to consider how in particular *this* detail from *this* painting deforms the meaning of the whole by reducing the complex aesthetic structure of Van der Goes's painting to a fragmentary representation. By doing so, I would like to open an investigation into how similar deformations and reductions are performed by readings of *The Recognitions* that mistake the position of critical partiality for the fullness of interpretive totality.

The *Portinari Altarpiece* depicts the adoration of the shepherds at the scene of Christ's nativity. The face on the cover of the Penguin edition of *The Recognitions* is one of these shepherds and the unseen object of his optical raptness is Christ himself. The look in his eye is his recognition of the Christian mystery of incarnation. In the *Portinari Altarpiece*, he is huddled together with two other shepherds on the right side of the center panel who are in turn surrounded by various angels and persons; on the cover, he appears in an individualized act of unshared vision. Thus by isolating one face from many, one loses the social context in which such recognitions happen. This erasure of social experience within the content of the image is duplicated formally by the erasure of the work's multi-perspectivist construction. In *The Recognitions*, Wyatt seeks to paint like Van der Goes and the other Flemish masters because "there isn't any single perspective, like the camera eye, the one we all look through now and call it realism, there ... I take five or six or ten ... the Flemish painter took twenty perspectives if he wished, and even in a small painting you can't include it all in your single vision, your one miserable pair of eyes, like you can a photograph."[3] In addition, the *Portinari Altarpiece* is constructed not merely with multiple perspectives, resulting in disproportionate figures, but also with multiple temporalities. The shepherds, for example, are fore-grounded in the central panel around the infant Jesus, but they are also portrayed in the far off background being greeted by an angel of the Lord. Likewise, Mary and Joseph are displayed in their traditional nativity positions, yet they are also depicted in the painting fleeing from Herod into Egypt. In short, the painting incarnates a spatiotemporal richness whose whole construction defies any attempt to be contained within the "single vision" of one spatial setting or temporality. Gaddis's maddening novel of pluralistic perception, structured as a Flemish triptych itself,[4] likewise demands that its spatiotemporal richness is not "miserably" reduced by single-minded criticism. More often than not, however, this has been the case.

I would suggest that the critical reductions typical of studies that address *The Recognitions* derive from the highly polemical position they invariably take. I will approach this polemic backwardly through Franzen's *New Yorker* essay in which he respectfully dismisses Gaddis as "Mr. Difficult," a writer of wrenchingly complex fictions that ultimately do not compensate the diligent reader's time and efforts with commensurate returns of pleasure. He argues that, especially in the books after *The Recognitions*, Gaddis's writing amounts to an act of bad faith against his readers, which in turn makes for crooked proselytizers. Franzen maintains that a Gaddis novel on one's bookshelf serves as little more than a status symbol among hipster, intellectual types who turn up their noses at character-driven, realist fiction. But, and this is important, he takes it for granted that nobody actually *reads* William Gaddis. At this critical point of readerly indifference, the pro-Gaddis polemics begin. Take, for example, the standard apologia Peter Wolfe offers at the start of his study, *A Vision of His Own* (1997): "'Gaddis remains one of the least read of major American writers' (1989, 1) says Steven Moore at the start of his book, *William Gaddis*. Not only has Moore judged well; he has raised an issue that needs raising at the start of any full-length study of his man [sic]."[5] This seems a reasonable problem for a critic to raise. A new problem is added, however, when the critic supposes that the old problem can be alleviated through the therapeutic intervention of one's critical perspective.

Initially, Wolfe quite sensibly suggests Gaddis writes large and difficult books that appeal to very few people. But then he attempts to explain this as a way for the author to get "revenge" on "the adult world of his parents," who always left him feeling physically small—writing big novels is an act of "masculine protest" comparable to that of Napoleon who "used imperial conquest to compensate for his littleness." Wolfe also implies that this sense of smallness extends to feelings of sexual anxiety, thereby offering that "Gaddis's attentiveness to penises is intriguing."[6] In another attempt to address (and redress) Gaddis's obscurity, John Johnston's *Carnival of Repetition* allows that "readers and critics alike have been deterred by its great length, perhaps even put off by its blend of extreme erudition with bald satire," but adds that "neglect seems egregious now."[7] Rather than claim a personal revenge strategy against the world as a reason for his public neglect, Johnston implies that Gaddis has been egregiously misunderstood due to his presence as a liminal figure between distinct historical periods. Seen from the vantage point of 1990, however, the "strategic position alone" of *The Recognitions* between modernism and postmodernism, "would seem to establish Gaddis's novel as a privileged locus for investigating the historical conditions of possibility for the emergence of 'textuality.'"[8] More than this, however, Gaddis's writing "demands the kind of theoretical approach" that Johnston offers because it anticipates, even "if sometimes only symptomatically," major tenets of contemporary approaches to literature, a "kind of deconstruction *avant la lettre*."[9] Thus, he "press[es] into service"[10] the work of Bakhtin, Deleuze, Kristeva, and others to reinvent *The Recognitions* as a carnivalesque romp across the fairground of postmodern theory.

I would like to consider one more critical approach. Steven Moore's impressive *Readers's Guide to William Gaddis's The Recognitions* (1982) contains both annotations of allusions in the text and an introductory essay that addresses the failure of the novel to accrue a large readership. The material conditions of sheer length and a spotty publishing history are noted. But a third problem of the text's hyper-referential design is the inciting factor for Moore's study. He summarizes:

> many critics have probably realized (as I did at the outset of this study) that before one could speak about the novel with confidence and authority, one would first have to identify the large number of sources, literary allusions, book titles, historical references, obscure subjects, hagiographies, details from church history, mythology, and anthropology, foreign phrases in over a half-dozen languages—in a word annotate the novel.[11]

Guiding Moore's project is his own understanding of *The Recognitions* as a mythical narrative of modern man's struggle for "integration of the personality, which can result only from an acknowledgement of the *White Goddess*."[12] Indeed, one might say that the annotations themselves are a catalogue of the novel's unconscious memory as channeled through the compiler's mediating consciousness. Moore elaborates his Jungian reading of *The Recognitions* by demonstrating how the theme of alchemy as understood by Jung (in whom Gaddis was deeply read) provides "a spiritual 'plot' to complement (and justify) the narrative of the novel."[13] In Gaddis's novel, the gold of myth redeems the leaden stuff of contemporary spiritual existence, and Moore's annotations provide the incantations necessary ("identified and codified for easy use") to reach the elusive Philosopher's Stone hidden beneath its 956 pages. Deservedly touting the merits of his own work and citing *The Recognitions*' in-print status, Moore insists that excuses for not reading it "can no longer be justified."[14]

I am not surprised by Gaddis's "egregious" or "unjustified" neglect. Indeed, failure to find a large audience seems to me one of the novel's basic strategies. Nor, more importantly, will I dare venture a reading of *The Recognitions* with "confidence and authority," whether this means "pressing into service" Graves's *White Goddess* (1948) or poststructuralism for conscription duties to wage some battle of exegetical attrition. Rather, this essay is (as the word "essay" implies) my attempt to gather together some related observations concerning *The Recognitions* and share them with an audience interested in reading it. If I stray somewhat from establishing an overarching thesis, it is because I agree with Gregory Comnes that "[b]ecause Gaddis's texts substitute heterogeneous example for argument and explanation to such a degree, the reader is forced to approach the object of the study in a different way."[15]

This different approach means foregoing supreme critical fictions to render the text intelligible. For example, Johnston positions his work against the Dark Age approaches that preceded post-structuralism like "myth study and the early kind of Freudian analysis,"[16] for which we might use Moore's alchemical Jungianism and Wolfe's intriguing penises as respective models. Johnston's triumphant narrative of theory's advance over "Anglo-American empiricism,"[17] the most recent reiteration of metaphysics that ever since Derrida has been described by theorists as the privileged form of Western thinking ever since Plato, recounts the post-structural transvaluation of a literary "work" into a "text" that finds itself embedded in a nexus of intertextuality. As in much theory-driven scholarship, one adopts the premise that there is nothing but the text, yet one proceeds as if certain textual terrains (particularly those marked "Bakhtin," "Deleuze," "Kristeva," etc.) occupy more of "nothing but" than most. This does not mean Johnston's readings, which demonstrate how Gaddis's writing engages in the overthrow of Platonism's insistence on univocal identity, are not persistently brilliant, only that *The Recognitions* so overtly addresses such themes that a redescription of its novelistic discourse into theoretical discourse is at best a work of critical translation, and at worst implies that novels cannot speak critically in their own time and in their own voices. Novels, the implication is, must be identified with certain concepts before they can make sense. They must be *represented* by another in order to be understood. And thus theoretical readings go the way of all Platonism.

Any extended gaze, we might say, that turns a given object into a given object of critical scrutiny, promotes blindness to the ground of one's own premises and, following the old allegory of the philosopher and the well, the unseen pitfall such blindness invites. Thus in their approaches to *The Recognitions*, Wolfe's bio-Freudian approach misses every mordant reference to quack Freudianism, Moore's Jungian criticism glances away from the bemused tone in which the hidden narrator satirizes the ridiculousness of so much alchemical lore, and Johnston's anti-representational ideal loses sight of where the novel holds up a symbolic of real presence similar to the Eucharistic ministers of modernism like T.S. Eliot. Borrowing the analogy from painting introduced in the beginning of this essay, one might say that the transposing of Gaddis's densely envisioned novel into one's individual perspective erases the figural fullness and multidimensional character of the work. One critic who seems to mostly avoid such fallacies of theoretical reduction is Comnes. In *The Ethics of Indeterminacy* (1994), he forgoes critical apology and approaches Gaddis's novels as cultural forms that historically represent the real ethical concerns that haunt an ironic and indeterminate world. He concludes that the process of reading Gaddis's writing enacts in its various moments "an idea of postmodern ethics," which can only be "grasped through experiencing the texts rather than reading criticism about them."[18] Comnes's most surprising critical move is to consider *The Recognitions* as a mimetic fiction with the "capacity to recognize and produce similarities—between both text and world and epistemology and ethics."[19] Such a mimetic function is unthinkable for Moore, whose Gaddis manipulates a hermetic codex of symbols to represent a primal myth of identity, and Johnston, whose Gaddis writes in an arbitrary language of unsignifying signifiers that trace themselves through a world of pure difference. That these readings both begin with an assumption that *The Recognitions* avoids a mimetic aesthetic is quite reasonable, given the often hallucinatory events that happen in the novel, the oblique manner in which time and character are established, and, of course, the obfuscatory prose that sometimes seems more intent on annihilating apprehension of its referent than presenting it to the reader's mind. Yet, by defamiliarizing the traditional formal understanding of Gaddis, Comnes provokes us to rethink Gaddis's project as containing a complex mimetic component that is too often overlooked by those critics who prefer a purely experimental Gaddis who wishes to repudiate a "real world," rather than an experimental Gaddis who wishes to repudiate reductive perceptions of what generally constitutes the "real."

Moore addresses Gaddis's own notes on the issue of realism: "Everything I have observed has been only for its symbolical value: anything is met with my frame of reference: exact opposite of Hemingway."[20] For Moore this directly refers to Gaddis's technique of resting his novel on a foundation of timeless myth, whereas Hemingway's work demonstrates a former journalist's approach to representing the world as it really is in readily apprehended prose. The "symbolical value" of Gaddis's writing, however, need not mean an esoteric signified for every exoteric signifier—he is quite good, for example, in representing newspaper prose for the purposes of satire. Nor must we, I think, give ourselves over to Gaddis's characterization of his writing as wholly antithetical to Hemingway, allowing only that it might be antithetical to a certain way of *seeing* Hemingway. A critical comparison between a sentence from *The Recognitions* and a sentence from *A Farewell to Arms* (1929) may be beneficial:

> **Gaddis**: The morning was exceptionally fine, the streets still comparatively unlittered by those tons of ingeniously made, colorfully printed, scientifically designed wrappings of things themselves expendable which the natives drop behind them wherever they go, wary as those canny spirits down under cluttering the path to paradise.[21]
>
> **Hemingway**: It was a fine country and every time that we went out it was fun.[22]

Gaddis writes a forty-one word sentence, averaging six characters per word; Hemingway offers a sentence of fifteen words, averaging three-point-four characters each. Upon inspection, however, we see that Hemingway gives us two whole independent clauses, whereas Gaddis gives us only a single, five-word independent clause which everything else depends on: "The morning was exceptionally fine." "Fine," as Hemingway readers know, is one of the paradigmatic adjectives in his writing, ranging in meanings from "less than okay" to "more than sublime," or, when used as an answer to the question, "How are you?" from "absolutely wonderful" to "I don't want to talk about it." But, as seen in the sentence quoted above ("It was a fine country"), he rarely upsets the already precarious semantics of this word with an adverbial intensifier like "exceptionally." One meaning of the word "fine," after all, is just this: "unexceptional." Therefore, "exceptionally" identifies a difference in style which may go some way toward explaining why Gaddis considered himself "the exact opposite of Hemingway." We might even read his sentence as a revision of the more famous novelist's reticent aesthetic.

Both Hemingway and Gaddis make ontological statements about the fineness of a certain object; for Hemingway, it is a place in space ("country"). When Hemingway wrote *In Our Time* (1925), he, along with much of post–World War I modernism, felt, as he called it in one of his stories, "the end of something," maybe Western civilization, or maybe his own sense of virility. "Fine," let us remember, comes from the French *fin*, that is, the "end." As he perceived it, the chaos of contemporary European history had little left for his generation that could be meaningfully represented — time itself having seemingly tapered itself into a fine point. His style so often mislabeled "blunt" actually deserves to be reappraised as "fine," indicating something exceptionally delicate, not unlike one of his female characters. We must not mistake Hemingway's blustering public image (as Gaddis himself seems to have done) for the basic vulnerability of his prose. This fragility is part of an essentially tragic vision that he offers up in works such as *A Farewell to Arms* which submit characters to the forces of history, abandoning messianic hope for, at best, the experience of a little "fun" before time swallows everything of value. "Every time that we went out it was fun," indexes fun *then*, but by the end of the story when the narrator's female lover dies during a miscarriage (the objective correlative of "lost generation"), we know it is not fun *now*. Hemingway's aesthetic strikes the familiar modernist dirge of nostalgia.

Gaddis, meanwhile, invests the moments of being in his novel with exceptional details that strive to hallow the time, rather than hollow it as Hemingway does. "The morning was exceptionally fine" is an onto-historical statement identifying the being ("was") of time ("morning"), and the clauses that follow are a diffusion of details that make this definitive time ("The") different ("exceptionally fine") in comparison to other times. Temporality is differentiated into individual historical moments that have a fullness unique to each of them, whereas Hemingway presents history as just one fine thing after another. An idealist would claim that Gaddis's sentences display a messianic understanding of temporal fulfillment, but a skeptic could claim that these individual moments do not add up to anything; rather, they demonstrate how time explodes our every attempt to wholly represent it. Gaddis's sentence doesn't resolve this problem of representation-in-time; instead, it unfolds as the problem itself. Unlike Hemingway, Gaddis is willing to generate lexical waste as a way of dramatizing the wasted products of a scientifically engineered and technologically rendered mass society that endlessly produces more than it can possibly consume. In this he *mirrors* the times. Yet within the waste of his sentence, emblem of a wasteful society, a "path to paradise" is contingently offered. In this, he holds a *lamp* out into the future (to borrow M.H. Abrams' helpful terms to distinguish between classical and romantic aesthetics).[23] "Unlittered" may connote a biological birthing process, just as what "the natives drop behind them" may connote excretion, in which case, mass economy can still be understood in terms of individual physiological processes. But "Unlittered" could also denote trash just as what the natives drop is trash — all of which reflects an American culture of trash. The Janus-faced syntax of "wrappings of things themselves expendable" identifies the difference in which both these readings arise. I understand this phrase as alluding to Kant (though Moore does not annotate), whose philosophy bridged idealism and empiricism by arguing that things-in-themselves may exist to the reason, but that ordinary understanding can only apprehend them through representational forms due to certain *a priori* restrictions of human consciousness. Thus, if the syntax renders "expendable" as modifying "wrappings," then waste is merely representative of "things themselves" more truly meaningful, indeed paradisiacal; if the syntax renders "expendable" as modifying "things themselves," than a culture of irredeemable waste triumphs, its natives cluttering up the confines of its own mass-produced hell with superficial values. As Kant struck a balance between Cartesian rationalism and Humean skepticism, Gaddis's language synthesizes representational and anti-foundational tendencies, and, in the manner of his favorite metaphor, the Gothic arch, exists as the articulation of tension between two irresistible forces.

Thus, we might say that Gaddis's prose takes *exception* to Hemingway's and clutters up the latter's style with his droppings of verbosity. This, however, is not to say that the styles are wholly opposed. In fact, one might easily argue that they derive from the same source. Hemingway's modernist reaction against mass culture took the form in his fine early prose of refusing to indulge the extravagant appetites he attributed to that culture. That he allowed himself to be commodified by mass consumer culture into "Papa," the adventurer, might have shown Gaddis the foolhardiness of that approach. Rather, Gaddis offers what we might call a mass style reflective of mass culture, but he does so as to critique (burying, he concedes, is impossible), not praise the massive capitalist system of superfluous overproduction. In this, he plants himself in a tradition of writing codified by Viktor Shklovsky's *Theory of Prose* (1929). Shklovsky, writing contemporaneously with Hemingway, already makes the American's writing seem symptomatic of a socio-economic system that it purports to reject. He describes a certain "principle of economy of effort" that leads to what he calls either an "algebrizing" or "automatizing" of the object being described, wherein a prosaic language of description keeps us from truly perceiving the object described because its terms are so familiar. An x is an x is an x is an x: "By means of this algebraic method of thinking, objects are grasped spatially, in the blink of an eye. We do not see them, we merely recognize them by their primary characteristics. The object passes before us, as if it were prepackaged."[24] A prose detailing the passing world of primary characteristics even if, as in Hemingway, economy of expression attempts to fine-tune our perception of the objects that matter most, will only augment the current level of automatized expression. Every thing else seems like everything else, just as newspapers place obituaries beside box scores, and, thus, "held accountable for nothing, life fades into nothingness. Automatization eats away at things, at clothes, at furniture, at our wives, and at our fear of war."²⁵ The inability of seeing the singularity of individual things, individual clothes, etc., due to our "prepackaged" exposure to them via algebraic language, keeps us alien to our own sensory experiences. We are left unable to perceive, as Shklovsky memorably puts it, that the "stone feel[s] stony."²⁶ The "stone's stoniness" would be an experience of the thing-in-itself that the wrappings of automatized prose make expendable. Conversely, "Every time we went out it was fun," as typical of Hemingway's doomed romances of historical escape, both renders the time atemporal and keeps the fun unfunny.

When Gaddis transfers Hemingway's "fine" into his own "exceptionally fine," when he recycles common trash on the street into "ingeniously made, colorfully printed, scientifically designed wrappings of things themselves expendable," his flouting of the principle of economy of expression aims to both refine fineness and to make trash trashy. Shklovsky recounts how strategies of verbal redundancy ("made," "printed," "designed"), circumlocutional phrasing ("the streets still comparatively unlittered,"), and repetition (the aboriginal tale of spirits spreading trash on the way to paradise returns throughout the novel) are integral to the making-strange-to-make-familiar process that an artistic deployment of language enacts. Gaddis and Shklovsky both adopt an aesthetic of waste that paradoxically lays bare a device for experiential renewal. As the spirits would cannily have it, the path to paradise is only made known by the miscellaneous clutter on its way.

The Recognitions penchant for lexical profligacy at the level of the sentence resonates as citational prodigality at the level of allusion. One need not agree with Steven Moore's assertion that understanding Gaddis's allusions helps to understand *The Recognitions* with "confidence and authority" to believe that the use of allusion is crucial both as a formal technique and as a mode of content. Let us take the beginning of part I, chapter 6, for example:

> "Why has man not a microscopic eye?" Writes Alexander Pope; "For this plain reason: man is not a fly." What of Argus, equipped with one hundred eyes to watch over the king's daughter turned into a heifer by a jealous goddess; how many images of the heifer did he see? How many leaves to the bracken where she browsed? After the death of Argus (his eyes transplanted to the peacock's tail), this wretched heifer, the metamorphosis of Io, was visited by a gadfly sent by the jealous goddess, and driven tormented across frontiers until she reached the Nile. What did the gadfly see? And Argus, suffering the distraction of one hundred eyes: did he sit steady? or move distracted from distraction by distraction, like the housefly now dashing and retreating in frenzy against the windowpane, drawn to a new destination the instant it halted, from the shade-pull to the floor, from there to the lampshade, back to the baffling window glass. No Argus, this miserable Diptera, despite its marvelous eyes, guardian of nothing.²⁷

There are at least three types of allusion at work here. The obvious Pope quotation (from "Essay on Man" [1733]) is directly given. The story of Io and Argus comes out of the *Metamorphoses* of Ovid, a writer understood to be present, though not cited. And third, the lifted phrasing from T.S. Eliot's "Little Gidding"—"distracted from distraction by distraction"—moves seamlessly through the paragraph as if it were originally produced there. The allusions continue to accumulate as Otto, whom the fly lands upon, awakens to the sound of Verdi's *Aïda* from the radio next door, which leads to more thoughts of Io's transformation into Isis at Egypt which evokes "the fly god, Baal-zebub," who, when "metamorphosed by a pun [...] becomes Beelzeboul, the dung god, Prince of Devils."[28] The ruse for this extended reflection on metamorphoses (Shklovsky's "motivation of the device") is the appearance of a fly while Otto sleeps. Pope's quote leads to the slow digestion of every metonymical possibility for the concept "fly," a series of tropings that culminates in the figure of the god of excrement. Rather than claim this highly allusive web of signifiers as further proof of the dead author, consisting of "a tissue of quotations drawn from the innumerable centers of culture," which in Barthes's classical formulation, "has no other origin than language itself,"[29] I offer that Gaddis's allusive practice functions like his sentence practice. The excessive accumulation of allusion within the novel strews itself across the page not to wholly lay waste the tradition it inherits, but rather to hold out the option that some droppings from the past may be made useful in the present. No doubt there's an execrable plenty of arcane learning as well. So if this involves unpleasantly imagining the writing of the past as a waste product, Gaddis's allusions conversely enact a situation that renders waste into a product worth our time and imaginative labor. Rather than experience the allusions as distracting to the real matter of the novel's narrative, I'd emphasize that this sense of general distraction created by the allusions is what really matters when reading *The Recognitions*.

The three major texts caught in the web of this passage are themselves "distracted texts," whose forms allow for intellectual digression, wandering meditation, and tangential storytelling to replace rigorous argument, thematic unity, and plot. Ovid's account of Io and Jove, for example, is interrupted in the middle while Mercury lulls Argos to sleep with another tale of metamorphosis, this one involving Pan and Syrinx, so that the god of writing can kill him. This "story within the story" structure is typical. Meanwhile, Pope's "Essay on Man" is an "essay" in the Montaignean sense of the word, an intellectually curious attempt to understand the nature of something — in this case, man himself: "Expatiate free o'er all this scene of man;/ A mighty maze! but not without a plan."[30] "Not without a plan" means something much different than "with a plan" and Pope's poem moves along as such, even meandering to consider the metamorphoses of "the dull ox" who "[i]s now a victim, and now Egypt's god,"[31] hence invoking Ovid's Io/Isis by way of the cow, rather than Gaddis's way of the fly. Finally, Eliot's "Little Gidding" from the *Four Quartets* (a work Gaddis thought so highly of that he considered inserting every line into *The Recognitions*) takes the form of a spiritual exercise in the manner of the Buddha and St. John of the Cross, placing itself "[w]here past and future are gathered. Neither movement from nor towards."[32] Movement without direction (neither "from" nor "towards" but movement, nonetheless) allegorizes the formal quality of Eliot's verse, which shifts metrics and subject matter suddenly and often. Moreover, these three poems in question all take the human experience of mutability to represent a fundamental fact of being; how they represent this, however, indexes particular historical attitudes, which Gaddis organizes and critiques in his own work "where past and future are gathered."

Ovid's poem of "things that change,"[33] inspired by the atomistic philosophy of Epicureanism, takes the perpetual flux of matter without steady form (of which god and humans are but a part) as the world itself. Pope allows for the chaos of matter to remain, but only as something for God, not poets, to dwell on: "Who sees with equal eye, as God of all,/ A hero perish, or a sparrow fall,/ Atoms or systems into ruin hurl'd/ And now a bubble burst, and now a world."[34] Pope's essay is a paean to Enlightenment science, which for him dictates the rationalized study of material with concern for neither first or final causes nor emotional investment, taking it for granted that outside the chaos of our perceptions, God keeps the universe as rational and neat as a heroic couplet. Meanwhile Eliot strives for an ascetic ideal in which the "weakness of the changing body"[35] is overcome by the conquering of desire, and thus "a release from action and suffering."[36] By this, the body's metamorphic state is regularized into a pattern of necessary motion freely purified from unnecessary motion. None of these representative strategies account for Gaddis's own chaotic study. Ovid offers materialism without idealism: gods and men are both physically and morally diffuse. Eliot offers idealism without materialism: submission to metaphysical pattern at the expense of erotic pleasure and its natural vicissitudes. Lastly Pope, whose rational skepticism of both idealist and materialist narratives alienates him from a claim to either: "proud Science"[37] sticks to the natural realm, giving up on transcendental experience in favor of empirical facts, yet empirical classification separates physical bodies from one another according to a rationalizing system of identities and differences, which neutralizes the very mutability matter has traditionally been associated with. Gaddis's metamorphic fly can represent not only a fly itself, but "a goddess, a princess, and a devil."[38] Contrarily, Pope is pleased to individually categorize "each beast, each insect, happy in its own,"[39] according to the rational pleasure that taxonomy affords. Indeed, the segregating science that Pope praises in his "Essay" consistently comes under the attack of Gaddis's pen. Drawing both on Ovid's sense of divine mutability and Eliot's irresistible desire for pattern, while also resisting certain claims of each, *The Recognitions* wages a general critique of how modern forms of rational perception mediate the complex experience of experience into the simple consumption of information.

As noted before, the intricate verbal structure of *The Recognitions* rejects a linguistic model of communicative transparency, which Gaddis associated (fairly or not) with Hemingway and a kind of artificial scarcity of reference that the later writer rejected. Remember that Gaddis wished to fuse his own subjective "frame of reference" with the objectively figured characters and events in his novel. This infusion of individual subjectivity into objective description comprises an aesthetic strategy that is explicitly set against objective formalisms, whether encountered in the dispassionate recording of experiment results by a nuclear scientist, or the anesthetic stoicism of a Hemingway hero's recorded thoughts. For Gaddis, disinterested language is one kind of mediating instrument that reduces the experience of experience, but *The Recognitions* sets its multiple sights on repudiating any act of mediation that offers stable reference by obliterating a proliferation of meanings and values. Elsewhere, Gaddis took to task those writers who "derive" from Hemingway and attempt "to teach us to tell precisely what happened" by maintaining that "the instant a thing happens it has happened, and when it has happened it has happened in a thousand ways none of which alone is true."[40] As mentioned before, Wyatt's desire to paint like the Flemish Masters is itself linked to this desire for the transcendence of a single "miserable" perspective. The "perspective fallacy" is what Gaddis condemns in both the Hemingway school of writing and post–Renaissance painting: the presumption that a single individual is alone capable of stabilizing the flow of experience.

In his classic essay, "Perspective as Symbolic Form" (1927), Erwin Panofsky demystifies the claim that the perfected technique of perspective line drawing in the Renaissance is the most "natural" form for representing "real" space. Rather, he demonstrates how a proportionally lifelike painting, constructed through the vanishing intersection of all lines at a single point on its horizon, marks just one of many of the artist's possible symbolic forms, by which he means an aesthetic configuration "in which spiritual meaning is attached to a concrete material sign and intrinsically given to this sign."[41] What makes perspective so attractive and thus lasting as a historical phenomenon, Panofsky suggests, is that it places the human observer in the traditional all-viewing role of God:

> Perspective seals off religious art from the realm of the magical, but opens it to the realm of the visionary, where the miraculous becomes a direct experience of the beholder, in that the supernatural events in a sense erupt into his own apparently natural visible space, so permitting him really to internalize their supernaturalness.[42]

Thus the figure of "man" is spiritualized, abstracted from his own dematerialized body, and the result is "a translation of psychophysiological space into mathematical space; in other words, an objectification of the subjective."[43] Nature submits to understanding through the all-knowing perspective of an unseen, all-powerful consciousness, which mistakes its own symbolic creation for creation itself, like that theoretically perfect magician of Borges who gets tricked into mistaking his own illusions for the truth. Moreover, the perceptual normalization in the aesthetic realm that perspective entails is analogous to modern science's normalization of empirical observation in the scientific realm. As an erroneous result, historically specific habits of observation are misclassified as eternal principles of trans-historical rationality.

One way of describing Gaddis's metamorphic language is that it aims to retranslate mathematical space into psychophysiological space, recalling Gaddis's criticism of Hemingway's truncated "frame of reference" that he sets against his more symbolically inclusive one. This critique against perspective is not simply one of Wyatt's gripes, it is an ongoing feature of Gaddis's own prose. The traditional metaphor of perspective, classically elaborated upon by Leon Battista Alberti in his seminal 1435–6 treatise, "On Painting," is that of a transparent window separating the painter's subjective gaze from the object of his painting. Alberti also recommends that no more than nine figures should be painted within the frame, due to consideration for the pleasures afforded by mathematical proportion.[44] But Gaddis, we remember, wishes to fuse his own symbolical frame of reference with that of the objects being described, favoring indeterminate meaning over transparency and referential exuberance over proportionate representation. We might term this, inverting Panofsky's phrase, a subjectification of the objective in which the clear pane of "miserable" representation is shattered in favor of a more diffuse aesthetic. Rather than signal, however, as Barthes would have it, "an anti-theological activity,"[45] Gaddis's destruction of the individual's self-authorized act of creativity aims to disfigure the notion of "man as watchful God" so as to open the chance that some transcendental presence (God, history, an ideal reader?) might rescue the referential frame from incoherence—that his mighty maze might have a plan.

So let's return to the amazing fly of chapter 6, which, we remember, enters the frame of part I, chapter 6 via a passage from Pope that is set off from the rest of the prose as a curious specimen within quotation marks, unlike the material of Ovid whose traditional presence passes fluidly into the text, or Eliot, whose language is so contemporary that it absently-mindedly drifts into the writing like it may be Gaddis's own (indeed, Moore does not bother to cite it). When the empirically "real" fly, "Diptera," appears, the narrator describes him as "dashing and retreating in frenzy against the windowpane, drawn to a new destination the instant it halted, from the shade-pull to the floor, from there to the lampshade, back to the baffling window glass."[46] The Diptera (the name itself captures a bit of Ovid's Latin in the isolating amber of Linnaeus's) is trapped by a single window, which is soon forgotten to exist as it comically explores the every particular of the landscape of Otto's face. There he studies "the caves of his nostrils," "the tanned peak of his nose," the cleft of his chin," and the "protruding" and "convoluted marvel" of his ear.[47] As Diptera, the fly is "[n]o Argus," the multi-perspectivist observer, nor is he "a goddess, a princess, and a devil" that Gaddis's writing metamorphosizes him into.[48] As through the microscope glass or inside of a cinematic close-up, his vision is made intimately familiar with the smallest details of Otto's face, yet his rapid "dashing and retreating" keeps him in a state of distraction, flitting from one captured image to the next. In this, he is the onlooker of everything but the "guardian of nothing," recalling Shklovsky's characterization of alegebraic perception as a world of nothingness, an endless repetition of meaningless images subjected to neither pattern nor meaning. This Diptera, evoking Wyatt's characterization of perspective painting and the camera, is no less than "miserable."

I would like to suggest that the "miserable" form of perception which Gaddis associates with simple empirical observation, Hemingwayesque prose, and perspective painting, he also associates with the film making process. Wyatt himself conflates the technique of perspective, developed alongside Renaissance use of the *camera obscura*, with cameras in general, just as Panofsky in "Style and Medium in the Motion Pictures" (1947) draws a direct historical line from perspective to the film camera.[49] And if perspective could lend single perception a spiritual dimension, so too could film. Writing out of the French New Wave in the 1940s and 50s, André Bazin insisted that film served such a sacramental function. In "Ontology of the Photographic Image (1945)," Bazin famously compares the photographic image as captured by the camera on film to the ancient Egyptian practice of mummification, an attempt "to snatch [the human body] from the flow of time, to stow it away neatly, so to speak, in the hold of life."[50] The process of filmmaking for Bazin, with its delight in transparently reproducing everything it beholds, consecrates every visibility inside the purview of the camera's mechanical gaze. Indeed, the movie camera offers an advance in this area over perspective painting and its descendant, still photography, because it appears to hold motion itself outside of time. "Motion pictures," unlike the still figures on Keat's Grecian urn, for example, can move. Gaddis, however, insists that an action "happen[s] in a thousand ways," and a filmed gesture simply isolates a set of motions from the full context of causal associations to which they belong.

"[U]nder the ingenious guidance of the camera," Walter Benjamin writes in his definitive essay on the subject, "filmed behavior lends itself more readily to analysis because of its incomparably more precise statements of the situation," making even the "muscle of a body" an object for its art, thus "exploding the prison-world" of ordinary optical perception, transforming the simplest gestures into something shockingly unfamiliar.[51] Just as Hemingway's literary progeny write "to tell precisely what happened," the medium of film seeks "precise statements of the situation," and like early Hemingway and early film, the results are indeed explosive. Yet, such initial shock value can just as easily, through constant exposure to filmed images, inure "the mass" into a habitual state of "distraction." Unless the public retains critical habits, film offers its observer a "position [that] requires no attention." In this sense, Benjamin adds that "[t]he public is an examiner, but an absent-minded one."[52] Less sanguine than Bazin, but more optimistic than Gaddis, Benjamin offers the hope that a publicly critical attitude toward mechanical reproduction may ward off a situation of tuned-out masses ripe for the machinations of capitalist ascendancy. Yet in the wake of a triumphant war against fascism, Gaddis concludes that the complacent patriotism of a Cold War U.S.A. had already tuned out the realities around them in favor of the fantasies that they both projected and had projected upon themselves.

Chapter 6 of *The Recognitions* includes Otto's peregrination around the city, leading to a scene on mass transportation where a distracted public cease to experience their lives and the world around as anything but a mass produced, Hollywood film:

> The downtown bus [Otto] boarded a quarter-hour later was driven by a mustached man in a leather jacket, whose swashbuckling motions recalled the devil-may-care bomber pilots of the motion-picture screen. His cap, its wiry frame removed, clung rakishly to the back of his oily head, as he guided his huge machine down the runway for another takeoff.[53]

The individual gestures of a bus-driver immediately lead to an image of an Errol Flynn "swashbuckling" pirate movie, which is imperceptibly transmuted into a hackneyed Hollywood image of patriotic propaganda that in turn provides a fully realized shot of unrealistic warfare. A culture of un-self-critical distraction will only triumph, Benjamin writes, with the aestheticization of war, in which "self-alienation has reached such a degree that it can experience its own destruction as an aesthetic pleasure of the first order."[54] When the masses desire bomber pilots, simple pirates will not satisfy. The bus-riders' distraction develops across several paragraphs as an extended metaphor whose runaway vehicle flattens the whole world of its original tenor. A physical world melts away at the blink of an eye, when a bus driver becomes a cartoonish bomber pilot whose bus becomes a plane taking off a runway that used to be a street. The eclipse of the real continues as "[the passengers] tore through clouds, shuddered at air-pockets, dove low over landmarks," merrily jetting through "phantastical domains"[55] on their way to incinerate ... where? Dresden? Hiroshima? Hanoi? Baghdad? New York? Perhaps only the "devil may care."

Gaddis's misgivings about film in *The Recognitions*, much like his suspicion of Hemingway, stems from a distrust of a certain kind of realism (it is no surprise that Humphrey Bogart and Gary Cooper starred as Hemingway heroes while the world still awaits to see Gaddis on film). Such mimesis embeds itself within a classical empiricist tradition that mistakes what is visible for what is valuable. "Mirrors dominate the people," Esme warns Otto at the end of chapter 6, shuddering to think of what it may mean to be "trapped in one."[56] The "distracted" and "absent-minded public" that Benjamin feared was one which bothered Gaddis as well. When the mass production of images overwhelms the ability of mass consumers to address such images as having complex histories of development, the critical mind is laid waste. As in Gaddis's runaway metaphor, collective disengagement imaginarily deforms vague transcendental longing into aggressive flights of aimless desire, projecting allegories of violence upon a blank screen in the space where no genuine historical consciousness can flicker. As part of its thoroughgoing critique of contemporary modes of mimetic reproduction (its "overthrow of Platonism," if you will), *The Recognitions* contends a mass medium like film offers images without substance in order to create human subjects without judgment. This uncritical public as represented in the novel, in turn, provides endless opportunities for money to be made by selling them sham products packaged as spiritual objects, whether saint relics, forged paintings, or Dale Carnegie's *How to Win Friends and Influence People*.

The epigraph to chapter 6 preceding Otto's encounter with the fly and subsequent bus ride is extracted from *The Brothers Karamazov* (1880) and deals with the arbitrary power that wealth exerts over individuals, its one goal to "conquer everybody."[57] Wealth "conquers everybody" just as "mirrors dominate the people." Both, recalling Wyatt's language, are "miserable." Gaddis's adjectival deployment of this word as an indicator of rationalized perception also critiques the capitalization of detailed empirical knowledge for the gains of monetary profit. When Recktall Brown, the novel's miserly arch-capitalist, observes Wyatt's multi-perspective paintings, he praises "all these God damn tiny little details,"[58] which he knows are central to the painting's ability to return a generous profit. Likewise, chapter 6 of the first part, one of the smallest chapters in the novel, may be seen as an extended engagement with the way capitalism thrives in a culture of attention to fragments of empirical detail that, given the meaningless-in-itself status that such information inhabits (God-damned indeed), is transformed from knowledge in the lab to power in the market place. Thus, we overhear ad copy from the radio boast that a hair removal product is "guaranteed to remove fifteen hundred hairs in a single hour," or of the odorless deodorant that is "[f]ifty-two percent more effective";[59] we learn about Stanley's letter from the "eye bank" that wishes him to "deposit [his] eyes" after death so that they may be sold to someone else.[60] Gaddis satirizes (and discursively employs) the power of statistical knowledge himself, representing New York City by how many aspirin tablets it buys in a year and at what cost it buys them (15,670,944,200 tablets for $85 million), as well as how many how many cigarettes smoked annually (40 billion).[61] Reality that exists for the brute extraction of detailed information constitutes a simple understanding of what is real within *The Recognitions*. It is in this sense that Recktall Brown corporately merges himself with a brute empirical worldview when he lectures Valentine and Wyatt: "Business is cooperation with reality."[62]

The reality business is what bothers Gaddis. Whether in the form of allegedly transparent prose, empiricism, perspective painting, or film, *The Recognitions* resists the sort of violent critical reductions of human experience he associates with the mass media strategies of his time and the profit motives that drive them. The atomization and fragmentation of everyday life associated with a twentieth-century society both democratic and capitalist in nature are only accelerated by those practices of representation that operate by shrinking plural moments of experiential chaos into single objects of known quantity. Yet unlike the high-Church monarchist Eliot, Gaddis shares with Benjamin an unwillingness to separate his work from the chaotic modern culture that provides the very base for its material production. In relying on Shklovsky, Panofsky, Bazin, and Benjamin, rather than contemporary theorists, I have attempted to resist the "alienated genius" model of Gaddis interpretation. Rather, *The Recognitions* may be safely contextualized in specific Euro-American currents of early to mid-twentieth century intellectual history. Too many readers do Gaddis a disservice when they take at face value Wyatt's priestly pretensions, or make Gaddis himself into a figure martyred for the eternal sanctity of art, an image as tiresomely reproducible as that of Papa Hemingway.[63] The cover image explored at the beginning of this essay is one such instance in which Gaddis's attempt to create a vast social canvas like those of Van der Goes or Bosch is hacked away into the image of a solitary, Romantic genius trapped in the throes of some private and unsharable religious experience.

Rather, resembling the undeluded Town Carpenter of his story, Gaddis refuses to give up on the folly of searching for transcendence, even as he knows his own two eyes are miserably inadequate for the task. Thus, *The Recognitions* struggles to develop a set of formal strategies meant to proliferate points of view so that at no point on the critical horizon can all lines of thinking be said to converge and vanish. But such proliferation requires additional eyes, a society of additional readers and, especially, critics. After all, as Wyatt would have it, criticism "is the most important art now, it's the one we need most."[64] In some notes he drafted for a possible documentary film about forgery based on much of the archival research he performed for *The Recognitions*, Gaddis dismisses Platonic idealism out of hand, yet he identifies the difference between the arts of "the creator" and "the forger" by deeming the former as one "who knows where he fails" while deeming the latter as one who "obviates this possibility by setting 'perfected' limitations beforehand."[65] We Gaddis critics might learn something from this distinction. Instead of limiting ourselves beforehand via perfected theories of reading or the desire to establish our object of study's undeniable worth, only to inadvertently deny the presence of details in that object less visible to our critical focus, we might begin by allowing that an exhaustive reading is neither possible nor desirable. Giving up the urge to forge a more perfect reading, we at least might open up our own writing for the chance to try to fail to express our critical objectives more creatively.

6

Agapē Agape:
The Last Christian Novel(s)

BIRGER VANWESENBEECK

> It is with fiction as with religion: it should present another world, and yet one to which we feel the tie.
> — Herman Melville, *The Confidence-Man*[1]

> Nihil cavum neque signo apud Deum.
> — Irenaeus, *Adversus Haereses*;
> Epigraph to William Gaddis's *The Recognitions*[2]

> I see myself as the rear guard, as the last of something.
> — William Gaddis[3]

One of the remaining enigmatic statements about *The Recognitions* (1955) is its author's belated acknowledgment, first made publicly in a 1986 interview with the *Paris Review* and reiterated eight years later during a university lecture in St. Louis, that it was originally conceived out of a desire to write nothing more or less than "the last Christian novel."[4] This curious and, as Gaddis self-mockingly admitted in the interview, particularly hubristic poetics should be understood in relation to the *Clementine Recognitions*, a fourth-century "theological romance" from which the novel draws its idiosyncratic title, and a text that, as one of Gaddis's own characters remarks, "[has] been referred to as the first Christian novel."[5] Detailing the story of a young man's quest for salvation after an initial lapse of faith, the *Clementine Recognitions* contains not only the oldest known version of the Faust myth in Western literature — as the same Gaddis character also eruditely insists — but also, and perhaps more relevant for the purpose of this essay, it provided the early Church, then but recently promoted to state religion by the Roman emperor Constantine, with an invaluable literary ally in its theological witch-hunt against heretics. Indeed, it may well have been the text's indictment of the Gnostic teachings of Simon Magus (one of those heretics singled out by the early church father Irenaeus in his second-century tract *Adversus Haereses*) that guaranteed its continued presence on the copyist's table during late antiquity in the first place.[6]

Yet knowledge of this historical precedent far from settles the hermeneutic difficulties that the phrase "last Christian novel" evokes, if only because of its pleading allegiance to a genre that, even after the publication of Northrop Frye's rigorous genre taxonomy *The Anatomy of Criticism* (published two years after *The Recognitions*), has remained mostly apocryphal and untheorized. Neither does it help that Gaddis criticism in the half-century since has remained remarkably silent on all matters religious, so much so that one cannot help but wonder whether, in a secondary literature now dominated by the media-savvy doctrines of first and second-order cybernetics,[7] religion constitutes perhaps that proverbial "blind spot" from which the critical observer is always making his observations. Or still more to the point, one wonders why it is that religion, itself an autopoietic system of sorts that is reliant — as Gaddis understood so well — on the recursive measures of rereading and recognition, has not been given a more prominent place in those cybernetic approaches in the first place.

Perhaps most striking, however, is the absence of religion from those (now often but incriminatingly cited) essays that have compared Gaddis to James Joyce in the past, an author that may or may not have "influenced" him while writing *The Recognitions* (a topic of continued debate among scholars), but certainly a writer that shares with Gaddis a far-reaching interest in the history of Christianity.[8] Indeed, Joyce and Gaddis stand almost alone among twentieth-century novelists in their deeply felt need to position themselves (and their characters) with regard to a religious doctrine that they nevertheless both claim to have outgrown. It is here that a comparatist approach might illuminate not just the related *aesthetic* of *Ulysses* (1922) and *The Recognitions*, as past analyses have done, but also the all but conventionally religious penchant of two writers (one a lapsed Catholic from Europe; the other a protestant apostate writing in the American grain) whose works are perhaps best considered in such chiasmic terms rather than through the *rigor sortis* of analogy.

The notion of "lastness," for that matter, constitutes a similarly neglected trope in Gaddis criticism as scholars— urged on by the an-archic, post-1968 philosophies of Jean Baudrillard, Gilles Deleuze and Jacques Derrida — have perhaps focused all too much attention on the critique of firstness and originality in novels such as *The Recognitions*, thus largely foregoing that novel's as profound interest in the process of termination. Indeed, although the posthumously published *Agapē Agape* has been hailed by some critics as "in some ways a final accounting,"[9] and even as a *Pincher Martin*-esque narrative "posted from beyond the grave,"[10] it should at the same time be obvious that this is hardly the first Gaddis novel to unfold from under the advancing pressure front of death. Already in *The Recognitions*, the beleaguered writer "Willie," a character that many scholars have read as a barely disguised alter ego of the author, is at work on an (as barely disguised) *Recognitions*-esque book that is explicitly referred to as "[e]schatological, the doctrine of last things."[11] Alternately, what reader can ever forget that novel's dramatic, apocalyptic finale where the Catholic composer Stanley, arguably the last Christian *artist* in Gaddis's oeuvre, is buried under the falling rubble of an Italian Renaissance church due to a fatal insistence to play the organ with the stops removed?

Long before the publication of *Agapē Agape* therefore, Gaddis's novels, and *The Recognitions* in particular, have always already been what Frank Kermode, in *A Sense of an Ending* (1967), calls "fictions of the End," quasi-apocalyptic narratives that not only offer a (usually) dark vision of the end of the world, but that also provide an inquiry into "the ways we make sense of the world."[12] For it is by projecting our own ends that we give expression to our anxieties and/or excitement about the world, and it is also through such apocalyptic "deadlines" that we impose a sense of order on the passing of time. So it is also with Gaddis's notion of the "last Christian novel," which indicates an eschatological poetics that constitutes as much a heretical gesture bent on provocation as it reflects an attempt to ground oneself within a pre-existing literary tradition, no matter how ill- or non-defined.

Provocation and orientation, however, are hardly the only meanings that lie embedded in the epithet "last Christian novel." As with so much in Gaddis, the phrase is likely meant to be taken as part quip, part hubris, but also part serious historiography of a sort typically shunned by other, more ironic late-twentieth-century writers such as Thomas Pynchon and Don DeLillo, yet very much on a par with some of Gaddis's other grand literary ambitions.[13] One way to start accounting for the phrase "last Christian novel" is therefore to take it simply at face value and to read it as the more or less conscious attempt on the part of a then thirty-two-year-old author to write himself loose from a religious doctrine, which, it is fair to say, he loathed as much as he, like Melville in the quotation preceding this essay, realized its deep contiguity to the art of fiction. This, at least, is the view that Gaddis had come to espouse by 1994 when, in an essay that had its origin in the earlier mentioned St. Louis lecture, he argued that both religion and fiction essentially capitalize on the same Coleridgian willing suspension of disbelief:

> Rather than initiating our undertaking with a confrontation—I am sure we will see plenty of that—I propose to extend the hand of fellowship from the criterion central to both: that which constitutes poetic faith for the writer in Coleridge's familiar "willing suspension of disbelief," and for the religionist the leap of faith enshrined in Augustine's misquotation of Tertullian, "Credo quia absurdum."[14]

Between the theater of the absurd that is religion and the often mystifying escapism of literature, there are, in other words, far more parallels than a post–Nietzschean, late twentieth-century novelist like Gaddis may be willing to endorse. Hence the obvious need to distinguish between the two, perhaps by insisting, as does the lapsed Jesuit priest Basil Valentine in *The Recognitions*, that "the priest is the guardian of mysteries. The artist is driven to expose them."[15]

Yet to interpret Gaddis's fervor to write the "last Christian novel" solely as an emancipatory gesture would be to miss some of the very specific resonances that it also has within the actual plot of *The Recognitions*. For instance, one also imagines Gaddis writing the last Christian novel as a kind of present-day analogue to the Flemish Primitives that his artist-character Wyatt forges in that novel. It was the Dutch historian Johan Huizinga who first pointed out in 1919 that these fifteenth-century artists should not so much be regarded as the pioneers of a "Northern Renaissance" — as painters such as the brothers Van Eyck, Rogier van der Weyden, and Hugo van der Goes were then commonly viewed — but rather as the last "cinders" of a medieval tradition then coming to a close. As Huizinga puts it poetically in the introduction to *The Waning of the Middle Ages* (1924):

> Here an attempt is made to see the fourteenth and fifteenth century, not as the announcement of the Renaissance, but as the end of the Middle Ages, as a medieval society in its last life cycle, as a tree bearing overripe fruit, matured and fully grown [....] The gaze of the writer has been directed as if into the depths of an evening sky, — but of a sky filled with bloodlike red, heavy and rugged with a lead-like grey, filled with a false shine of copper.[16]

Gaddis, who relies heavily on *The Waning of the Middle Ages* throughout *The Recognitions* (including for the novel's epigraph cited above) may have felt more than just a little bit of literary kinship to this curious Dutchman who, like himself, wrote with such remarkable fervor and empathy about a culture not his own (the fact that Huizinga was Dutch and not Flemish is often seen as one of the primary reasons he was able to write with such great insight about the culture of fourteenth- and fifteenth-century Flanders). Similarly, Huizinga's stubborn refusal to allow any spelling updates in later editions of *The Waning of the Middle Ages* might also have appealed to the author of *The Recognitions* whose own novels notoriously hang on to curiously archaic and/or British spelling forms.[17]

A second intratextual parallel for the phrase "last Christian novel" is that it aptly reinforces the presence of Goethe's Faust in *The Recognitions*, perhaps the eschatological literary stock-character par excellence, who famously makes his entrance into Goethe's play declaring that "I have alas studied, philosophy / Jurisprudence and medicine, / And, worst of all, theology / With keen endeavor, through and through —/ And here I am, for all my lore / The same wretched fool I was before."[18] It is exhaustion rather than pride that brings Faust to make a pact with Mephistopheles, an irony — one might call it the "banality of the devil" — that could hardly have escaped the author of *The Recognitions*. Not only would Gaddis have heartily seconded Faust's diagnosis of theology as "the worst [discipline] of all," but his own Faustian protagonist Wyatt gets lured into an international forgery scheme largely because, after a flopped art show in Paris and a failure to connect with the post–World War II art society of Greenwich Village, Mephistopheles is the only art commissioner left. As Wyatt tells his future employer upon their first encounter: "It's as though ... there's no direction to act in now."[19] In a national literature long dominated by the youthful (if often failed) pioneer-narratives of the likes of Huckleberry Finn and Jay Gatsby, the worldly fatigue of Goethe's Faust certainly introduces an uncommon and unprecedented theme into American letters, but it fits in perfectly with the kind of terminal fiction that Gaddis envisioned *The Recognitions* to be, a "last Christian novel" weighed down by two millennia of religious history coming to an end in the very genre that originally contributed so much to the spreading of its teachings.

And yet the paradox is that, judged by the standard of its own eschatological poetics, one must conclude that *The Recognitions* is a failure. For not only is the last Christian novel a book that has been written time and again both before and after Gaddis's time (by Melville, by Dostoyevsky, by José Saramago, or by Harry Mulisch), but also the very creation of such an absolute *nec plus ultra* is of course nothing short of an impossibility. After all, as any seasoned concert-goer knows, one can always imagine yet another encore after the final chord has been struck—so that even after the world has ended in fire, as Robert Frost famously hypothesizes in "Fire and Ice" (1920), there is still the possibility that "if it had to perish twice," it still might end in congealment. This apocalyptic relativity explains why, as Frank Kermode argues, eschatological narratives, both fictional and cultic, are not so much discredited once their projected ends peacefully expire; but rather, such a "disconfirmation" is typically "followed by a consonance" with a newly projected end that newly restores "our confidence of the end."[20]

So it is also, in a way, with Gaddis, who not only significantly ends *The Recognitions* with an epilogue (a kind of end after the end) and then still with "outlined notes ... for spinning out the novel's conclusion"[21] on his desk, but who, as I want to argue in this essay, also returned to the project of writing the last Christian novel with each new fiction that he published. Indeed, unlike what Joseph Tabbi suggests in his introduction to Gaddis's essay collection *The Rush for Second Place*, the author's interest in religion never so much "went away,"[22] but resurfaces time and again in each one of his novels. Thus, following a debut novel that essentially explored the distinctly Christian origins of "modern" Western art, it did not take the author of *The Recognitions* long into his subsequent self-styled "novel about business" *J R* before finding out that the presence of Christianity also loomed large. As one audibly overworked corporate employee in that novel puts it,

> Well go up to the library dig out some of the President's speeches whole Protestant work ethic head of General Motors on free enterprise whole utilitarian pragmatism angle what works, sees how things are not how they ought to be whole approach is what works sort of a two-edged sword forged from.[23]

Ironically (or perhaps fittingly), it is this same Calvinistic ardor that drives the musical compositions of the novel's main artist-character, Edward Bast (named, so one suspects, after the Tudor king who established Protestantism in Britain), who also labors under the never-waning pressure of a Protestant work aesth-ethic that he can't redeem.

Similarly, Gaddis's third and arguably most difficult novel *Carpenter's Gothic*, a present-day *Heart of Darkness* (1899) featuring a fundamentalist evangelical missionary as the maniacal Kurtz to whose making the whole of America contributed, hinges on the impossibility of viewing the history of Western colonialism loose from that of Christianity. As the Reverend Ude self-asserts, his mission is "bringing Africa to the foot of the cross"[24] and that foot, as Gaddis makes clear, is one that goes shod in the sinister Orwellian boot of the future, "stamping on a human face — forever."[25] Gaddis's legal satire *A Frolic of His Own*, finally, is perhaps his least overtly "last Christian novel," yet there is the inescapable sense that so much of its legal rhetoric, such as Judge Crease's warning against "the atheistic subversion of our moral values as a Christian nation,"[26] tailors to its audience's identification with Christian values.

• • •

All of this brings us to *Agapē Agape*: the razor-thin novella that was published five years after Gaddis's death and that brought on a final, unprecedented storm of mostly laudatory praise from European and American critics alike, who took the publication apparently more as an occasion to celebrate (or in the case of Jonathan Franzen, condemn) the author's *overall* career than as an object to be reviewed.[27] Far less of this top-down approach should be attributed to a belated *noblesse oblige* of a medium that, until then, had mostly negatively responded to Gaddis's work, than to the fact that *Agapē Agape*, as Gaddis no doubt knew, is quite simply and insurmountably a near-impossible text to judge. Part rant, part historiography, part personal settling of accounts (most notably with the book reviewing staff of the *New York Times* and the trustees of the Pulitzer Prize), and part deathbed monologue, Gaddis's final novella perplexes more than it pleases, amazes more than it amuses, and perhaps comes closest in tone to the maddening prose of *Pierre* (1852), the work that plummeted Melville's career and that Gaddis's narrator refers to as "that terrible Pierre you can't get thirty pages into."[28] The reference is in fact most revealing for, just as Gaddis's narrator suspects Melville of having written *Pierre* "out of revenge" following the disappointing reviews and sales of *Moby-Dick* (1851),[29] so it also seems to be with Gaddis himself who, following a life-long career at odds with the reviewing business, left it, at the very height of his literary fame, with a book that was (and is) entirely unreviewable. "[A]nd what is your book about Mister Joyce?" he tellingly has one journalist ask of James Joyce in *Agapē Agape*, letting the latter reply with an anti-critical riposte that is likely also his own: "It is not about something Madam, it is something."[30]

Yet interpret and criticize *Agapē Agape* we must if only because the same Gaddis also unreservedly endorses criticism as "the most important art the one we need most [...] now,"[31] and, unlike Melville, he never abandoned his profound belief in the novel as a vehicle for social critique. Indeed, even the dying narrator of *Agapē Agape*, weakened by prednisone shots and frequent bloodletting, still sounds remarkably pugnacious in his attachment to "the artist the real artist Plato warned us about, the threat to society."[32] In what follows, I will elaborate on this rather peculiar engagement of *Agapē Agape* with criticism before turning to a discussion of the novella as yet another (though now literally *the*) last Christian novel of William Gaddis. The two are related closely, as I hope to make clear, in their common concern with community, a notion of which Gaddis retraces the critical, as well as religious significance.

That the young Gaddis should have praised criticism as an "art" (let alone one of which we are in dire need) may come as a surprise to contemporary readers of his fiction who have become perhaps all too accustomed to the irony of the author's continued exclusion from the canon, as well as to the failed initial reception of *The Recognitions*.[33] Yet, this autonomistic, elevated view of criticism would have come naturally to any English undergraduate who completed his education, as did Gaddis, at Harvard in the early forties. This was after all the heyday of New Criticism, propagated by the likes of I.A. Richards (who started teaching at Harvard while Gaddis was still a student there), which left the future author of *The Recognitions*, among others, with a life-long affinity for T.S. Eliot's impersonal, proto-New Critical approach to literature. Indeed, in hindsight it can easily be established that so many of the compromised critics that permeate Gaddis's fiction — Crémer and Basil Valentine in *The Recognitions*; the Village party evaluating the *L'Ame d'un Chantier* artwork in part II, chapter 5 of the novel; Judge Crease's indictment of the sculpture *Cyclone 7* in *A Frolic of His Own* — are in fact guilty of one of the critical "fallacies" that New Criticism famously warns against. The same, for that matter, could be said about Wyatt's own oft-cited rhetorical query: "What is it they want from a man that they didn't get from his work?,"[34] which obviously reiterates the New Critics' emphasis on close reading, as well as W.K. Wimsatt and Monroe Beardsley's intentional fallacy.

Given this, the final published format of *Agapē Agape* resembles neither the "social history" that the character Jack Gibbs imagined it to be in *J R*,[35] nor the fictionalized autobiography that some scholars have made it out to be, but rather it comes closest to being a work of criticism, not that of a New(er) Critic, but one that follows in the eminent continental tradition of thinkers like Nietzsche, Huizinga, and Benjamin (all of whom are cited in *Agapē Agape*). It is Gaddis's narrator himself who encourages such a perspective in telling us right from the start that the purpose of his writing is expository rather than aesthetic:

> No you see but I've got to explain all this because I don't, we don't know how much time there is left and I have to work on the, to finish this work of mine while I, why I've brought in this whole pile of books notes pages clippings and God knows what.[36]

The primary purpose of his narrative, as he further explains, is to "get it all sorted and organized" and to test his "thesis," revealed only gradually to the reader in bits and pieces, that the driving force behind technological innovation is the desire for entertainment.[37] Hence, for instance, the novella's recurring references to Johan Huizinga's *Homo Ludens* (1938), a study of the play-element in culture, whose "criterion of the charm"[38] is one of the theories—along with the Pleasure Principle of "my golden Sigi" (Sigmund Freud)—by which the narrator tests the validity of this thesis.

Yet within American literature proper, too, there are important precedents for the peculiar narrative format of Gaddis's final fiction, most notably Melville's *Moby-Dick* and Pynchon's *The Crying of Lot 49* (1966), novels that, like *Agapē Agape*, dramatize the act of criticism itself by featuring as their main protagonist a scholar-like character in search of truth. Like Oedipa sorting through the will of a recently expired former lover in Pynchon's novel; and like Ishmael evaluating and optimizing the existent research on cetology in *Moby Dick*, Gaddis's scholarly narrator studiously rummages through the relevant secondary literature on technology, and, like any exemplary doctoral candidate, even vows to "publish a paper separate from this big project."[39] In each of these three texts—one might call them "critical narratives"—the gesture of criticism moreover occurs, in conformity with the original Kantian notion of *Kritik*, in opposition to authority and dogma: against the published naturalists and historians whose whaling data Ishmael vehemently contests, against the official government history which Oedipa so boldly (and eventually desperately) resists, and, in Gaddis's case, against the doxic view that the social impact of our technologies has been and is merely instrumental.

Yet as a critical narrative, *Agapē Agape* also goes further than each of these two precedents in that it does not just adopt the anti-authoritarian nature of *Kritik*, but at the same time harkens back to criticism's older Greek etymological origin *krinein* (to decide, to separate, to judge) from which the modern English word "crisis" is derived. Criticism and crisis evoke one another in *Agapē Agape* in the sense that Gaddis's narrator obviously operates from the premise of a perceived impasse in the present, which is what prompts him to retrace a lost authenticity in the past. "Where did it tip?" he asks repeatedly in the novella, desperately trying to retrieve the point of divergence "where it came from."[40] "It," as Gaddis's narrator gradually reveals to the reader, refers to the increasing technologization of society and more particularly to the detrimental effects that this has had on the arts including Gaddis's own literary practice. As criticism, *Agapē Agape* is, therefore, in the first place, a work of self-reflection in that it scrutinizes the very media—literature, criticism, art—in which the narrator addresses himself to us. It is this self-reflective approach that, according to Paul de Man, is precisely that which binds what he calls "authentic criticism" to the idea of crisis:

> In periods that are not periods of crisis, or in individuals bent on avoiding crisis at all cost, there can be all kinds of approaches to literature: historical, philologi-

cal, psychological, etc., but there can be no criticism. For such periods or individuals will never put the act of writing into question by relating it to its specific intent.[41]

De Man goes on to show that it is precisely this self-reflective approach that characterizes "the Continental criticism of today,"[42] but he also harkens back to one early twentieth-century text: the "Vienna Lecture" of Edmund Husserl, arguably Western philosophy's most sustained theoretical reflection on the link between crisis and critique.[43]

In this lecture, originally delivered under the title "Philosophy in the Crisis of European Mankind" to the Vienna Cultural Society on May 7 and 10, 1935, Husserl identifies "a crisis of European humanity"[44] that according to him has its origin in the increasing "specialization"[45] of the European sciences since the Renaissance. This specialization — of which Husserl singles out behaviorist psychology and historicism — has transformed the European sciences into a strictly mechanical endeavor where previous insights are now being adopted as ready-made concepts without any renewed inquiry into the conditions by which they were originally brought to light. There has, in other words, been a lapse away, so Husserl argues, from philosophy's original Greek ideal of *theōria*, from the "interest in the All," that conceived of thinking as an "infinite task."[46] Consequently, Husserl's lecture urges the European sciences to return to this original philosophical ideal of *theōria*, just as Gaddis's narrator in *Agapē Agape*, seeks to retrieve "what we destroyed, what we tore away"[47] from what he sees as the original sense of community associated with the arts.

Yet there are other ways, too, in which the Vienna lecture and *Agapē Agape* invite an analogous reading. Both are texts that were composed at career's end — Husserl died three years after giving the lecture — by two authors whose works are notoriously conflicted with regard to the very crisis that they treat. Indeed, as de Man perceptively points out, the tragedy of Husserl's "Vienna Lecture" is that its author ultimately fails to live up to the very ideal of infinity that he embraces,[48] just as Gaddis's narrator in *Agapē Agape* remains deeply conflicted regarding the *kind* of community that art establishes. According to one tradition, represented by the elitist Flaubert, that community can only be that of "a small group of minds, ever the same, which pass on the torch,"[49] whereas another tradition, represented by Leo Tolstoy, wants such a community to be one that is first of all *of* the people:

> "Perhaps they don't understand and don't want to understand our literary language because it's not suited to them and they're in the process of inventing their own literature" Tolstoy wrote that, we must write what they want or not write at all "we are thousands and they are millions" Tolstoy writes, obey the law of the greatest number talk about tyranny of the majority.[50]

It is the narrator's indecision with regard to these two traditions that indicates that perhaps far less of the crisis of community in the arts should be attributed to technology's impact than to an interior conflict that rages within the arts themselves, forever caught between elitism and populism.

Secondly, it is interesting to note that both Husserl and Gaddis conceive of this crisis in pathological terms with the former arguing that "the European nations are sick,"[51] whereas the latter refers to the craze of technologization in the arts as "the epidemic, it was the plague spreading across America a hundred years ago."[52] In addition, both Husserl and Gaddis's texts are obviously permeated by an overall sense of despair. In Husserl's case, the object of that despair is all too clear given the particular date and place of the Vienna lecture—Austria in the late 1930s— and is at once general and personal. Because of his Jewish heritage, Husserl had then already been stripped of his professorial privileges at the University of Freiburg just as the "European crisis" was soon to reach its sinister climax in World War II. In Gaddis's case, this tone of despair similarly concerns at once the legacy of literature itself in a society dominated by technology, and the gradual deterioration of his own body due to illness and age: "they keep me here to be cut up and scraped and stapled and cut up again my damn leg look at it, layered with staples like that old suit of Japanese armour in the dining hall feel like I'm being dismantled piece by piece."[53]

Another parallel between the two texts is the fact that both Gaddis and Husserl see the crises that they treat — specialization and technologization — as part of a larger problem affecting the possibilities for community. Indeed, like Gaddis, Husserl's hypothesis about a crisis of "European humanity" (*Europäische Menschentum*) should first of all be understood as referring to a sense of community that has gotten lost. According to him, what emerged with the Greek ideal of *theōria* was not just a self-reflexive ideal of thinking but also

> a new type of communalization (*Vergemeinschaftung*) and a new form of enduring community whose spiritual life, communalized through the love of ideas, the production of ideas, and through ideal lifenorms, bears within itself the future-horizon of infinity.[54]

It is this community of infinity that, according to Husserl, has gotten lost through the ever-increasing specialization of the sciences.

Gaddis, for his part, makes a much similar claim in *Agapē Agape* in that, according to his narrator, it is the increasing technologization of society that has caused the traditional sense of community associated with the arts (referred to by Gaddis with the Greek term *agapē*, or brotherly love) to come undone (agape). More specifically, it is Gaddis's claim, one that appears not just in *Agapē Agape*, but also throughout his fiction that the arts foster a kind of community through the participation that they demand from the reader or viewer. This, for instance, is the idea that underlies Wyatt's guild aesthetic in *The Recognitions*, where forgery becomes such a way of participating in the community, as Rave argued elsewhere.[55] Also Gaddis's own hypothesis, reiterated in numerous interviews, that the dialogical structure of novels such as *J R* and *Carpenter's Gothic* is meant to invite a "collaboration" between author and reader obviously bespeaks such a communitarian aesthetic.[56] Once artistic participation gives way to technological efficiency—a process that *Agapē Agape* traces back to the introduction of the player piano in 1876—the arts are deprived of this communitarian significance and are reduced to mere entertainment media. Consequently, for Husserl and for Gaddis, the crisis is one that cannot be dissociated from a larger crisis of community.

Finally, some words need to be said on the term "crisis," which, even though it is used nowhere in *Agapē Agape*, constitutes a notion that is as dear to Gaddis's thinking as it is to Husserl's. It appears, for instance, in the title of an unpublished 1979 essay, "Literature and Crisis," where, as in *Agapē Agape*, Gaddis discusses the problems posed to contemporary society by the "dominance of science and technology."[57] He concludes the essay by zooming in on the deep interconnectedness of the terms crisis, art, and community in this matter:

> It is, in short, a time of crisis. But it has always been a time of crisis, and it is not the purpose of literature to solve it, as a mathematical problem finds a solution. It was, after all, the mathematician Pascal who observed three centuries ago that "the heart has its reasons that reason knows nothing of." And it is these reasons with which literature "knits together the loneliness of innumerable hearts." It is these reasons that "bind together all humanity" in the permanent crisis of the human condition, these areas of intuitive as well as rational knowing, of individual frailty and sheer perversity, that literature has never ceased to explore, and so long as we have it, never will.[58]

Perhaps coming as close in tone to the Nobel Prize acceptance speech that Gaddis never got to give (the two quotations in the texts are taken from Saul Bellow's 1976 Nobel acceptance lecture),[59] this text fragment offers us yet another example of Gaddis's profound belief in the communitarian nature of art. It also draws attention to the peculiar fact that literature does not so much "solve" the crisis of technology as it transports the notion of crisis unto a different plane. Indeed, the paradox of de Man's "authentic criticism," one that both the "Vienna Lecture" and *Agapē Agape* exemplify, is that, while it operates from the premise of a perceived crisis in the present, its approach to this demise is not, as in mathematics, to solve or overcome it, but rather to take up the very idea of crisis as a part of the methodology. In Husserl's case, this occurs through the adoption of the perpetual crisis of philosophy as an infinite task; in Gaddis's case—as the above fragment indicates—the crisis is reassigned and interiorized by reminding us of our common share in the perpetual crisis that is the human condition.

· · ·

If the above observations reveal the deep-running similarities between Gaddis's views on community and those of Husserl, an author that he may or may not have read,[60] then the place where they part — that is the "crisis" between them — is even more interesting in that here the two texts appear as complements of each other. Whereas Husserl rather univocally retraces the community of European mankind to the theoretical insights of the Greeks, Gaddis, while plainly dismissive of the societies proposed by Plato and Pythagoras, locates the model for his art-mediated community instead in the one Western tradition notoriously overlooked by Husserl: Christianity. This, at least, is how the narrator urges us to understand the titular term *agapē*, not as a reference to some general idea of love or brotherhood, as most critics have read the phrase,[61] but rather as a return to "that love feast in the early church."[62] More specifically, the term "love feast" refers to the early Christians' re-enactment of the Last Supper and, in particular, to the transubstantiating event of the Eucharist—first performed by Christ *at* the Last Supper — where bread and wine take on the symbolic identity of his body and blood, thus allowing the believer to become one with Christ through consumption. It is this (loving) internalization of the body of Christ by the believer — later institutionalized as the sacrament of the Holy Communion during mass service — which Gaddis's narrator reappropriates in *Agapē Agape* as model for the community of art. The latter, so he argues, similarly consists of a "natural merging" of one artist's work with that of another "in love that transcends it, a celebration of the love that created it."[63]

Like the Christian believer's consumption of the host, the artist's compositional practice also consists of the internalization of an inspirational (and divinely capitalized) "Other,"[64] whose felt artistic kinship "transfigures you yourself into the self who can do more."[65] The latter phrase, an expression that recurs in each of Gaddis's five novels, is adapted from a sonnet by Michelangelo where, appropriately enough, it refers to a state of religious ecstasy. As quoted (in Michelangelo's original Italian) and self-translated by Gaddis in *Agapē Agape*, the relevant passage reads:

> O Dio, o Dio, o Dio, Chi m'a tolto a me stesso Ch'a me fusse più presso O più di me potessi, che poss'io? O Dio, o Dio, who has taken the one closest to me who could do more than no, no it's not that pedestrian it's fifteenth, sixteenth century Italian nearer poetry, Who nearer to me Or more mighty yes, more mighty than I Tore me away from myself.[66]

Given this, it would not go too far to read *Agapē Agape* itself as an extended *hoc est corpus meum* by which the dying narrator offers up his narrative — in the manner of the Christian host — for it to be internalized by the reader. With the narrator's prednisone-affected skin already eerily reduced to "parchment,"[67] not to mention the wafer-like thinness of the novella itself, such a eucharistic reading of the text — literature as the transubstantiated body of the author — seems naturally implied and is further reinforced by the overall sense of mourning that inevitably accompanies our reading of it. After all, like

Christ at the Last Supper, the narrator (and indeed Gaddis himself) addresses us in *Agapē Agape* with the knowledge that his end is near and that "we don't know how much time there is left."⁶⁸ Reading *Agapē Agape*, therefore, essentially becomes an exercise in mourning in the same manner as the sacrament of the Eucharist carries that significance for the Christian believer. Indeed, it is this internalization of the deceased Other's (textual) body that, as Jacques Derrida has shown,⁶⁹ in fact mirrors traditional psycho-analytical approaches to loss, where the glaring absence of the dead is absolved by letting him or her live on into our own thoughts and gestures, or — as with the host — into our very own bodies.

Alternately, the very premise of a community agape (as well as the attempt at a recuperation thereof) is, as Jean-Luc Nancy has perceptively noted, itself a distinctly Christian reflex, one that is fueled by a nostalgia for the Eucharist:

> [T]he true consciousness of the loss of community is Christian: the community desired or pined for by Rousseau, Schlegel, Hegel, then Bak-ouine, Marx, Wagner, or Mallarmé is understood as communion, and communion takes place, in its principle as in it is ends, at the heart of the mystical body of Christ.⁷⁰

In bemoaning the lost sense of *agapē* in the arts, in "looking back at what we destroyed, what we tore away from the self who could do more,"⁷¹ *Agapē Agape* therefore rather explicitly inscribes itself into a long Christian tradition of communitarian nostalgia, one that runs from the thinkers mentioned above all the way to Gaddis's own debut novel *The Recognitions*, whose two main artist-characters both express a nostalgia for the religious-artistic community of the medieval guild.

Yet why would Gaddis choose to present the community of art in analogy with a religious doctrine which his fiction otherwise so vehemently opposes? I believe it indicates an awareness on his part of the impossibility for any Western writer to conceive of community outside of the Christian paradigm of communion. In this, *Agapē Agape* mirrors the approach taken by Nancy who argues in *Being Singular Plural* (2000) that any contemporary revaluation of community first of all requires "the deconstruction of theological and/or sentimental Christianity, of the 'love one another'"; that is, of *agapē*.⁷² It is such a deconstruction that Gaddis also undertakes in *Agapē Agape* by evoking on the one hand the Christian notions of love and loss — pithily combined in the novella's anaphoric title — but by also forcefully reinscribing these two terms at the same time. After all, the idea of a Eucharist-like communion is what haunts the narrator of *Agapē Agape* as much as he recognizes its (historically inherited) appeal since such a "natural merging" would also imply the destruction of artistic individuality. As the narrator puts it, such a symbiotic process is what "[puts] me in danger of deadening myself out of existence,"⁷³ or, still more to the point, of having one's artistic work "plagiarized [...] before I've even written it."⁷⁴ Gaddis is therefore far from fully endorsing the art-mediated community as communion-like model of love, but he rather sets out to redefine the term *agapē* from a more individualized point of view. Gaddis's communitarian ideal, after all, unlike that of the early Christians, is that of a "*self* who can do more," an enlarged subjectivity that, like the multitudinous self of Walt Whitman's *Leaves of Grass* (1855) ("I am large, I contain multitudes"), engages with his artistic others from within the inalienable stronghold of the ego.

The distinction between Gaddis's own reappropriated model of *agapē* and that of the early Christians can perhaps best be summarized by the Latin prepositions *apud* and *cum*. Both are commonly translated as "with" in English: yet *apud* refers to the idea of proximity and symbiosis, while *cum* always evokes a sense of spacedness and individuation. *Apud* is what expresses the "nearer to me" ("Ch'a me fusse più presso") that appears in Michelangelo's original formulation of the self "who could do more,"[75] an ecstatic sense of symbiosis that annexes that with which it is paired. Tellingly, *apud* is also the word that is commonly used by Christian writers to refer to the becoming one with God: it is the term that appears in the famous opening line of the Gospel of John (*Et verbum erat apud Deum*; "And the word was with God"), as well as in the quotation from Ireneaus that serves as the epigraph (quoted in Latin) to Gaddis's *The Recognitions*: *Nihil cavum neque signo apud Deum* ("Nothing that is with God is devoid of meaning").

The preposition *cum*, by contrast, refers to a bringing together of entities which nevertheless retain a certain distance or "gaping" between each another. When we speak of a novelist *cum* entrepreneur, for instance, we do not so much suggest that these two professions are being sublated into one symbiotic whole as that they co-exist, as separate personalities, within that person. This is why Nancy refers to the preposition *cum* as an "interiority that has no interior"[76] since it is precisely this implied distance, this gaping, that prevents the joined entities from acquiring a symbiotic identity of its own except for the interiority of the "with-ness" itself. It is this spatialized model of *agapē* that Gaddis also endorses in *Agapē Agape* as a viable model for community in the arts, an *agapē* agape that joins together even as it also maintains a distance between its members. It is in this sense that the novella displays what Michael Wutz has called a "writing from between the gaps,"[77] neither fully identifying itself with the works of the artists that he cites nor denying the contiguity of their work to that of his own.

It is through this spatialization of the original Eucharist that *Agapē Agape*, like each of Gaddis's previous novels, can be said to situate itself within the horizon of Christianity, if only to reappropriate the latter's traditional symbology. Indeed, *Agapē Agape*'s focus on the deep kinship between community and religion in many ways mirrors Gaddis's earlier concern in *The Recognitions* with the deep-running parallels between fiction (and art in general) and religion. The realization of this parallelism is what forces him, in both novels, as well as in the "Old Foes with New Faces" essay, simultaneously to endorse, as well as to reappropriate and deconstruct them. *Agapē Agape* therefore adds a dignified and appropriate coda to the religio-eschatological aesthetic that Gaddis began with *The Recognitions* and that was to characterize every one of the novels published in between. Fittingly, the novella ends with a reference to "that Youth who could do anything,"[78] as if to emphasize yet one more time the youthful, hubristic poetics that occupied the author throughout his literary career and that never left him, not even in those ill-stricken months leading up to his death: that of writing the last Christian novel, nothing less.

7

"A disciplined nostalgia": Gaddis and the Modern Art Object

LISA SIRAGANIAN

> *Meanwhile, the arts are the only currency left which cannot be counterfeited and which may be passed from nation to nation and from people to people.*
> — James Thrall Soby (March 1942)[1]

In his 1953 autobiographical novel, *The Subterraneans,* Jack Kerouac writes about an evening with "a young novelist looking like Leslie Howard who'd just had a manuscript accepted and so acquired a strange grace in my eyes I wanted to devour."[2] The evening becomes a long night, involving various Beat poets, a car ride out of the city, flirtations and jealous arguments, and lengthy conversations with this Leslie-Howard-look-alike (called "Harold Sand" in the novel). Harold Sand, writes Kerouac, is a "flushed successful young author but 'ironic' looking," who is both "very interesting" and very determined.[3] In fact, Sand is so determined that he applies to an unpleasant car ride "the same grit that made him write the half million words of his novel."[4] And while the Kerouac character is too preoccupied to participate in the activities, Sand and a fellow poet, "Austin Bromberg," spend much of the next twenty-four hours "deeply engrossed in the music, the books, the brilliant conversation" and "chattering about every tom dick and harry in art."[5] The Kerouac character and his girlfriend brood, while Sand and Bromberg talk "of literary and musical and artistic matters, the kitchen littered, Bromberg rushing up (in pajamas) to fetch three-inch thick French editions of Genet or old editions of Chaucer or whatever he and Sand'd come to."[6]

"Harold Sand," as critics such as Barry Gifford and Lawrence Lee have pointed out, is Kerouac's pseudonym for William Gaddis.[7] And the depicted scene accurately captures Gaddis in his Greenwich Village days of 1953, at the moment when he had secured an advance for *The Recognitions,* his massive novel about art and forgery, but had not yet completed the "half million words of his novel" (as Kerouac quite correctly describes). In turn, Kerouac's descriptions of Sand and Bromberg resemble Gaddis's descriptions, in *The Recogni-*

tions, of the characters Wyatt Gwyon and Otto Pivner carousing late at night around New York City. The artist-protagonist Wyatt and his author-friend Otto are both equally determined to establish their notoriety as to invent new styles of art. Otto provides perhaps the best example in the novel of someone who plagiarizes the literary avant-garde to achieve social success, while Wyatt provides the key voice for an intense, unapologetic discourse about painting.

I begin with this example from *The Subterraneans* not to focus on the potential biographical connections between Gaddis and the characters in his novels (connections that Gaddis more or less acknowledged yet nonetheless loathed discussing), but to underscore Kerouac's indispensable observation about Gaddis's aesthetic interests.[8] Gaddis had a very real and deep engagement with the New York art movements of the late 1940s and early 1950s, a point that has been neglected in many critical discussions of Gaddis's work and which my essay seeks to redress. His understanding of modern art is mirrored in the shadowy art world of forgeries represented in *The Recognitions*. This conception of art also appears in Gaddis's later novels—specifically, in the fictional legal case about the various, dangerous, site-specific *Cyclone Seven* sculptures (either a direct reference to Richard Serra's "Tilted Arc" or an uncanny coincidence) which first appear in *J R* and play a larger and more critical role in *A Frolic of His Own*.[9] Not only was Gaddis attentive to major twentieth-century trends in art, such as Post-Impressionism, Surrealism, Abstract Expressionism and Minimalism, he also understood the particular directions and possibilities that were being negotiated at mid-century by artists such as Jackson Pollock, Robert Rauschenberg and Andy Warhol. Namely, while one strand of the Abstract Expressionist movement would develop into the performance-based, theatrical work ("Happenings") of artists such as John Cage, Rauschenberg and Warhol, another strand developed into site-specific or Earthworks art of Minimalists such as Richard Serra, Carl Andre and Robert Morris. Starting with *The Recognitions*, my subject here, and continuing thorough *J R* and *Frolic*, Gaddis not only reveals his familiarity with these divergent strands of post-war art, but he also pointedly engages with—and criticizes—debates within avant-garde art as they develop throughout the second half of the twentieth-century.

Of course, this literary interest in avant-garde painting is not Gaddis's alone. A wide range of twentieth-century writers are concerned with the status of the art object—whether that art object is a painting, a poem, or a novel—particularly in its phenomenological relation to the beholder. Writers such as Gertrude Stein, William Carlos Williams, and Gaddis are interested in the art object *not* in the service of a modernist critique (or an anti-modernist redemption) of referentiality. That modernist critique is most often understood as the attempt to displace the nineteenth-century naturalistic emphasis on external reality by problematizing the relation between a representation and the thing represented. Instead, writers like Gaddis are interested in the relation between an art object (a representation) and its beholder (a viewer or reader).

In his various novels, Gaddis reflects on — but, crucially, doesn't agree with — the idea that the spectator's or reader's experience is an inseparable part of art's meaning. This notion was increasingly prominent after mid-century and relates to broader trends in cultural studies and literary theory, such as Reader-Response criticism. Yet this question of an art object's relation to the reader or viewer is developed in a very sophisticated way by American writers — such as Stein, Williams and early Gaddis — even before it appears on the scene in its most explicit form in debates about Minimalist, Performance and Earthworks art in the 1960s and 1970s. Gaddis remains attentive to the art world throughout his career, satirizing these later artistic debates in *Frolic*: when the sculptor Syzrk initially defends *Cyclone Seven*'s existence and placement (the sculpture is dangerous to approaching humans and animals), he is implicitly relying on the idea that the spectator can only understand his work, whatever the mortal consequences, in its site-specific location. According to Syzrk, because the town of Tantamount "'epitomiz[es] that unique American environment of moral torpor and spiritual vacuity' requisite to his artistic enterprise," the sculpture *Cyclone Seven* must sit directly in front of that particular town.[10]

In *The Recognitions*, the question is whether or not the spectator's body — specifically, her particular visual perspective on the world — is relevant to a painting's meaning. Near the beginning of the novel, there is a scene of Wyatt Gwyon as a young boy. Even at a young age, he is a precocious painter, and here he begins to paint a remarkable picture of his mother who died on a transatlantic crossing when he was a toddler (she was the victim of a botched appendectomy by the quack ship's doctor). The painting, while beautiful, greatly bothers Wyatt's puritanical father, the Reverend Gwyon, for one reason in particular:

> [The painting] was done in black on a smooth gesso ground, on strong linen, a stark likeness which left its lines of completion to the eye of the beholder. It was this quality which appeared to upset Gwyon: once he'd seen it he was constantly curious, and would stand looking away from it, and back, completing it in his own mind and then looking again as though, in the momentary absence of his stare and the force of his own plastic imagination, it might have completed itself. Still each time he returned to it, it was slightly different than he remembered, intractably thwarting the completion he had managed himself.[11]

For Reverend Gwyon, still grief-stricken by his wife's premature death, the unfinished quality of his son's painting presents a problem not unlike the anxiety Dorian Gray faced in front of his portrait in Oscar Wilde's novel. Specifically, in both instances, to the men's fascination and horror, the representation keeps changing. Just as Dorian's bad deeds cause sneers to suddenly appear in his portrait, so every time Gwyon looks at the image of his wife, "it was slightly different than he remembered." Of course, for someone traumatized by such a loss, the mutability of the image of his wife seems to stand in, distressingly, for the mutability of the woman while she was alive. Just as people age day by day, the portrait of Gwyon's wife changes day by day. But in contrast to Wilde's novel, in Gaddis's novel her portrait does not change because it is a constant, accurate referent to his wife's life, and thus (as Wilde puts it) a "visible symbol of the degradation of sin."[12] Instead, in *The Recognitions*, Wyatt's portrait of his dead mother changes because the painting was *never* finished to begin with and requires the beholder to do this work of completion. In fact, Wyatt explains to his father that he made a deliberate choice to leave the work unfinished because, unlike a complete portrait, an unfinished work still has the possibility of perfection, while "all the time you work trying to uncover" that perfection. In contrast to Dorian Gray's portrait, which requires the referent of the sinning Dorian to be complete, Wyatt's original painting needs not the original referent to be complete, but the "eye of the beholder."

Wyatt's period of unfinished portrait painting is short-lived, not because he actually finishes his original paintings (he never does), but because he can no longer tolerate the beholder's involvement in his work's meaning. In other words, the incompleteness of his early paintings becomes a tremendous problem not only for his father, but more crucially, for Wyatt himself. Paradoxically, by the time he fully develops as a painter he stops painting original pictures entirely. Instead, he lives sequestered in his Greenwich Village apartment, painstakingly reproducing Dutch Old Master portraits. His forged paintings are then sold on the black market as utterly convincing counterfeits of Jan van Eycks and Hans Memlings. Wyatt decides that if an artist is faced with the choice of either producing works which require the beholder for their completion, or copying works which are complete in and of themselves in their original form, the artist must choose to copy.

Throughout the novel, Gaddis's central move is to represent the ontological relation between the spectator and an art object's meaning by contrasting the idea of a representation with that of a counterfeit. According to the world of *The Recognitions*, a counterfeit's status differs from a representation's status in that the former relies wholly on its ability to fool the spectator and, consequently, the spectator *entirely* determines the object's meaning. Wyatt's, and the novel's, central dilemma is how to create art while living in a world in which art's meaning has collapsed because spectators create (or, at least, finish) art. In stark contrast to the quotation with which this essay begins (i.e., James Thrall Soby's claim that "the arts are the only currency left which cannot be counterfeited"), Gaddis explores a world in which art's currency is just as degradable as any other. In particular, what has collapsed is the idea of representation, replaced by counterfeits that vary in their ability to compel conviction. Gaddis invokes painting as an example in order to illustrate his commitment to the irrelevance of the spectator's experience to the meaning of the art object.

In *The Recognitions*, Impressionism and Surrealism are tacitly blamed for having created this situation, negatively altering the possibilities for future art.

These movements, as Gaddis critiques them, create a situation in which painting reduces originality to a merely *physical* perspective. His claim is that if Impressionism reduces originality to a mechanized reproduction of what is in front of your face, then Surrealism reduces originality to a simple reproduction of the "view" of dreams behind your eyes. In either case, painting has become an automatic, almost photographic activity. Wyatt's is the voice of Gaddis's critique, here observing his fellow painters in Paris:

> He might walk up there occasionally and see them, the alleys infested with them painting the same picture from different angles, the same painting varying from easel to easel as different versions of a misunderstood truth, but the progeny of each single easel identical reproduction, following a precept of Henner who called this the only way of being original. Passing, he showed all the interest for them he might have for men whitewashing walls.[13]

Wyatt is dismissive of these contemporary painters he sees in Parisian alleys because they mistake their particular perspective (being in one particular alley and not another) for originality of vision (having something unique to show the world). They might each have "different angles" on the world, but the pictures they paint are identically flawed, hence their "different versions of a misunderstood truth." Wyatt carefully distinguishes between particularity and originality when it comes to modern art, and lambastes artists who confuse the two.

Thus, one reason why Wyatt produces art as if he is a fifteenth-century Flemish painter is to combat the idea that painting has no choice but to imitate the purely physical perspective of the camera. The view from the camera is a view from a single perspective, and this singular perspective is also—as he understands it—the flaw of modern art. Defending himself to the critic Basil Valentine, Wyatt explains that in a Flemish painting, in contrast to a modern one,

> There isn't any single perspective, like the camera eye, the one we all look through now and call it realism [...] the Flemish painter took twenty perspectives if he wished, and even in a small painting you can't include it all in your single vision, your one miserable pair of eyes, like you can a photograph, like you can painting when it ... when it degenerates, and becomes conscious of being looked at.[14]

Wyatt rejects modern art — and Impressionism and Surrealism seem to be his particular targets here — precisely because these movements aim to embody a particular, individual perspective on the world, just as a camera captures the particular perspective, light and time of a moment and place. Modern painting, according to this logic, has become too much like photography. Instead of capturing an artist's imagined vision, modern painting limits itself to capturing a single person's (albeit the artist's) perception of the world. Wyatt makes one more important point: as soon as an artist values his physical perspective on the world (the view from his eyes) over his entire vision, he has reduced his art to the literal world of his audience. A painting becomes something that "knows" it has an audience and plays to that audience. Such painting loses its status as a representation because its consciousness of spectators suggests it has become of the world of spectators (an embodiment of reality) instead of a *representation* of that world. So, as Wyatt puts it, "when it degenerates, and becomes conscious of being looked at," a painting is losing the essential characteristic that distinguishes a representation from just an object in the world. Instead of a representation of reality, Wyatt fears that modern art has become simply a poor embodiment or counterfeit of reality — and an unconvincing one at that.

Thus the counterfeit in Gaddis's novel is not simply a trope for the feelings of total falseness in mid-century life; it is also an important idea for establishing the changing conception of how art objects work in the mid-century world. When representation has lost its value as something distinct from a reproduction (to put it in Walter Benjamin's terms), art must compete with reality as one in a series of high-quality fakes. And from the very beginning of the novel, Wyatt's representations — his drawings and paintings — are depicted as counterfeits, even when they are, in all senses of the word, his original creations. By using the notion of a "counterfeit" to refer to original works of art, Gaddis implies that art objects are of the world in the way that a rock or a breath of air is of the world. In a certain sense, the problem as he sees it is that paintings have become objects that do not have the status of art objects.

According to the novel, the degeneration of representation had begun earlier in the twentieth century, epitomized at the very moment when young Wyatt (as a child) produces a drawing of a bird and his Aunt May chastises him for competing with nature. According to Aunt May, the drawing of a robin he shows her, "which looked like the letter *E* tipped to one side," is an attempt "to become original [...] to steal Our Lord's authority, to command his own destiny, to bear his own light!"[15] Despite Aunt May's warnings, Wyatt secretly continues to make drawings, "terrified with guilty amazement as forms took shape under his pencil," which he then wraps in newspaper and buries behind the barn. By burying his art, Wyatt seems implicitly to consent with this understanding of the artist as satanic usurper, for he is unable to distinguish the actions he commits in the world from the drawings he commits to the page. The burying of his art suggests an abject relation to the work (one thinks of cats burying feces in out of the way places). But this art is also something physical and original to him (in the way that feces is an unmistakably original substance).[16] When we then continue to read that "once, digging back there, he came upon the rotted remains of the bird he had killed that day he had burst into tears at Aunt May's conjectural challenge and punishment," we are most likely given pause — is Gaddis alluding to Wyatt's drawing of the robin? Did drawing the robin kill the robin being used as a model? Or did Wyatt kill it in order to draw it? Can art, wrapped in newspaper, rot like a rotted bird? Certainly a painting or drawing can rot, but we are not used to thinking of the *representation* as rotting too. Finally, is Wyatt unable to distinguish between his representation of a bird and the actual animal? The next few lines explain the conundrum: "He had thrown a stone at the wren, and could not believe it when he hit it square and picked it up dead."[17] In other words, Wyatt had happened to kill a wren the same day he drew the picture of the robin, and both were buried: one in the earth, the other in his unconscious. But the delayed explanation does not entirely eliminate his lingering doubts about art's mortality. The effect of Gaddis's narrative strategy here not only suggests that, from young Wyatt's perspective, all art is a counterfeit of God's handiwork, but also reveals how art, for him, is of the world in which we live and breathe and is something we quite literally live and breathe.[18] Like dead birds, art, when buried, rots in the ground. Moreover, this understanding of art is completely opposed to a High Modernist conception of the art object as depicted by Wyndham Lewis, for example. Lewis writes in *Tarr* (1918) that "art is peculiar; it is anything that lives and yet you cannot imagine as dying," even if the physical painting happens to be destroyed when buried in the ground. Wyatt's problem is that he believes the reverse: art both lives and dies ... and rots.[19]

As he understands it, once representation is understood as mortal, a new economy is produced. This economy of counterfeiting ranks counterfeits of varying skill and effectiveness against one another. Wyatt's, of course, are at the top of the heap. Yet from the second page of the novel, generated out of the original forgery, counterfeiting — however ingeniously and artistically done — is identified as a "false economy."[20] It might be a working economy, but Gaddis suggests that it is not an economy which incorporates and values art objects at their true value. Furthermore, as Steven Weisenburger points out, one of the perils of counterfeiting is that "bad currency drives out good."[21] The fake, then, raises problems regarding the status of art objects. If the modernist claim as it is typically understood is that any and all viewers are irrelevant to the status of an art object's meaning, the fake painting, by definition, presents a problem, particularly if the painting is convincingly executed. The issue here is that because the value of a fake is dependent on the critics who evaluate it, the door is open to a charlatan such as Crémer, who offers to write positive reviews of Wyatt's early paintings (the only ones that are not fakes) for a cut of one-tenth of their sale price. And a fake's value is also dependent on the wealthy art buyers who equate a high price with aesthetic excellence. While these same factors also *could* be indicators of aesthetic excellence when it comes to "real art," Gaddis, and certainly Wyatt, seem to think that these are not necessarily the only indicators of good, authentic art. As Wyatt puts it to Crémer, when rejecting his offer of puff-piece reviews, success in selling his pictures is "up to the pictures" themselves.[22] The fake painting, in contrast, cannot rely on its integrity to compel conviction in order to sell itself, and so must by definition rely on an outside economy: the economy of the critic and art buyer. In contrast to authentic art, fake art relies on the world of the spectator for its value, and the economic world of the spectator is dominated by false economies of counterfeiting.

Exactly who are these spectators determining art's value? Some relevant background on the art world in the 1950s might help explain how these spectators were seeing and thinking. Mid-century spectators, critics and art buyers were a varied group. In part, this is because the immediate post-war period was not only the moment when "New York Stole the Idea of Modern Art" from Europe, as Serge Guilbaut has so strikingly argued, it was also the moment when there was a great deal of uncertainty about the future development and direction of art. As Wyatt puts it, during his first meeting with the demonic art collector Recktall Brown, "It's as though ... there's no direction to act in now."[23] Although Cubism and Dadaism had been immensely popular in earlier decades, by this point their popularity was on the wane. Instead, Surrealism, with its emphasis on one individual's automatism and psychological free association, and Abstract Expressionism were on the rise. And despite the fact that *The Recognitions* depicts copies of fifteenth-century Old Master art more often than contemporary art, it is precisely the popular ideas of Surrealism and the burgeoning movement of Abstract Expressionism that concern Gaddis here, and which he pointedly rejects.

Before the Second World War, Wyatt follows the path that many American visual artists took, traveling to Germany and Paris to study art. A whole host of American modernists were part of this contingent: photographers Man Ray and Edward Steichen and the painters Stuart Davis, Alexander Calder and Charles Demuth, among many others.[24] Yet Wyatt's decision, while in Europe in the late 1930s, to emulate fifteenth-century Flemish painters such as Memling and Van Eyck instead of the painters most Americans in Paris were emulating (that is, Picasso, Léger, Breton, Mondrian, and so on), not only reveals his rejection of modernism in general, but also his rejection of the Paris School and the fashionable trends of Abstraction and Surrealism, in particular. As Gaddis writes,

> [Wyatt] did not spend time at café tables talking about form, or line, color, composition, trends, materials: he worked on this painting, or did not think about it. He knew no more of *surréalisme* than he did of the plethora of daubs turned out on Montmartre for tourists, those arbiters of illustration to whom painting was a personalized representation of scenes and creatures they held dear; might not know art but they knew what they liked, hand-painted pictures (originals) for which they paid in the only currency they understood, to painters whose visions had shrunk to the same proportions.[25]

Gaddis portrays his protagonist as a "natural"; he is an artist of action instead of an artist of café chats. Wyatt's neglect of Surrealism as just one more form of insipid, naturalist illustration reveals his low regard for the movement. He values it about as much as he values tourist art for the upper-classes: something largely beyond his notice and his contempt, and wholly distinct from the currency of art that he values.

Wyatt could afford to ignore Surrealism (at least from a financial perspective) by living his life as a high-end forger. But the rest of the art world would not or could not be similarly uninterested in the movements of the day. By the time Gaddis was envisioning *The Recognitions*, also around the time we are reunited with Wyatt in New York after the war (in approximately 1946), Surrealism's effects on the New York art and commercial scene were widespread. As Serge Guilbaut describes, by the mid–1940s "the public had become used to [the Surrealists's] extravagances."[26] Salvador Dali presented some of his exhibitions in the windows of New York department stores, and, in 1944, he illustrated a cover of *Vogue* magazine (perhaps as shocking a sight at the time as it would be today on the cover of *Vogue*). Early Abstract Expressionists such as Arshile Gorky, Robert Matta, and Jackson Pollock were particularly influenced by Surrealist ideas. For them the experience of unconscious life (dreams, hallucinations, memories) and one's perceptions of the metaphysical world was as or more important than the reality of the physical one.[27] Arshile Gorky's paintings, for example, containing vaguely anthropomorphic forms, melting and dripping in lush washes, were given pointed titles alluding to his traumatic past during the Armenian Genocide. Pollock's paintings from the early 1940s are quite unlike his later iconic drip painting; they too reveal Surrealist influences. Small sections of paintings such as *Male and Female* (1942) or *Guardians of the Secret* (1943) reveal passages of unconscious automatic writing and iconic figures that purportedly emerged out of his Jungian analysis.

Surrealism, of course, wasn't the only game in New York City in the mid–1940s, and one of the more vigorous cultural battles was between two museums and their two respective philosophies of art, as Serge Guilbaut outlines in fascinating detail. Specifically, the battle was between the Metropolitan Museum of Art on the one hand and the younger MoMA on the other, and Gaddis's novel reflects upon this battle.[28] Both institutions were trying to achieve cultural supremacy in the City and the country at this moment, with the Met standing for the prudent academic culture of the past while the MoMA represented the *nouveaux riches* and a blossoming American avant-garde. In a sense, the Met represented the older philosophy of naturalism and realism, while MoMA represented the turn to Surrealism and Expressionism. And, to add to these matters, at this same moment in the mid–1940s there was an unprecedented art boom in the States with some New York art dealers selling more than 250% more work each year. Thus, the battle between the Met and MoMA implied certain socio-economic class distinctions, as well as a changing consumption pattern for art. If the upper-classes (composed of Peggy Guggenheim and Nelson Rockefeller — and in *The Recognitions*, those people who attend Recktall Brown's parties) were buying Pollocks and Mattas, large numbers of the middle class became first-time consumers of paintings, specifically, old paintings.[29] In 1943, New York department stores began to sell Old Master paintings to supply this new demand for authentic art. Duchamps and Dalis were on the cover of *Vogue*; Légers and Mondrians helped advertise dresses in *Harper's Bazaar*; and, most incredibly, that same year Macy's sold small-sized Rubens canvases and Gimbel's sold Rembrandts.[30]

Returning once more to Wyatt, living in New York City in the late 1940s: he is now frustrated with his domestic situation and has chosen, reluctantly, to work for the villainous Recktall Brown. We also know that he visits the Met on occasion[31] and forges Memlings for income.[32] Wyatt is more acquainted with Surrealism than he was while in Paris (thanks to the movement's enduring popularity), yet he is just as vehemently opposed to it. In a comic scene, he mimics one of Esther's acquaintances who, as Jackson Pollock also did with his early work, uses paintings in the service of Jungian analysis, as "pure symbols in the process of individuation."[33] Also in a veiled allusion to Pollock, Wyatt reveals that he is now aware of, and disgusted by, Abstract Expressionist painting. Pollock famously claimed that "when I am in a painting, I'm not aware of what I'm doing. It is only after a sort of 'get acquainted' period that I see what I have been about."[34] In contrast to this claim of near obliviousness in the act of painting, Wyatt's notion of art requires not a sense of automatism, but an overarching feeling of deliberateness, "that this is the way it must be [...] when you paint you don't just paint, you don't just put lines down where you want to, you have to know, you have to know that every line you put down couldn't go any other place, couldn't be any different."[35] Pollock's vigorous drip paintings—however planned as they might or might not have been—are precisely opposed to Wyatt's obsessively exact reproductions. Wyatt's vaunted ability to create marks on a canvas through a highly controlled technique of brush on surface is the very opposite of Pollock's aims of painting whilst unaware.

From all of these examples, it would seem fairly uncontroversial to argue that Wyatt is rejecting modern, contemporary art: he chooses the Met over MoMA, naturalism and academicism over abstract expressionism, Memling and Van Eyck over Picasso and Pollock. But the story doesn't quite end here, even though Wyatt's apparently retrograde decision to stop producing his own, original painting and forge Flemish Old Masters has distracted critics. *The Recognitions* appears, in other words, to have created its own misleading, critical misrecognition. Serious literary critics of the novel have more or less followed Wyatt's lead in rejecting, or at least ignoring, the avant-garde scene of American painting as I have sketched it so far. In the process, critics have failed to take into account Gaddis's complicated interest in avant-garde American painting.

Instead of referring back to the New York art scene described above, critics have developed their aesthetic theory based on *The Recognitions* using two alternate models: on the one hand, critical accounts have focused on the redemptive, religious and humanist aspects of art. As Joseph Salermi puts it, "Gaddis's position seems to be that genuine art atones not only for false art, but for false life as well."[36] On the other hand, post-structuralist accounts have focused on the novel's proto-postmodernism, and in particular on its Baudrillardian theory of art as simulacrum. Wyatt's forgery, according to John Johnston's view, "eludes the very opposition between an original and a copy."[37] Moreover, Johnston's postmodern account does not derive from the postmodern visual art scene (Minimalism, Conceptual art, Earthworks), but from the literary scene (Thomas Pynchon, Don DeLillo, and David Foster Wallace).

In a way, both of these alternative models make sense. Wyatt's rejection of modern painting, Stanley's interest in baroque music, the mocking account of the site-specific Minimalist sculpture *Cyclone Seven* in *A Frolic of His Own*, are all instances in the novels which might seem to suggest that Gaddis's main characters are rejecting modern art. And, by extension, Gaddis himself would appear to be contemptuous of current trends in the art world, beginning with Post-Impressionism and continuing through Surrealism, Abstract Expressionism, Minimalism, Site-specific art and so on, throughout his literary career.[38] According to this view, Gaddis would be condoning Wyatt's and Stanley's atavistic return to historical art by rejecting the contemporary avant-garde aesthetic. Certainly the Greenwich Village party scene, where an artist's (perhaps Max Schling's) new painting is being "honored"—but really more or less ignored—is an apt satire of Abstract Expressionism:

> On the gray chipped mantel lay a spray of flowers, which someone had gaily lifted from the door of a bereaved Italian family downstairs. Above it hung the painting. No one was looking at it. The unframed canvas was tan. Across the middle a few bright spots of red lead had been spattered. The spots in the lower left-hand corner were rust, above them long streaks of green paint, and to the upper right a large smudge of what appeared to be black grease. It looked as though the back of an honest workman's shirt had been mounted for exhibition, that the sleeves, collar, and tails might be found among the rubble in the fireplace.[39]

Whether this "honored" painting actually is an honest workman's shirt, or a dishonest workman's shirt, or a painting of a workman's shirt, or a painting designed to counterfeit a workman's shirt, we never really know. What we do know, however, is that this painting (or counterfeit of a painting), is meant to allude to an Abstract Expressionist painting. Perhaps it's supposed to be a Kline, a De Kooning, or an early Rauschenberg such as "Bed" (1955), a paint-splattered quilt and pillowcase mounted on a canvas. Whosoever it is exactly, the allusion isn't meant to be flattering. Abstract Expressionist art, Gaddis seems to be saying, is precisely the sort of stuff one is unable to distinguish from life (that is, a shirt is mistaken for a representation). We never know whether it is a shirt as art, or simply a shirt that is misidentified as art. This art, failing to make its status as representation clear, competes with life.

But the point to be made here is that instead of trying to mediate between these two interpretive poles—art as atonement on the one hand and art as simulacra on the other—Gaddis's theory of art and the art object's relation to the beholder occupies a different position in the genealogy of modernism and cultural theory. Specifically, what Tom Wolfe, in his 1975 monograph *The Painted Word*, ironically laments as art's demise, Wyatt in *The Recognitions* imagines as art's future. At this moment, Gaddis's satire of the contemporary art world becomes a real vision of avant-garde art's future development. In the final pages of *The Painted Word*, Wolfe describes a scene of painting's future in America, and more specifically, in New York City:

> I am willing [...] to predict that in the year 2000, when the Metropolitan or the Museum of Modern Art puts on the great retrospective exhibition of American Art 1945–75, the three artists who will be featured, the three seminal figures of the era, will be not Pollock, de Kooning, and Johns—but Greenberg, Rosenberg, and Steinberg. Up on the walls will be huge copy blocks, eight and a half by eleven feet each, presenting the protean passages of the period [...] beside them will be small reproductions of the work of leading illustrators of the Word from that period, such as Johns, Louis, Noland, Stella, and Olitski.[40]

The year 2000 exhibition of Wolfe's anxious (and possibly anti–Semitic) fantasy imagines the triumph of art theory over art practice—Clement Greenberg, Harold Rosenberg and Leo Steinberg have trumped Jackson Pollock, Willem de Kooning and Jasper Johns. In this dystopic fantasy, visual experience and creative imagination lose out to critical art theory, as art becomes an illustration of powerful art criticism. Artists abnegate their technical mastery, training, and imaginative capabilities in order to fall in line with the new doxology theory produces, "The Word."

Although Wolfe's prophetic art show did not become a reality in 2000, the example is pertinent: the scene of criticism displayed as art that Wolfe imagines with despair is essentially the same scene that Wyatt, in *The Recognitions*, envisions with hope and longing. The future of painting, according to Wyatt, *must* incorporate criticism. Trying to convince Basil Valentine of the value of his forgeries, Wyatt explains: "Criticism? It's the most important art now, it's the one we need most now. Criticism is the art we need most today. But not, don't you see? Not the 'if I'd done it myself....' Yes, a, a disciplined nostalgia, disciplined recognitions."[41] Wyatt argues that real criticism is something he values deeply and tries to incorporate into his own work because real criticism respects and requires the mastery of a discipline.[42] The "disciplined nostalgia, disciplined recognitions" describe the very method and aim of his forgeries. For example, his dedication to his craft extends to details of method: he uses special farm-fresh eggs for his tempera and real lavender oil for his medium. He does these things to be accepted, in theory, into the Flemish painter's guild (long since disbanded). But he also follows such an exacting technique in order to put his "disciplined nostalgia" into practice. In other words, by using an archaic and exacting technique to forge old Flemish paintings, Wyatt performs a disciplined act of remembering that he intends as a cultural critique of modern painting. In a sense, his forgeries are intended as both an art object and a form of criticism, precisely because they are not intended as merely automatic reproductions of a cultural artifact. The artist painting as a disciplined "nostalgist" is staying true to her imagined vision of the world instead of reducing her vision to a physical view of reality (like the view from a camera).⁴³ These forged reproductions, and the techniques Wyatt uses to create them, involve the mannered and methodological act of recognizing, transforming and placing that cultural artifact into one's own personal and bodily memory.

Or consider an earlier scene: when Wyatt complains about the role of "'cheap fakes,'" by which he means photographs or print reproductions in magazines, Basil dismisses his argument by pointing out that "every piece you do is calumny on the artist you forge."⁴⁴ Basil's point is that Wyatt is not in any position to condemn reproductions of art since his own counterfeits aim to injure the reputation of the original paintings. At this accusation, Wyatt defends himself fiercely:

> Do you think I do these the way all other forging has been done? [...] the recognitions go much deeper, much further back [...] some of them [the experts] aren't fools, they don't just look for a hat or a beard, or a style they can recognize, they look with memories that ... go beyond themselves, that go back to ... where mine goes.⁴⁵

He is arguing that forgery is not calumny on art when the forgery is, effectively, creating something new. The new art object created by Wyatt incorporates the recognition of art's disciplinarity. In other words, the art Wyatt understands himself to be creating is art that incorporates a cognizance — a recognition — of art historical trends and developments. This is why his forgeries do not simply entail imitating "a style." These forgeries also involve an understanding of painting as a discipline, an understanding which accompanies the recognition of great art. In a somewhat perverse manner, Wyatt's act of forging the great masters of art is also, according to him, the act of one man willfully instantiating a discipline and a cultural memory in himself, and via his art. Or as Stanley puts it later, "The memory that was himself, his own interpretation."⁴⁶

Later in the novel, Stanley notes that not just the artist's, but also the spectator's process of absorption and integration is a form of recognition: "Everybody has that feeling when they look at a work of art and it's right, that sudden familiarity, a sort of ... recognition, as though they were creating it themselves, as though it were being created through them while they look at it or listen to it."⁴⁷ Stanley, like Wyatt, emphasizes the active engagement involved in viewing art, and suggests that there is an element of creativity in the spectator's act of recognition. You make it your own, by seeing it on your own. But here is a crucial point: according to Stanley, the spectator's recognition does not complete the painting, for the act of recognition is only analogous to, and not identical to, the painter's act of creation: "*As though* they were creating it themselves, *as though* it were being created through them while they look at it or listen to it" (emphasis added). While a successfully executed "disciplined nostalgia" might make the reader feel as if she is taking part in the art work's completion, this feeling is a ruse that merely confirms the success of the writer or artist. In fact, the work does not at all rely on the beholder for its completion, in contrast to the degraded modern art (whether "original" or not) that Wyatt observes around him. Gaddis's personal statements about his writing are articulated with an almost identical deliberateness: "The reader is brought in *almost as* a collaborator in creating the pictures that emerge" (emphasis added).[48] His dialogic method prompts an engaged and active reader who feels she is the writer's partner, while in reality her role is not entirely collaborative.

And while it is undeniable that Wyatt's and Stanley's "disciplined nostalgia" resembles academicism, a retreat from avant-garde painting and a rejection of prevailing forms of modernism, in various other ways Wyatt is very much the avant-garde artist hero. Modeled on Goethe's title character in *Faust* (1832), (and thus also invoking Mann's *Doctor Faustus* [1948]), entrenched in art as a discipline from an early age by studying in Germany and living in Paris, Wyatt is one, doubtfully the last, in a whole series, of artist-heroes populating modern novels. He resembles Claude Lantier in Émile Zola's *The Masterpiece* (1886), the brilliant artist who is unable to finish his most brilliant painting; later taking on the name Stephen, Wyatt echoes Stephen Dedalus in Joyce's *Portrait of the Artist as Young Man* (1916), as many commentators have noted.[49] Wyatt is alone, rejected by society and, in turn, rejects society, struggling with a vision the profiteers around him cannot accept. All of these details read as vintage *Künstlerroman*, for Wyatt's artistic heroism, in the end, is his way of disciplining himself in art and disciplining avant-garde art in the process. *The Recognitions* is not only a satire and cultural criticism of American post-war life, it is also a thorough aesthetic critique, grounded in the mid-century art debates that Gaddis knew so well. Wyatt's unusual, satirical forgery instantiates a new avant-garde, backed up by a theory of art that Gaddis continues to promote and develop in a succession of masterful novels.

8

The Recognitions *and* Carpenter's Gothic: *Gaddis's Anti-Pauline Novels*

JOHN SOUTTER

Throughout his career, William Gaddis was preoccupied with fictions that were assumed as reality; or, as his first novel, *The Recognitions*, phrased it, with the mask that "presumes itself as reality."[1] When interviewed shortly before his death, Gaddis said that it is

> best to act as if conventional ethics were true. They are only hypotheses, fictions and we live in hypotheses and fictions. I think Hans Vaihinger is relevant. He was a German philosopher, who wrote that pure morality must always be based on a fiction. We must do so the same as if our duties were imposed upon us by God, as if otherwise we would be punished for our misdemeanours. But as soon as the *as-if* is turned into a *because,* ethics evaporate and our behaviour is ruled by base instinct.[2]

To assume a conditional fiction to be absolutely adequate for reality imposes that which Nietzsche describes as an *"interpretation according to a scheme that we cannot throw off."*[3] Not only do we thus imprison ourselves in a fictional construct that has no bearing on reality, but we also allow ourselves to be controlled by our own creation of an absolute and unyielding ethic that, although a fiction, causes our conduct within reality to become destructive and inhumane.

Gaddis takes his preoccupation from Hans Vaihinger's *The Philosophy of 'As if,'* which argues that all morality is a fiction. Although reality can never be absolutely known, we, nonetheless, construct representations around it. These representations, however, only reflect our notions of reality — therefore, our notions of *a* reality, rather than reality itself condition our actual behavior.

These fictions, Vaihinger argues, "must not be transformed into dogmas" which misinterpret "the 'as-if'" as "a 'that' and 'because.'"[4] A fiction consciously designed to give purpose, but unconsciously assumed as an unquestionable truth, becomes an unyielding and hence a debased dogma. Even if a fiction does reflect reality adequately, it is still a "construction, arising in our heads" and not the thing-in-itself.[5] *The Recognitions*' Otto Pivner paraphrases Vaihinger when he says, "We have to live in the dark and only assume postulates as true."[6] But, if even on an accidental basis, fictions must reveal some truth; from which truth however, as Plato (a philosopher Gaddis often references) puts it, we are all "thrice removed."[7]

Yet one establishment ignored the gap between its representation and reality by prioritizing the unconscious dogma of the disciples over the conscious fiction of the master. Insisting that its ethical fiction was no happenstance construction, but a divine and hence exact revelation of reality, any inconsistencies between its representation and everyday experience had to be ignored. This establishment was Christianity. Vaihinger demonstrates how the prioritization of a single representation over the represented arises from an avowal made by a "founder of a religion"—Christ no less—which "was originally meant" as a "conscious fiction," but was "transformed into the unconscious dogma of the disciples." The fiction is that God "is our father in heaven," but Christ probably meant: "You must regard God [...] *as if*, just as though he were your father and as if, just as though he were present in the heavens as a constant external observer of your actions."[8]

In *The Recognitions*, Gaddis demonstrations how, over the centuries, successive empires abused Christianity in order to justify their domination to the exclusion of all others. Despite the separation between Church and State in the present-day republic of the United States, a politically powerful strain of Christianity insists that the fundamental version of Christ's words is literal truth. The "Moral Majority's Reverend Jerry Falwell" asserts that "material wealth" is God's "way of blessing people who put him first."[9] A powerful group's ascendancy is immortalized by a dubious recognition of a dubiously *higher* reality rather than reality itself. A smug salvation is basely promoted for the fortunate at the expanse of the unfortunate.

For Gaddis, such arguments originate in the corruption of Christ's words: a literal interpretation of Christ's message about how to behave in everyday reality that ignores the spirit of Christ's words and encourages followers to concentrate on a materialistic acquisition. Following the letter of the law, in this case, results not only in reversing Christ's teaching, but also creates an indifference to everyday reality. In his essay "Old Foes with New Faces,"[10] Gaddis quotes St. Augustine's "*Credo quia absurdum*" stressing that the slavish acceptance of some absurd representation as truth despite the evidence against its existence also means the blind acceptance of further absurdities such as the Church's dogma of immortality.[11] Not only does an *a priori* dogmatic interpretation become an obstacle to seeing reality, it also causes reality to lose that which is already difficult to find within it—that is, some logical cohesion. As Gaddis puts it, "'Who do you believe?' Groucho Marx asked. 'Me? Or your own eyes?'"[12]

The acceptance of an absurd representation defies Gaddis's "present testimony of the senses" and demands an unwilling rather than a willing suspension of belief.[13] This pattern of absurdity was set up by Christianity, the whole of which

> hangs on a resurrection that only one lunatic saw, one and then twelve and then five hundred, for visions are contagious, and resurrections were a stock in trade, and the streets were full of messiahs spreading discontent, that Jesus Christ and John the Baptist would both be arrested on the street today, and jailed for the same reason.[14]

We are all trapped in absurd representations of our own creation that have disjointed us from the world. Yet all representations are false. We are all stuck in Plato's cave guessing at the world from the reflections of images cast upon the cavern wall. For all that, Christianity has been and still is the Western World's means of viewing and interpreting "reality," an episteme that has been prioritized over alternate worldviews, forcing an ascetic "indifference" to "worldly activity" or the reality around us.[15]

Gaddis based *The Recognitions* on the ascetic indifference to reality that is to be found in the circa fourth-century *Clementine Recognitions,* also known as the *Pseudo-Clementines.* This fiction was assumed as reality by the Church to incorporate its power. The work is a theological romance attributed to Saint Clement of Rome giving "fictional details of Clement's conversion to Christianity" by Saint Peter, as well as Peter's battle with Simon Magus.[16] Simon Magus, traditionally, is the origin of Faust because he "bore the Roman cognomen Faustus."[17] The Faust legend is a "revolt against human limitations" to fulfill a "thirst for knowledge."[18] Simon Magus had already "used sorcery, and bewitched the people" as though with hocus-pocus in order to make them believe that he was "the great power of God."[19] He wanted to fulfill his desire for knowledge and power by gaining the Apostles' laying of hands that symbolizes their succession from Christ. The Church took up the *Clementine Recognitions* because the work hereticizes Simon Magus; its portrayal of Peter's indoctrination of Clement (traditionally he was the first Pope) also confirms apostolic succession upon the Church via Clement. Apostolic succession, therefore, is made to seem to be no accident, but an act of design by a fiction whose assumption as truth is "dependent on a supreme sanction": God.[20]

The Church, therefore, used the *Clementine Recognitions* to bolster its teaching as absolute, but so did other sects. In fact, the *Clementine Recognitions* was composed by a heretical sect. Gaddis read about the *Clementine Recognitions* in Robert Graves's *The White Goddess* (1948), published when Gaddis was twenty-five. Graves writes that the *Clementine Recognitions* was the work of the "Essene Ebionites" who "embraced Christianity" as the "Clementine Gnostics" and "popularized" their heretical beliefs in "a novel called *The Recognitions.*"[21] The Church, however, did not flinch from the absurd position of adopting a heretical work to argue its own "apostolic succession against Gnosticism" which just happened to be the very sect that concocted the work.²² It also ignored the Ebonite heresy in which they "utterly repudiat[e]" the Apostle Saint Paul and him "as an apostate."²³

In other words, there has always been an anti–Pauline tradition.²⁴ Paul is thought to be "the best candidate" for Herman Melville's Cosmopolitan in *The Confidence-Man* (1857)²⁵ and in *Moby-Dick* (1851), Paul is criticized for "preaching to others" while being "himself a castaway."²⁶ Max Weber condemns Paul for his ascetic indifference to worldly activity, which gives more importance to Paul's vision than it does to the world. Paul has even been called "a Walter Mitty," because "the plans of God" as revealed to him "just don't work out."²⁷ Nietzsche, whose anti–Pauline stance Vaihinger continues, argues that the world "manifestly is not saved" despite Paul's insistence that it is.²⁸ For his opponents, Paul's fiction has neither roots in nor any bearing on reality. Furthermore, Nietzsche calls Paul's fictional construction "a process of decay which commenced with the death of the redeemer."²⁹ It is "the progressively cruder misunderstanding of an *original* symbolism."³⁰ Paul's theology was not based on any direct experience of Christ, Nietzsche avers, and consequently, Paul cannot offer any direct knowledge of him. Moreover, another of Gaddis's sources for *The Recognitions* argues that the Simon Magus of the *Clementine Recognitions* is Paul "under a mask."³¹

Gaddis was aware of the anti–Paulinism in the *Clementine Recognitions* early in his career. Five years before publication of *The White Goddess,* the twenty-year-old Gaddis read Spengler's *The Decline of the West* (1923), whose "pessimistic vision," Gaddis himself says, "overwhelmed" him.³² Spengler, continuing the anti–Pauline tradition of his predecessors Nietzsche and Vaihinger, refers to the *Clementine Recognitions* as "the anti–Pauline Pseudo-Clementines."³³ Spengler's Paul is a fanatic who would "compel" the "old comrades of Jesus" to admit that his "creation contained the true doctrine." Paul turned his "salvation-yearning"—his *as-if*—into "a *salvation*-certainty"—a *because*.³⁴ The Church turned Paul's hypothetical figment into a political authority to which all must submit.

> Let every soul be subject unto the higher powers. For there is no power but of God; the powers that be are ordained by God.
> Whosoever therefore resisteth the power, resisteth the ordinance of God: and they that resist shall receive to themselves eternal damnation.³⁵

An epileptic fanatic prone to hallucinations, Paul and his "visions and dreams" were prized "more highly" than reality.³⁶ His salvation certainty, however, is like that of Spengler's Faust, who shows a "tendency towards the infinite."³⁷ Their systems' transcendental drive for pure and limitless space intends to represent a "spiritual something" that "*could* not be represented" previously.³⁸ Yet the two, having reached their goals are spent of energy and now decline into entropy that Spengler defines as the "*world's end as completion of an inwardly necessary evolution.*"³⁹ This system's lack of energy turns into Gaddis's "spiritual entropy."⁴⁰

Gaddis's novels are concerned about the "secularization of salvation."[41] He doubts the efficacy of a soteriology that is but a personal "hodgepodge system" assumed as a collective absolute.[42] He is skeptical of a system whose basic tenet — salvation for all — is not even formulated upon another's personal experience of Christ's crucifixion and resurrection, but upon a theory taken from a hallucination of these improbable events. He challenges the dubious but permanent solution applied by an institution, whose authority, however, is maintained upon a "stupid salvation-mechanism."[43] Referring to Christianity, Reverend Gwyon in *The Recognitions*, asks, "Cannot they see, it is exhausted?"[44]

Institutionalized Christianity has lost sight of its origins. Yet, while fictions and representations lose sight of their author's original vision, something of the original still remains—"*semper aliquid haeret.*"[45] *The Recognitions*, like the *Clementine Recognitions*, works optimistically for a personal "religious experience" that is "unencumbered by the theology of Paul, the fathers of the church and later thinkers."[46] Systems treated formulaically suppress any fresh experience or intuition, thereby denying any reinvigorating prospect of the original vision's power. Despite a rigorous system's over-conceptualization of reality, it is still within that system that any fresh personal experience must be intuited. Indeed, *The Recognitions* condemns the "world where first-hand experience is daily more difficult to reach," a result caused by an all-encompassing system whose determined homogenization depersonalizes experience and encourages its counterfeit.[47] Yet Gaddis's novel focuses upon a specific "religious experience"—crucifixion, which is mediated, and consequentially can give only "some idea."[48] Were he a priest, Otto Pivner would acknowledge his redemption and affirm "I am the man for whom Christ died"; but Otto has copied this line from Wyatt.[49] Already, hearsay and forgery interfere with the original experience. For Fuller, a servant of Recktall Brown, who with Basil Valentine heads the novel's counterfeiting ring, a picture of God is "quite a hindrance to the faith" especially were it to be absurdly assumed as a collective truth.[50] Fuller's Reverend Gilbert Sullivan is "a hindrance too" because his preaching Christ's death dissipates Christ's message.[51] Amidst this increasing dispersion, Wyatt asks, "Father ... *Am I the man for whom Christ died?*"[52] An "engine of human frailty" — Paul's mediation — has "interfered with the miracle so preternatural" — the crucifixion — that the miracle is taken "for granted" in being an institutionalized mediation.[53]

Gaddis maintains that first-hand experience must be intuited in the counterfeit or second-hand world. Nonetheless, as if trying to escape mediation to experience first-hand beyond the given, Wyatt would "work in the sight of God."[54] He wants "credit for it," and "not from you, and not from them," but "from the thing itself," which is not God, but his own idea of God.[55] Yet to express his experience of God, Wyatt pursues a medieval religious praxis by counterfeiting late-medieval Dutch paintings for a contemporary counterfeiting ring. He must "attempt to reconcile old custom with new reason, to find sound theory for absurd practices" from a personal picture (or fiction) must come some rational ethical conduct.[56]

Yet Wyatt fails to realize that his quasi-religious calling interferes with the original paintings as Paul's vision does with Christ. When disseminated, a vision is "scattered everywhere, and they have no right to do that. It cheapens the whole ... it's a calumny, that's what it is."[57] The calumny arises from one individual's distorting perspective; yet there "isn't any single perspective, like the camera eye, the one we all look through now and call it realism" because "you can't include it all in your single vision, your one miserable pair of eyes, like you can a photograph."[58] Any picture, including Wyatt's, dissipates the original; yet a revelation that purports to make God tangible, visible, and even reproducible becomes a soulless mechanism like "the Machine" of the "'Recording Rosary,'" whose button is pressed to "'Keep tabs on Mystery!'"[59] God becomes tenuous and absurd through over-accessibility.

An externalized God, moreover, becomes an "insane upside-down apology." A fiducial system when manifesting its vision of God actually expresses a "profound mistrust in God." People "need every idea out where they can see it, where they can get their hands on it" to counter the possibility that "maybe God isn't watching" as though to insist a hypothesis to be more than a hypothesis makes it a certainty.[60] God is a personal intuition of the infinite. Yet a system that is constructed around the fiction of God conditions the thoughts and deeds of its adherents and imposes a convention that forces the "creators" to bow "down to their creatures."[61] Faith in an *a priori* system is prioritized over the *a posteriori* experience arising from that system which in its turn conditions us to a "'yes' or 'not-yes'" response to a reality that we have ourselves created.[62] All systems "expect that we will comply with them."[63]

Seeing that all systems suppress personal experience, Wyatt insists on "living it through" and not "locking yourself up with your work, until it becomes a gessoed surface, all prepared, clean and smooth as ivory."[64] Any system's "smooth functioning" becomes an "oppressive mechanism."[65] It ignores any irregularity to eliminate "life's oddities and incongruities" and creates a world where everything is already defined.[66] Society bows itself down to a fictional "automaton of 'duty'" in order to live without any "inner necessity" or "deep personal choice."[67] Despite this, Wyatt's *living it through* is a striving for "firsthand experience," even if it is within a mechanically schematized system.[68]

In *J R* (1975), it is money that is obeyed "something like Divine Law."[69] It expresses a "feeling which is closely connected with certain religious ideas."[70]

> The trust of our people in God should be declared on our national coins. You will cause a device to be prepared, without unnecessary delay, with a motto expressing in the fewest and tersest words possible this national recognition [Abraham Lincoln's treasurer, to the director of the mint].[71]

An at best second-hand reproducible recognition made by one person on the orders of another is applied. Gaddis's eleven-year-old J R is forced to listen to

Bach's "Komm, mein Jesu, und erquicke." In the duet from Bach's Twenty-first Cantata *Ich hatte viel Bekümmernis,* the soul mourns its damnation despite Christ's assertion that it is saved. Gaddis too would force another perspective than that which the system produces. The system in *J R*, however, is "set up to promote the meanest possibilities in human nature and make them look good."[72] Its mediation deliberately promotes pretence so that *seeming* is prioritized over *being. J R*'s system of money conceals the chaos of reality and does nothing to redeem it. Its fictional construction of reality is mediated with "no tricks," or so people "pretend" until "they finally believe that they really believe that the way they saw it is the way it is."[73] A false picture of how the world *should be,* or *seems* but not how it *is,* is established.

Gaddis's novels condemn institutional perspectives that get things upside-down or backwards. His third novel, *Carpenter's Gothic* (1985), does so with a vengeance. The one "text that dominates" it "is the Bible," but its influence is not so simple.[74] A question arises: "What's the Bible doing here. It's in here upside down. What's it doing upside down?"[75] A perspective is imposed that, despite distorting reality, must be coaxed to reveal more than it allows. Paul Booth — Gaddis's "parody" of the "first and most effective PR man for Christianity" — is a media representative for the novel's Christian fundamentalists.[76] He broadcasts their beliefs as a cover to grab power for himself. Booth's imposition of the fundamentalists' view of the world makes everyone become "convicts locked up in some shabby fiction doing life without parole and they want everybody else in prison with them."[77] Here Gaddis draws upon Nietzsche's anti–Pauline *The Anti-Christ* (1895), a text in which Nietzsche calls convictions "prisons."[78]

In fact, for Nietzsche, there is no "difference whatever between a lie and a conviction."[79] Nietzsche condemns Christianity for teaching "that most mendacious mode of interpretation," which is "of a supposed 'moral world-order'" that causes the world to be "once and for all stood on its head."[80] These abuses to the system turn the message of Christ the "'Evangel'" into "the opposite of what *he* had lived: '*bad* tidings,' a *dysangel*" that is "false to the point of absurdity."[81] To maintain power, a "'revelation' is required"; but it reveals not the "'will of God,'" but the "parasitism of the priest."[82] The priest is a "pale vampirism of pale subterranean bloodsuckers."[83] For Gaddis however, Nietzsche's priestly problem is now "more of a secular, which is to say political, threat."[84] The parasitism of *Carpenter's Gothic* is of financial corporatism, which, in doing "business with the greatest work ever produced by western man"— the Bible — degrades it.[85] Paul Booth is as parasitical. His purpose is to take over a corporation that once employed him as a bagman. He was used as a parodic redeemer, *delivering* corporate bribes to ensure the continuation of the system to the detriment of the system's adherents. Paul's vampirism uses a religious sect — fundamentalism — as a cover for his own pursuit of power. Gaddis alludes to Nietzsche's vampirism by not only giving Booth the cliché "I've always been crazy about the back of your neck," but also by using it again to close the novel.[86]

Carpenter's Gothic also depicts a war that arises from the thinnest of connections. Paul's fiction is as insensible to reality. A Vietnam veteran, he believes that "he's still out there on the Mekong Delta" and "everybody he sees is a gook."[87] His hallucination victimizes everyone, including himself. In revenge of the "*sons of bitches*" that sent him to Vietnam, the "apostate" Booth would victimize everyone with his vision that is not only life-denying, but also follows the law of the jungle.[88] When asked why he "couldn't have just knocked [...] down" instead of killing the young black man who mugs him, Paul whispers, "Don't you see? They never taught us how to fight" in Vietnam, "they only taught us how to kill."[89] Paul's ethic gives no promise of life. Like Nietzsche's Saint Paul, Gaddis's Paul is the greatest of the "apostles of revenge."[90]

Paul claims superior vision, telling his wife, "Maybe you can't see quite as clear as I can" as he tries to impose his hallucination by violence.[91] Like Saint Paul, his plans do not work out as intended; Booth would impose a personal fiction on the world, but the fiction is not of his creation. It might protect him by making his inglorious past look glorious, but it also victimizes him. His conduct in Vietnam was meant to follow the stereotype of the Southern officer. After demobilization, he claims that he was attacked by the Vietcong when asleep, when in fact he was assaulted by his own men, "two thirds" of whom were "black from Detroit and Cleveland." They did not "give a shit for being a hero," but Paul, the Southern officer, was "going to show them" by forcing them to substantiate his ideal.[92] Because Paul reported his crew chief for taking heroin, the crew chief, in revenge, rolled a grenade under Paul's bed, yet failed to kill him. It was the recruits that "made up" the "whole story" to protect the crew chief who had "passed the word that he'd fragged" Paul; the recruits "covered it up" with the fiction about the Vietcong.[93] A fiction is used to conceal. Its *logos* or *word* enslaves and Paul's Southern officer fiction paradoxically enslaves himself. The black recruits create a concealing fiction that isolates Booth and forces him to maintain the fiction to hide his own failure in emulating his ideal. In revenge for this, Paul kills the black mugger under the delusion that he is the crew chief.

Paul's system barely helps him "to get through the night."[94] It not only fails to bring about any revelation, but it is also one into which he cannot fit. He is no White-Anglo Saxon-Protestant Southern officer as he pretends, but an adopted Jew. He is an outsider trying to be an insider in a system that, although originating from Judaism, is blighted by its anti–Semitism. No matter if the enemy is Vietcong or an African American recruit, the Jewish outsider's attempt to become an insider is undermined by other outsiders' attempts to fit in; but the various methods get in each other's way.

Paul is set on "delivering God's word," but all he delivers is Reverend Ude.[95] Ude leads a fundamentalist movement named the Christian Recovery of America's People. The title's acronym — C.R.A.P.— comments clearly on Ude's distortion of God's Word. *Ude* suggests a distortion of God (*deus*), invoking Nietzsche's "God, as Paul created him, is the negation of God." Paul and

Ude have the "resolute *determination*" to call their "own will 'God'" and "confound 'the wisdom of this world'" by creating a system that "is at no point in contact with actuality."[96]

Ude wants to renew the broadcasting license of his "nickel and dime radio station": the Voice of Salvation that broadcasts the gospel in Africa.[97] Coincidentally, the station is on a mineral vein. Although Gaddis deliberately leaves it unclear whether this vein is spent or not, Ude's station becomes a convenient cover for the United States to pursue its imperialist program to claim the deposit as its own. Since Ude's mission broadcasts the gospel against that "instrument of Satan," Marxism, this becomes the opportune excuse for the United States overtly to protect Ude's station as its own, but covertly claim the mineral seam.[98] There is, however, another participator in this plot, Vorakers Consolidated Reserve: the firm that employed Booth as a bagman, and which Booth would control. Although referred to by its "familiar acronym, VCR," it may also "refer to videocassette recorders" as the means by which a mechanically reproducible message is institutionalized and accepted as truth by being constantly broadcast.[99]

Ude's claim to be the way to salvation is quickly undermined by the novel when he accidentally drowns a boy in a baptismal ceremony. Paul must peddle a newspaper account of it attempting to make the accident look good, but being a cover for suspect ends, no redemption for the boy's drowning is made. The boy becomes "the opening salvo in God's eternal war against the forces of superstition and ignorance throughout the world and elsewhere."[100] A botched baptism is deliberately used not to open some prospect of *salvation,* but the *salvo, bombardment, pretext,* or *expedient* to release a nuclear bomb at the novel's end. These maneuvers start a war, in which both sides are prepared to "kill each other over something," in this case the gold in the mineral vein "that's not even there."[101] In fact, "there's nothing but bush."[102] The origin of the novel's chaos—the fiction of God—is not only used up, but the belief in it is used for perverse ends. Likewise, Paul's surname, Booth, recalls not only a "polling booth," as well as William Booth, the founder of the Salvation Army, but also John Wilkes Booth: the "first presidential assassin."[103] His militaristic and deathly grab for power is the expression of an ascetic indifference to his actions in the world, as well as to Christianity. That which ought to be a crusade spreading glad tidings is debased into "higher piracy, that is all!"[104] Wyatt's "Thank God there was the gold to forge" is wearing thinner.

Moreover, Paul knows Ude is a sham. He comments on Ude's harvesting of souls: "What harvest, it hasn't rained there in three years everybody starving, going blind."[105] Ude's symbolic harvest does nothing about the actual harvest but blind people to its lack of sustenance. His metaphor is empty and mendacious. Ude creates a lie, but the difference in using a lie or fiction is "whether one preserves" or "*destroys* with it." Paul and Ude "'eternalize'" the lie as "a grand organization of society" of the world. The organization, however, is established neither for "the benefit of the most distant future," nor for the "most complete harvest possible." As ever in Gaddis's novels, an intention ensues in its opposite, producing semantic debasement and an impoverishment of reality. Instead of creating "the most grandiose form of organization," Paul and Ude create a system that is "patchwork, bungling" and "dilettantism." It expresses a "*deadly hatred* towards everything that stands erect, that towers grandly up, that possesses duration, that promises life a future."[106] A symbol of regeneration is vampirically drained of any "harvest of *Renaissance*."[107] Booth, Ude and VCR use "a little sectarian movement" to "ignite a 'world conflagration.'"[108] "'Salvation of the soul'"—an unattainable salvation, but maintained as attainable to hold on to power—is set up on the belief that the "world revolves around me."[109]

Carpenter's Gothic, however, has a fiction that tries to withstand the final holocaust and hold, like Nietzsche's Christ, to a life of love without deduction or exclusion: Elizabeth Booth. She is the daughter of the head of VCR. Although she might produce "a more accommodating order," her representation is discounted by the abuse that the novel inflicts on her: but her greatest abuser is her husband, Paul.[110] The narration's *leitmotif* for Paul's entrance is his calling out of "Liz," suggesting *lies* and *distortion*; but *Elizabeth* means *the oath or fullness of God* and, hence, implies an abusive curtailment.

She too creates a fiction—a novel—but cannot finish it. Since she makes nothing of her creation, she is embroiled in the plot for the mineral site, which the geologist, McCandless, claims is spent. When Elizabeth goes to bed with McCandless, his hands move "to sequester the white of her breast," as if she were an economic asset like the mineral seam up for grabs.[111] His fingertips run "light as breath down skirting the top of the rift" of her vagina "tracing down its edge."[112] McCandless, like Paul, wrenches any symbolic value from Elizabeth into another distorted vision that is imposed on reality for a suspect end. Her body is made subject to a piratical and colonizing rape. She becomes a fiction as an excuse for a war over a debased and debasing fiction.

McCandless might be "Gaddis's strong seer," but does nothing to establish order: he allows the war to escalate.[113] A thumbnail sketch of Gaddis, he is "the old God" who "*could* no longer do what he formerly could. One should have let him go" for his existence proves and solves nothing.[114] Elizabeth brings his attention to a window "so fogged with smoke" that "you can hardly see through it." McCandless replies, "I don't especially want to see through it."[115] His vision is one that paralyses, although he has the key that might stop the war.

Elizabeth also finds no place to fit in. Even the reader abuses her after death, as Gaddis—the "true god of the novel"—embroils the reader into his deceitful fiction.[116] A conjecture begins: *who killed Elizabeth?* She suffers "two near falls, and then her final fall," which connect her "to the Christian narrative, for Christ also falls three times on his way to Golgotha."[117] Another distorting fiction—a readerly one—is underway that ought to reflect a realm immersed in symbols and incomprehensibilities, but is distorted into a crude means for a suspect end. As the novel's striking narratorial rejoinder remarks, this fiction is simply "like the inside of your head" and must not be mistaken as reality.[118]

Gaddis's works are all imbued with a religious impulse. *The Recognitions* is bemused by the religious irrational impulse to find some means of salvific redemption within a secular society; the novel even provides an example of an unlikely redemption in Wyatt Gwyon that is brought about by his chance meeting with the forger Frank Sinisterra: but in fact, there is no purpose or guiding hand within this favorable redemptive design as its consequences as indifferently unroll in the mistaken canonization of Camilla Gwyon, Wyatt's mother, as much as in Stanley's accidental death in the collapse of a church. In *J R*, money is forced as if there were no other available system upon the world in the same way as the boy, J R, is forced by Bast to listen to the Bach cantata, a musico-artistic religious system: the systems of money (or capital), religion, and of art can be imposed upon society "to make you hear, to make you feel [...] to make you *see*" that nonetheless impose a mindless mindset in which people perfunctorily keep within its limits.[119] In *Carpenter's Gothic*, Paul Booth, a mixture of a fanatical St. Paul and of William Booth's Salvation Army that has now shed the problems of salvation in order to concentrate more on assumed certainties for all to live by made mandatory by paramilitary force, is Gaddis's anti–Enlightenment priest and at the secular level one of those "solitary, self-interestedly acting monads who merely turn their subjective rights like weapons against one another."[120] He surrenders himself "to mechanisms of success-orientated action that are orientated toward individual preferences" against which, however, the area subject to the needs of public legitimating also shrinks.[121] For Gaddis, Booth is the priest [who] is the guardian of mysteries, [but] the artist is driven to expose them.[122] The manifest difference between them is in the writer as a secret-teller grappling with his audience one reader, one page at a time, whereas the priest engages the collective delusion of his entire congregation all at once.[123]

Under Gaddis's deceitful and coercive priestcraft using deception to maintain a dysfunctional system to the detriment of those within it, humanity becomes "the *object* of our political decisions and of our economic activity, yet in which it is not yet the *subject* of its activity."[124]

9

This Little Prodigy Went to Market: The Education of J R

TIM CONLEY

> We do not know what our nature permits us to be. None of us has measured the distance which can exist between one man and another. What soul is so base that he has never been warmed by this idea and does not sometimes in his pride say to himself: "How many men I have already surpassed! How many I can still reach! Why should my equal go farther than I?"
>
> —Jean-Jacques Rousseau[1]

> Rarely is the question asked: is our children learning?
>
> —George W. Bush[2]

Although *J R* is gradually becoming recognized as perhaps the most blistering satire on unfettered capitalism of the last half-century, its author's attitude toward competitive struggles for economic survival is notably ambivalent rather than directly oppositional. In an interview given a few years after the publication of *J R*, Gaddis speaks of "the turning upside down of what I see as the great system of private capitalism because of abuses. I would still like to think that the problems are not inherent to the capitalist system and that they could be corrected."[3] In the 1987 *Paris Review* interview, which Gaddis explains he undertakes in order to establish a kind of record he "can simply refer people to," he solidifies this view of capitalism as "the most workable system we've produced."[4] Gaddis's unease with this "most workable system" lies in the unresolved question of whether, as Edward Bast claims to an uncomprehending J R, "there's such a thing as as, as intangible assets," or instead, as an imagined Walter Benjamin agrees with an imagined Johan Huizinga in *Agapē Agape*, "[e]verything becomes an item of commerce and the market names the price. And the price becomes the criterion for everything."[5]

Part of this intrinsic conflict within both novel and author can be observed in the concurrent discussions of aesthetic "difficulty" represented in the novel and (all too often) reiterated in its critical considerations. Jack Gibbs wants to make his book on mechanization as "[d]ifficult as I can make it,"[6] though he repeatedly challenges others, when he awkwardly reads from his manuscript, to tell him where the difficulty lies. It is not the case that Gibbs merely wants to write a book and that Bast wants to write music and the world, too much with them and easily blamed, prevents completion of any significant work (bumper-sticker wisdom: "Life is what happens to us while we are busy making other plans").[7] Rather, their own contradictory ambitions defeat them: Gaddis's artists aspire to transcend if not negate the shallow, commercial "trash"[8] that so offends and perversely obsesses them, but they in fact require the "trash" as something against which to define themselves and their art. The revealing title of Gaddis's 1981 meditation on failure in American history and culture, "The Rush for Second Place," points to a belief in and a barely concealed yearning for "first place." Apart perhaps from the ironic exception of Wyatt at the end of *The Recognitions*, none of Gaddis's artists comes close to winning first place or transcending anything. The closest candidate to a "winner" in Gaddis's novels — if that designation is understood to mean a character who, through his art (or at least a kind of artfulness), supercedes both his own expectations and those of others who underestimate him — is the boy J R, who by his own admission "plays to win."

It is unexpectedly illuminating to read the novel's final paragraph —

> —for all these here letters and offers I been getting because I mean like remember this here book that time when they wanted me to write about success and like free enterprise and all hey? And like remember where I read you on the train that time where there was this big groundswill about leading this here parade and entering public life and all? So I mean I got this neat idea hey, you listening? Hey? You listening...?[9]

Against the journal entries that conclude *A Portrait of the Artist as a Young Man*, in which Stephen Dedalus vows "to encounter for the millionth time the reality of experience and to forge in the smithy of my soul the uncreated conscience of my race."[10] Both monologues exude raw, even rapturous ambition at the same time that they register the isolation of the speaker: no one but the reader is "listening" to J R, no other character has access to Stephen's diary. Both want to write a book, though the younger of the two is less metaphysical about it (and, depressingly, perhaps more likely to see his project accomplished), but that is only a narrow part of the larger dream expressed. Stephen craves independence, flight, and the power to create; J R wants none of these things. His vision is of a "groundswill" of fame and power over others bestowed upon him by others, and his latest "neat idea" is left ominously undefined, though given the reference to "entering public life," it is hard not to think of the puerile "Jr." who occupied the Oval Office at the beginning of the twenty-first century.[11]

J R is, like Joyce's *Portrait*, a Bildungsroman, a point that tends to get obscured in busy discussions of the novel's other classifications (the postmodern epic, the novel of cybernetic systems, and so on). The novel's attacks on hypocrisy, sloth, and stupidity are encompassed by a carefully observed inversion of the ideals of liberal education. The model of education presented in the novel streamlines, if you will, Mandeville's infamous formula and posits these same (ostensibly) private vices as themselves public virtues. This model of education is found not merely within the representation of a given institutional mandate and system, such as those of the sorry school in which Jack Gibbs, Amy Joubert, and (very briefly) Edward Bast at least try to teach, but also in the general arc of the story: a young boy learns about the world and looks for his place in it. Moreover, the text itself constitutes an education for the reader, challenging as it is. Its structure and style inculcate virtues of patience and perceptiveness and ultimately the capacity to recognize the interconnectedness of persons and things in a frantic and disorienting world.

When this model of education is thus observed as both the novel's subject and form, it becomes plausible to read *J R* as an educational treatise, just as Rousseau insists that Plato's *Republic* ought to be.[12] To do so reveals the novel's implicit understandings of human nature, a necessary step if we are to appreciate its depiction and estimation of the world in which those humans find themselves.

• • •

Let me repeat, for the sake of closer examination, the claim that *J R* attacks hypocrisy, sloth, and stupidity. Greed is, significantly, not one of the novel's target vices, or at least not in and of itself. In the *Paris Review* interview, Gaddis refers to J R's "good-natured greed" and "simple, cheerful greed."[13] It is only "unmitigated greed" that Gaddis warns against, in much the same way that McCandless excoriates stupidity as "the deliberate cultivation of ignorance," rather than ignorance per se.[14] In both cases, innocence of intent not only pardons the lesser evil, but it also renders it as a default or basic property, a "natural" human quality.

Steven Moore has noted that Gaddis "follows an American tradition in giving his most trenchant criticism to children," offering *Huckleberry Finn* (1884) as the readiest comparison.[15] Twain was able to condemn racism and slavery in highly dramatic terms by suggesting that such things are anathema to the innocent observer, the child — but this effect is prefaced by and altogether dependent upon the implied assertion that the child is, because ignorant of the iniquitous ways of world, a good and honest witness. Huck is mischievous, Twain allows, but not wicked. The reader who does not comprehend or refuses to accept even conditionally this premise about the innocence of children will get nothing of the satire. It is unlikely that such a reader will "learn" anything at all from *Huckleberry Finn*.

Gaddis has referred to J R as "undeveloped" and having "nothing inside"[16] and if the first of these descriptions seems apt the second is a puzzle. The statement invokes the so-called "nature versus nurture" among psychologists, philosophers, and pedagogues. Perplexingly long-lived though it has been, the debate became a more public affair in America from the late 1950s into the early 1970s, when Gaddis was working on his novel. Ideas and expressions that had been the province of scholarly journals and professional seminars were then noticeably afforded greater space in popular media. In *How Children Fail* (1964), called by Gaddis an "excellent, profoundly saddening book,"[17] John Holt remarks on how "still very much in fashion" is behaviorism in the 1960s,

> despite all it cannot explain. It is also comforting to teachers, who have felt all along that their job is to drop, or push, one at a time, little bits of information into those largely empty minds that are moving slowly before them down the academic assembly line. And finally, it has set into motion the apparently endless gravy train of programmed instruction and machine teaching, onto which everyone and his brother seem to be happily clambering.[18]

Although behaviorism's notion of the child as an "empty" vessel — the titular "blank slate" of cognitive scientist Steven Pinker's 2002 demolition of the myth[19] — has lost a good deal of its intellectual credibility at least since Noam Chomsky's famous review of B. F. Skinner in 1959. Postmodern culture has (as many critics have commented) proved habitually uncomfortable with almost any conception of "nature."[20] Holt's argument is that both teachers and the system in which they operate badly underestimate students. They effectively ensure that students will not learn to think for themselves by treating them as "empty minds," expecting them to parrot "little bits of information" and give prescribed answers on demand. Students learn, Holt observes, how to satisfy the teacher (sometimes with ready help from unaware teachers) and pass the tests or, if they (rather reasonably) find these rituals pointless, they fail. "Assembly line" conformity is both the practice and the measure of its success.[21]

This state of affairs is reflected in Gaddis's novel, where the schoolchildren are likewise underestimated and the classroom mechanized. By turns laughable and pitiful, the inadequacies of the standardized, closed-circuit model of the education system — most ably reconnoitred by Christopher J. Knight[22] — yield a dumbshow sort of constant, unconstructive competition among the students. Nicholas Spencer remarks how the routine testing "measures the extent to which subjects behave according to the logic of the reception and restatement of information."[23] The individual identities of children are overlooked by design: the mystery-fiasco of the child "lost" during a class field trip aptly represents the trend ("no child left behind" indeed). When a photograph of Amy Joubert's class is retouched to add black faces to an all-white crowd to raise the "quota of blacks," principal Whiteback (the opposite, one might suppose, of blacktop) merely mutters "don't recognize them myself," confirming yet again how little aware the school administration is of the students themselves.[24] Though he is an obvious irritant to his teachers and a bragging point for his father, Major Hyde's son is never named ("my boy"). Nor is J R usually named apart from these initials, and if he is summed up as "that grubby boy"[25] by his teachers, it is little wonder that the altogether more fantastical portrait of himself that he reads to Bast holds such appeal for him.[26]

While the school treats the children as "blank slates" and "empty minds," it is far from clear that Gaddis himself does. The initial problem lies in determining exactly what he means by J R's having "nothing inside," as well as how much weight to give this retrospective opinion. Gaddis has also admitted to being "awfully fond of the boy,"[27] implying that there is indeed "something" within him to like. It is obvious that J R is not a social nullity, a being without personality—far from it, since much of the novel's humour and pathos come from the very distinct character that so many adults and educators miss. Probably the most thoughtful of the school's teachers, Amy Joubert offers this description of J R:

> When you talk to him he doesn't look at you but it's not as though, not like he's hiding something. He looks like he's trying to fit what you're saying into some utterly different, some world you don't know anything about he's such an eager little boy but, there's something quite desolate, like a hunger....[28]

Apart from the ironic foreshadowing of events to come, there is a quiet revelation here. Such comments intimate that J R is in fact an ideal pupil, capable of not only absorbing information—the entire, limited and limiting mandate of education critiqued by Holt—but also of further extrapolation and applications, some of which may be beyond the individual teacher's purview at a given moment. The combination of loneliness and calculation ought to make him worthier of attention than students like Major Hyde's obtuse son. The "hunger" is not "nothing"; it is that same "good-natured greed" that Gaddis does not censure precisely because it is in his view an elementary part of human nature.

It is neither J R nor children generally who are "empty," but the school itself. Education is the absent centre of the book, just as the absence of authenticity (particularly love, which Gaddis seems to see as itself a kind of elusive authenticity) is the centre of *The Recognitions* (and to some extent, perhaps, of all of Gaddis's work). In the various conversations in the principal's office, subjects range from the catch-22 logic behind bank loans to the acceptable kinds of patriotic affirmations, but "[e]ducation is never discussed. This absence was a conscious effort to show that the educators were wholly concerned with administrative problems, rooms, schedules, machines."[29] As Gibbs bluntly puts it, "the function of this school is custodial,"[30] but he leaves out (possibly out of grim awareness of his own complicity in it) the corollary function of socialization, which here means the instilling of due deference to the iron laws of mass production and mass consumption. Just as the language lessons Liz half-heartedly listens to in *Carpenter's Gothic* concentrate on the niceties of banking,[31] sixth grade math poses problems about gross and net profits, sales and costs.[32] Even Bast's rebellious Mozart lesson cannot resist making money its focus, ultimately equating creativity with poverty. Blind greed is encouraged: this is the only lesson.

Gaddis has stated, in the same interview in which he said J R "has got nothing inside," that at the end of the novel "even though he has been put out of business, destroyed, he is still ready to go again and is looking for some new way to do it. He hasn't learned anything."[33] This is, on both points, an oversimplification. True, the boy has "learned" none of the humanist or aesthetic values that Amy and Bast have — fairly incidentally and impatiently, it must be said — tried to open his senses to, and what might be called his "Language Arts"[34] remain unimpressive apart from his splendid knack for malapropisms. On the other hand, J R has come to understand the fundamental drive of corporatism as simply an extension of human nature, both in theory and in practice. How far J R has been "put out of business" can be reliably measured by consulting Gaddis's revisiting his character in 1987 in "Trickle Up Economics: J R Goes to Washington," published in *The New York Times Book Review*. Now a White House official, the young man's "neat idea" about "entering public life" has clearly come to fruition, and if his diction has not changed much, neither has his zeal. Not unlike how George W. Bush won the presidency despite his trail of entrepreneurial disasters, the public success of J R depends on unapologetic, monomaniacal avarice in the face of all challenges, obstacles, or inconveniences. Here, for example, is policymaking J R on educational standards:

> Like you start off with all these here schoolteachers? I mean right at the start they were always getting paid worse than anybody, so they were mostly these ladies, right? So you create this second class profession you get second-class people, so now you get all these pupils which can't hardly read so they have these here remedial reading programs. See if these teachers got it right in the first place then all of these remedial teachers would be out of work which that's what we call this here ripple effect, where each new job creates like three more new ones. Like half the teachers will retire this next six years and they figure the replacements will be off the real bottom of the academic ladder, so each new one should degenerate like maybe five remedial ones, that's how it works.[35]

With the same candour with which Huck Finn rejects the culture of slavery, J R has put his finger squarely on capitalism's fundamental need for imperfection, mediocrity, and inequity. Reaganomics and like ideologies justify the existence and the maintaining of a "second class" by equating it with more employment, regardless of such adverse effects as operational redundancies, lower standards, and of course ever more finely divided incomes because they, unlike the money, trickle down.

• • •

It is instructive to look beyond the "American tradition," observed by Moore, of employing children as moral barometers in fiction (though this practice is by no means exclusive to American literature, however recurrent therein). Particularly since the education so lacking in both the novel and its eponymous hero is moderation, the arguments of Jean-Jacques Rousseau, who fashions himself a "preacher of moderation" in his own novel-cum-treatise

Emile (1762), provide an edifying comparison.[36] Indeed, it is not perhaps too fanciful to read the initials "J R" as those of "Jean-Jacques Rousseau"; to do so is to open a wide and bright window on Gaddis's text.

Gaddis scholars have found valuable ore in the subjects and sources of the author's various abandoned writing projects, re-woven into subsequent fiction, particularly in connection with cybernetics, entropy, and the mechanization of the arts. Oscar's "unfinished monograph on Rousseau" in *A Frolic of His Own*,[37] flashes of which can be seen in his play, points to a mine still largely unexcavated. Of note to the reader of *J R* are the first three books of *Emile*, in which Rousseau somewhat unevenly splits his attentions between ridiculing the practices and mores of contemporary education and spelling out his formula for raising his ideal pupil while he is yet a boy. In imagining his Emile, Rousseau peremptorily dismisses the importance of parents—"It makes no difference whether he has his father and mother"[38]—and offers this warning about childhood:

> The most dangerous period of human life is that from birth to the age of twelve. This is the time when errors and vices germinate without one's yet having any instrument for destroying them; and by the time the instrument comes, the roots are so deep that it is too late to rip them out. If children jumped all at once from the breast to the age of reason, the education they are given might be suitable for them. But, according to the natural progress, they need an entirely contrary one.[39]

Gaddis is as "awfully fond of"[40] his invented child as Rousseau is of his, a child at the "most dangerous" age of eleven with a largely absent (because overworked) mother and no father in sight. Both children are models, presented as bright but not exceptional, with which to demonstrate the respective benefits and deficiencies of the education depicted. Whereas Rousseau takes his child very much under his wing, Gaddis remains outside the narrative—"disconnected," as I have put it elsewhere[41]—and allows the "invisible hand" of Adam Smith to do most if not all of the guiding. Rousseau is self-styled as his ward's "governor," and though J R lacks a constant tutor, the most affecting lesson he receives is gubernatorial: "The trick's to get other people's money to work for you, get that?"[42]

J R gets it. He gets it so clearly that by the novel's end he will outdo and supplant even this would-be master, just another adult who underestimates children. Often, as in this instance, such underestimation is dramatized by the conspicuously little faith a teacher has in either the clarity of the lesson being given, the capacity of the student to understand, or both. When, for example, the slippery public relations man Davidoff tells Amy Joubert's class that as shareholders they can exercise certain rights, it is not expected that they will do so—quite the contrary. Yet J R readily assimilates all of the suggestions and expressions that come his way: Gaddis's claim that the boy is "completely *sui generis*" notwithstanding,[43] J R is not himself the author of his own "neat ideas," but an avid collector of discards. Instead of being creative or even learning to think critically, J R is indisputably resourceful. Rousseau contends that

[t]he most brilliant thoughts can come into children's brains, or, rather, the best lines into their mouths, as diamonds of the greatest value might come into their hands, without either the thoughts or the diamonds thereby belonging to them. There is no true property of any kind at that age.[44]

While the apparent coincidence of Rousseau's metaphor with the Diamond Cable stock that comes into J R's hands is tantalizing, a more pressing concern lies in the questions of how and why children develop the notion of property (since it is not, in the philosopher's view, a natural phenomenon) and whether Gaddis agrees on these points or not.

"The political knowledge of a child," according to Rousseau, "ought to be distinct and limited; he ought to know about government in general only what relates to the right of property."[45] J R grows to understand that government is simply an extension of this central "right of property"—a right that neither Rousseau nor Gaddis challenge, or even show might be challenged[46]— by absorbing both the official information that is being doled out and the unofficial, sometimes covert connections and implications within and behind that information. Invited to ask the tycoon Moncrieff about "the secret of his success," Amy's class is quickly able to find the literal truth behind this insincere catch phrase:

— Well I'd just say boys and girls, as long as you're in the game you may as well play to win.
— I hoped he'd say hire smart people, Davidoff winked disappointment past his shoulder to them.
— That's right hire smart people ... he paused folding away his glasses from a glance down at the pencil stub grinding on the yellow pad, — but run things yourself.
— Is that what you're going to do at Washington?
— What's, where'd she....
— Where this says here taking leave of his leading role in private industry to join the official family as undersec....
— Where did, that in this damn kit too Dave?
— Must have, one of the girls must have dropped it in we, boys and girls? That's just a, it's what we call a news release it's just a story about something that's going to happen and we write it to help out the newspapers so that when the....
— Like you get to write this here news which it didn't even happen yet?
— Well that's not exactly what, what I mean boys and girls a story like this we haven't told anybody yet because Mister Moncrieff's appointment hasn't really been made yet officially so let's, yes let's keep it a club secret shall we?[47]

When much later in the novel J R rethinks his strategies to try taking the banks rather than the manufacturers, and then ultimately to "entering public life and all," his career path seems less a surprise than merely a perversely more candid version of those he has noted in other successful plutocrats. So too will the cynical wisdom to "hire smart people ... but run things yourself" guide his dealings with Bast.

Rousseau despairs of the polarity that so often characterizes the master-disciple relationship: "Each sets up his own little separate system; and both, engrossed by the time when they will no longer be together, stay only reluctantly. The disciple regards the master only as the insignia and the plague of childhood: the master regards the disciple only as a heavy burden of which he is burning to be relieved."[48] The uneven business partnership between Bast and J R represents a comic inversion of this relationship. These two fatherless sons adopt each other at the suggestion of J R, in his words, to "use each other."[49] Crass though the suggestion is, it is far from antithetical to the kinds of ongoing dependency Rousseau encourages, some of which might well strike twentieth- and twenty-first-century educators and parents as a bit on the creepy side.[50] J R literally becomes an insignia ("wanted to stress the profit motif without hitting you over the head with it name of the game after all"),[51] and a "parent" in a "family" of companies: "The paper's always saying the parent this the parent that I mean that's me the parent!"[52] He becomes the abstract and invisible father to the downtrodden avatar son, Bast, who is forever running the asinine and even dangerous errands that constitute "his father's business." (As the syllabic rhythm of his name hints, Edward Bast is another of Gaddis's distorted Christ-figures.) The image of the damaged marionette being played with by simple-minded Freddie repeats and deftly encapsulates the scenario.[53]

When J R usurps the role of the master/teacher, nearly every character follows his lead. He becomes the "prominent conductor" that he imagines Bast's father to be (his confusion between the kinds of conductor found in a symphony and aboard a train is a joke borrowed from the 1959 film *Some Like It Hot*), leading such varied individuals as Davidoff, Crawley, Brisboy, Rhoda, and Gibbs to play parts in his imperial march. No other tune interferes with his, so even radio stations swallowed up by his growth market are compelled to make their music subservient to advertisements for other J R Corp commodities. When Bast forces J R to listen to Bach, effectively (and belatedly) trying to reclaim the role of teacher, he is alarmingly rough about it ("could you, I mean could you let go my shoulder") and his frustration and impatience get him nowhere.[54] In *Emile*, Rousseau presents a corresponding scene as a cautionary tale for teachers. The master tries to convey the beauty of birdsong, "enchantment which no man can resist":

> Full of the enthusiasm he feels, the master wants to communicate it to the child. He believes he moves the child by making him attentive to the sensations by which he, the master, is himself moved. Pure stupidity! [...] The child perceives the objects, but he cannot perceive the relations linking them; he cannot hear the sweet harmony of their concord [....] How will the song of the birds cause a voluptuous emotion in him, if the accents of love and pleasure are still unknown to him? [...] how can he be touched by the beauty of nature's spectacle, if he does not know the hand responsible for adorning it?[55]

Bast's futile attempts to instill some sort of respect for, if not outright awe of, Bach fatally lack any history or context. No thought is given to the fact that his student cannot understand German, let alone know what a cantata might be. The assumption that beauty speaks for itself and genius is instantly and universally recognizable is demolished in this scene. Gaddis is in apparent agreement with Rousseau that a taste for beauty is cultivated rather than constitutive and, further, that such cultivation is dependent on prior understandings. Of particular note in this last regard is the "voluptuous emotion" to which Rousseau refers. Not only does this resonate with Gaddis's "absence of love" theme, but it also highlights another irony in the novel. A few of J R's favorite borrowed expressions display an aggressive sexuality of which he has little genuine comprehension: he speaks of getting competitors "by the short hairs" and fears being "screwed" by them.[56]

Asked what he has heard in the Bach recording, J R fearfully reverts, in precisely the manner detailed by Holt in *How Children Fail*, to the manner expected in the classroom and offers Bast the answer he guesses is wanted, namely that which Bast himself has already supplied: "like it lifted me out of [myself]."[57] However meaningless this easily repeated bromide is, it is worth noting both that here again J R declines to invent, preferring (as capitalism has taught him) to make other people's work do his work for him, and that Bast is no better an expositor of the significance of music than Crawley, whose windy rhapsodies about how music can express the "grace and dignity" of the shot zebra, "soaring tones that conjure up the vastness of the plains, the purple mountains' majesty," and so on, are the embossed tokens of a philistine's affectation of culture.[58]

Bast's reification of Bach as the great composer whose talents transcend the particulars in history, against which he struggled (and, in the romantic picture Bast paints in his controversial lecture, valiantly lost), is based on an understanding that some artists are greater than others. In this, too, he is disturbingly comparable to his patron. Nicholas Spencer's observation that "[w]hile representatives of corporate culture in *J R* belittle the aesthetic meaning of art, they nevertheless insist that art's value is rooted in hierarchical notions of greatness"[59] extends to the attitudes of Gaddis's artists themselves, who aspire to be on some abstract higher "level" than others. The competition between art and business is, in this view, a mutual understanding, and both Bast and Crawley conform to their projected roles. Bast has (a sometimes muted) contempt for worldly matters as beneath art ("if we can't rise to his level no at least we can, we can drag him down to ours")[60] and Crawley, a self-styled man of the world, can in turn offer contemptuous wages. Tug-of-war only works if both sides agree to pull against the other.

In the face of Bast's scorn, J R himself poses the eminently reasonable question about Bach: "What's the difference if maybe I couldn't even understand it."[61] The value of understanding Bach has never been made clear to the boy. He does, however, fully appreciate the notion of an originating genius without a history, and these wondrous heroes are called "millionaires," a designation that neatly expresses their value. Insofar as J R is the prodigy who composes and sits at the center of the fugue of events in the novel, he is ironically more like Bach than Bast could be. (Bach shared his father's first name, making him a kind of "J R" himself.) Besides constituting poor teaching practice, Bast's assumption that the value of Bach's music is self-evident is a substitution of one form of capital for another.

How different is J R's "hunger" from Bast's wish to "rise above?"[62] Gaddis may or may not believe, as Rousseau does not, that the concept of property is "natural," but they do share the position that the competitive drive, the desire to be esteemed above others, is (see the first epigraph to this essay: "no soul is so base that he has never been warmed by this idea"). The measure of this esteem, whether it is a dollar value, a grade in school, or cultural canonization, is determined by education. Gaddis's satire pillories the education systems and schemes for the crassness of their measures of success, but not the desire to succeed over others.

• • •

In "The Rush for Second Place," Gaddis points out how the competitive streak in American culture is symptomatic of and perpetuated by a fear of losing (again, the same fear that Holt detects in children in the classroom). He notes how the Vietnam war has provided an overwhelming source for such anxiety: "Gerald Ford, speaking as our unelected president at the moment of that final humiliating withdrawal from Vietnam, chose the metaphor of the game. It seems a shame, he said, 'that at the last minute of the last quarter we don't make that special effort.... It just makes me sick.'"[63] J R's most acrid rejoinder to this rhetoric comes from Isadore Duncan, the former wallpaper manufacturer. Financially destroyed and dying at the end of the novel, he might be recognized as "collateral damage" in the wars of Wall Street. Duncan gives his hospital room-mate Bast an earful: "people think winning's what it's all about just ask those son of a bitches who ran that war."[64]

This fear of losing is palpable in both Gaddis's characters (especially men) and his novels, no matter how absurd the game or stakes involved. Games are everywhere in J R, a conspicuous variety including golf,[65] craps,[66] Mah-jongg,[67] and horse races (Gibbs's weakness). If these largely masculine pastimes were not enough, there are invented games, like Gibbs's misogyny-inspired "pregnancy sweepstakes" and elaborate "parlor game" to be called either "Divorce" or "Split."[68] Men with professional titles and bearing are particularly conspicuous in their gaming and fondness for the all-purpose "metaphor of the game," men such as Coach Vogel, Governor John "Black Jack" Cates (whose nickname links him to Gibbs as a gambler), and Major Hyde. The last provides an example of how furiously the metaphor can be mixed:

> That's what I'm talking about Whiteback, dramatize the issue. Fire him and you'll have the whole outfield behind you running interference, there's too much milksop management sitting back in the defense zone while the opposition marches up

to the basket and drops one in. Let us carry the ball for a change, I know Vern's with me on this one. Put the ball over in their court for a change."[69]

Hyde swerves from baseball ("outfield") to football ("running interference") to basketball ("the basket"), back to football ("carry the ball"), and finally to tennis ("court"), thus embracing all of the highly subsidized American collegiate sports at once. All are essentially the same game to him, as indeed all of the games in J R are what game theorists categorize as "zero-sum" games. These are games which declare as winner the player who possesses the most of the closed set of resources at game's end; any other player is a loser.

The incessant refrain of "play to win" underlines the obvious connection between the arbitrary, but seriously taken, rules of games and those of market capitalism. In studying the entrepreneurial mania represented in the novel, Peter Wolfe writes of "the game of high finance" and Knight reflexively uses the same metaphor: "The game becomes an addiction."[70] Certainly the shared language of the novel's market professionals and politicians is bursting with versions of this metaphor, to the point that they seem to claim it as their exclusive property: Cates moans, "Damned amateurs don't know the rules come in and ruin the whole damn game for everybody."[71] Yet the elasticity of the metaphor permits its use for virtually any occasion, thereby constraining the discourse to a competitive framework.[72]

This constraint has a number of effects. First, it means concealing or eliminating certain facts and opinions contrary to or incompatible with the "play to win" doctrine. As Knight observes, "Even as the language of sport obscures real issues, it constitutes the form in which the community constructs its most important narratives about itself."[73] Ford's hackneyed war-as-game analogy not only obscures the suffering and destruction of war, but its wider purchase also compels the history of wars to become a history of games. Second, the game metaphor gives its subject a patina of honor, a reliable means to ensure against challenges to the rules, which are ultimately governed by the user of the metaphor. Naysayers can be dismissed as sore losers, those who would try to change the rules as cheaters. Third, the "play to win" doctrine can be endlessly expanded, prolonging a game in which the status of "winner" always seems to be threatened, in much the same way that mythology suggests that competitive market capitalism has no historical beginning or end. One of the few glimmers of J R forming anything resembling a critical judgement of the wisdom he has collected and the game he is zealously playing comes when he realizes this point: "They said if you're playing anyway so you might as well play to win but I mean even when you win you have to keep playing!"[74] Fourth and last, it demands that there be losers, and losers are by definition to be reviled. Amy says that her father only watched football games on television "because he liked to see someone lose."[75] When Gibbs uses the metaphor as he fumbles to convey his frustration to his ex-wife, he guarantees continued opposition: "Can't you just once can't you, just once couldn't you, once just not have to win...?"[76] In a zero-sum game — in football and in the way Gibbs envisions divorce — the only alternative to winning is losing, so all necessarily opposing players are enemies.[77]

It is worth noting that Gaddis is at least as critical of sore losers as he is of blithe winners — perhaps more so. Losers, in the competitive world beheld and represented by Gaddis, continuously strive to "drag down" others. Consider how Eigen understands the rules of the Winnie the Pooh board game that he plays with his son, David:

> — You skipped this blue back here. You're back here.
> — Oh.
> — And I got green. Here. Now really shake the bag.
> — I did. I got red, Papa if you got black you'd go all the way there.
> — That's why there are only two blacks in the whole bag.
> — Why.
> — To make it harder to get.[78]

His rigid insistence on the rules is part of a campaign to teach his son that "nobody always wins,"[79] the sorry last gasp of which is David's catching him cheating. The lesson Eigen thus delivers is more complicated and even more bitter than he intended. The lesson to David is that the odds of winning easily are against all players, but the game need hardly be fair, since even those who most stridently enforce the rules can and do violate them. The lesson to the reader is that losers will do anything to win.

Concurrent with *J R*'s deluge of games is a preponderance of infantile behaviour in adult males. If Gaddis generally tends to give his central women characters greater composure and moral dignity than his men — and the truth of this common observation notwithstanding, a sustained critical analysis of the subject has yet to be undertaken — his women seem less concerned with the inevitable quandary of what is worth doing. Gaddis's men are more likely to throw the tantrum, more likely to reject blame, and more likely to seek succour when things fall apart. In *J R*, this general trend is exacerbated by the theme of games and the inevitable contrast with the title character.

One of the unresolved legal questions that prevents Bast from receiving his rightful inheritance is whether he is an adult: indeed, this question effectively frames the book. Even by the time the harried lawyer Coen manages to meet him — picking him up in his car, quite by accident, within the novel's last sixty pages — the matter is no clearer, for his maturity is impossible to judge:

> — Get to start over right?
> — Mister Bast I'm afraid you no sit up! You've, there's simply not room for you to lie down in the front seat while I'm...
> — Not pissed off at me are you Mister Coen?
> — Why why, why no but...
> — I mean why is everybody always getting mad at me![80]

His master's voice: at this point the J R-Bast/master-student reversal is complete. In the hospital, where nurses say things like "now let's act our age,"[81] Bast will be reduced to writing with crayon.

Yet this transformation is only a defeated acceptance of the way he is seen and treated by others, particularly women. His aunts, as doting as they are dotty, manage to avoid clarifying whether he is a minor (a desperate Coen tries: "On your income taxes for instance do you recall listing him as a deduction?") at the same time that they speak of him as defenseless and guileless, "poor Edward."[82] Amy becomes similarly fond and protective of Edward, inspiring some jealousy in Gibbs, and both of the women who seduce him, successfully or no, clearly take the lead.

Jack Gibbs, himself a caring but absent and distracted father, is no less juvenile. When Amy, irritated with his jaded ramblings, asks Gibbs, "What did you want to be when you grew up," he answers, "A little boy." He explains that "he never really expected to [grow up]."[83] Later, at her place, he rhetorically asks, "Do you think I'm eleven years old"—the age of J R—and Amy truthfully responds: "You're behaving like one."[84] Certainly, Gibbs's boyish antics constitute part of his charm, but his frequent subterfuges and Bunburying habits reveal an unwillingness to accept responsibility. His success at using a child's ticket to catch a train by pretending not to understand English shows him to be resourceful at changing identities, but the fact of the event is that he passes for a child. Brigitte Félix hears "high man" within "Hyman"[85] Grynszpan, Gibbs's tax-dodge persona, though one could just as well note that the name simply means "life" (from the Hebrew *chaim*). For Gibbs, "a genuine rascal,"[86] life is a series of disguises and dissimulations, and in this respect he is quite comparable with the boy who uses a handkerchief when speaking on the telephone.

Knight remarks upon the frequent use of the word "crèche" in *J R*, a word which connotes both the nativity of Christ and "a home for foundlings,"[87] though the appearance of "cradle" is equally common. Davidoff enthuses to visiting schoolchildren about "standing here in the cradle of American history," and when Amy later wonders about the absurdity of this image, Gibbs assures her that there is "always somebody standing in your cradle."[88] It could be any one of the peevishness, the resentment, or the irreverence of this phrase that prompts her to ask

> why you can't simply, simply act like a grownup...
> He'd recovered his hand, busied it now digging a matchbox from a pocket.—
> Never really expected to ... he dug elsewhere, came up with a broken cigarette.
> —To what, to grow up? she looked away from his hands,—do you think any of them do?[89]

In making this challenge, Amy has to look away from Gibbs's hands because they attract her. When they become lovers, this close pairing of "hands" with "cradle" recurs: "Moving *hands* stilled and, stilled, moving again as though life had stopped threatened only to seize it where her breast yielded, to flee that and descend to climb the *cradled* rise of bone."[90] One need not overestimate the suggestion that Gibbs is symbolically trying to climb back into the cradle to see that, after this moment, Amy assumes a rather maternal demeanor in how she treats him: cleaning him up, buying him new clothes, giving him medicine. Their brief relationship wobbles between a mother-son dynamic and a daughter-father one ("I've always gone with older men," says Amy,[91] taking her place with Liz in *Carpenter's Gothic* and Christina in *A Frolic of His Own* as Gaddis's Daddy's girls).

In a culture of infantilism, no one expects to grow up. The confusion between adult occupations and childish things—manifest in candy cigarettes and toy guns—is symptomatic of the shared "play to win" mandate of education and business. When Whiteback calls Bast "our Peter Pan," the allusion is apt and resonating.[92] Bast is only one of several characters in the novel who could be called a "boy who wouldn't grow up." Gaddis revisits this allusion shortly thereafter, when Marian Eigen reads to David:

> Nana had filmy eyes, but all she could do was to put her paw gently on her mistress' lap. They were sitting thus when Mister Darling came home from the office. He was tired. Won't you play me to sleep on the nursery piano? he asked. And as Mrs Darling was....[93]

Moore's admirable online annotations dutifully refer one to "Sir J. M. Barrie's children's classic *Peter Pan* (1911)," but the Eigen family's version of the book appears to be an abridgement of the original. This passage comes from the next-to-last chapter of the novel, in which the narrative returns to the forlorn Darling household just before the missing children themselves do. The alterations to the original text, whether they are attributed to Gaddis or to Marian, omit the absurdity of the scene (in abjection for having tied up the dog Nana the fateful night his children flew away with Peter Pan, Mr. Darling has confined himself to the dog's kennel), leaving a different impression of the Darling family's situation than what one finds in Barrie's text:

> Nana had filmy eyes, but all she could do was put her paw gently on her mistress's lap; and they were sitting together thus when the kennel was brought back. As Mr. Darling puts his head out to kiss his wife, we see that his face is more worn than of yore, but has a softer expression.[94]

By comparison, the Mr. Darling in the Eigens' *Peter Pan* seems insensitive, even demanding: a man of the office rather than of the family. While this scene in Barrie's novel directly precedes the reunion of the returned children with their parents, Marian's reading anticipates the break-up of the Eigen family.

As Marjorie Garber has succinctly put it in another context, "Transgression without guilt, pain, penalty, conflict, or cost: this is what Peter Pan—and *Peter Pan*—is all about."[95] The same might be said about *J R*. The novel's title character is far from being alone in wanting to reap every potential benefit at the lowest personal cost, minimal effort, and without obligation. Only he, however, has the excuse of ignorance, and when he asks, "So what am I suppose to do!"[96] he receives no decent answer. His question, which despite its syntax is as pointed as any a teacher can hear from a pupil, reflects the very same anxiety and uncertainty in the nominally adult male characters about what in life is worth doing. This philosophical problem is in equal measure profound and inescapably childish.

• • •

Jeff Bursey and Anne Furlong contend that "the worlds of art or finance are too large, amorphous, and pervasive to be comprehended by an individual,"[97] but Gaddis's novel-systems are simultaneously comprehensive and comprehensible. They effectively *teach* the individual reader to discern connections, causalities, and responsibilities. Although the poor typically have little difficulty recognizing the rich, the machinations of an increasingly corporate economy are so obscure as to nearly dissolve relationships between manufacturer and purchaser. With her usual perspicacity, Rebecca Solnit laments in a 2003 essay how the way "every object spoke — some of them must have sung out — in a language everyone could hear, a language that surrounded every object in an aura of its history" has faded in the shopping mall era in which advertising "constitutes an aggressive attempt to displace the meaning of the commodity from its makers."[98] An individual *can* comprehend these systems within systems, *can* connect with the makers and hear their stories, but only with considerable attention and diligence.

The reader of *J R* demonstrates this point. Brigitte Félix argues that the characters and events of Gaddis's novel are not visualized by the reader, as Wolfgang Iser has suggested generally occurs in reading fiction: "*Il est difficile de se faire une image des personnages, des choses ou des lieux, quand ils sont présentés comme des entités abstraites*" (It is difficult to form an image of characters, things, or connections when they are presented as abstract entities).[99] The abstractness of these elements in *J R* reflects the abstraction in operation in the intertwined market and school systems it represents, and the novel's reader learns to identify and compare patterns, expressions, and ultimately ideas and feelings. In learning to revert the abstract to the concrete, the reader gets the education that J R is not given.

Musing about the autobiography that his PR agents assure him he would not have to write himself, J R makes a substantial distinction between "make" and "earn": "Like they said they want to name it How To Make a Million see only I think earn, like How To Earn a Million I mean it sounds more dignified you know?"[100] *Earn* "sounds more dignified" because *make* implies labor; it suggests some active, creative effort (perhaps too, risk and even hardship) rather than passive accruement of wealth.[101] Just as there is no apparent content to the classrooms of the novel, J R never has any clear idea what he would do with the great sums of money he "earns," apart from using it to "earn" even more. J R becomes the most abstract character in the novel because he most aspires to abstraction. According to Davidoff, his invisible employer "sees how things are not how they ought to be,"[102] but it would be more accurate to say that he sees neither; he sees only an abstracted, distorted version of how things are without a thought for what ought to be.

To diminish the attractions of material wealth, Rousseau proposes to take his Emile

> to dine in an opulent home. We find the preparations for a feast — many people, many lackeys, many dishes, an elegant and fine table service. All this apparatus of pleasure and festivity has something intoxicating about it which goes to the head when one is not accustomed to it. I have a presentiment of the effect of all this on my young pupil. While the meal continues, while the courses follow one another, while much boisterous conversation reigns at the table, I lean toward his ear and say, "Through how many hands would you estimate that all you see on this table has passed before getting here?"[103]

This question acts as a bombshell. Emile is thereafter incapable of blind delectation, so taken is he with imagining the complex histories of production and so vexed by so many attendant uncertainties. As he did with the anecdote about appreciating birdsong, Rousseau insists that value can only be determined by one who first comprehends these histories, who senses the "language" and "aura" that Solnit refers to (borrowing the latter term from Walter Benjamin). Gaddis's own prodigy is never asked such a revelatory question; the closest thing to it is Amy's "Does there have to be a millionaire for everything?" which fails to introduce even the notion of any other possible origins.[104]

The author's claims about his hero having "nothing inside" to the contrary, *J R* affirms that Gaddis agrees with J. M. Barrie that children are, in the concluding words of *Peter Pan*, "gay and innocent and heartless."[105] The unexceptional "good-natured greed" of J R is comparable to the natural nobility of Rousseau's "savage made to inhabit cities"[106] and, if anything, is to be praised rather than reproved. If "unmitigated greed" is censurable, however, it follows that an ideal teacher should convey and explain the benefits of moderation. No such teaching occurs in *J R*, and its absence is painfully felt. What remains unresolved — and a source of anxiety — in the novel is whether the "play to win" doctrine of education, art, and free enterprise, "a system that's set up to promote the meanest possibilities in human nature and make them look good,"[107] is indeed "the most workable system we've produced."

10

Fields Ripe for Harvest: Carpenter's Gothic, *Africa, and Avatars of Biopolitical Control*

MATHIEU DUPLAY

"Think you could write me some zebra music...?" Crawley asks in *J R*, seemingly out of the blue, a few minutes after his first encounter with the hapless composer Edward Bast.[1] Selfishness alone motivates Crawley's obsession with Africa and his madcap scheme to import various exotic animals from Uganda: a compulsive hunter, he cannot wait to set up a private game preserve in the Florida Everglades,[2] and, with Bast's help, he hopes to "wake up some people down in Washington to the idea of stocking our public lands with something more suitable than a lot of trailers and beer cans."[3] However influential Crawley may be in the boardroom and beyond, his sense of priorities certainly does not earn him much respect in this novel, and readers perceive him as a richly comic figure, worried though they may be that such people "throw off your balance of nature and leave it off," with potentially disastrous consequences.[4] Still, the fact is that "zebra music," albeit of a very different kind, echoes through much of Gaddis's fiction: the theme is first sounded in the North African sections of *The Recognitions* and recurs in the later novels, so that there is ample ground for regarding it as a satire on the lingering spirit of colonialism and its many manifestations in postwar American discourse.

So far, this has been largely ignored by commentators, probably because Gaddis's stronger emphasis on matters of much more immediate interest to most Western readers, along with the formal brilliance and inventiveness of his writing, have shifted critical interest away from what may, in comparison, appear to be a minor issue. This is unfortunate, for there are strong reasons to argue that the politics of (post)colonialism significantly interact with the epistemological concerns on which most critics have chosen to concentrate: while Crawley sees Uganda as a prime hunting ground, the legacy of colonial domination provides for an even more fruitful exploration of issues, such as the pragmatics of "ordinary" discourse and its complex relationship with various definitions of "nature" (especially of the "human" variety). Nowhere is the absence of any reference to Gaddis's interest in the fate of Africa more regrettable than in discussions of *Carpenter's Gothic*, where it unquestionably occupies a central position, as the site of the major ideological conflict upon which the entire plot hinges.

As formulated by McCandless, the terms of the debate seem relatively familiar and straightforward. Scientists view the so-called "Dark Continent" as a repository of first-rate research material, with its "earthquakes, volcanoes, boiling springs," not to mention "that site on Lake Rudolf up in the Gregory Rift, hominid fossils, stone tools, hippo bones all of it caught in a volcanic burst two or three million years ago."[5] However, politics constantly interfere with the objective study of nature: in the post–colonial age, and at the peak of the Cold War, Africa is a pawn in the hands of developed nations in search of supremacy, while the religious right does its best to prevent proper Darwinian science from being taught in American schools.[6]

This simple, not to say simplistic, account is summarily dismissed by Lester,[7] with good reason since the narrative as a whole clearly suggests that there is no such thing as "disinterested" science: McCandless's own research is directly to blame for the military escalation that leads to a "10 K 'demo' bomb" being dropped off the African coast,[8] and he is in no position to criticize abuses for which he himself is largely responsible. Judging from the satellite scans with which McCandless's private office is littered, one would be tempted to conclude that geology is best practised at a remove from its object, like bird-watching, which requires the observer to be as self–effacing as possible.[9] However, the quest for neutrality quickly proves fruitless. Like undue proximity, excessive distance interferes with the pursuit of "objectivity," as the reference to satellite technology implies; for in gazing at other celestial bodies — or in looking at the Earth from a point in outer space — it quickly becomes necessary to take into account the distortions induced by factors such as the speed of light. Scientists do not describe the world "as it is," but study what can be perceived from a particular position in space-time, and thus end up describing themselves instead of "neutrally" contemplating the stars. "[S]et up a mirror on Alpha Centauri [...], you'd sit right here [on Earth] with your telescope watching yourself four, about four and a half years ago."[10]

If scientific inquiry actually fashions its own objects, it follows that "nature" is not a given, but a theoretical construct which politics and ideology have no difficulty putting to their own more or less judicious uses. The Masai warrior whose picture appears on the cover of *Natural History* magazine is a particularly telling example. The editors apparently treat him as an object of anthropological study, not as a potential enemy, as if war and conquest were some kind of "natural" phenomenon in which the Western reader takes no part.[11] However, the text is careful to point out that there is a very real connection between the Masai's archaic weapons and the state-of-the-art nuclear technology wielded by developed countries: in the relativistic universe of *Carpenter's Gothic*, to look away is to look into the past, and the African warrior is merely an exotic counterpart of the English archers whose pioneering use of the longbow at the battle of Crécy marked "the beginning of firepower."[12] Thus, the picture serves as an ironic reminder of the West's willful indifference to the true nature of its relations with the rest of the world, a mistake that later proves costly when Senator Teakell's plane is shot down by African rebels.[13]

In the end, and despite McCandless's protestations, the real question is not whether science can defeat the forces of obscurantism, but why and how the scientific invention of "nature" turns into an instrument of sovereignty, not to say tyranny. What brings the matter home and, at the same time, justifies the choice of Africa as the prime example of nature's complex involvement in political discourse is the cluster of images associated with the word "rift."

McCandless' interest in the Great Rift is justified on scientific grounds, as this exceptionally interesting geological feature is one of the world's richest sources of hominid fossils.[14] In *Carpenter's Gothic*, the word "rift" also refers to various intimate body parts, for instance when McCandless has sex with Elizabeth, or when she looks up a word in the dictionary, "confusing rift for cleft, and there waylaid by the anal ~ of the human body."[15] The connection is not purely lexical, since the reader may more or less consciously recall that "the northern end of the Great Rift" at which Elizabeth gazes in wonder is shaped like a triangle,[16] with the Sinai Peninsula lying between the Gulf of Suez (to the west) and the Gulf of Aqaba (to the east). While this is not pointed out in *Carpenter's Gothic*, the text does mention the Afar Triangle, a fork in the Great Rift located in the Horn of Africa ("Lucy," the first known specimen of *Australopithecus afarensis*, was discovered there in 1974).[17] Thus, by way of analogy, the signifier "rift" progressively comes to stand for the origins of human existence, for the site where the human species arose out of its hominid ancestors, and where "babies [...] demanding to get born" finally carry out their purpose, according to Elizabeth's naïve account of childbirth.[18]

For semantic reasons alone, the term "rift" is particularly well suited to describing the process whereby humanity diverges from animality: humans are to animals what one side of a valley is to the other, since the gulf that divides them also expresses their deeper interconnectedness, geography serving as a metaphor for genealogy. What is true of the species as a whole just as easily applies to the individual. However different they may be from other living beings, modern humans are biologically indistinguishable from animals, a point underlined by Elizabeth's numerous ailments, ranging from her bruised skin to the asthma attack which presumably kills her; thus, the individual's humanity must constantly be redefined and defended against the encroachments of "mere" animality, which comes to the fore in sickness, in death, or, less dramatically, in the aftermath of sexual intercourse:

> He stood there, looking down at her [...] as though years and her very identity had fled taking with them any intelligence or the hope of it and surely any beauty,

or the claim to it, legs flung wide and her arms loose beside her, her thumbs still crushed in the palms of her hands.[19]

McCandless is equally affected by the constantly shifting boundary between the "natural" (or "animal") and the "human," if for somewhat different reasons. As he caresses her, "easing the rift wider to the moistened breadth of his hand," he harps on his usual themes—the dangers of revealed religion and the stupidity of his fellow Americans.[20] The striking discrepancy between what he does and what he says, between the ideological points McCandless makes for the benefit of his largely unresponsive audience of one and the sexual stimulation he provides—apparently to little avail, for Elizabeth suddenly "pull[s] away, up on that damned elbow again"—, sets up a complex relationship between the (male) discourse of power and the supine (female) body, to which he hardly refers at all except maybe as an allegory of "the one thing in life that's absolutely inevitable," i.e., mortality considered as a fact of nature. On the one hand, McCandless, the proud ideologue ever ready to "bully and browbeat everybody in sight,"[21] needs to elevate himself far above physical contingencies, the better to survey world history from a position of absolute authority; on the other hand, he needs everyone else to be hopelessly enslaved to biology, so that he can dismiss whatever other people say as an "evasion" of reality. Thus, the "rift" between nature and politics indeed gets "wider," as it also seems to do when the power-grabbing clique for whom he used to work treats Africa as a mere storehouse of "mineral resources" to be exploited or destroyed at will. This strategy is not immediately successful, as the weaker party proves unwilling to cooperate: when Elizabeth pulls away, her reaction foreshadows that of the African rebels who shoot down Teakell's plane. The reader is thus reminded that there is more to femininity than mere physicality; what erases the distinction is not a law of nature, but a rhetorical strategy, just as nothing would predestine an entire continent and its inhabitants to be considered as a "field" literally "ripe for harvest"[22] were it not for the likes of Elton Ude, whose cynical abuse of the English language knows no bounds. However, in both cases, resistance proves futile, and Elizabeth dies—possibly worn down by Paul's constant harassment and McCandless' inconsiderate chain-smoking, among other instances of autocratic behavior—only a few short pages before Africa is ravaged by nuclear war.

Considered in this light, *Carpenter's Gothic* vividly illustrates the central paradox of sovereignty, as described by the Italian philosopher Giorgio Agamben. Suppose, he writes, that the power to suspend the law is inseparable from the power to make the law—that is to say, that sovereign authority is understood as the ability to proclaim a state of exception, following Carl Schmitt's now classic definition. It follows that the sovereign occupies a paradoxical position, both inside and outside the political order. She has the unique ability to decide whether or not the law shall be applied; thus, she is not bound by the same legal restrictions as everyone else, and stands free of otherwise universal constraints, a sovereign exception to the general rule. Yet the privilege thus enjoyed by a particular individual or group (such as an elected parliament) violates neither the spirit nor the letter of the law, as many constitutions explicitly provide for situations in which the general welfare requires the suspension of ordinary legal procedures, for instance in wartime. In other words, an extra-legal status is granted to a particular person or institution; yet, this exception is not only legal, but also constitutes the guarantee on which all law ultimately rests.

Agamben observes that the Schmittian paradox oddly resonates with Foucault's exploration of the politics of selfhood, although Foucault himself explicitly turns his back on traditional investigations of the legal and institutional expressions of power.[23] Evidence of the link is provided by the concept of *homo sacer*, a term which, in ancient Roman law, designated individuals whom anyone could kill without being guilty of homicide, and yet who could not legally be sacrificed to the gods.[24] To Agamben, this means that *homo sacer* stands outside both human and divine law, deprived of all legal protection and reduced to the status of an unclean animal. The ultimate outcast, *homo sacer*, is nonetheless essential to the preservation of the legal order, as Agamben also observes: for by thus identifying properties a person might hold without therefore being entitled to a place in the community, ancient Roman law implicitly defined the boundaries of its own jurisdiction and sharply distinguished the "merely natural" from the proper object of legislation.[25] This typically biopolitical gesture whereby power asserts its own legitimacy by singling out the body as the key site of segregation and control is uncannily similar to the complex procedure of "inclusive exclusion," which gives rise to the sovereign exception described by Carl Schmitt.[26]

Agamben further proposes that the sovereign and *homo sacer* are ultimately indistinguishable (as demonstrated by taboos affecting the person of the sovereign in many traditional monarchies). Both straddle the boundary between what the Greeks called *bios*, i.e., the purposeful living enjoyed by humans, and *zōē* or "bare life," i.e., the biological process of survival in which all living beings have an equal share; both therefore embody the fundamental distinction drawn by Aristotle between *polis* (political existence considered as the privilege of the human race, *zōion politikon*) and *oikos* (the strictly private or a-political sphere of reproduction and subsistence).[27] While Agamben's argument explains why, in the Western tradition at least, all sovereignty immediately assumes a biopolitical form. It also accounts for the specifically modern forms of biopolitical control identified by Foucault: whereas, in ancient times, the figure of *homo sacer* was largely repressed and essentially served as the negative point of comparison which brought into sharper focus the boundaries of the truly political, modernity's major innovation has consisted in allowing this repressed other to return and invade the entire field of politics, as its identity with the person of the sovereign indeed predisposed it to do. This has resulted in the emergence of a new biopolitical state whose major concern is to monitor and control the bare processes of life, health, and sexuality, at the cost of reducing human existence to the level of mere animality.

A similar logic is at work in *Carpenter's Gothic*. In this novel, the exercise of power requires a sharp distinction to be drawn between *bios*, intelligent life as lived by "civilized" members of the *polis*, and *zōē*, or mere survival. The numerous references to Elizabeth's bodily functions (sex, defecation, "confusing rift for cleft") and her forcible — if comically inadequate — identification with the traditional figure of the "homemaker" turn her into a quintessential *homo sacer* figure, a kind of universal scapegoat whom anyone can persecute with complete impunity and whose sudden death from unexplained causes not only illustrates the breakdown of causality and meaning, but also irreversibly compromises her humanity.[28] Africa likewise stands for the biopolitical "other" whose supposed inability to rise above the dictates of mere survival justifies by contrast the smugness of self-styled "missionaries" such as Ude. The same process is at work in both cases, and the only difference is a matter of scale. Paul's insistence that his business files be kept away from the kitchen exactly parallels Teakell's "Food for Africa" program,[29] since both enact a clear separation between *polis* and *oikos*, between political decision-making — a privilege of American males — and such mundane realities as "bag[s] of onions": food is for Africa because Americans presumably have more important matters to worry about.[30]

As if this were not sufficient, every available technological device is called upon to circumscribe the sphere of "bare life" and emphasize, by contrast, the self-sufficiency and detachment of the agents in charge of managing it from a distance: the sophisticated medical equipment trained upon Elizabeth's bruised and battered body serves exactly the same purpose as the satellites hovering over the Great Rift, as the point is not to heal or save, but to permit a strictly utilitarian evaluation of the "resources" and "services" each may be able to provide. This attitude finally proves self-defeating, as scientific inquiry reveals that no one, not even the proudest politician or ideologue, is exempt from participation in "bare life." Ude and the religious right still cling to the archaic belief that humanity is radically distinct from animality, and therefore reject Darwinism, whereas McCandless, along with modern science, insists that very little would actually distinguish *Homo sapiens* from *Proconsul africanus* were it not for the former's pretentious claim to uniqueness: "If you want ignorance you can find it right there, that site on Lake Rudolf [...] that was ignorance, that was the dawn of intelligence what we've got here [i.e., among Ude's followers] [i]s its eclipse."[31] The "rift" does not divide one group or country from another, but cuts right across the body of each individual, whose exalted sense of sovereignty is compromised by clear evidence of subjection to the demands of biology. Paul's scars and bleeding shoulder are no less vividly evoked than his wife's asthma attacks; the circumstances of

Teakell's death ironically recall what it means to be bodily lifted up into heaven; one of the reader's earliest glimpses of Billy is as "the denimed swell of ribs creased under the rocker panel" of a dangerously swaying car, while Paul thinks of him less as Elizabeth's brother than as the man who invariably floods the downstairs bathroom ("Try to live like civilized people your brother comes in here pisses all over the floor"); and McCandless himself is reminded by Lester that alcohol and tobacco are taking their toll on his aging body: "See where there's no hair growing till way above your ankle there? That's what I told you, that's the whisky and the cigarettes working on you together that's your circulation failing, that's when your toes turn green."[32]

It should not come as a surprise that violence and death are ubiquitous in a novel where all the characters are *homines sacri*: for what defines *homo sacer* is precisely that she has been shorn of all human characteristics save one, namely the mortality shared by the human species with the rest of the animal kingdom. In such a world, as Paul points out, all life is constantly threatened with sudden elimination, and death carries no political or spiritual meaning, as it is strictly synonymous with the mere cessation of bodily functions: "Walk down the street everybody's got high blood pressure, [...] probably got it myself, heart attack drop in the street and they'll just step around you."[33] Elizabeth likes bird-watching, and McCandless is fond of referring to various literary animals such as Faulkner's "buzzard" or Robinson Jeffers' "grasshoppers."[34] This ominously recalls the fate of the helpless bird tortured by sadistic children in the novel's opening lines. However, what best illustrates the condition to which Gaddis's characters have been reduced may be the image of Cettie Teakell lying comatose on her hospital bed,[35] a chilling instance of life reduced to a bare vegetative process.

To a certain extent, the pessimistic vision detailed in *Carpenter's Gothic* unquestionably reflects the mood of the period in which the novel was composed. In the sharply polarized world of the mid–1980s, the risk of nuclear war was more real than it had ever been since 1962 and the Cuban Missile Crisis, as the hard-line attitude adopted by the Reagan administration in response to the Soviet invasion of Afghanistan (1979) and the perceived threat of Soviet expansionism increased the likelihood of a direct military confrontation between the two superpowers. While the widespread anxiety caused by this situation left its mark on popular culture—as evidenced by the resounding success of the 1983 disaster movie *The Day After*—, it also struck a chord both among evangelical Christians interested in end-time prophecies, and among liberal intellectuals concerned that the rise of the religious right might prove destructive of civil liberties (Margaret Atwood's *The Handmaid's Tale*, which depicts the transformation of the United States into a theocratic dystopia, came out in 1986, one year after *Carpenter's Gothic*).[36] Although the East-West dispute did not escalate into full-scale war, the tension generated by the international situation gave rise to a number of conflicts in countries such as Angola, Nicaragua, and El Salvador, where the United States sought to prevent Communist factions from seizing power. *Carpenter's Gothic* offers a recognizable picture of a world in which Cold War tactics and the politics of decolonization frequently overlapped, and where the probability of imminent and near universal destruction provided the foundation for the entire international order. Gaddis's point, however, is probably less to comment on actual situations than to parody contemporary modes of discourse, ranging from Ude's cynical handling of biblical references to McCandless's liberal paranoia. Contrary to what both evangelical Christians and secular intellectuals feared, Gaddis's world ends neither with a bang — there are still newspapers the "day after" — nor with a whimper, unlike Elizabeth's final struggle for survival, since talk, the only reality of any substance, is able to proceed unimpeded in the midst of global catastrophe.[37]

However, the text actually invokes a much broader historical context and may be less concerned with current events than with an earlier, and much more significant, biopolitical shift. Toward the end of the novel, Elizabeth gazes at the back of her hand as it rests on the kitchen table, "searching [...] for relevance in the smallest particular, finding wood grain and skin follicle all the same."[38] This equation accurately reflects the status of human life once it is stripped of all significance or purpose and becomes a more or less expendable "resource"; and it has particularly sinister implications, for if flesh and wood are essentially identical, they can be treated, or destroyed, exactly the same way. Earlier on, Lester recalls that there was indeed a time when people were burned in furnaces like so much firewood: "It's like Dachau in here, you know that?" he exclaims, irritated by the cigarette smoke which fills McCandless's office.[39] Tasteless as it is, Lester's chilling joke is not altogether unfounded. Agamben recalls that the Nazis defined politics as the "art of making possible what seems impossible" (in Goebbels's words: "*Politik ist die Kunst, das unmöglich Scheinende möglich zu machen*").[40] And in this they succeeded all too well, for by creating a state in which "bare life" was the norm, the threat of mass extinction a tangible, daily reality, and *bios* a practical impossibility, they paved the way for the previously unthinkable forms of biopolitical management, which have left an indelible mark on postwar strategies of governance, as Agamben points out.

According to Hannah Arendt, "The totalitarian hell proves [...] that the power of man is greater than [average persons] ever dared to think, and that man can realize hellish fantasies without making the sky fall or the earth open."[41] Agamben argues that this lesson has been heeded in the postwar period to such an extent that the death camp has become the main biopolitical paradigm of modernity,[42] that is, of a time in which it is not absurd to imagine an entire continent being wiped out together with its inhabitants for the sake of "mineral resources" that are not even there. In this, as in other matters, the rhetoric of the religious right is deliberately archaic, for it is unable, or unwilling, to admit such a possibility, unless it is sanctioned by the intervention of a vengeful Providence: "They can't wait to be snatched up to meet the Lord in the clouds and sit there watching the rest of us tormented with fire and brimstone in the presence of his holy angels."[43] Ever on the side of technological modernity, McCandless knows that this kind of theological alibi is utterly superfluous and that belief in a jealous God has been consigned to irrelevance now that the human race is fully capable of annihilating itself without any help from on high (or, as the narrator of *Agapē Agape* would add, now that Blake's "little lamb" has been supplanted in the popular imagination by Dolly, the first cloned sheep).[44] As Arendt further points out, this guilty, destructive knowledge "is positively dangerous to those who know from their own imaginings what they themselves are capable of doing [...] (and they are more numerous in any large city than we like to admit)."[45] McCandless may be one of their number, as Elizabeth implies when she finally confronts him:

> Because you're the one who wants it[....] And it's why you've done nothing... [...] to see them all go up like that smoke in the furnace all the stupid, ignorant, blown up in the clouds and there's nobody there, there's no rapture no anything just to see them wiped away for good it's really you, isn't it.[46]

Ultimately, the crisis whose effects are detailed in *Carpenter's Gothic* cannot be circumscribed within the limits of a given historical situation, no matter how broadly defined, for it takes place on an ontological level, or rather because it is associated with the breakdown of *onto-logy*, of the traditional links between discourse (*logos*) and the entities (*onta*) it designates. The opposition between *zōē* and *bios* which, according to Agamben, underpins the entire Western tradition of political thought obviously resonates with Aristotle's equally seminal characterization of the human race as *zōion logon ekhon*, as the animal endowed with speech, where *zōion* refers to the biological features that serve to establish humankind's generic status and *logos* identifies the unique, specifying feature which distinguishes it from other members of the same class.[47] Since *logos* also means the ability to make plans, the implication is that, in humans as opposed to all other animals, *zōē* can be made subservient to a freely chosen purpose. This argument leads to the unforeseen consequence that when *bios*, or purposeful living, is supplanted by the "bare life" which it was originally supposed to hold in check, the reason must be that the human species is no longer able to give voice to what constitutes its world. In conditions of extreme biopolitical regimentation, human beings (if indeed they still deserve to be called such) are no longer "endowed with" speech, but view language from the outside, as an alien reality which somehow concerns them and yet over whose workings, or meaning, they do not have the slightest control. The consequences are no less fateful regarding *logos* itself, which thereby loses touch with whatever else exists in the world, as it is no longer handled by beings who straddle the divide between "bare life" and rational, meaningful existence.

This is exactly what happens in *Carpenter's Gothic*. Whereas, in strictly historical terms, Gaddis's novel can be said to depict a post–human universe, that is to say the kind of world which can come into being only after belief in the human has been virtually abandoned, it would be more accurate to describe this book as a novel about human degeneracy or involution, that is to say as a dramatization of what happens when the concept of the "human" is resolved into its component parts, like a decaying mass of organic matter.[48] In such a situation, language appears increasingly mysterious and alien, as the once familiar *logos* edges ever closer to the status of found object, like the quaint furnishings which clutter Elizabeth's living room: "Because it's all, I mean some of it's quite lovely isn't it it's, c'est comme un petit musée isn't it. I mean ces chaises? they're rosewood aren't they."[49] Lovely or not, the "little museum" houses difficult foreign words, as well as rosewood chairs, and the reader who gazes at the page is no less puzzled than Elizabeth herself by these delicate artifacts whose relevance and purpose are no longer clear. By demoting the human to the status of mere living matter, the text implicitly, albeit inevitably, problematizes the status of language, which mysteriously breaks loose and becomes an autonomous entity with a life of its own at the very moment when it loses touch with biological data. Elizabeth's, and McCandless's, interest in the literary depiction of animals may be fateful since it foreshadows their own reversion to mere animality. At the same time, it suggests that literary texts themselves may be compared to strange living organisms, viewed by the reader with the same mixture of perplexity and fascination, as if they were buzzards or grasshoppers.

• • •

Despite McCandless's protestations to the contrary, the African controversy is not truly about reason's struggle for supremacy against the forces of obscurantism, but about the tyrannical (mis)management of so-called "natural" resources after the demise of *logos*, hence of the very rationality McCandless purports to defend. This has far-reaching implications, for if the fate of language indeed hangs in the balance, it follows that the question of supremacy and power has an immediate bearing on the biopolitics — not to mention the ethics — of fiction itself. Far from being a "minor" problem to which the critic interested in theoretical and/or epistemological issues can afford to turn a blind eye, the post–colonial debate articulated in *Carpenter's Gothic* thus turns out to be inextricably linked to Gaddis's interest in redefinitions of writing, so that a proper awareness of the context in which the novel was written may significantly enrich critical discussions of its broader agenda. Conversely, hermeneutic issues of the kind favored by most commentators may turn out to have unsuspected political implications, to which a reader less attuned to the narrative's contextual resonance runs the risk of remaining oblivious.

Elton Ude's African project is a case in point, as it depends, not just on his alliance with Senator Teakell, but also on a deliberate overhaul of language aimed, in particular, at altering the status of reference. In order to provide his friends in high places with the theological alibi they need, Ude makes extensive use of biblical phraseology, and particularly of the word "harvest," to which he is so partial that even Paul, his public relations adviser, has to take this preference into account.[50] This eminently biopolitical figure proves serviceable because it widens the rift between *zōē* and *bios*, between "bare life" (recalled by the word's "literal" meaning) and Ude's professed interest in the spiritual welfare of those waiting to be converted. Although he claims to defend revealed truth, he is best described as a purveyor of particularly shameless fictions, for the emphasis he places on imaginary, as opposed to tangible, harvests conveniently justifies his callous indifference to the death of millions and creates rich opportunities for irony when the reader realizes that a word semantically associated with food is being made to provide a particularly cynical justification for its absence: "Citing the drought conditions now prevailing in Africa, he [Ude] identified that dark continent as the dry land named in the prophecy where millions of souls are waiting to be harvested in the name of the Lord."[51]

Thus, McCandless is not quite right to claim that the discourse of Christian fundamentalism, as exemplified by Ude's speeches, relies on a strictly "literal" interpretation of biblical language.[52] It would be more accurate to say that Ude's rhetoric heavily relies on the possibility of such an interpretation, needed in order to circumscribe the territory over which fundamentalists claim a sovereign authority. Biblical literalism allows Ude to proclaim the linguistic equivalent of a state of exception by pointing to a non–verbal reality, declaring it to be irrelevant, and thereby justifying language's total domination over it, as indeed all priests and preachers do regardless of nationality or creed, at least according to Gaddis, who describes religion in one of his essays as "the grandest fiction to be concocted by man."[53]

Since the trick cannot be pulled off unless the "literal"/"figurative" dichotomy remains in place, it is futile to try and undo the effects of Ude's rhetoric by simply turning the process on its head, recalling the "literal" meanings he discounts and defending an allegorical reading of the Bible in response to its alleged mishandling by evangelical preachers. McCandless attempts something of the kind when Teakell's death gives him a gruesome opportunity to make fun of evangelical Christians' belief in the rapture of the Church: his reinterpretation of St. Paul's prophecy brutally silences its allegorical resonance, thus turning the foolish Senator into a perfect example of "bare life," of the human animal's meaningless existence and even more absurd destruction.[54] However, such a reaction is unlikely to embarrass Ude, since Wayne Fickert's equally inglorious death from drowning provides him with a perfect opportunity to describe his victim as a hero of the true Church. In the end, McCandless's self–indulgent response simply produces yet more dubious fictions, as Lester gleefully points out by reading a few choice excerpts from his novel.

> This part here? Where he's proceeding on a sea of doubt? that's pretty bad, proceeding on a sea of doubt that's pretty bad, you know that? And that part where he's trying to give his life a course of inevitability? where he wants to rescue his life from chance and deliver it to destiny? I wouldn't believe that, if I didn't know you I wouldn't believe anybody would talk like that.[55]

Interestingly, Lester objects to these phrases on ethical rather than aesthetic grounds: his point is not that they exhibit a total lack of literary taste, but that the use of such portentous language in an obviously autobiographical narrative is self–aggrandizing to the point of untruthfulness. Nothing disguises the unwelcome truth so well as "fine writing," that is to say prose filled with intricate figures of speech, and the only proper response is to seek out the unpalatable facts hidden beneath the rhetoric, or, better yet, to "pull out" while McCandless "rant[s] and rav[es]."[56]

McCandless attempts to defend himself by claiming that he wrote a novel, and that it is pointless to try and read allusions to real life — let alone his own past — into what was intended as a fictional narrative.[57] In other words, McCandless argues that fiction does not actually refer to anything outside itself, so that whoever chooses this mode of writing thereby assumes a position of complete irresponsibility. This, however, is precisely the root of the problem; for a discourse without a specific referent can be applied indiscriminately, like a prophecy in the hands of a self–serving preacher, or a vaguely worded law enforced by an unscrupulous government in a time of national emergency. The Masai invoke a "serviceable fiction" of this kind when they claim that "all the cattle in the world belong to them," so that "[w]hen they raid other tribes they're just taking back what was stolen from them long ago."[58] It seems that nothing is so widely shared as the human tendency to evade all responsibility, and McCandless's inflated but somewhat cryptic prose admirably serves this purpose, for it establishes his claim to authority while absolving him from the obligation to offer justifications for it.

If this is truly what novels are all about, and there is no middle way between the "serviceable fictions" used to justify the worst abuses and the "desperate fictions" on which most people base their strategies of denial,[59] then the reader may legitimately wonder why the text not only gets written at all, but actually remains suspended in mid–sentence, suggesting that a sequel may yet be expected.[60] A tentative answer might be that Gaddis's narrative is not, in fact, fiction of the kind it satirizes — or, in other words, it manages to avoid falling into the same biopolitical trap as its foolish or dishonest characters.

The counter–intuitive claim that "fiction" consists not so much in a certain type of narrative as in the normative use of language treated as an all-purpose rule to be subjected to wholly arbitrary interpretations recalls a well-known paradox whose classic formulation can be found in Ludwig Wittgenstein's *Philosophical Investigations* (1953). As Wittgenstein points out, there is a sense in which "no course of action [can] be determined by a rule" because "*any* action can be made out to accord with the rule."⁶¹ Whatever the rule may state, any given situation can be described as an exception of some kind, and the rule may therefore be invoked to justify anything as long as it is interpreted creatively enough, as Gaddis brilliantly demonstrates in *A Frolic of His Own* (1994).

If all discourse is to be perceived as a kind of rule, as it is in *Carpenter's Gothic* for purposes of biopolitical (mis)management, Wittgenstein's argument leads to the unsettling conclusion that no word can have a definite meaning: on such a basis, any utterance may be interpreted to mean just about anything, which is tantamount to saying that where a state of exception prevails, there is no such thing as meaning at all. It is easy to understand why Gaddis was drawn to this idea, since he felt that the "great fictions" have always been about "fighting off," or "succumbing to," "the ultimate chaos where everything equals everything else: the ultimate senseless universe."⁶² However, "fighting off" a threat is not the same as facing up to an established fact, let alone one that is inscribed in the nature of things. In any case, as Wittgenstein is quick to suggest, the paradox may result from a mere logical fallacy. It arises only if one assumes that it is necessary to begin by working out what the rule dictates so as to perceive how it is to be put into practice in the situation at hand. This turns out to be impossible, for the rule, being formulated in very general language, does not in fact refer to anything specific. However, these assumptions are by no means natural, as common experience suggests; in ordinary circumstances, "obeying a rule" means applying it, not substituting one expression of the rule for another, and is a matter of correct practice rather than explanation.⁶³ By analogy, it should not trouble anyone that language does not spontaneously refer to anything. The truth is that it is up to each individual speaker to make words refer to whatever happens to be at stake in a given context; indeed, this is the reason why it makes sense to speak at all: for, if meaning did in fact pre-exist in some form or other, speech as we know it would be futile (just as action would lose all ethical and political relevance if it followed automatically from a rule).

Gaddis's fictions, whether serviceable or desperate, are fictions of language—that is to say, they are concerned with fictive linguistic states, they describe and explore imaginary modes or definitions of verbal expression. They frequently turn into narratives of sovereignty because some of the most common misconceptions as to what it is to speak and write both result from, and support, our belief in the grand delusions of power promulgated by the modern state in its attempt "to flee from reality in fictions of such magnitude and audacity that we are swamped in admiration and dismay."⁶⁴ However, the point is not so much to echo widespread prejudices as to draw attention to their extreme strangeness. *Carpenter's Gothic* depicts a world of cynical televangelists and corrupt politicians, of dishonest researchers and venal journalists, in which the suspension of disbelief is literally a matter of life and death — if indeed this opposition still makes sense, considering that "life," when lived on such terms, means little more than the temporary avoidance of "the one thing [...] that's absolutely inevitable."[65] The novel's outrageous but weirdly plausible plot, and its comically exaggerated, albeit familiar and recognizable language provide a much needed reminder that this suspension is an act of free will — that mere credulity is not a sufficient explanation for the general regard in which the most extravagant fabrications are held, and that stupidity, far from being an involuntary deficiency for which people cannot be held responsible, in fact results from the active and "deliberate cultivation of ignorance."[66] Thus, Gaddis's approach to writing can indeed be described as a form of resistance against senselessness, as a withholding of consent which, by contrast, reveals just how much of the chaos against which we struggle can be blamed on our own tendency to accept absurd fictions at face value.

In practice, this cannot be accomplished by championing the "facts" as an antidote to the lies purveyed by the likes of Paul Booth and Elton Ude, for this would simply recreate the "literal"/"figurative" dichotomy in a disguised, but no less detrimental, form. The only way of rejecting all claims to sovereignty consists in rejecting both "fact" and "fiction" in order to explore the dynamics of language as it is actually spoken, the endless variety of contexts in which individual words acquire an ever renewed significance, and the unpredictable ways in which every utterance invents new forms of reference. This choice accounts for Gaddis's peculiar brand of embattled realism, whose aim consists not so much in showing "things as they are" as in offering the reader a sample of the myriad kaleidoscopic effects on which all verbal expression relies, the better to challenge the regimentation of meaning for purposes of totalitarian control. This may no doubt appear disappointing to a reader who feels that wide-ranging issues of biopolitical regimentation require solutions of a comparable scope, rather than a series of infinitesimal responses suspiciously similar to Wittgensteinian language games. However, the very nature of the problem precludes one from addressing it on any other terms, as the forcible reduction of human existence to "bare life" cannot be resisted unless the workings of language are more correctly apprehended, which in turn entails the realization that words actually function best on a microscopic scale alien to the sweeping generalizations and indiscriminate pronouncements that are so potent an instrument in the service of biopolitical domination.

It is tempting to search *Carpenter's Gothic* for signs of a coherent strategy capable of salvaging the last surviving remnants of the compromised *logos* and of rescuing humankind from the biopolitical quagmire of which the tragedy that befalls Africa in the novel's final pages is so potent an illustration. This, however, is a mistake against which Gaddis takes care to caution his readers when he argues in one of his essays that "outrage," not the impulse to preach, is what fuels writing: to claim that indignation alone is a proof of superior wisdom would be "naïve," and the novelist's aim is not to lecture the public on the folly of its ways, but to "embrace reality," a more arduous and thankless task.[67] In other words, fiction beyond the state of exception recognizes that there is no simple way of overturning such grandiose delusions as religion and the modern state, let alone the entire world "order," however much it may resemble a form of organized chaos. Overt rebellion is futile when it is not frankly counter–productive, as in the case of the African guerillas whose successful attack on Teakell's plane brings disaster upon their entire continent. Indeed, the ultimate outrage may consist in the realization that such global devastation does not thwart dreams of global domination, but actually fulfills them as nothing else could: as Hannah Arendt puts it, "Men insofar as they are more than animal reaction and fulfillment of functions are entirely superfluous to totalitarian regimes. Totalitarianism strives not toward despotic rule over men, but toward a system in which men are superfluous."[68] In contemporary parlance, the supreme "technological fix" is none other than the atom bomb, as all political problems will be resolved once and for all when there are no more people capable of raising them, and any form of rebellion likely to encourage retaliation on such a massive scale not only does not challenge the system, but actively assists it.

Writing in the immediate aftermath of World War II, at a time when humankind was learning to live in the twin shadow of Auschwitz and Hiroshima, Arendt was understandably pessimistic about the world's immediate future, and her doubts as to the viability of concerted efforts at resistance stem as much from philosophical considerations as from the experience of recent years in which the human race had entered the darkest times of all despite a hard-won victory against Nazi oppression. However, she does offer her reader a gleam of hope when she points out that even the most determined totalitarian government cannot altogether suppress what she terms "spontaneity," i.e., the individual's ability to act in unpremeditated ways, thus defeating attempts at complete control. "Total power can be achieved and safeguarded only in a world of conditioned reflexes, of marionettes without the slightest trace of spontaneity. Precisely because man's resources are so great, he can be fully dominated only when he becomes a specimen of the animal-species man"[69] — and possibly not even then: for supposing that it is indeed possible to reduce human existence to the modicum of "bare life" necessary to survival, there is a form of spontaneity pertaining to zōē, as childbirth demonstrates, since "with each new birth, a new beginning is born into the world, a new world has potentially come into being."[70] Elizabeth's "babies demanding to get born" thus stand for the inarticulate hope that a fresh start may yet be contemplated, and her barren life and premature death for the fear that total domination will "ravage the world as we know it — a world which everywhere seems to have come to an end — before a new beginning rising from this end has had time to assert itself."[71]

Gaddis's vision is even more pessimistic than Arendt's, since he envisions a future in which even the "animal-species man" is threatened with immediate extinction, and birds and trees alone still testify to *zōē*'s continued vitality. The characters' interminable conversations may make an increasingly discordant sound, but "zebra music" of a kind fills the intervening prose descriptions, or rather its American equivalent, since there is no need to import antelopes from Uganda when there is enough wildlife in Elizabeth's backyard to surprise and delight the most demanding reader:

> She looked up for the cry of a jay, for the sheer of its blue arc down the length of the fence and then back to lark bunting, red crossbill, northern shrike, lesser yellowlegs fluttering by on the pages of the bird book opened on her lap while here, in the branches of the mulberry tree above her, nothing moved but a squirrel's mindless leap for the roof of the house.[72]

The likes of McCandless may rail against the stupidity of their fellow human beings, not without some justification since there is no point in having a mind unless one is prepared to try and think. However, the proudest teacher is not exempt from blame, since using one's intelligence in the service of global domination may be even worse than not using it at all. Seen in this light, the squirrel's "mindless leap" offers a tempting alternative to humankind's self-destructive behavior, as it points to a form of spontaneity and freedom beyond the control of the most scheming ideologues and suggests that Arendt's "new beginning" is indeed about to assert itself, right under the eyes of the novel's unlucky protagonist, in a parallel universe where problems of sovereignty do not arise since it does not make sense to single out "bare life" where "purposeful living" is not, and has never been, an option.

There are good reasons to believe that the text is indeed offering an ecological solution to the abuses of biopower, for a similar burst of uninhibited energy also affects language, as words leap across the pages of the "bird book" like a squirrel hopping from tree to tree. One of the most dangerous symptoms of the modern biopolitical crisis lies in the widening gap between discourse and life, between the dynamics of actual physical existence and the medium in which its meaning can be articulated; thus, language's renewed ability to mimic the erratic trajectories of birds may be taken to indicate that the split has been temporarily healed, allowing words to behave with as much spontaneity as the animals they designate, and thus to exempt themselves from all forms of regimentation and control. While this may sound encouraging, it nonetheless confirms that no solution can be found save on a microscopic scale incompatible with human life as we know it: there may be some hope for squirrels, or words, but there is none for Elizabeth, who simply sits there, a bemused spectator of processes in which she takes no part. However, this is unlikely to stop the text in its tracks, since there is no reason why fiction should automatically side with the doomed human race rather than with jays or Northern shrikes. It may be too late to solve Africa's problems; indeed, the final moment of reckoning may be at hand for the entire human species caught in a lethal trap of its own devising. Yet this does not entail that fiction is at an end, since it alone is not complicit with the global attempt at self-destruction, and is therefore capable of envisioning a future beyond the current biopolitical quandary, even though there may be no place for it except in a post–human world. When push comes to shove, the side with the feebler imagination goes down, which, at least, "is good news for the writer."

11

After Gaddis: Data Storage and the Novel

STEPHEN J. BURN

> American life is crowded with facts.... Men work for nothing more than to know how to classify their facts, what to do with them, how to govern them and how far to be governed by them.
> —J.G. Holland, *Atlantic Monthly* (1865)

In "Mr. Difficult," a now-infamous essay that first appeared in the *New Yorker* in 2002, Jonathan Franzen offered an account of his ambivalent experiences reading and not reading Gaddis's novels. When the essay was reprinted in his nonfiction collection, *How to Be Alone* (2003), it was wedged between an essay about correctional facilities and one about sex manuals—a frame that seemed to encapsulate the mixed sense of punishment and desire that Gaddis's work apparently provoked in Franzen.[1] But despite this ambivalence toward Gaddis, at the heart of "Mr. Difficult" was a series of "Fallacies" about literature—propounded by supposedly-ignorant critics—which Franzen wanted to dogmatically expose. Amongst these was the Fallacy of Capture, in which a book is falsely considered to be an ethnographic device for capturing some elusive essence of daily life. Then there was the Fallacy of the Symphonic, in which a book is falsely praised for motifs that supposedly wash over the reader, like an orchestral movement. Attached onto the end of this list was, implicitly, another fallacy: the Fallacy of Data Storage, in which the purpose of a novel is falsely assumed to be its ability "to capture and efficiently store data."[2]

Against these supposedly-false analogies, Franzen posed the erotic and culinary arts, ultimately imagining the novel as a kind of fruitcake to be served to the reader. But the refutation this counterargument proposes is less than convincing. By attempting to dismiss a series of false analogies by simply suggesting different analogies, Franzen does not so much refute other conceptions of the novel as much as he attempts to replace a conception that he dislikes with another model that he prefers. This decision to resolve an apparently objective argument by filtering it through the lens of his own personality is, as several critics have noted,[3] a strategy that Franzen employs in many of his essays. But rather than provide another critique of Franzen's mode of argument, I want to explore one of the analogies that he rejects in his Gaddis essay—the novel as a medium of data storage. I'd like to suggest, firstly, that Gaddis's use of data goes beyond merely using the novel as a storage device, and actually provides a careful critique of the role of facts and data in American life. Secondly, I'd like to demonstrate that Gaddis's approach to information has influenced Franzen and several of his contemporaries.

That Gaddis's novels use their often-vast scale to embed an encyclopedic range of data has long been the starting point for Gaddis criticism. John Kuehl and Steven Moore introduce this idea in their *In Recognition of William Gaddis* (1984) by calling *The Recognitions* "encyclopedic";[4] while Christopher Knight begins his study, *Hints and Guesses* (1997), with the assumption that his readings will be constrained by the novels' "encyclopedic range and complexity."[5] But while Franzen criticizes both Gaddis's fascination with embedding diverse information in his novels and the scholarly defenses of this aspect of his work, it is worth observing that encyclopedic knowledge actually plays a dual role in Gaddis's novels. On one level, Gaddis's novels *are* structured (as Franzen implies) to amass data, using multiple examples to thicken Gaddis's thematic explorations, and widen the context in which his critiques of fraudulence might be understood. But, on another level, data collection also becomes a thematic exploration, as Gaddis demonstrates the limitations of encyclopedic knowledge to show that in a world of proliferating information we can never master enough data. In doing so, Gaddis, in a sense, pre-empts Jean-François Lyotard's announcement of the splintering of knowledge in the postmodern world, a world in which "the diminished tasks of research have become compartmentalized and no one can master them all."[6] But beyond the bounds of Franzen's argument with Gaddis, this is particularly worthy of note because so many critics have seen the novel of encyclopedic scope as entirely antithetical to the age of postmodernism.[7] I will suggest here, however, that Gaddis's books actually use their vast scale to explore the fracturing of holistic models of knowledge, and are, as such, very much in tune with the philosophical substratum of postmodernism.

The dominant metaphor Gaddis employs to explore data storage is the encyclopedia,[8] but his skeptical attitude toward encyclopedic knowledge is neatly encapsulated in an episode near the middle of *The Recognitions* (1955). In Gaddis's first novel, Wyatt's father owns the fourteenth edition of *Encyclopaedia Britannica*[9] and consults "volume eighteen [...] PLANTS to RAYM"[10] in part II, chapter three of the book. Later in that chapter Gaddis reveals that Wyatt's grandfather has borrowed volume eighteen, as the Reverend Gwyon sends him a note requesting that he "return vol. 18."[11] The relevance of this missing volume is twofold: first, the difficulty Wyatt's father has in getting hold of his encyclopedia when there is "a great deal of work to be done"[12] offers a metafictional commentary on Gaddis's own struggle to keep track of the disparate resources needed to write his data-filled novel, but at the same time the Town Carpenter's use of the volume signals one of the difficulties of data. The Town Carpenter reads up on Prester John in this volume, but his enthusiasm for the subject leads him to subsequently mistake his own grandson for the legendary King. Acting upon data drawn from the encyclopedia, in this instance, leads to one of the novel's many misrecognitions and should remind us that, as Emerson notes, "all the wisdom is not in the encyclopædia."[13]

Elsewhere in Gaddis's three long, data-filled books problems arise not just from characters misusing information, but also from the proliferation of data in the modern world.[14] As knowledge becomes more specialized, Gaddis suggests, no one can know enough. Stanley's tragicomic death in Fenestrula at the end of *The Recognitions* comes because, in spite of his mastery of musicology, he has insufficient mastery of languages, and so cannot translate the Italian priest's warning about the cathedral's shaky architecture. In a more literal comment on the problems caused by runaway data, Edward Bast's attempts to work in *J R* (1975) are encumbered as volumes of a corrupt ten-part children's encyclopedia gradually fill up the 96th Street apartment where he is staying. As if to underscore Gaddis's account of the compartmentalization of knowledge, it is only "samples of volume four" that are "blanketing the city" and the apartment.[15]

Gaddis's last long fiction, *A Frolic of His Own* (1994), seems to represent the natural culmination of this development, since the novel threatens to embed "the whole Britannica"[16] and centers around Oscar Crease, who is nearly always shown helplessly surrounded by "every piece of paper he's ever had his hands on, letters, old Playbills, scraps of newspaper, invitations, papers written by his illiterate students, recipes he's never tried."[17] Drowning in this deluge of information, Oscar seems to embody Gaddis's conception of the postmodern individual, but unlike the undeniably talented Stanley and Bast, Oscar's ability to master even a single body of information amid this deluge seems doubtful. On a basic level, the noise of the world is much louder in this book, eroding Oscar's vain attempts to hold onto literary data: "Justice and slavery, war, destiny, things are in the saddle and ride mankind in Emerson's voice cut short by the tin trivial interruption of Jack Preswig."[18] But more subtly, Gaddis has structured the world of this novel around a series of circles that seem to doom Oscar's efforts to master his data to failure.

Circles are everywhere in the plot of *A Frolic of His Own*, from the gyres of Yeats's "The Second Coming" (a poem alluded to four times in the novel, on pages 251, 304, 321 and 532), to the dreary soap-opera "If the World Turns,"[19] but the underlying driving force of the narrative is also patterned around the idea of circularity. This is partly true in terms of a kind of narrative recycling, where Gaddis recasts elements of his earlier novels (the sculpture *Cyclone Seven* from *J R*, or Liz Booth's death from *Carpenter's Gothic*), but more prominently circularity governs the fate of information in the novel. Gaddis introduces the tendency of information to circulate futilely when Trish tells Christina that "someone should simply shoot" Spot (the dog that has become trapped in *Cyclone Seven*) only to have Christina almost immediately repeat the same phrase to Harry.[20] But Gaddis's satire, here, is not directed simply at these two rather helpless women. The tendency for information to be pointlessly recycled occurs endlessly in the novel, even infiltrating the high legal language that intersperses the text. When Judge Crease, for example, establishes in the novel's first legal brief that "a dog is not a boy," he does so only to move forward to the observation that "a boy is not a dog,"[21] nouns circling from one end of the sentence to other. If the etymology of *encyclopedia* suggests the circle of knowledge,[22] then Gaddis's last long book examines the failed circulation of that knowledge. The dominant loop of *A Frolic of His Own* is the vicious circle of a closed system, where data flows only back to itself. This movement is darkly summarized when Spot dies, only to have an "enterprising glover in San Francisco" produce a range of mittens from "Simulated Spotskin(r)."[23] The passage of these mittens through the culture, however, grotesquely parallels the movement of knowledge: the dogskin returns to a dog, as Lily's dog, Pookie, chokes to death on the mittens.[24] This closed system, as Gaddis notes later in the book, operates on the principle of "dog eat dog,"[25] as everything circles destructively back to its point of origin.

Gaddis, then, does not simply use the novel to store data, but rather explores the negative impact endlessly proliferating information has upon the lives of his characters. His books set up an implicit dialogue between form and content, where the novels' vast and layered erudition is called into question by the lives imprisoned within their pages. But while Franzen criticizes this approach, it is worth noting the breadth of Gaddis's influence. In the past ten years, the work of scholars and the testimonies of writers have combined to underline just how significant Gaddis's impact has been upon the American postwar novel. A host of important American writers contributed to a feature devoted to Gaddis in *Conjunctions* in 2003, while Steven Moore has coordinated a project that catalogues mainly American writers who have alluded to Gaddis within their own fictions.[26] But beyond the U.S., British novelists, such as David Mitchell, also seem to have learned from Gaddis. Mitchell's first novel, *Ghostwritten* (1999), clearly shares Gaddis's fascination with data, since it self–consciously refers to the "Tree of Knowledge"[27] and is structured around nine-principal narrators who are geographically arranged in different locations (from Okinawa, moving gradually west to finally arrive in New York) to present an encyclopedic totality of vision. Within this ambitious structure, Mitchell uses his many nested stories to nod to Gaddis's first two books. In *Ghostwritten*'s sixth section, for example, Mitchell apparently recreates Wyatt Gwyon in Jerome, whose "only marketable talent is his ability to paint copies of masterpieces."[28] Like Wyatt, whose talent is commandeered by Recktall Brown, Jerome is exploited by an unscrupulous gang, and the resemblance between the two is further strengthened when Mitchell reveals that Jerome has "never owned a mirror" because "whenever he looks into one he sees a man inside it,"[29] just as Esme says that Wyatt's mirrors are dangerous because "they trap him."[30] In a more formal parallel, the ninth section of *Ghostwritten* seems to recall *J R*, as Mitchell relays the only section of his novel to be based in America entirely through dialogue.

To map the full extent of Gaddis's impact upon the topography of global, or even just American, fiction is, however, beyond the scope of this essay. Instead, I'm going to settle for the smaller goal of briefly assessing the impact of his use of data upon three American writers: Richard Powers, David Foster Wallace, and Franzen, himself.

• • •

The author of nine complex, erudite novels in twenty-one years, Richard Powers belongs in the front rank of late-century novelistic achievement, beside other contemporary writers who have simultaneously engaged with the legacy of postmodernism while mapping out new directions. But when tracing his genealogy as a novelist most introductions to his work normally stress his affinities with Thomas Pynchon.[31] Powers, however, also records a debt to Gaddis:

> I read *The Recognitions* in 1980, having recently dropped out of graduate school and got [a] job working as a second-shift computer operator in an isolated facility on a renovated, nineteenth-century wharf in Boston. I had recently read *V.*, and I could feel the direct genealogy. The book just amazed me, and I am still living with it and working my way through all the material he opened up for me.[32]

The influence of his experience reading Gaddis is discernable in several places in Powers's oeuvre. Echoes of *The Recognitions* might be detected in his account of "unsponsored recognition"[33] in his first novel, *Three Farmers on Their Way to a Dance* (1985), or in Franklin Todd's critique of "the cult of originality"[34] in *The Gold Bug Variations* (1991). Perhaps more tenuously, *Plowing the Dark* (2000) refers to "Carpenter Gothic,"[35] and (as Joseph Tabbi notes) preempts *Agapē Agape*'s thesis that "entertainment [is] the parent of technology," when Steve Spiegel observes that "*Hollerith got his idea for the punched data card from the player piano.*"[36]

More substantial affinities, however, can be located in Powers's approach to data and the novel. Powers, like Gaddis, sees data (and particularly scientific data) as an irrefutable aspect of contemporary existence that must be acknowledged by the modern novel. As he explained to Harvey Blume, "If the novel's task is to describe where we find ourselves and how we live now, the novelist must take a good, hard look at the most central facts of contemporary life — technology and science. The 'information novel' shouldn't be a curiosity. It should be absolutely mainstream."[37] Powers's conception of the way data has shaped modern life is (again, like Gaddis) built around a demonstration of the limitations of the encyclopedia. This can be clearly seen in *Three Farmers on Their Way to Dance*, in which one of the quests hinges on a flawed search through "a thousand encyclopedias and references."[38] At the start of the novel, an unnamed narrator has become fascinated with a photograph by August Sander, but because an exhibition incorrectly lists his name as Zander, the narrator's desire to learn more about the photographer is doomed from the moment he begins his investigation in "the *Xerxes to Zygote* volume of a multivolume encyclopedia."[39] Because of the explosion of data in modern times and the subsequent need to divide knowledge alphabetically into separate volumes, the narrator's initial mistake means that he will not find enlightenment in the encyclopedia.

But while *Three Farmers on Their Way to a Dance* illustrates the problems of data storage, it is significant that Powers also takes pains to demonstrate the use of that data. He does this via an argument the novel makes about art. *Three Farmers* begins at the Detroit Institute of Arts with the assumption that "art can only hope to be an anaesthetic, a placebo,"[40] but soon challenges this notion by replacing the anesthetizing story the reader may have expected (after all, chapter one begins with a nursery rhyme) with a narrative that makes challenging forays into the thought of such diverse figures as Alfred Jarry, Charles Darwin, and Charles Péguy. On one level, this data about intellectual history serves to enlarge the novel's context, reminding the reader that life does not simply take place at the level of the individual in the present moment, but rather unfolds amid an accumulation of vaster social, economic, scientific, historic, and artistic trends. But at the same time, Powers links his narrative excursions throughout the novel to quantum physics' recognition that "there is no understanding a system without interfering with it."[41] Developing this parallel between the arts and the sciences, Powers asks the reader not to simply observe the writer's knowledge, but to return to the world armed with greater understanding, ready to interfere in these larger impersonal systems. This imperative is encapsulated by the novel's first-person narrator, who recognizes that he must make use of the knowledge embedded in the novel "to continue the daily routine of invention and observation, to dirty my hands in whatever work my hands can do."[42] In this way, Powers's novel is not simply a structure that (in Franzen's phrase) is designed "to capture and efficiently store data" but is rather a kind of guidebook, preparing the reader to make use of the data shaping her life.

• • •

Like Powers, David Foster Wallace has been both praised and condemned for writing learned fiction that (especially in his masterful novel about addiction, *Infinite Jest* [1996]) unfolds on an epic scale, and Wallace has been equally forthcoming about his debt to Gaddis. In 1997, Wallace praised Gaddis for exposing hypocrisy in the world of "abstract capital,"[43] and Steven Moore has traced a pattern of allusions to Gaddis's work that Wallace has embedded in *Infinite Jest*.[44]

Composed of 1079 dense pages, packed with allusions that range from Descartes to DeLillo, the encyclopedic project of *Infinite Jest*, with its detailed "data-retrieval,"[45] overlaps significantly with the model used by Gaddis and Powers. Like Gaddis's novels, in particular, the fundamental process of Wallace's book is to seek exhaustive accounts and to accumulate information, but most of these efforts (like one character's attempt to list everything blue in the headmaster's waiting room)[46] prove empty and futile exercises. The limitations of data collection are at the forefront of the novel in a narrative devoted to Hal Incandenza, a teenage prodigy who has memorized the *Oxford English Dictionary*. But while Hal's story is pertinent, here, it resists curt summary,[47] and Wallace's approach to data can be summarized equally well by surveying some of the novel's minor characters. Of particular importance is the stepfather of Don Gately (a recovering alcoholic, who shares the novel's spotlight with Hal), and the father of Hugh Steeply (a political agent). Both of these characters are obsessed with "Data Analysis."[48] Gately's stepfather, for example, is a violent alcoholic, who balances his emotional disorder by precisely recording every drink he has in his notebook. He is, Wallace explains, "the sort of person who equated incredibly careful record-keeping with control."[49] The cruelty of Steeply's father is more emotional; he withdraws from his family so that he can catalogue insane details from syndicated reruns of *M*A*S*H*. As he is gradually consumed by this obsession, he increasingly gives his time to the "scrupulous recording of tiny details, in careful order,"[50] and developing "baroque systems of cross-reference."[51] Whether physically or emotionally, both are destructive characters, and it is, of course, not coincidental that they are both addicts. Encyclopedic data storage is, for Wallace, just another of the many potentially dangerous addictions he explores, and he sets these characters against more positive examples, such as Hal's brother, Mario, and fitness guru, Lyle, who "take data pretty much as it comes."[52] They may seem to know less, but they are in many ways more alive than Wallace's other "data-entry drone[s]."[53]

• • •

For Gaddis, Powers, and Wallace, then, the novel is uniquely suited to both investigate the limitations of data collection and to represent the ways in which American life is crowded with facts. But it would be misleading, however, to take Franzen's 2002 rejection of Gaddis strictly at face value, and set him entirely in opposition to the large-scale novels of information discussed here. The novels of Powers, Wallace, and Franzen, are, in a sense, homologous forms—each emerging from the same engagement with major modernist and postmodernist writers to develop their own late-century shape — and Franzen's relationship to Gaddis is a good deal more complex than it might first appear. Not only do Franzen's early novels — in spite of his criticism of data collection — reveal a fascination with information that parallels Gaddis's, but *The Corrections* itself has a shadowy relationship to Gaddis's work that Franzen has not acknowledged.

In "Mr. Difficult," Franzen freely admits that he titled his third novel, *The Corrections* (2001), "partly in homage to" *The Recognitions*.[54] But while there are a few overlaps between the two novels — as is often noted, Chip's email address is "exprof@gaddisfly.com,"[55] while, nearer the beginning, Chip resembles Gaddis's money-obsessed writer Otto Pivner[56] — Franzen's ire is really reserved for Gaddis's later works. *A Frolic of His Own*, for example, is criticized for having "a very large child" as its central character: "the selfish, unreasonable, self–pitying, incapable, insatiable Oscar [...] a suffering artist who (ha ha!) happens to have little talent [....] His long play about the Civil War is obviously and unfunnily bad."[57] Yet in criticizing this central narrative situation, consciously or unconsciously, Franzen is (minus the Civil War reference) describing the kernel of his own novel. How else can Chip Lambert — a 39 year-old man who dresses (and acts) like a teenager — be described other than as a "very large child"? How else to describe his behavior, talents, and his sexual appetites other than as "selfish, unreasonable, self-pitying, incapable," and "insatiable"? The more these characters are compared, the more the parallels accumulate: both Chip and Oscar are simultaneously repulsed and seduced by American commerce. Both are estranged from their fathers, but move toward something of a reconciliation with fathers who die at the end of each novel. Both are writers and, indeed, both could be described as "a suffering artist who [...] happens to have little talent." Crucially, however, there is a significant overlap in the realization that both come to concerning their "literary" works' (which in each case, are largely written as self–vindications) relationship to the movies. As Chip scrambles toward an exit from Franzen's cartoonish Lithuania, he realizes suddenly why his self–indulgent screenplay has been such a failure: "All of a sudden he understood why nobody, including himself, had ever liked his screenplay: he'd written a thriller where he should have written a farce."[58] This epiphany marks one of the climaxes of Chip's story, but in allowing his character this recognition, Franzen is doing little more than rewriting Oscar's recognition of the limitations of *his* self–justifying script at the end of *Frolic*: "No, no I cast myself a hundred years too early didn't I, with those tragic heroics [...] when it was farce all the time."[59] The broad arc of Chip's story in *The Corrections*, then, significantly recasts Oscar Crease's story, which makes Franzen's attack on *Frolic* seem ripe for what *Infinite Jest* calls one of "Professor H. Bloom's turgid studies of artistic influenza."[60]

Beyond these notable overlaps, however, one of the clearest indications of the depths of Franzen's ambivalent relationship to Gaddis is that despite his criticisms he has, like his contemporaries, used own his early books to explore the limits of data collection. In *The Twenty-Seventh City* (1988), for example, Franzen mocks the cold certainty of data through the paratextual apparatus that frames his text. Franzen begins the book with an apparently helpful prefatory note explaining that "this story is set in a year somewhat like 1984." Although most contemporary reviews of the novel accepted the veracity of this date,[61] the information Franzen offers the reader is exactly a half-truth. In actual fact, the novel is evenly split between 1984 and 1985 (twelve of the novel's twenty-four chapters are devoted to each year), and with only a few exceptions the novel's action can be directly traced onto the calendars for those years.[62]

Franzen follows his prefatory note with more paratextual data to apparently aid the reader, this time presenting a map of St. Louis and vicinity. Although the map's clear lines seem to offer a neat grid on which the novel's action can be plotted, this is—again—misleading. In fact, the limitations of the map's quaint regionalism are sharply exposed by the very first sentence of chapter one, which announces Jammu's arrival from "Bombay, India."[63] As the novel progresses it becomes clear that Jammu is not the only important character whose movements take place beyond the boundaries of the map's neatly fenced-off territory. Luisa Probst has recently returned from Paris, Duane Thompson has come back from Munich, Asha Hammaker and Balwan Singh have traveled from India to St. Louis, and near the end of the book Devi Madan travels to Edinburgh and back. By contrast, many of the local charms that the map does pick out—a Shriner's Hospital in Ladue, a Junior League field in Brentwood—do not feature in the novel at all.

From the very beginning of this novel, then, Franzen toys with the reader's faith in received data by presenting her with layers of information that cannot be properly understood until the novel itself is over. And his fascination with data extends beyond this book. While writing his first novel, Franzen worked as a researcher in the Earth and Planetary Sciences department at Harvard, studying seismograms, "rejecting bad data and accepting good data."[64] The immediate result of this work was that Franzen appeared as co-author on twenty surveys of seismic activity,[65] but his interest in this work filtered into his second novel, *Strong Motion* (1992), whose narrative he thickened by including seismograms alongside mini-essays on seismology.

Beyond *Strong Motion*, Franzen seemed inclined to continue his explorations of the limits of data collection. An early draft of *The Corrections* entitled "How He Came to Be Nowhere" was based around Andy Aberant, a character who is evidently defined by his ambivalent relationship to information, since Franzen describes him as having "the breadth and depth of knowledge of a card catalog. He was full of data which often proved not very reliable."[66] But somewhere in the five-year gap between this draft and the final version of the novel Franzen excised him from the book, bestowing his fraudulently-won science fair trophy upon Chip Lambert.[67] With the removal of Andy Aberant went Franzen's engagement with the novel as an epistemological study of our engagement with data. His rejection of encyclopedic fictions culminated in a dogmatic essay about Gaddis that offers an oddly narrow account of what a novel should be. But Gaddis's demonstration of how the novel can interrogate and store data lives on in the work of writers, such as Wallace and Powers, as well as writers I have not mentioned, such as Zadie Smith, William T. Vollmann, and Evan Dara, who have broadened our understanding of what a novel may contain.

Chapter Notes

Introduction

1. Quoted in *Enron: The Smartest Guys in the Room*, dir. Alex Gibney, 1 hr. 50 min., Magnolia, 2005, DVD.
2. Ibid.
3. See the case of Jonathan Lebed, as documented on the Gaddis Annotations website at http://www.williamgaddis.org/jr/jlebedindex.shtm.
4. Quoted in Christopher Walker, "All in Order, Thanks," review of William Gaddis, *A Frolic of His Own, The Observer*, 27 February 1994: 18.
5. Zoltán Abádi-Nagy, "The Art of Fiction: An Interview with William Gaddis," *Paris Review* 105 (Winter 1987), 79–80.
6. Formerly Box 1a2, Folder 11. William Gaddis Papers, Washington University, St. Louis.
7. William Gaddis, *The Recognitions* (New York: Penguin Classics, 1992), 96; ellipses Gaddis's.
8. Steven Moore, *A Reader's Guide to William Gaddis's* The Recognitions (Lincoln: University of Nebraska Press, 1982).
9. J.R. Ackerley, *Hindoo Holiday*, quoted in Moore.
10. William Gaddis to John Napper. 27 January 1951. William Gaddis Papers. Harry Ransom Center. University of Texas, Austin.
11. John Johnston, *Carnival of Repetition: Gaddis's "The Recognitions" and Postmodern Theory* (Philadelphia: University of Pennsylvania Press, 1990), 195.
12. William H. Gass, personal interview with Crystal Alberts, November 2000.
13. William Gaddis to William H. Gass. 25 August 1980. William H. Gass Papers. Washington University, St. Louis.
14. William Gaddis, *The Recognitions* (New York: Penguin, 1993), 251.

Chapter 1

1. Most criticism of Gaddis's first novel, *The Recognitions*, is buried under a summary of it, which considering the fact that it is 956 pages long, something that scholars also compulsively mention, is almost understandable. In order to avoid this critical trap, the present study will provide only the briefest summary. For a complete synopsis of *The Recognitions*, see Steven Moore, *The Reader's Guide to the Recognitions* (Lincoln: University of Nebraska Press, 1982) also available at http://www.williamgaddis.org/recognitions/preface.shtml.
2. "Statement of Personal History." 24 June 1963. William Gaddis Papers. Washington University Special Collections Library (St. Louis, Missouri).
3. William Gaddis, *Agapē Agape* (New York: Viking, 2002), 2.
4. John Kuehl and Steven Moore, "An Interview with William Gaddis," *Review of Contemporary Fiction* 2.2 (Summer 1982): 4–6.
5. Ibid.
6. Interview with author, 6 September 2003.
7. William H. Gass, *Finding a Form* (Ithaca, NY: Cornell University Press, 1997), 35.
8. Raymond Williams, *The Long Revolution* (New York: Columbia University Press, 1961), 32.
9. Zoltán Abádi-Nagy, "The Art of Fiction: An Interview with William Gaddis," *Paris Review* 105 (Winter 1987), 57–58.
10. John Kuehl and Steven Moore's *In Recognition of William Gaddis* (Syracuse: Syracuse University Press, 1984) and Steven Moore's *William Gaddis* (Boston: Twayne, 1989) have been quite resourceful in spite of not being based on Gaddis's own archive. However, numerous other published criticisms on Gaddis contain biographical errors, such as Bernard Benstock, "On William Gaddis: In Recognition of James Joyce," *Wisconsin Studies in Contemporary Literature* 6 (Summer 1965): 177–89.
11. Given space constraints, this essay maps only select parts of Gaddis's movements in Spain and their corresponding appearances in *The Recognitions*. However, this method could be used to map the movements of William Gaddis and *The Recognitions* through Central America, Western Europe, Northern Africa, and New York City.
12. William Gaddis to John Napper. 12 April 1987. William Gaddis Papers. Harry Ransom Center, University of Texas, Austin.
13. William Gaddis to John Napper. 27 January 1951. William Gaddis Papers. Harry Ransom Center. University of Texas, Austin.

14. William Gaddis, *The Recognitions* (New York: Penguin, 1993), 89.

15. See for example, John Johnston, *Carnival of Repetition: Gaddis's "The Recognitions" and Postmodern Theory* (Philadelphia: University of Pennsylvania Press, 1990); Gregory Comnes, *The Ethics of Indeterminacy in the Novels of William Gaddis* (Gainesville: University Press of Florida, 1994); Joseph Tabbi and Rone Shavers, eds., *Paper Empire: William Gaddis and the World System* (Tuscaloosa: University of Alabama Press, 2007).

16. Johnston, 20.
17. *Ibid.*, 4.
18. *Ibid.*, 7.
19. *Ibid.*, 24.
20. *Ibid.*, 195, quoting Baudrillard.
21. *Ibid.*, 17, emphasis in original.
22. *Ibid.*, 107.
23. *Ibid.*, 109.
24. *Ibid.*, 169.

25. *Ibid.*, 170. Johnston's primary evidence for this contention is that Gaddis includes a monk named Eulalio, which Johnston declares "odd." After some impressive etymological and allusive gymnastics, Johnston concludes that the "representation function" is "more or less suspended [...] in the interest of self-reflexivity and textual play" (Johnston, 171–172). However, according to the William Gaddis Papers, while in Seville in 1949, Gaddis became friends with Eulalio Abril Morales. The friendship between Eulalio and Gaddis, as well as the correspondence from Eulalio in Spanish, has always piqued my interest. While paging through Gaddis's reading notes for *The Recognitions*, I stumbled upon these scrawled notes: "of the modern lower middle class Spaniard caught in the middle isolation from world, national pride, Catholicism, small money, food, His army position, his wife and children her mother's death, the 100 pesetas *What* incident?," with a single word heading the page, *Eulalio*. From these notes, Gaddis created Friar Eulalio, who "was in his twenties, a fact which he never allowed to interfere with those exercises of gravity so necessary to his profession, which was not so much being a monk, as being a Spaniard" (*The Recognitions*, 859). We are further told that "he had made that historic choice between church and state because, under present conditions, there were few other choices to be made." Moreover, choosing the priesthood "was certainly no question of fear, or bravery: a recent civil war had shown the cowl as dangerous costumery as the uniform" (*The Recognitions*, 859). Hence, with this brief introduction of Friar Eulalio, Gaddis managed to incorporate class, Catholicism, and national pride, as well as allude to Eulalio's actual profession, for, according to the manuscripts, he had been a brigadier in the Spanish army.

However, Gaddis, who in his own words was an "inveterate researcher," needed more than generalities to bring Friar Eulalio to life. Further investigation in the William Gaddis Papers revealed that the real Eulalio practiced "that primeval method of becoming friends: the exhibition and inspection of each other's worldly goods." This is also echoed in the first interaction between Friar Eulalio and the distinguished novelist in *The Recognitions*, "He had that primeval way of becoming friends, which was to go through the possessions of any new acquaintance, busy with comment on anything he recognized, questions for what he did not" (859). We are told Friar Eulalio is also extremely interested in the distinguished novelist's typewriter and that he has a large, private scrapbook that "the breathless owner turned the pages, slowly enough that each might be thoroughly perused. They were all pictures of typewriters" (*The Recognitions*, 860). At first glance, the description of such a scrapbook may seem odd, all the more so when one finds out it actually existed. For, found scrawled on another manuscript page is "E's collection in scrapbook of American portable typewriters." Moreover, Gaddis's notes reveal that just as when Friar Eulalio "gives everyone the feeling that they were in a crowded room" (*The Recognitions*, 880) when the real Eulalio leaves the room, "it is as though a crowd had left, after a party, when the guests tumble through the door, calling goodbye in seven languages, calling the elevator, calling each other fool, and lover: and then they are gone." Friar Eulalio and his real counterpart share many other characteristics from the spitting on the floor to concerns over American suits. There are many more similarities between the two Eulalios, which I will elaborate on at a later date.

26. Johnston, 170.
27. *Ibid.*, 181.

28. Allison Russell, *Crossing Boundaries: Postmodern Travel Literature* (New York: Palgrave, 2000), 25.

29. *Ibid.*, 32.
30. *Ibid.*, 28.
31. *Ibid.*, 28.
32. *Ibid.*, 31.
33. *Ibid.*, 29.
34. *Ibid.*, 34.
35. *Ibid.*, 34.
36. *Ibid.*, 40–41; 47.
37. *Ibid.*, 47.
38. *Ibid.*, 48.
39. *Ibid.*, 8.

40. As he explains on a page found within one of his notebooks, most likely written in the late 1950s or in the 1960s, "I don't theorise or work from a theory dont like othr ppls) [sic] exprmntlism dont object to label experimental but dont feel I'm experimenting: work till I'm as sure as I can be of what I'm doing." William Gaddis Papers. Washington University in St. Louis. (Unless otherwise noted, all manuscript references refer to the Washington University collection.)

41. Russell, 45, emphasis added.

42. While travel by airplane was possible from the United States to Europe in the 1950s, many, including Gaddis, traveled by ship.

43. For a description of Italy in 1947–48 through the eyes of another great American au-

thor, see Arthur Miller, *Timebends: A Life* (New York: Penguin, 1995), 156–176.
44. William Gaddis Papers.
45. The Gaddis working library does contain Francis Ambriere's *Blue's Les Guides France*; however, it was published in 1959, four years after the publication of *The Recognitions*.
46. Gaddis's movements in New York City and their significance for *The Recognitions* will be investigated elsewhere.
47. "Statement of Personal History"; Formerly Box 1a2 Folder 11, page marked 98. William Gaddis Papers.
48. After another trip to Paris, according to a passport stamp, Gaddis reentered Spain through Hendaye on July 21, 1950.
49. Gaddis's movements in France, Switzerland, Italy, Belgium, and England will be addressed in another essay.
50. William Gaddis to John Napper. 5 April 1951. William Gaddis Papers. Harry Ransom Center University of Texas, Austin.
51. Gaddis, *Recognitions*, 4. The assertion that the port of entry was Gibraltar is based on Gaddis's own port of entry as evidenced in his passport, as well as the later allusion to Gibraltar. The alternate option of Algeciras again is based on information found within Gaddis's passport, as well as the allusion in *The Recognitions* to the Spanish port of entry, which would be Algeciras.
52. *Ibid.*, 6.
53. *Ibid.*, 7.
54. Formerly Box 1a2, Folder 11. William Gaddis Papers.
55. In 1950, John Napper, an English artist, and his wife Pauline met William Gaddis while lying on a nearly deserted beach in Spain. In a letter written to me on September 16, 2003, Pauline Napper recounts "[the beach] wasn't quite deserted — about 25 [yards] away from us was a solitary figure, a man sitting surrounded by sheets of writing paper which kept shifting in the slight wind and which he was desperately trying to hold down." Some sheets blew in the Nappers' direction and when John helped to retrieve them, John "asked him if he was English and Willie replied rather abruptly 'No, I am American and I am working!'" A short while later, Gaddis came over to "apologize for his abruptness and suggested [they] meet for a drink later at a café by the harbour." This initial meeting would lead not only to an invitation to Gaddis to visit the Nappers in England a few months later, but also a lifetime friendship, as evidenced by the abundant correspondence found in the William Gaddis Papers.
On another trip to England, Gaddis again met up with the Nappers. As Pauline relates, "we were having a drink in a pub in Chelsea, I think the 6 or 8 Bels in the King's Road near Oakly Street. A friend of ours, an antique dealer, joined us and from his waistcoat pocket he brought out a pair of gold earrings. He told us how they were ancient — Byzantine. They were beautiful and I fell in love with them. He then said 'I will give them to you if you can wear them.' I wasn't sure what he meant but looking more closely I could see that the gold hoop was quite thick and of course with no modern fastening. I went off to the cloakroom and managed with a certain amount of agony, I had just recently had my ears pierced, to put the earrings on and returned triumphant. I still have the earrings and also a Greek pair similar to those illustrated in certain editions of *The Recognitions*."
This historical event, of course, appears in slightly altered form in the first chapter of *The Recognitions*: "And before they closed that casket for the last time, Gwyon had stopped them, to reach in and remove Camilla's earrings, heavy Byzantine hoops of gold which had contrasted the fine bones of her face all these last years of her life. In the first week of his marriage, a friend, an archaeologist whom he had not seen since, had shown them to Camilla, and noting the delicate pricks in her ears (done with needle and cork years before), said laughing, — you may have them if you can wear them..., not knowing Camilla, not knowing she would run from the room clutching the gold hoops, and surprised (though Gwyon was not) when she burst in again with wild luster in her eyes, wearing the gold earrings, blood all over them" (*The Recognitions*, 14).
56. Gaddis, *Recognitions*, 9.
57. According to Steven Moore, Abd-er-Rahman was the "sultan of Fez and Morocco (1822–59)" (*Reader's Guide*, 9.14).
58. *Ibid.*, 9.
59. *Ibid.*, 12–15.
60. *Ibid.*, 16.
61. *Ibid.*, 18.
62. *Ibid.*, 769.
63. *Ibid.*, 776.
64. *Ibid.*, 784. On his way to Italy, based on passport stamps, Gaddis passed through Switzerland.
65. *Ibid.*, 784–823.
66. *Ibid.*, 857.
67. *Ibid.*, 877.
68. *Ibid.*, 877, 898.
69. The use of the term "notebook" is deliberate. According to William H. Gass, "With the notebook we break out of chronology. Entries do not require dates. I can put anything in it I like, even other people's thoughts. The notebook is a workshop, a tabletop, a file [....] Henry James's *Notebooks* are the real thing: a place to plot novels, to ponder problems, to consider strategies and plan attacks. All three — diary, journal, notebook — are predicated on privacy. They are not meant to be read by anyone else, for here one is emotionally naked and in formal disarray" *Finding a Form*, 188.
70. Johnston, 24.
71. *Ibid.*, 17.
72. Formerly Box 1a2, Folder 10. William Gaddis Papers.
73. Christopher Knight, *Hints and Guesses: William Gaddis's Fiction of Longing* (Madison:

University of Wisconsin Press, 1997), 249, quoting Gaddis from an unpublished interview.

74. Raymond Williams, *The Long Revolution* (New York: Columbia University Press, 1961), 24–25.

75. Williams, 34.

76. T.S. Eliot, *The Four Quartets* (New York: Harcourt, Brace, 1943), 28.

77. Eileen Battersby, "The Elusive Interviewee," *The Irish Times* Literary Supplement, 30 June 1994: 9.

78. William Gaddis to Dr. J. Robert Oppenheimer. 4 January 1955. William Gaddis Papers.

79. Formerly Box 1a2, Folder 11. (24). William Gaddis Papers.

80. Formerly Box 1aZ, Folder 11. (48). William Gaddis Papers.

81. William Gaddis Papers.

82. Moore, *The Reader's Guide to The Recognitions*, 3.9.

83. In my longer project I will investigate how the basic allusions to other geographical locations mimic Gaddis's own methods—*The Recognitions* "find[s] the situation [...] not[es] it down [...] knowing that later [it] shall have the requisite actuality to fill out."

84. Gaddis, *Recognitions*, 16.

85. *Ibid.*, 776.

86. Formerly Box 1a2, Folder 10. "Real Monasterio de Guadalupe Estremadura March 49." William Gaddis Papers.

87. Gaddis, *Recognitions*, 16.

88. *Ibid.*, 776.

89. Formerly Box 1a2, Folder 10, page marked 55. William Graddis Papers.

90. Gaddis, *The Recognitions*, 96.

91. "Real Monasterio de Guadalupe Estremadura March 49." Formerly Box 1a2, Folder 10. William Gaddis Papers.

92. Padre J. most likely refers to Padre Julio who is referenced elsewhere in the manuscripts in relation to the monastery.

93. "Real Monasterio de Guadalupe Estremadura March 49." Formerly Box 1a2, Folder 10. William Gaddis Papers.

94. Gaddis, *Recognitions*, 857.

95. *Ibid.*, 9.

96. *Ibid.*, 10.

97. *Ibid.*, 11.

98. *Ibid.*, 11.

99. *Ibid.*, 12.

100. *Ibid.*, 856.

101. *Ibid.*, 856.

102. *Ibid.*, 857.

103. *Ibid.*, 857.

104. *Ibid.*, 888.

105. Paul Carter, *The Road to Botany Bay: An Exploration of Landscape and History* (New York: Knopf, 1988), xiv.

106. William Gaddis Papers.

107. *Ibid.*

108. Gaddis, *Recognitions*, 769.

Chapter 2

1. William Gaddis, *Carpenter's Gothic* (New York: Viking, 1985), 158.

2. *Ibid.*, 134–5.

3. *Ibid.*, 20.

4. *Ibid.*, 23.

5. *Ibid.*, 35.

6. *Ibid.*, 166.

7. *Ibid.*, 166–7.

8. *Ibid.*, 167.

9. *Ibid.*, 167.

10. *Ibid.*, 167.

11. H.L. Mencken, *The American Language* (New York: Knopf, 1947), 533.

12. Gaddis, *Carpenter's Gothic*, 134.

13. *Ibid.*, 135.

14. *Ibid.*, 135.

15. *Ibid.*, 136.

16. *Ibid.*, 229–230.

17. Douglas Bush, *English Literature in the Early Seventeenth Century* (London: Oxford University Press, 1945), 328.

18. E.P. Thompson, *Witness Against the Beast* (New York: New Press, 1993), 28

19. Gaddis, *Carpenter's Gothic*, 151.

20. *Ibid.*, 149.

21. *Ibid.*, 150.

Chapter 3

1. In an elaborate comedy of misrecognition, Otto actually winds up with a shipment of phony twenty-dollar bills given him by the counterfeiter, Frank Sinisterra. Rather than meeting his own father, Otto has unwittingly just dined with the father of his rival for the poet Esme's affections, the heroin dealer Chaby.

2. William Gaddis, *The Recognitions* (New York: Penguin, 1993), 523.

3. The almost universally accepted clearinghouse of sources for *The Recognitions* is housed at http://www.williamgaddis.org, a website maintained by Victoria Harding and largely based upon the tireless scholarship of Steven Moore. The current entry on this passage, to be found at http://www.williamgaddis.org/recognitions/25anno3.shtml, notes it as "unidentified." This chapter recognizes such a minor lacuna precisely because of my ceaseless consultation of this invaluable resource.

4. Gaddis, *Recognitions*, 829.

5. My source for this is Michael Williams, *The Shadow of the Pope* (New York: McGraw-Hill, 1932), 124. Because Anselm repeatedly appeals to a magazine, it is possible that Guy Fitch Phelps's publisher, The Rail Splitter Press, advertised this book elsewhere. Given Gaddis's fascination with religion, and particularly with intolerant fundamentalisms, it would not be altogether surprising if he consulted William's anti–Catholic history in the research preparing for his volume.

6. This essay will use the name William Gaddis and the idea of a collection of fictions and es-

says penned by the man also named William Gaddis interchangeably. Due to his extremely reclusive lifestyle until almost the end of his life, little biographically is known about the man William Gaddis. The available information is perhaps best left in the hands of those who knew him well, and those with a familiarity with his personal effects— scholars like Crystal Alberts, whose essay "Mapping William Gaddis: The Man, *The Recognitions*, and His Time" appears in this volume.

7. The *Oxford English Dictionary*, 2nd Online Edition, defines "aporia" as "a perplexing difficulty," but it is my contention that Gaddis is actually drawing from the Greek root *aporos*: that both suggests "to be at a loss" and "impassable." To this end, it may be helpful to think in terms of the opposite of "porous."

8. Stephen Schryer, "The Aesthetics of First- and Second-Order Cybernetics in William Gaddis's *J R*," *Paper Empire: William Gaddis and the World System*, eds. Rone Shavers and Joseph Tabbi (Tuscaloosa: University of Alabama Press, 2007), 79.

9. For the sake of clarity, although Oscar introduces historical artifacts into his play, it is only done to essentialize that experience to a Platonic mode, thereby eliding historical contingency in favor an enduring (if not perverse, as his own stance towards the law would indicate) ideal form of justice. So, even though he uses material from the historic record, this material is de-historicized.

10. Schryer, 77.

11. Schryer, 83.

12. "[S]econd-order observations, the observation of others' blind spots, cannot themselves stand out of the systems that they observe and thus do not promote objectivity; rather, they only produce more blind-spots in an endlessly recursive manner.... [T]his recursive model of observation describes the manner in which organisms cognitively construct their environments.... [S]econd-order cybernetics sets up a 'theatrical' model of scientific investigation, one that insists that the scientific object only takes on meaning in relation to a possible viewer." *Ibid.*, 84.

13. Though the narrative strategy of *The Recognitions* does not align as well with Schryer's reading as the later novels do, his claim about the art-work nevertheless holds. In attempting to copy his "palimpsests" to a final, perfect score while left alone in his cabin in a trans-Atlantic sea voyage, Stanley "made more mistakes than he ever had before [...] just this morning, writing in a throbbing bass which, as he realized when he stopped, was the steady vibration of the engines." Gaddis, *Recognitions*, 827.

14. Schryer, 87.

15. Norbert Wiener, *The Human Use of Human Beings: Cybernetics and Society* (1954; rpt., New York: Da Capo, 1988), 21. It would be wise to note here that Claude Shannon turned this notion of entropy and information on its head: this development is tracked wonderfully in N. Katherine Hayles's *Chaos Bound: Orderly Disorder in Contemporary Literature and Science* (Ithaca: Cornell University Press, 1990). As Joseph Conte pointed out to me in private correspondence, "Gaddis's big novels are ridiculously noisy with overheard, overlapping conversation. So his process seems to inculcate a theory of information rich because [of] complex, rather than redundant, messages." I agree this is an accurate reading, easily sustained by the text and worthy of further consideration. Indeed, these novels support competing notions of entropy. As Hayles argues, "It makes no sense to ask what entropy 'is,' as though it were possible to find in this protean signifier a transcendent signification. Instead we must ask what it meant to whom, for what reasons, in what context, and with what consequences" (38). Therefore, it is also imperative to consult the sources from which Gaddis draws, despite advancements in those fields. After all, the claim here is that tracking such sources is a part of the process of understanding his project. That science would come into dispute with itself is only further evidence to a claim that Gaddis's artistic process forges productive impasses, and encourages rather than resolves aporias.

16. Gaddis, *Recognitions*, 870.

17. See Wyatt's continued explanation, *Ibid.*, 874–875.

18. William Gaddis, *Agapē Agape* (New York: Penguin, 2002), 1.

19. *Ibid.*, 1–2.

20. *Ibid.*, 13.

21. *Ibid.*, 6. Emphasis added.

22. Sven Birkerts, "Introduction," William Gaddis, *Agapē Agape* (New York: Penguin Classics, 2002), xvii.

23. Gaddis, *Agapē Agape*, 6.

24. Joseph Tabbi, "Introduction," William Gaddis, *The Rush for Second Place*, ed. Joseph Tabbi (New York: Penguin Books, 2002), vii– xvii.

25. William Gaddis, *A Frolic of His Own* (New York: Scribner, 1994), 32.

26. Because Gaddis believes the institution of the private collection (which he identifies as a creation of the Roman Empire) has done so much damage to art, I contend, it is important that his solution to the impasse of artistic interpretation return to the Greek world.

27. Tabbi, x.

28. See *Agapē Agape*, 13–14: "Here's a German ad 1926 holding the line for the class act against here they come, here they come, 'a still larger class of people who cannot successfully operate the usual type of player, because they lack a true sense of musical values. They have no "ear for music," and for that reason they play atrociously upon pianos equipped with even high grade player actions' talking about the class act? about defending these elitist music lovers? Not here no, talking about what we're talking about. Sales! 'Hence, too often, potential sales in a neighborhood are killed by someone unable to do justice to the possibilities of the player-piano he has purchased. To reach the enormous markets of the non-musical and half-

musical and to conquer the growing prejudice of the truly musical' what are we going to do, educate this pleasure seeking rabble? There's Plato again agreeing that the excellence of music is measured by pleasure, but for this gang out there playing You're a Dog-gone Daisy Girl with its feet? Good God no, for them Plato rhymes with tomato, it can't be the pleasure of chance persons, he says, it's got to be music that delights the best educated or you get your poets composing to please the bad taste of their judges and finally the audience instructing each other and that's what this glorious democracy's all about, isn't it?" A common theme in Gaddis is one that indicates the danger of the extreme commodification of the artifact: if art is produced to be sold, it will inevitably aim to the lowest common denominator. See also *The Recognitions*, on 179, 243 and again on 356, Gaddis raises the specter of a potential "review board" or "assembly line" to produce novels, where the content and form is developed to match the highest number of representatives of the public taste.

29. Birkerts, xv.
30. Gaddis, *The Rush for Second Place*, 48–49.
31. Gaddis, *Recognitions*, 356.
32. Gaddis, *Frolic*, 248.
33. Birkerts, xii.
34. See Genesis 11:1–9.
35. Gaddis, *Frolic*, 297.
36. By conflating history, the language of history, and the historian himself, Gaddis is arguably mounting a critique on the production of history as a narrativized act. In this instance, to read the language given in this description in an either/or manner, to say that it either refers to Oscar or Grant, but not both, is to impose an understanding on the material that limits the possibilities of understanding that are created. In this way, Gaddis confuses the tongues of the historical and the fictive to both level a criticism and suggest possibilities for a type of historical construction that allows for the types of interpretive maneuvering that totalizing historical accounts prevent.
37. See Thomas Pynchon, *The Crying of Lot 49* (1966, New York: Perennial Classics, 1999), 68: "'Sorting isn't work?' Oedipa said. 'Tell them down at the post office, you'll find yourself in a mailbag headed for Fairbanks, Alaska without even a FRAGILE sticker going for you.'"
38. Jonathan Raban, "At Home in Babel," *New York Review of Books*, Vol. XLI, No. 4 (17 February 1994): 3–4, 6.
39. Gaddis, *Recognitions*, 299.
40. Gaddis, *Frolic*, 28.
41. *Ibid.*, 33.
42. *Ibid.*, 373: "You understand that this is a civil and not a criminal case. In other words, it is a suit brought by one private citizen against another, and the fact that a death is involved does not mean that the defendant, if found guilty, would be subject to criminal penalties leading to his imprisonment or worse, but limited to the payment of money damages to the plaintiff."
43. *Ibid.*, 260–261.
44. *Ibid.*
45. According to Marx, capital is itself an expression of a system of relations between men, in much the same way that law and language are, though capitalism seeks to ignore this fact.
46. Gaddis, *Frolic*, 320.
47. Gaddis, *Recognitions*, 290–291.
48. This, and the rest of the exchange reproduced, is taken from William Gaddis, *J R* (1975; rpt. New York: Penguin, 1993), 655–658.

Chapter 4

1. Robert Frost, "Education by Poetry," in *Frost: Collected Poems, Prose, & Plays* (New York: Library of America, 1995), 719–720.
2. W. H. Auden, *Lectures on Shakespeare*, ed. Arthur Kirsch (Princeton: Princeton University Press, 2000), 162.
3. A. D. Nuttall, *Shakespeare the Thinker* (New Haven: Yale University Press, 2007), 1.
4. William Gaddis, *The Rush for Second Place: Essays and Occasional Writings*, ed. and introd. Joseph Tabbi (New York: Penguin, 2002).
5. Tobias Wolff, *Old School* (New York: Alfred A. Knopf, 2004), 118.
6. Quoted in Paul J. Contino, "This Writer's Life: Irony & Faith in the Work of Tobias Wolff," *Commonweal* (21 October 2005), 18.
7. *Ibid.*, 18.
8. Paul Ricoeur, responding to Jesus's statement that "[w]hoever loses their life for my sake will find it," writes,

> In many parts of the world, men and women do actually lose their lives because they are not ashamed of Jesus or of his words in front of other human beings. But what are we to make of this saying in a pluralistic society where persecution is no longer practiced? In such a society as our own, being ashamed of Jesus and his words takes on the more subtle forms of abstention and silence. I admit that the answer to the question of Christian witness in a liberal society is an extremely difficult one to formulate. Most of us, myself included, feel repugnance when confronted with the advertising-like quality much Christian witnessing has taken on in the media. Between the arrogance, the indiscretion, and the vulgarity of such testimony, on the one hand, and the flight into polite and prudent silence in the name of the private character of belief and respect for others, on the other, the most honest and courageous form of testimony, where it is needed and required

by both the situation and our fellow human beings, is neither easy to discover nor to formulate. On both the individual and the communal planes, the question remains open what such honest and courageous testimony would look like in a liberal society (*Figuring the Sacred: Religion, Narrative, and Imagination*, ed. Mark I. Wallace, trans. David Pellauer [Minneapolis: Fortress, 1995], 286–87).

9. *The Norton Shakespeare: Tragedies*, edited by Stephen Greenblatt et al. (New York: Norton, 1997), Act I, scene 2, line 76.

10. Quoted in Charles McGrath. "Word Freaks," *New York Times Magazine* (19 November 2006), 63.

11. Christine Atkins, "Paul Muldoon," New York Writers Institute's *Writers Online*, http://www.albany.edu/writersinst/webpages4/archives/olv2n2.html. Accessed 24 January 2009.

12. T. S. Eliot, *Selected Prose*, ed. and introd. Frank Kermode (San Diego: Harcourt Brace Jovanovich, 1975), 65.

13. William Gaddis, *The Recognitions*, (New York: Penguin, 1993), 113.

14. Samuel Taylor Coleridge, *Biographia Literaria* (London: J. M. Dent & Sons, 1975), 169.

15. William Gaddis, "The New York State Writers Institute Tapes," ed. Christopher J. Knight, *Contemporary Literature*, 42.4 (2001), 669.

16. William Gaddis, *Agapē Agape*, afterword Joseph Tabbi (New York: Viking, 2002).

17. Christopher J. Knight, "William Gaddis's Parthian Shot: Social Criticism in the Posthumous *Agapē Agape* and *The Rush for Second Place*," *Critique: Studies in Contemporary Fiction* 49.2 (2008): 207.

18. Gaddis, *Agapē Agape*, 90–91.

19. Coleridge, 169.

20. Joseph Conrad, Preface to *The Nigger of the Narcissus* (Garden City, NY: Doubleday, 1914), 14.

21. William Gaddis, *J R* (New York: Penguin, 1993), 658.

22. Quoted in Ihab Hassan, *The Postmodern Turn* (Columbus: Ohio State University Press, 1987), 207–8. Italics added.

23. Quoted in Jacques Barzun, *The Use and Abuse of Art* (Princeton: Princeton University Press, 1974), 92.

24. Gaddis, *Recognitions*, 143.

25. Quoted in Geoffrey Hartman, *Minor Prophecies: The Literary Essay in the Culture Wars* (Cambridge: Harvard University Press, 1991), 144.

26. Tom LeClair, "An Interview with William Gaddis, circa 1980," *Paper Empire: William Gaddis and the World System*, eds. Joseph Tabbi and Rone Shavers (Tuscaloosa: University of Alabama Press, 2007), 19.

27. *Ibid.*, 26.

28. Eileen Battersby, "The Elusive Interviewee [William Gaddis]," *The Irish Times* (30 June 1994), 9.

29. Giles Gunn, *The Culture of Criticism and The Criticism of Culture* (Oxford: Oxford University Press, 1987), 180.

30. LeClair, 20; 21.

31. *Ibid.*, 21.

32. Cf. T. S. Eliot: "Indeed, in much romantic poetry the sadness is due to the exploitation of the fact that no human relations are adequate to human desires, but also to the disbelief in any further object for human desires than that which, being human, fails to satisfy them." *Selected Essays: 1917–1932* (London: Faber and Faber, 1932), 376.

33. George Steiner, *Real Presences: Is There Anything in What We Say?* (London: Faber and Faber, 1989), 218.

34. Edward Rothstein, "Classical Music Imperiled: Can You Hear the Shrug?" *The New York Times* (2 July 2007 [national ed.]), B1+.

35. Gaddis, *J R*, 287.

36. *Ibid.*, 658–59.

37. Rothstein, B1.

38. W.H. Auden, *In Memoriam A.H.H.*, 96, 11–12.

39. Eliot, *Selected Prose*, 278.

40. William Gaddis, *Carpenter's Gothic* (New York: Viking Penguin, 1985), 155.

41. T. S. Eliot, *Four Quartets* (San Diego: Harcourt Brace Jovanovich, 1971), ll. 186–88.

42. Gaddis, *Recognitions*, 160.

43. Eliot, *Four Quartets*, ll. 1–5.

44. LeClair, 19–20.

45. Marie-Rose Logan and Tomasz Mirkowicz, "Interview with William Gaddis," *Literatura na Swiece* (Warsaw), no. 1: 150 (1984), 178–89. Unpublished, unpaginated translation provided by Julita Wroniak.

46. LeClair, 18.

47. T. S. Eliot, *The Varieties of Metaphysical Poetry*, ed. and introd. Ronald Schuchard (New York: Harcourt Brace, 1993), 219.

48. T. S. Eliot, *The Letters of T. S. Eliot, Vol. 1: 1898–1922*, ed. Valerie Eliot (New York: Harcourt Brace Jovanovich, 1988), 84.

49. Quoted in Lyndall Gordon. *T. S. Eliot: An Imperfect Life* (New York: W. W. Norton, 1998), 189.

50. Henry Adams, *The Education of Henry Adams* (New York: Penguin, 1995), 276.

51. Joseph Tabbi, "Introduction," *Paper Empire: William Gaddis and the World System*, 9–10.

52. Gregory Comnes, *The Ethics of Indeterminacy in the Novels of William Gaddis* (Gainesville: University Press of Florida, 1994), 2.

53. Quoted in Gordon, 253.

54. Lloyd Grove, "Gaddis and the Cosmic Babble," interview with William Gaddis, *Washington Post* (23 August 1985), B 10.

55. Quoted in Gordon, 253.

56. Quoted in Grove, B 10.

57. Henry James, *The Bostonians* (New York: Penguin, 1984), 35.

58. Eliot, *Selected Prose*, 287.

59. Ralph Waldo Emerson, *Selected Essays* (New York: Penguin, 1982), 113.

60. William James, *The Varieties of Religious Experience* (New York: Penguin, 1982), 337–38.
61. Andrew Shranks, *Faith in Honesty: The Essential Nature of Theology* (Aldershot, UK: Ashgate, 2005), 125.
62. Quoted in *The Oxford Companion to English Literature*, 5th ed., ed. Margaret Drabble (Oxford: Oxford University Press, 1985), 536.
63. "He said to them, 'Then render to Caesar the things that are Caesar's, and to God the things that are God's.' And they were not able in the presence of the people to catch him by what he said; but marveling at his answer they were silent." Luke 20: 25–26.
64. William Gaddis, "Old Foes with New Faces," *The Rush for Second Place: Essays and Occasional Writings*, ed. and introd. Joseph Tabbi. (New York: Penguin, 2002), 88–89.
65. *Ibid.*, 93–94.
66. *Ibid.*, 89.
67. *Ibid.*, 96.
68. *Ibid.*, 101.
69. *The Winter's Tale* IV, iv, 573–75.
70. Quoted in Steven Moore, *A Reader's Guide to William Gaddis's The Recognitions* (Lincoln: University of Nebraska Press, 1982), 298–99.
71. Ricoeur, 292. Cf. T. S. Eliot: "One can conceive of blasphemy as doing moral harm to feeble or perverse souls; at the same time one must recognize that the modern environment is so unfavorable to faith that it produces fewer and fewer individuals capable of being injured by blasphemy. One would expect, therefore, that (whatever it may have been at other times) blasphemy would be less employed by the Forces of Evil than at any other time in the last two thousand years. Where blasphemy might once have been a sign of spiritual corruption, it might now be taken as a symptom that the soul is still alive, or even that it is recovering animation: for the perception of Good and Evil — whatever choice we make — is the first requisite of spiritual life. We should do well, therefore, to look elsewhere than to the blasphemer, in the traditional sense, for the most fruitful operations of the Evil Spirit today." *After Strange Gods* (New York: Harcourt, Brace, 1934), 52–53.
72. Gaddis, "Old Foes," 89.
73. *Ibid.*, 107.
74. *Ibid.*, 89.
75. Paul: "Now faith is the assurance of things hoped for, the conviction of things not seen." Hebrews 11: 1.
76. Ricoeur, 43. Cf. Denis Donoghue: "Stendhal said that beauty 'is only the promise of happiness.' It is not even so much; but it is a figure of happiness, not a promise but a hint of possibility. The criterion is elaborated in [Ernst Bloch's] *The Principle of Hope*, where beauty and even sublimity represent an existence for objects 'which has not yet become'; a 'thoroughly formed world, without external chance; without the inessential, the unrendered.' At any moment there is by definition no such place, it depends for its realization on the combined forces of desire, hope, and imagination." *Speaking of Beauty* (New Haven: Yale University Press, 2003), 86–87.
77. Shanks, 159–60.
78. *Ibid.*, 160.
79. Ricoeur, 223.
80. Gaddis, "Old Foes," 99.
81. *Ibid.*, 91. Cf. Jacques Derrida: "Between the fragments of the broken Tables the poem grows and the right to speech takes root[....] The necessity of commentary, like poetic necessity, is the very form of exiled speech. In the beginning is hermeneutics. But the *shared* necessity of exegesis, the interpretive imperative, is interpreted differently by the rabbi and the poet. The difference between the horizon of the original text and exegetic writing makes the difference between the rabbi and the poet irreducible. Forever unable to reunite with each other, yet so close to each other, how could they ever regain the *realm*? The original opening of interpretation essentially signifies that there will always be rabbis and poets. And two interpretations of interpretation." *Writing and Difference*, trans. Alan Bass (Chicago: University of Chicago Press, 1978), 67.
82. *Ibid.*, 91–92.
83. *Ibid.*, 98–99.
84. Quoted in Gabriel Josipovici, *The Singer on the Shore: Essays 1991–2004* (Manchester, UK: Carcanet, 2006), 131.
85. Gaddis, "Old Foes," 91.
86. *Ibid.*, 91.
87. Cf. the exchange between Basil Valentine and Wyatt Gwyon in *The Recognitions* on 261:
— In a manner of speaking. You have something of the priest in you yourself, you know.
— Damned little.
— Far more of that than the renegade painter.
— Are they so ... separate then?
— My dear fellow, the priest is the guardian of mysteries. The artist is driven to expose them.
— A fatal likeness, then.
— A fatal dissension, and a fatal attraction.
88. Gaddis, *Recognitions*, 152.
89. Mark 4: 11–12.
90. Iris Murdoch, *Metaphysics as a Guide to Morals* (New York: Allen Lane, 1993), 87.
91. Gaddis, "Old Foes," 107–8.
92. Gaddis, *Recognitions*, 119.
93. Hans-Georg Gadamer, *Dialogue and Dialectic: Eight Hermeneutical Studies on Plato*, trans. and introd. P. Christopher Smith (New Haven: Yale University Press, 1980), 117.
94. Gunn, 186.
95. Zoltán Abádi-Nagy, "The Art of Fiction: An Interview with William Gaddis," *Paris Review* 105 (Winter 1987), 56–89. Gaddis is alluding to the following passage, spoken by Wyatt to Esther, in *The Recognitions*: "What is it they want from a man that they didn't get from his work? What do they expect? What is there left out of him when he's done his work? What's any artist, but the dregs of his work? the human shambles

that follows it around. What's left of the man when the work's done but a shambles of apology," 95–96.

96. Eliot, *The Varieties of Metaphysical Poetry*, 60.

97. Gadamer writes, "In an early Freiburg lecture[....] Heidegger spoke of a 'haziness' of life instead of the principle of clear and distinct *perceptio* of the *ego cogito*. That this life is hazy does not mean so much that the little ship of life cannot see a clear and free horizon around itself. Haziness does not simply mean the clouding of one's vision; rather, it describes the basic constitution of life as such, the very movement of life itself. It shrouds itself in fog. Here lies the inner tension, the internal struggle [*Gegenwendigkeit*] that Nietzsche had pointed out: Not only to strive toward clarity and to know, but also to conceal in darkness and to forget. When Heidegger named the basic experience of the Greeks' *aletheia*, unconcealness, he did not simply mean that truth was constantly in danger of receding back into darkness, that efforts at conceptualization must involve efforts to keep truth from receding back, and that even this receding back must be thought as an event of truth." *Heidegger's Ways*, trans. John W. Stanley, introd. Dennis J. Schmidt (Albany: State University of New York, 1994), 63.

98. Wallace Stevens, *Letters of Wallace Stevens*, ed. Holly Stevens, foreword Richard Howard (Berkeley: University of California Press, 1996), 863.

99. Gaddis, *Recognitions*, 590.

100. William H. Gass, *Habitations of the Word* (New York: Simon and Schuster, 1985), 21.

101. Søren Kierkegaard, *The Sickness Unto Death: A Christian Psychological Exposition for Upbuilding and Awakening*, ed. and trans. Howard V. Hong and Edna H. Hong (Princeton: Princeton University Press, 1983), 95.

102. Quoted in Ronald Schuchard, *Eliot's Dark Angel: Intersections of Life and Art* (Oxford: Oxford University Press, 1999), xv.

103. LeClair, 26.

104. *Ibid.*, 21.

105. Gaddis, *Recognitions*, 589.

106. *Ibid.*, 589.

107. Gaddis, *Agapē Agape*, 95–96.

Chapter 5

1. Jonathan Franzen, "Mr. Difficult: William Gaddis and the Problem of Hard-to-Read Books," *The New Yorker*, 30 September 2002, 102.

2. *Ibid.*

3. William Gaddis, *The Recognitions* (New York: Penguin, 1993), 251.

4. I refer explicitly to the tripartite division of the novel. Ted Morrissey, following Brian Stonehill, makes this clear: "Stonehill points out, and I believe rightly so, that the novel resembles a Renaissance triptych, where 'the central panel is twice the width of its wings'; and, moreover, the two sides 'mirror each other in details large and small [...]' (130). In the 1993 Penguin edition, the central section, with 439 pages, is roughly twice as long as the first and third sections, 274 and 233 pages, respectively." See Morrissey, "Recognizing a Masterpiece: William Gaddis's Reinterpretation of Flemish Art" (http://www.williamgaddis.org/critinterpessays/morrisseyrecsart.shtml, accessed 17 September 2009). Also Stonehill, "Plagiarizing *The Recognitions*," *The Self-Conscious Novel: Artifice in Fiction from Joyce to Pynchon* (Philadelphia: University of Pennsylvania Press, 1988), 114–40.

5. Peter Wolfe, *A Vision of His Own: The Mind and Art of William Gaddis* (Cranbury, NJ: Associated University Presses, 1997), 15.

6. *Ibid.*, 50–1.

7. John Johnston, *Carnival of Repetition: Gaddis's The Recognitions and Postmodern Theory* (Philadelphia: University of Pennsylvania Press, 1990), 1.

8. *Ibid.*, 3.

9. *Ibid.*, 4; 3.

10. *Ibid.*, 5.

11. Steven Moore, *A Reader's Guide to The Recognitions* (Lincoln: University of Nebraska Press, 1982), 4.

12. *Ibid.*, 7.

13. *Ibid.*, 10.

14. *Ibid.*, 4.

15. Gregory Comnes, *The Ethics of Indeterminacy in the Novels of William Gaddis* (Gainesville: University Press of Florida, 1994), 10.

16. Johnson, *Carnival*, 3.

17. *Ibid.*, 2.

18. Comnes, *Indeterminacy*, 15.

19. *Ibid.*, 9.

20. Moore, *Guide*, 5.

21. Gaddis, *The Recognitions*, 205.

22. Ernest Hemingway, *A Farewell to Arms* (New York: Scribner, 2003), 303.

23. M.H. Abrams, *The Mirror and the Lamp: Romantic Theory and the Critical Tradition* (Oxford: Oxford University Press, 1953). While Abrams holds up the romantic tradition as a critic of the new science prophesized by Bacon, practiced by Newton, and celebrated by Pope, *The Recognitions*, with its deep suspicion of originality or romantic genius, critiques Romanticism as one more gesture toward an utter atomization of Western thought, culture, and history. Thus Gaddis, whose contempt for empirical methodology is well documented in the novel, finds comfort in neither mirror nor lamp. But rather than "choose a side," as in this historical moment academic literary study was divided into the "conservative" camp of New Critical classicism (i.e., Cleanth Brooks and John Crowe Ransom) and the "radical" theorists of romanticism (i.e., Abrams and Northrop Frye), Gaddis sustains the dialectical energy generated by their oppositional tendencies.

24. Viktor Shklovsky, *Theory of Prose*, trans. Benjamin Sher (Normal, IL: Dalkey Archive Press, 1991), 5. A grouping of Shklovsky and Gaddis serves another purpose. Shklovsky's prose tradition roots itself in the work of Cervantes and Sterne. Placing Gaddis into this tradition hopes to restore an appreciation for the humor in *The Recognitions*, as well as its satirical intentions. Wyatt's dedication to the old Masters is "noble" in the way Don Quixote's dedication to the books of knight-errantry is "noble." Let us not forget that both are madmen. Also, *The Recognitions* begins as a *bildungsroman*, becomes a Faustian allegory, gets lost in hundreds of pages of disembodied conversation, and concludes with the dispassionate recounting of an operatic death scene for a character that is fairly marginal to what we might call "plot considerations." One might fruitfully imagine the narrator as a descendent of Tristram Shandy, albeit one with a guilt-wracked, Calvinist conscience.

25. *Ibid.*, 5.
26. *Ibid.*, 6.
27. Gaddis, *Recognitions*, 202.
28. *Ibid.*, 203.
29. Roland Barthes, "The Death of the Author," *Image/Music/Text*, ed. and trans. Stephen Heath (New York: Hill and Wang, 1977), 146.
30. Alexander Pope, "Essay on Man," *Essay on Man and Other Poems*, ed. Stanley Applebaum (Mineola, NY: Dover, 1994), 46.
31. *Ibid.*, 47.
32. T.S. Eliot, "Little Gidding," *The Four Quartets* (New York: Harcourt Brace Jonavich, 1943), 15.
33. Ovid, *The Metamorphoses*, trans. Horace Gregory (New York: Viking, 1958), 1. The line comes from Ovid's invocation to the muses.
34. Pope, "Man," 48.
35. Eliot, "Gidding," 16.
36. *Ibid*.
37. Pope, "Man," 48.
38. Gaddis, *Recognitions*, 203.
39. Pope, "Man," 48.
40. Thanks for the permission to quote from the William Gaddis Papers from the Special Collections Library at Washington University in St. Louis.
41. Erwin Panofsky, *Perspective as Symbolic Form*, trans. Christopher S. Wood (New York: Zone, 1991), 41.
42. *Ibid.*, 72.
43. *Ibid.*, 66.
44. Leon Battista Alberti, *On Painting*, trans. John R. Spencer (New Haven: Yale University Press, 1970). On perspective as a window art: "When [painters] fill the circumscribed places with colours, they should only seek to present the forms of things seen on this plane as if it were of transparent glass" (29). On the number of figures proper to a painting: "In my judgment no picture will be filled with so great a variety of things that nine or ten men are not able to act with dignity. I think pertinent to this the statement of Varo who admitted no more than nine guests to a banquet in order to avoid confusion" (54). One need think only of one of the Village party scenes to see how Gaddis discards Alberti's advice.
45. Barthes, "Death," 147.
46. Gaddis, *Recognitions*, 202.
47. *Ibid.*, 203
48. *Ibid.*, 203
49. Erwin Panofsky, "Style and Medium in the Motion Pictures," *Critique* 1, no. 3, January-February 1947.
50. Andre Bazin, "Ontology of the Photographic Image," trans. Hugh Gray, *Film Theory and Criticism: Introductory Readings*, eds. Leo Braudy and Marshall Cohen, 5th ed. (New York: Oxford University Press, 1999), 195.
51. Walter Benjamin, "The Work of Art in the Age of Mechanical Reproduction," trans. Harry Zohn, *Illuminations*, ed. Hanna Arendt (New York: Shocken, 1968), 236.
52. *Ibid.*, 240–1.
53. Gaddis, *Recognitions*, 205.
54. Benjamin, 242.
55. Gaddis, *Recognitions*, 205–206
56. *Ibid.*, 221.
57. *Ibid.*, 202.
58. *Ibid.*, 250.
59. *Ibid.*, 204.
60. *Ibid.*, 211.
61. *Ibid.*, 213.
62. *Ibid.*, 243.
63. This would require, of course, that critics use someone other than Wyatt as their point of interpretive departure. Franzen, to his credit, reads Gaddis through Otto rather than Wyatt, thus deromanticizing the Gaddis-hero myth, even as he goes some way toward romanticizing a new Gaddis-failed-hero myth. Also, I would add, Esme provides a persistent deflation of Wyatt's values (it is he that she imagines trapped in a mirror). A feminist reading of *The Recognitions* that makes Esme its focus might provide a much needed counterweight to the "masculine protest" and "White Goddess" readings typical of Wyatt-based earlier studies (Comnes and Johnston are welcome exceptions here).
64. Gaddis, *Recognitions*, 335.
65. Gaddis, "First Notes for a Television Program on Forgery," in the Keith Botsford Papers, 3, Beinecke Library, Yale University. Though undated, the notes were compiled sometime in 1957.

Chapter 6

1. Herman Melville, *The Confidence-Man: His Masquerade* (New York: Norton, 2006), 187.
2. William Gaddis, *The Recognitions* (New York: Penguin, 1993), ii. The Latin phrase can be translated as "Nothing that is with God is devoid of meaning."
3. Quoted in Christopher Walker, review of *A Frolic of His Own* by William Gaddis, *The Observer*, 27 February 1994, 18.

4. William Gaddis, interview by Zoltán Abádi-Nagy, *Paris Review* 105 (Winter 1987), 79–80. On October 23, 1994, Gaddis was a guest speaker (together with J.M. Coetzee) at "The Writer and Religion" conference at Washington University in St. Louis (organized by his longtime friend and admirer William Gass), where he stated, with similar hindsight irony, that "[the Clementine Recognitions] was called the first Christian novel, and I, at the age of 25, would write the last" (sound cassette, William Gaddis Papers, Special Collections, Washington University). In addition, Gaddis also mentions the phrase "last Christian novel" in the interview with Eileen Battersby, *Irish Times Literary Supplement*, 30 June 1994, 9.

5. Gaddis, *Recognitions*, 373.

6. The *Clementine Recognitions* survives in a Latin Church translation whereas the Greek original has been lost.

7. The most recently published collection with essays on Gaddis, Rone Shavers and Joseph Tabbi's *Paper Empire: William Gaddis and the World System* (Tuscaloosa: University of Alabama Press, 2007), devotes an entire subsection of the book to systems theory and the cybernetic notion of "autopoiesis." Earlier essays that analyze Gaddis's fiction from a cybernetic point of view include Thomas LeClair's *The Art of Excess: Mastery in Contemporary American Fiction* (Urbana: University of Illinois Press, 1989) and Joseph Tabbi's "The Technology of Quotation: William Gaddis's *J R* and Contemporary Media," *Mosaic* 28, no. 4 (1995): 143–64.

8. On the parallels between Gaddis and Joyce, see, among others, Bernard Benstock, "On William Gaddis: In Recognition of James Joyce," *Wisconsin Studies in Contemporary Literature* 6 (Summer 1965): 177–189; and Stephen Burn, "The Collapse of Everything. William Gaddis and the Encyclopedic Novel," *Paper Empire* 45–4.

9. Joseph Tabbi, "Afterword," *Agapē Agape* (New York: Viking, 2002), 102.

10. Joseph Tabbi, paraphrased by Crystal Alberts, "Valuable Dregs: William Gaddis, the Life of an Artist," *Paper Empire: William Gaddis and the World System*, 253.

11. Gaddis, *Recognitions*, 478.

12. Frank Kermode, *The Sense of an Ending* (New York: Oxford University Press, 1967), 31.

13. One can think here of the research on the player piano that occupied Gaddis throughout his literary career, or the 84-volume *American Jurisprudence*, donated to him by the New York attorney Donald Oresman, which Gaddis duly consulted while at work on *A Frolic of His Own*.

14. William Gaddis, "Old Foes with New Faces," *The Rush For Second Place: Essays and Occasional Writings*, ed. Joseph Tabbi (New York: Penguin, 2002), 89.

15. Gaddis, *Recognitions*, 261.

16. Johan Huizinga, *Herfsttij der Middeleeuwen: Studie over Levens- en Gedachtevormen der Veertiende en Vijftiende Eeuw in Frankrijk en de Nederlanden* (Amsterdam: Olympos, 2006), 13. My translation.

17. As William Gass notes elsewhere in this volume, Gaddis's spelling remains largely "untouched by contemporary practice."

18. Johann Wolfgang Goethe, *Faust*, trans. Walter Kaufmann (New York: Anchor, 1961), 93.

19. Gaddis, *Recognitions*, 143.

20. Kermode, 18.

21. Personal letter to Steven Moore, quoted in Joseph Tabbi, "Afterword," *Agapē Agape*, 101.

22. William Gaddis, quoted (without reference) in Joseph Tabbi, "Introduction," in *The Rush for Second Place: Essays and Occasional Writings*, xv.

23. William Gaddis, *J R* (New York: Penguin, 1975), 530.

24. William Gaddis, *Carpenter's Gothic* (New York: Penguin, 1985), 190.

25. George Orwell, *1984* (New York: Signet Classic, 1977), 220.

26. William Gaddis, *A Frolic of His Own* (New York: Scribner, 1994), 36.

27. Given this quasi-unanimous praise for *Agapē Agape*, it is somewhat surprising that so much critical attention has focused on the one negative review by Jonathan Franzen.

28. Gaddis, *Agapē Agape*, 51.

29. *Ibid.*, 55.

30. *Ibid.*, 18.

31. Gaddis, *Recognitions*, 335.

32. Gaddis, *Agapē Agape*, 3.

33. Still the best introduction to this failed initial reception are the issues of Jack Green's proto-blog "newspaper," a one-man New York periodical that in 1962 devoted three issues to the media reception of *The Recognitions*, lambasting its national reviewers under the rather blatant title "Fire the Bastards!" The three issues of "newspaper" were later republished (against Green's own wish) in *Fire the Bastards!*, ed. and intro. Steven Moore (Normal, IL: Dalkey Archive Press, 1992).

34. Gaddis, *Recognitions*, 95.

35. See page 242.

36. Gaddis, *Agapē Agape*, 1.

37. *Ibid.*, 1; 45.

38. *Ibid.*, 7.

39. *Ibid.*, 45.

40. *Ibid.*, 8.

41. Paul de Man, *Blindness and Insight: Essays in the Rhetoric of Composition* (Minneapolis: University of Minnesota Press, 1983), 8.

42. *Ibid.*

43. The original title of the lecture was "Philosophy and the Crisis of European Humanity," which was later published under the slightly changed title "Philosophy in the Crisis of European Mankind."

44. Edmund Husserl, *The Crisis of European Sciences and Transcendental Phenomenology: An*

Introduction to Phenomenological Philosophy, trans. by David Carr (Evanston, IL: Northwestern University Press, 1970), 269. Hereafter cited as *Crisis*.
45. *Ibid.*, 283.
46. *Ibid.*, 276.
47. Gaddis, *Agapē Agape*, 96.
48. This inconsistency shows itself, for instance, in an infamous passage where Husserl argues that "[i]n the spiritual sense the English Dominions, the United States, etc., clearly belong to Europe, whereas the Eskimos or Indians presented as curiosities at fairs, or the Gypsies, who constantly wander about Europe, do not" (*Crisis* 273).
49. Gaddis, *Agapē Agape*, 50.
50. *Ibid.*, 59.
51. De Man, *Crisis*, 270.
52. Gaddis, *Agapē Agape*, 11.
53. *Ibid.*, 1.
54. Husserl, 277.
55. Birger Vanwesenbeeck, "Art and Community in William Gaddis's *The Recognitions*," *Mosaic* 42.3 (2009):141–156.
56. See, for instance, the interview with Zoltán Abádi-Nagy, 79–80.
57. William Gaddis Papers, Special Collections, Washington University.
58. *Ibid.*
59. The second quotation is actually taken from Joseph Conrad's preface to *The Nigger of the Narcissus*.
60. Although it is doubtful whether Gaddis actually read any Husserl, it should not be ruled out. After all, as a philosopher, Husserl is very much in the line of some other, generally rather conservative thinkers that Gaddis cites approvingly in his fiction such as Ortega Y Gasset, Johan Huizinga, and T.S. Eliot. Moreover, Gaddis's personal library, now at the William Gaddis Papers at Washington University, indicates that he did own a copy of *Introduction to Metaphysics* by Husserl's most influential student Martin Heidegger. *Introduction to Metaphysics* is not only composed of university lectures that Heidegger gave around the same time as Husserl also delivered his "Vienna Lecture," but it similarly evokes the idea of a Europe in crisis. Finally, Gaddis's personal library also indicates that he owned a copy of (and read) *Man and Crisis* by Ortega Y Gasset, a philosopher very much influenced by Husserlian phenomenology.
61. See for instance Gregory Comnes's 1994 study *The Ethics of Indeterminacy in the Novels of William Gaddis*, who introduces his discussion of the term *agapē* — which first surfaces in Gaddis's 1975 novel *JR* — with a "cautionary note." "Throughout this book," Comnes notes, " I will deliberately avoid any discussion of *agapē* love in the situation of the Christian believer. Reading Gaddis makes it clear that his concern is not with any conventional Christian doctrine — except as the object of satire — but rather with the general structure of a consciousness informed by the virtues of alterity, risk, and responsible suffering" (5). Comnes's rather crude suggestion that Christianity is but an "object of satire" in Gaddis's fiction is symptomatic of the way in which critics have failed to take the topic of religion seriously even as it resurfaced in each one of his novels.
62. Gaddis, *Agapē Agape*, 37.
63. *Ibid.*
64. *Ibid.*, 95.
65. *Ibid.*, 96.
66. *Ibid.*, 94.
67. *Ibid.*, 11.
68. *Ibid.*, 1.
69. See Jacques Derrida, "By Force of Mourning," trans. Pascale-Anne Brault and Michael Naas, *Critical Inquiry* 22, no. 2 (1996), 187–8.
70. Jean-Luc Nancy, *The Inoperative Community*, trans. Peter Connor, et al. (Minneapolis: University of Minnesota Press, 1991), 10.
71. Gaddis, *Agapē Agape*, 96.
72. Jean-Luc Nancy, *Being Singular Plural*, trans. Richard D. Richardson and Anne E. O'Byrne (Stanford: Stanford University Press, 2000), 203.
73. Gaddis, *Agapē Agape*, 20.
74. *Ibid.*, 12.
75. *Ibid.*, 94. Both versions (in Italian and in English) of this line are quoted by Gaddis.
76. *Nancy*, 63.
77. Michael Wutz, "Writing from between the Gaps: *Agapē Agape* and Twentieth-Century Media Culture," *Paper Empire*, 185–210.
78. Gaddis, *Agapē Agape*, 96.

Chapter 7

1. Quoted in Serge Guilbaut, *How New York Stole the Idea of Modern Art: Abstract Expressionism, Freedom, and the Cold War* (Chicago: University of Chicago Press, 1983), 64. James T. Soby, originally published in the unpaginated catalog for the "Artists in Exile" show held at the Pierre Matisse Gallery from March 3 to March 28, 1942.
2. Jack Kerouac, *The Subterraneans* (New York: Grove, 1958), 82–3. Kerouac wrote this novel five years earlier, in 1953, more or less concurrent with Gaddis's writing of *The Recognitions*.
3. *Ibid.*, 84–85.
4. *Ibid.*, 87.
5. *Ibid.*, 89, 90.
6. *Ibid.*, 87–88.
7. Barry Gifford and Lawrence Lee, *Jack's Book: An Oral Biography of Jack Kerouac* (New York: St. Martin's, 1978), 326.
8. In an interview published in the *Paris Review*, Gaddis frequently refers to Wyatt's comments on art when answering questions about his own views on art: "I'd go back to *The Recognitions* where Wyatt asks what people want from the man they didn't get from his work, because presumably that's where he's tried to distill this 'life and personality and views' you speak of. What's any artist but the dregs of his work: I gave that line to Wyatt thirty odd years ago and as far as

I'm concerned it's still valid" (Zoltán Abádi-Nagy, "The Art of Fiction: An Interview with William Gaddis," *Paris Review* 105, Winter 1987, 57–58). The quotation from *The Recognitions* that Gaddis is referring to is as follows, in Wyatt's voice: "What is it they want from a man that they didn't get from his work? What do they expect? What is there left of him when he's done his work? What's any artist, but the dregs of his work? The human shambles that follows it around. What's left of the man when the work's done but a shambles of apology," 95–96.

9. Richard Serra's *Tilted Arc* was a large, site-specific sculpture located on the Federal Plaza at Foley Square in Manhattan that aroused controversy and legal action. Larry Wertheim's book review of *A Frolic* considers the case at length and also provides an extended discussion of the relationship between the legal cases involving *Tilted Arc* and the fictional *Cyclone Seven*. As he explains, Serra's *Tilted Arc* was criticized by the public leading the government to remove it from the plaza. Serra unsuccessfully fought this action in court. See "Symposium: Proposed Restatement (Third) of Torts: Products liability: Book Review: Law as Frolic: Law and Literature in a Frolic of His Own," *William Mitchell Law Review* 421 (Winter 1995). See also Richard Posner's discussion of the novel in *Law and Literature*, revised and enlarged edition (Cambridge, MA: Harvard University Press, 1998), 32–7.

10. Gaddis, *A Frolic of His Own* (New York: Simon and Schuster, 1994), 35.

11. William Gaddis, *Recognitions* (New York: Harcourt Brace, 1955), 57.

12. Oscar Wilde, *The Picture of Dorian Gray*, ed. Michael Patrick Gillespie, 2d ed. (New York: W.W. Norton, 2007), 81.

13. Gaddis, *Recognitions*, 67–8.

14. *Ibid.*, 251.

15. *Ibid.*, 34.

16. The other character in the novel that comes to mind here is Rektall Brown, whose name is both a pseudonym of "asshole" and descriptive of the only original thing he can create.

17. Gaddis, *Recognitions*, 35.

18. There are other locations in the novel where Gaddis slyly gives the impression that Wyatt's art is "alive." Consider the scene when Esther admires the portrait of herself as it is drying in Wyatt's studio: "A drying lamp had been turned on the portrait, and she looked at it. He had done an excellent job and she, fresh from her mirror, stared at the flesh of the face on the easel as clear as her own.—I'll miss it, she said.—I'll be glad to see it gone but ... but I'll miss it. Something moved. She turned, but it was not he. In the mirror ('to correct bad drawing...') she caught his reflection and realized he was behind the table" (Gaddis, *Recognitions*, 108). Gaddis's narration moves seamlessly between depictions of Esther, her portrait, the reflecting mirror and the room they are in, in effect blurring the distinctions between them. The "something moved" reads like the scene of the buried bird—we are momentarily led to suspect a scene of gothic creepiness, i.e., that something in the painting moved. In fact, the movement is Wyatt's reflection in the mirror.

19. Wyndam Lewis, *Tarr* (New York: Alfred A. Knopf, 1918), 352.

20. Mr. Sinisterra's outfit is the first indication of his fraudulent status. He is pretending to be a physician in order to travel undetected, but his shabby clothes give him away to the careful observer: "The buttons down the front of those duck trousers had originally been made, with all of false economy's ingenious drear deception, of coated cardboard" (*Recognitions*, 4).

21. Steven Weisenburger, *Fables of Subversion: Satire and the American Novel, 1930–1980* (Athens: University of Georgia Press, 1995), 218.

22. Gaddis, *Recognitions*, 71.

23. *Ibid.*, 143.

24. Sophie Lévy, ed., *A Transatlantic Avant-Garde: American Artists in Paris 1918–1939* (Berkeley: University of California Press, 2003).

25. Gaddis, *Recognitions*, 67.

26. Guilbaut, 73.

27. Stewart Buettner, *American Art Theory, 1945–1970* (Ann Arbor: UMI Research Press, 1981), 68.

28. Guilbaut writes: "The painters and their works were caught up in the battle between the two museums, MoMA and Metropolitan, for cultural supremacy in New York. The trustees of the Met represented old wealth in America, and the museum consequently stood for a tame, prudent, and academic culture oriented toward the past. Young, liberal, and dynamic, the Museum of Modern Art represented new wealth, the 'enlightened rich' [...] the future of American culture" (Guilbaut, 76–77).

29. Guilbaut, 91–94.

30. Marcel Duchamp's *Bride Stripped Bear by Her Bachelors, Even*, with a fashion model behind it, was on the cover of *Vogue* in July 1945, and Léger's and Mondrian's paintings appeared next to high fashion items in *Harper's Bazaar* in 1944. Janis Mink, *Marcel Duchamp, 1887–1968, Art as Anti-Art* (Köln: Taschen, 2000), 80 and Guilbaut, 95. Guilbaut describes the sale of art at New York department stores (93–94).

31. Gaddis, *Recognitions*, 123.

32. Scene 45 of *J R* also takes place at the Met, but largely in the men's bathroom, where J R (taking a break from a school trip he is not legitimately supposed to be on) is conducting business with Edward Bast. William Gaddis, *J R* (New York: Knopf, 1975), 290–309. Also relevant here is a biographical detail: Gaddis's second wife worked at the Met.

33. Gaddis, *Recognitions*, 108.

34. Jackson Pollock, interview with William Wright, "My Painting" (1950). Reprinted in *Jackson Pollock: Interviews, Articles, Reviews* (New York: MoMA, 1999), 18.

35. Gaddis, *Recognitions*, 144.

36. Joseph Salemi, "To Soar in Atonement: Art as Expiation in Gaddis's *The Recognitions*,"

In Recognition of William Gaddis, John Kuehl and Steven Moore, eds. (Syracuse: Syracuse University Press, 1984), 46-57.

37. John Johnston, *Carnival of Repetition: Gaddis's* The Recognitions *and Postmodern Theory* (Philadelphia: University of Pennsylvania Press, 1990), 12.

38. Various critics have made such observations about Wyatt's view of contemporary art: "As Wyatt sees things, contemporary painting is little more than a reflection, and in this sense a part, of the modern situation or, as he might describe it, malaise. His contemporaries, Wyatt feels, are unable to distance themselves from what they see. Their art offers neither an effective judgment nor a higher standard by which to measure the events of the age"; Christopher Knight, "Flemish Art and Wyatt's Quest for Redemption in William Gaddis's *The Recognitions*" in John Kuehl and Steven Moore, eds., *In Recognition of William Gaddis* (Syracuse: Syracuse University Press, 1984), 58-69. Knight continues, "In working in a style outside the range of modernism, Wyatt is also doing something else. He is trying to work himself free of self-imposed intellectual boundaries that modernism has tended to reinforce. Modern art, in its affirmation of materialism, has disengaged itself from the whole area of metaphysics." See also Knight, *Hints and Guesses: William Gaddis's Fiction of Longing* (Madison: University of Wisconsin Press, 1997).

39. Gaddis, *Recognitions*, 176.

40. Tom Wolfe, *The Painted Word* (New York: Bantam, 1975), 119-120.

41. Gaddis, *Recognitions*, 335.

42. This respect for serious critics and criticism also surfaces in *Frolic*, when the lawyers Jawaharlal Madhar Pai and Harold Basie debate, among other things, the distinction between amateurs and professionals, form and content, and homage and plagiarism. At one point during Oscar Crease's deposition, Madhar Pai defends book critics as superior to mere book reviewers: "I did not say book critics I said reviewers, there's a world of difference although the reviewers are delighted to be referred to as critics unless they're on the run, then they take refuge in calling themselves journalists" (Gaddis, *Frolic*, 193).

43. Gaddis uses the same comparison when describing his own writing: "things don't happen [...] in a single light, the single light which is very effective in Hemingway for instance, and so damned boring in those who 'derive' from him" (Gaddis Papers, Washington University). Gaddis also was trying to produce writing that followed a specific vision of the world instead of a writing that imitated the world from a single, physical point of view or, as he nicely puts it, from "a single light." An artist's vision of the world is a representation, while the camera's view of the world is here understood to be a devalued embodiment, or copy, of that world. I am grateful to Crystal Alberts for pointing out this quotation from the Gaddis papers at Washington University.

44. Gaddis, *Recognitions*, 250.

45. *Ibid.*

46. Stanley explains to Max the notion of the embodiment of cultural memory by referring to a comment by Van Gogh about his process of composition: "when he would take a drawing of Delacroix as a subject and improvise with colors, not as himself, he says, but searching for memories of their pictures, the 'vague consonance of colors,' the memory that was himself, his own interpretation" (Gaddis, *Recognitions*, 461). The key phrase here is the last part: memory of the self and interpretation have become interchangeable ideas.

47. Gaddis, *Recognitions*, 534-535.

48. Abádi-Nagy, 13.

49. Soon after its publication, *The Recognitions* was associated with Joyce's *Ulysses* and *A Portrait of the Artist as a Young Man*. See, for example, Bernard Benstock's "On William Gaddis: In Recognition of James Joyce," *Wisconsin Studies in Contemporary Literature* 6 (2) Summer 1965, 177-89, and Craig Hansen Werner's *Paradoxical Resolutions: American Fiction Since James Joyce* (Urbana: University of Illinois Press, 1982), 169-181. Gaddis, however, vehemently denied this Joycean connection and claimed not to have read *Ulysses* before writing *The Recognitions*. In the *Paris Review* interview with Abádi-Nagy, Gaddis dismisses the apparent debts to Joyce: "Many of these similarities which critics and doctoral students have dug up are absolutely coincidences" (Abádi-Nagy, 62).

Chapter 8

1. William Gaddis, *The Recognitions* (New York: Penguin, 1993), 3.

2. Paul Ingendaay, "Agent der Veränderung. Ein Gespräch mit William Gaddis," *Rowohlt Literatur Magazin* 39 (1997), 90-91. ("Agent of Change: A Conversation with William Gaddis" [My emphases and translation].

als ob bestimmte ethische Grenzziehungen wahr sind. Es sind natürlich nur Hypothesen und Fiktionen. [...] echte Moralität immer auf einer fiktiven Basis beruhen muß. Wir müssen uns so verhalten, als ob unsere Pflichten uns von Gott auferlegt wären, als ob wir sonst für unser Fehlverhalten bestraft werden würden. Aber sobald dies Als-Ob zu einem Weil gemacht wird, verflüchtigt sich der ethische Charakter, und unser Verhalten wird von niederen Instinkten bestimmt.

3. Friedrich Nietzsche, *The Will to Power*, trans. Walter Kaufmann and R. J. Hollingdale (New York: Vintage, 1968), 283.

4. *Ibid.*, 297.

5. *Ibid.*, 63.

6. Gaddis, *Recognitions*, 120.

7. Plato, *The Republic*, Book X (Cleveland: Fine Editions, 1946) 354.

8. Hans Vaihinger, *The Philosophy of 'As if': A System of the Theoretical, Practical and Religious Fictions of Mankind,* trans. by C. K. Ogden (New York: Barnes and Noble, 1966), 264. Vaihinger's emphases.
9. William Gaddis, "The Rush for Second Place," *The Rush for Second Place: Essays and Occasional Writings,* ed. Joseph Tabbi (New York: Penguin, 2002), 43.
10. Delivered at "The Writer and Religion Conference" at Washington University in St. Louis in 1994, published by Southern Illinois University Press in 2000.
11. William Gaddis, "Old Foes with New Faces," *The Writer and Religion,* eds. William H. Gass and Lorin Cuoco (Carbondale: Southern Illinois University Press, 2000), 36.
12. *Ibid.,* 46.
13. *Ibid.,* 37, quoting David Hume.
14. Gaddis, *Recognitions,* 384.
15. Max Weber, *The Protestant Ethic and the Spirit of Capitalism,* trans. Talcott Parsons (New York: Charles Scribner's Sons, 1958), 84.
16. Peter Koenig (a.k.a. David Koenig), "'Splinters from the Yew Tree': A Critical Study of William Gaddis' *The Recognitions*" (unpublished doctoral dissertation, University of New York, 1971), 50.
17. Rodger Cunningham, "When You See Yourself: Gnostic Motifs and Their Transformation in *The Recognitions,*" *Soundings — An Interdisciplinary Journal,* 71:4 (1988), 620.
18. Philip Mason Palmer and Robert Pattison More, *The Sources of the Faust Tradition: From Simon Magus to Lessing* (New York: Oxford University Press, 1936), 3.
19. Acts of the Apostles 8:9–10. *King James Version.*
20. Tony Tanner, *City of Words: American Fiction 1950–1970* (New York: Harper and Row, 1971), I, 414.
21. Robert Graves, *The White Goddess: A Historical Grammar of Poetic Myth,* amended and enlarged ed. (New York: Octagon, 1972), 160.
22. Elaine B. Safer, *The Contemporary American Comic Epic: The Novels of Barth, Pynchon, Gaddis, and Kesey* (Detroit: Wayne State University Press, 1988), 117.
23. Michael Grant, *Saint Paul* (New York: Charles Scribner's Sons, 1976), 171.
24. Philip Carrington, *The Early Christian Church: Volume I The First Christian Century,* 2 vols. (London: Cambridge University Press, 1957), I, 414.
25. Warwick Wadlington, *The Confidence Game in American Literature* (Princeton: Princeton University Press, 1975), 168.
26. Herman Melville, *Moby-Dick,* ed. Harrison Hayford and Hershel Parker (New York: W.W. Norton, 1967), 50.
27. A. N. Wilson, *Paul: The Mind of the Apostle* (New York: W.W. Norton, 1997), 208.
28. Grant, 128.
29. Nietzsche, *The Twilight of the Idols and The Anti-Christ: or How to Philosophize with a Hammer* (New York: Penguin, 1990), 169.
30. *Ibid.,* 161.
31. Montague Rhodes James, *The Apocryphal New Testament: Being The Apocryphal Gospels, Acts, Epistles, and Apocalypses,* corrected ed. (Oxford: Oxford Clarendon Press, 1953), xxiv.
32. Ingendaay, 87. "Als ich als Zwanzigjähriger Spengler habe gelesen, war ich überwältigt von seiner pessimistischen Vision des Untergangs der westlichen Welt."
33. Oswald Spengler, *The Decline of The West,* vol. II, *Perspectives of World History,* trans. Charles Francis Atkinson (New York: Alfred A. Knopf, 2000), 237.
34. *Ibid.,* 221. Original emphasis.
35. Romans 13:1–2. *King James Version.*
36. F. C. Coneybeare, *Myth, Magic, and Morals: A Study of Christian Origins* (London: Watts & Co., 1909), 3.
37. Oswald Spengler, *The Decline of The West,* vol. I, *Form and Actuality,* trans. Charles Francis Atkinson (New York: Alfred A. Knopf, 2000), 75.
38. *Ibid.,* 183. All emphases are Spengler's.
39. *Ibid.,* 424.
40. Zoltán Abádi-Nagy, "The Art of Fiction: An Interview with William Gaddis," *The Paris Review* 105 (1987), 77.
41. Steven Moore, *A Reader's Guide to William Gaddis's* The Recognitions (Lincoln: University of Nebraska Press, 1982), 18.
42. William James, *Pragmatism and Other Writings* ed. Giles Gunn (Harmondsworth, UK: Penguin, 2000), 12.
43. Nietzsche, *Anti-Christ,* 149.
44. *Ibid.,* 437.
45. *Ibid.,* 336.
46. John Stark, "William Gaddis: Just Recognition," *The Hollins Critic* 4:2 (1977), 5.
47. Gaddis, *Recognitions,* 952.
48. *Ibid.,* 356.
49. *Ibid.,* 127.
50. *Ibid.,* 347.
51. *Ibid.,* 348.
52. *Ibid.,* 440.
53. *Ibid.,* 727.
54. *Ibid.,* 250.
55. *Ibid.,* 362.
56. *Ibid.,* 535.
57. *Ibid.,* 250.
58. *Ibid.,* 251.
59. *Ibid.,* 826.
60. *Ibid.,* 690.
61. Karl Marx and Frederick Engels, *The German Ideology,* ed. C.J. Arthur (New York: International, 1970), 37.
62. William Gaddis, "Treatment for a Motion Picture on 'Software,'" *The Rush for Second Place: Essays and Occasional Writings,* ed. Joseph Tabbi (New York: Penguin, 2002), 17.
63. Hugh Kenner, *The Counterfeiters: A Historical Comedy* (Bloomington: Indiana University Press, 1968), 41.
64. Gaddis, *Recognitions,* 896.

65. *Ibid.*, 559.
66. Peter Wolfe, *A Vision of His Own: The Mind and Art of William Gaddis* (Cranbury, NJ: Associated University Presses, 1997), 17.
67. Nietzsche, *Anti-Christ*, 134.
68. Wolfe, 16.
69. Steven Weisenburger, *Fables of Subversion: Satire and the American Novel, 1930–1980* (Athens: University of Georgia Press, 1995), 210.
70. Weber, 53.
71. Gaddis, *Recognitions*, 487.
72. William Gaddis, *J R*, corrected ed. (Harmondsworth, UK: Penguin, 1993), 463.
73. Gaddis, *Recognitions*, 113.
74. Gregory Comnes, *The Ethics of Indeterminacy in the Novels of William Gaddis* (Gainesville: University Press of Florida, 1994), 129.
75. William Gaddis, *Carpenter's Gothic* (New York: Penguin, 1999), 128.
76. Joseph Dewey, *In a Dark Time: The Apocalyptic Temper in the American Novel of the Nuclear Age* (West Lafayette, IN: Purdue University Press, 1990), 192.
77. Gaddis, *Carpenter's Gothic*, 186.
78. Nietzsche, *Anti-Christ*, 184.
79. *Ibid.*, 185.
80. *Ibid.*, 148.
81. *Ibid.*, 163.
82. *Ibid.*, 150.
83. *Ibid.*, 177.
84. William Gaddis, "Old Foes with New Faces: Discussion," *The Writer and Religion*, eds. William H. Gass and Lorin Cuoco (Carbondale: Southern Illinois University Press, 2000), 56.
85. Gaddis, *Carpenter's Gothic*,134.
86. *Ibid.*, 22.
87. *Ibid.*, 193.
88. *Ibid.*, 242.
89. *Ibid.*, 241.
90. Nietzsche, *Anti-Christ*, 173.
91. *Ibid.*, 77.
92. *Ibid.*, 91.
93. *Ibid.*, 240.
94. *Ibid.*, 111.
95. *Ibid.*, 111.
96. *Ibid.*, 175.
97. Gaddis, *Carpenter's Gothic*, 19.
98. *Ibid.*, 179.
99. Wolfe, 249.
100. Gaddis, *Carpenter's Gothic*, 78.
101. *Ibid.*, 242.
102. *Ibid.*, 238.
103. Wolfe, 233.
104. Nietzsche, *Anti-Christ*, 196.
105. Gaddis, *Carpenter's Gothic*, 111.
106. Nietzsche, *Anti-Christ*, p. 192.
107. *Ibid.*, 196.
108. *Ibid.*, 193.
109. Nietzsche, *Anti-Christ*, 168.
110. Christopher J. Knight, *Hints and Guesses: William Gaddis's Fiction of Longing* (Madison: University of Wisconsin Press, 1997), 150.
111. Gaddis, *Carpenter's Gothic*, 151.
112. *Ibid.*, 157.
113. Cynthia Ozick, "William Gaddis and the Scion of Darkness," *What Henry James Knew* (London: Vintage, 1994), 223.
114. Nietzsche, *Anti-Christ*, 148.
115. Gaddis, *Carpenter's Gothic*, 63.
116. Ozick, 225.
117. Knight, 279.
118. Gaddis, *Carpenter's Gothic*, 228.
119. Joseph Conrad, "Preface" to *The Nigger of The Narcissus* (London: Dent & Sons, 1945), 5.
120. Jürgen Habermas, "On the Relation Between the Secular Liberal State and Religion," *The Frankfurt School on Religion: Key Writings by the Major Thinkers*, ed. Eduardo Mendieta (New York: Routledge, 2005), 343.
121. Habermas, 344.
122. Gaddis, *Recognitions*, 261.
123. Gaddis, "Old Foes," 38.
124. Helmut Peukert, "Enlightenment and Theology as Unfinished Projects," *The Frankfurt School on Religion: Key Writings by the Major Thinkers*, ed. Eduardo Mendieta (New York: Routledge, 2005), 351.

Chapter 9

1. Jean-Jacques Rousseau, *Emile, or On Education*, trans. Allan Bloom (New York: Basic, 1979), 62.
2. "Remarks by the President at the Radio-Television Correspondents Association 57th Annual Dinner," 29 March 2001. Available at http://www.whitehouse.gov/news/releases/2001/03/20010330-1.html accessed on 14 December 2008.
3. Tom LeClair, "An Interview with William Gaddis, circa 1980," in *Paper Empire: William Gaddis and the World System*, eds. Joseph Tabbi and Rone Shavers (Tuscaloosa: University of Alabama Press, 2007), 23.
4. Zoltán Abádi-Nagy, "The Art of Fiction: An Interview with William Gaddis," *Paris Review* 105 (Winter 1987), 57, 68. Given these statements, it is hard to find the basis for Johan Thielemans' suggestion that "[t]he drift of Gaddis' argument is clear: money is a curse. Ideally, we should be able to do away with it" ("Art as Redemption of Trash: Bast and Friends in Gaddis' *J R*," *In Recognition of William Gaddis*, eds. John Kuehl and Steven Moore [Syracuse: Syracuse University Press, 1984], 136). Money is merely one of the signs of capital, and just as *J R* begins with a remembrance by Edward Bast's aunts of the advent of paper money, the novel's unfolding shows how abstract both the values and the commodities in exchange become in an ever-expanding "free market" system. (Thielemans' reading includes factual errors, too, such as J R's age and a puzzling confusion of Gibbs with Bast [142].) Just as *J R* appropriately begins with the word "money," *A Frolic of His Own* opens with "justice," both accompanied by question marks; and it would, accordingly, be as groundless to suppose that Gad-

dis conceives of *justice* as a curse ideally disposed of as it is to imagine the same of *money*. For Gaddis, these are needs that the byzantine systems deny many people, and it is these systems that he attacks.

5. William Gaddis, *J R* (New York: Penguin, 1993), 655; William Gaddis, *Agapē Agape* (New York: Viking, 2002), 34.

6. Gaddis, *J R*, 244.

7. *Ibid.*, 486.

8. *Ibid.*, 656.

9. *Ibid.*, 726.

10. James Joyce, *A Portrait of the Artist as a Young Man* (Oxford: Oxford University Press, 2000), 213. In no small part because of Gaddis's own reactions to such suggestions, critics have in recent years grown shy of drawing connections with Joyce. Gaddis wrote to Grace Eckley in 1975, "I believe I read *Portrait of an Artist* but also think I may not have finished it" (quoted in Steven Moore, *William Gaddis* [Boston: Twayne, 1989], 7) but, apart from noting the uncertain wobble to that statement, my point here is not to argue an "influence," but rather to highlight how *J R* is *comparable* to Joyce's Bildungsroman in this regard.

11. It is frighteningly easy to compare J R's wisdom ("this whole bunch of rules"), such as "hire smart people but run things yourself" (Gaddis, *J R*, 647), with Bush's wit: "I'm the decider."

12. Rousseau, 40. The reader will note that the translation I've elected to cite in this essay was published after *J R*, and so could not have been used by Gaddis. My reason for using Allan Bloom's version is to invite consideration of how it, together with Bloom's 1987 best-seller *The Closing of the American Mind* (in which his *Emile* and Plato's *Republic*, which he also translated, figure prominently as prescribed antidotes to American heathenism) represents a very different but in some ways parallel discourse on education's failings to that found in *J R* and *Carpenter's Gothic*.

13. Abádi-Nagy, 60, 70.

14. *Ibid.*, 69; William Gaddis, *Carpenter's Gothic* (New York: Penguin, 1985), 182; see also Abádi-Nagy, 67. Given this important qualification, Nicholas Brown is slightly off the mark then he writes that J R "embodies the innocence of Capital" ("Cognitive Map, Aesthetic Object, or National Allegory? *Carpenter's Gothic*," *Paper Empire: William Gaddis and the World System*, 152). In Gaddis's novel it is the desire to acquire wealth, not wealth itself or even the concept of wealth, that is innocent.

15. Moore, 73.

16. Quoted in Moore, 12.

17. William Gaddis, *The Rush for Second Place: Essays and Occasional Writings*, ed. Joseph Tabbi (New York: Penguin, 2002), 54.

18. John Holt, *How Children Fail* (New York: Pitman, 1964), 105.

19. Steven Pinker, *The Blank Slate: The Modern Denial of Human Nature* (New York: Penguin, 2003).

20. Gibbs explains one item in his collection of smudged newspaper clippings to Amy: "That's nothing yes, this behaviorist B F Skinner just intrigued the way he's parlayed all his infantile ideas into such a successful" (485).

21. In the words of President Bush, the much-touted "No Child Left Behind" program means "we're going to spend federal money, and we want you to develop an accountability system that will show the parents and taxpayers that the schools are meeting high standards" (www.ed.gov/news/speeches/2007/07/07262007.html). Note that the standards themselves, whatever they might be, are ultimately less important than a measuring system (i.e., tests) by which to assure voters that the standards are met.

22. See Christopher J. Knight, *Hints and Guesses: William Gaddis's Fiction of Longing* (Madison: University of Wisconsin Press, 1997), 106–16.

23. Nicholas Spencer, "Critical Mimesis: *J R*'s Transition to Postmodernity," *Paper Empire: William Gaddis and the World System*, 144.

24. Gaddis, *J R*, 460.

25. *Ibid.*, 246.

26. *Ibid.*, 651.

27. Abádi-Nagy, 85.

28. Gaddis, *J R*, 246–47.

29. LeClair, 25.

30. Gaddis, *J R*, 226.

31. Gaddis, *Carpenter's Gothic*, 32.

32. Gaddis, *J R*, 29.

33. Quoted in Moore, 12.

34. Gaddis, *J R*, 34.

35. Gaddis, *The Rush for Second Place*, 64–65.

36. Rousseau, 447.

37. William Gaddis, *A Frolic of His Own* (New York: Simon and Schuster, 1995), 21.

38. Rousseau, 52.

39. *Ibid.*, 93.

40. Abádi-Nagy, 85.

41. Tim Conley, "William Gaddis Calling: Telephonic Satire and the Disconnection of Authority," *Studies in the Novel* 35.4 (2003): 526–42.

42. Gaddis, *J R*, 109.

43. Abádi-Nagy, 68.

44. Rousseau, 106.

45. *Ibid.*, 189.

46. Rousseau spells out the conditions for this right within his larger conception of the social contract near the end of *Emile*: "The right of property is inviolable and sacred for the sovereign authority as long as it remains a particular and individual right. But as soon as it is considered as common to all the citizens, it is subject to the general will, and this will can suppress it" (461). As ambivalent as Rousseau can be about private property, here and in *The Social Contract*, it is always posited as a "right" and linked, if not synonymous, with powers of government.

47. Gaddis, *J R*, 107.
48. Rousseau, 53.
49. Gaddis, *J R*, 59.
50. This is to say nothing of his views on women, expounded at unfortunate length in Book V of *Emile*.
51. Gaddis, *J R*, 536–37.
52. *Ibid.*, 653–54.
53. *Ibid.*, 622.
54. *Ibid.*, 655.
55. Rousseau, 168–69.
56. Perhaps the most absurd instance of such usage is Davidoff's repetition of J R's expressed desire "to get Mickey Mouse by the short hair ... what's he got against Mickey Mouse" (*J R*, 540).
57. Gaddis, *J R*, 657.
58. *Ibid.*, 203, 439.
59. Spencer, 140–41.
60. Gaddis, *J R*, 42.
61. *Ibid.*, 661.
62. *Ibid.*, 658.
63. Gaddis, *The Rush for Second Place*, 40. Ford is, of course, hardly alone among excited American leaders, policy makers, media pundits, and military personnel in this rhetorical habit. It comes as no surprise that, according to an Associated Press report, "In the Bush [II] White House, sports are a metaphor for life" (Ben Feller, "Bush sees life in sporting terms," *USA Today* [15 July 2007]). In a speech on 22 August 2007, Bush effectively adopted Ford's "last minute of the last quarter" interpretation of events to suggest that withdrawal from Iraq would be as calamitous as was, apparently, the withdrawal from Vietnam.
64. Gaddis, *J R*, 672–73; also 683.
65. *Ibid.*, 529, 630.
66. *Ibid.*, 686.
67. *Ibid.*, 587.
68. *Ibid.*, 450, 410, 630.
69. *Ibid.*, 177.
70. Peter Wolfe, *A Vision of His Own: The Mind and Art of William Gaddis* (Madison, NJ: Fairleigh Dickinson University Press, 1997), 275; Knight, 92.
71. Gaddis, *J R*, 432.
72. The polysemy is active even within the word itself. In the same way that Cates complains about amateur investors ruining the game of big business, Crawley complains about African people ruining the business of big game: "the rate Africa's developing it's going to be nothing but a lot of niggers driving around in hats and neckties no place left for the game at all" (Gaddis, *J R*, 204). This and other imperial intonations of "game" point to similar usages in the ongoing history of colonization.
73. Knight, 93.
74. Gaddis, *J R*, 647.
75. *Ibid.*, 499.
76. *Ibid.*, 597.
77. More acutely than he knows, Davidoff recommends against using "the team player image" in the invented biographical profile of J R (530).

78. Gaddis, *J R*, 263.
79. *Ibid.*, 265.
80. *Ibid.*, 667.
81. *Ibid.*, 711.
82. *Ibid.*, 15, 13.
83. *Ibid.*, 477.
84. *Ibid.*, 481.
85. Brigitte Félix, *William Gaddis: L'alchimie de l'écriture* (Paris: Éditions Belin, 1997), 52.
86. Gaddis, *J R*, 725.
87. Knight, 268, note 17.
88. Gaddis, *J R*, 82, 118.
89. *Ibid.*, 118–19.
90. *Ibid.*, 483; emphasis added.
91. *Ibid.*, 502.
92. *Ibid.*, 236.
93. *Ibid.*, 267.
94. J. M. Barrie, *Peter Pan* (New York: Bantam, 1985), 151.
95. Marjorie Garber, *Vested Interests: Cross-Dressing and Cultural Anxiety* (New York: Routledge, 1992), 184. The psychological dimensions of the *Peter Pan* theme in *J R* are beyond the scope of this paper. Relevant to such a discussion are Garber's analysis of transvestism (most especially in connection with Amy Joubert's playful flirtations with her "mustache" and smoking cigars), representations of warlike Native Americans, and Rhoda's sad failure to fly.
96. Gaddis, *J R*, 172.
97. Jeff Bursey and Anne Furlong, "Cognitive Gothic: Relevance Theory, Iteration, and Style," *Paper Empire: William Gaddis and the World System*, 119.
98. Rebecca Solnit, "The Silence of the Lambswool Cardigans," *Storming the Gates of Paradise: Landscapes for Politics* (Berkeley: University of California Press, 2007), 323, 325.
99. Félix, 64 (parenthetical translation mine).
100. Gaddis, *J R*, 651.
101. It is interesting in this context to consider the differences implicit in pedagogies that privilege the phrase "to have earned the grade" over "to have made the grade." They may even be as different as "believing and shitting" (*J R* 42).
102. *Ibid.*, 530.
103. Rousseau, 190.
104. Gaddis, *J R*, 474.
105. Barrie, 168.
106. Rousseau, 205.
107. Gaddis, *J R*, 463.

Chapter 10

1. William Gaddis, *J R* (New York: Penguin, 1993), 202.
2. *Ibid.*, 291.
3. *Ibid.*, 202.
4. *Ibid.*, 204.
5. William Gaddis, *Carpenter's Gothic* (New York: Viking, 1985), 182–3.
6. *Ibid.*, 180.

7. *Ibid.*, 136.
8. *Ibid.*, 259.
9. *Ibid.*, 36, 165.
10. *Ibid.*, 153.
11. *Ibid.*, 121.
12. *Ibid.*, 147.
13. In this as in other respects, the seemingly extravagant scenario laid out in *Carpenter's Gothic* now appears remarkably prescient: on April 6, 1994, the airplane carrying Rwandan president Juvenal Habyarimana and the president of Burundi was shot down by rebels as it approached Kigali, sparking off a genocide in which up to a million people were killed. The similarity should not be exaggerated, as the target of the rebellion was not the United States, but the ruling Tutsi minority and its moderate Hutu allies, reflecting a centuries-old dispute whose origins long predate European colonization. However, Western countries did eventually get involved, as French troops intervened to quell the genocide, followed by a UN peacekeeping force to which the United States largely contributed. While humanitarian concerns undoubtedly played a part in this decision, political motivations were far from absent, since the stability of the Great Lakes region is a matter of strategic importance to former colonial powers such as France. In a post-colonial context, "humanitarian" missions are seldom wholly disinterested; in this respect, they resemble Teakell's apparently innocuous "fact-finding trip."
14. Gaddis, *Carpenter's Gothic*, 165.
15. *Ibid.*, 157, 163, 248.
16. *Ibid.*, 165.
17. *Ibid.*, 181.
18. *Ibid.*, 155–7.
19. *Ibid.*, 163.
20. *Ibid.*, 157.
21. *Ibid.*, 136.
22. *Ibid.*, 102.
23. Agamben, *Homo Sacer*, 5–6.
24. *Ibid.*, 73.
25. *Ibid.*, 81–2.
26. *Ibid.*, 21.
27. *Ibid.*, 2.
28. Gaddis, *Carpenter's Gothic*, 253.
29. *Ibid.*, 39–40, 46.
30. *Ibid.*, 40.
31. *Ibid.*, 182.
32. *Ibid.*, 11, 20, 139.
33. *Ibid.*, 208.
34. *Ibid.*, 127, 157, 161.
35. *Ibid.*, 221.
36. Gaddis's own sympathies are not in doubt. In an unpublished letter to William Gass dated August 25, 1980, he expresses indignation at the rise of the religious right: "the only thing that rouses me these days all these god damned born-agains & evangelicals." William H. Gass Papers, Washington University Special Collections Library, St. Louis, Missouri.
37. Gaddis, *Carpenter's Gothic*, 253, 259, 262.
38. *Ibid.*, 239.
39. *Ibid.*, 133.
40. Agamben, *Remnants of Auschwitz*, 77.
41. Arendt, *The Origins of Totalitarianism*, 446.
42. Agamben, *Homo Sacer*, 117.
43. Gaddis, *Carpenter's Gothic*, 185.
44. Gaddis, *Agapē Agape*, 35.
45. Arendt, *The Origins of Totalitarianism*, 446.
46. Gaddis, *Carpenter's Gothic*, 243–4.
47. "But obviously man is a political animal in a sense in which a bee is not, or any other gregarious animal. Nature, as we say, does nothing without some purpose; and she has endowed man alone among the animals with the power of speech." Aristotle, *The Politics*, 1253a, 60.
48. Gaddis, *Carpenter's Gothic*, 228–9.
49. *Ibid.*, 29.
50. *Ibid.*, 102.
51. *Ibid.*, 78.
52. *Ibid.*, 134.
53. William Gaddis, "How Does The State Imagine? The Willing Suspension of Disbelief," *The Rush for Second Place: Essays and Occasional Writings* (New York: Penguin, 2002), 123.
54. Gaddis, *Carpenter's Gothic*, 237.
55. *Ibid.*, 136–7.
56. *Ibid.*, 137.
57. *Ibid.*, 136.
58. *Ibid.*, 121.
59. *Ibid.*, 157.
60. *Ibid.*, 262.
61. Wittgenstein, *Philosophical Investigations*, §201, 69^e.
62. Abády-Nagy, "The Art of Fiction: An Interview with William Gaddis," 77.
63. Wittgenstein, *Philosophical Investigations*, §201, 69^e.
64. Gaddis, "How Does The State Imagine? The Willing Suspension of Disbelief," 124.
65. Gaddis, *Carpenter's Gothic*, 157.
66. *Ibid.*, 182.
67. Gaddis, "How Does The State Imagine? The Willing Suspension of Disbelief," 123.
68. Arendt, *The Origins of Totalitarianism*, 457.
69. *Ibid.*, 457.
70. *Ibid.*, 465.
71. *Ibid.*, 478.
72. Gaddis, *Carpenter's Gothic*, 36.

Chapter 11

1. Jonathan Franzen's essay on Gaddis, "Mr. Difficult," was reprinted in the paperback revision of *How to Be Alone* (New York: Farrar, Straus and Giroux, 2003), but was not included in the first edition, published a year earlier. That doesn't mean, however, that the essay on Gaddis had no impact on the first edition — in fact, it seems to have significantly directed some of Franzen's revisions to his so-called *Harper's* essay, "Perchance to Dream," which he retitled "Why Bother?" For

example, in "Mr. Difficult" Franzen describes himself as "a slattern of a reader" (241), who has started, but never come anywhere near finishing, *Remembrance of Things Past*, and has checked Coover's works out of the library, only to return them after reading a few pages. This admission presumably explains why in the revised version he has deleted some of the sections of "Perchance to Dream" that most strongly romanticized reading, notably the descriptions of long nights spent "swallowing whole the oeuvres of Dickens and Proust, Stead and Austen, Coover and DeLillo" ("Perchance to Dream In the Age of Images: A Reason to Write Novels," *Harper's* [1996], 37.

2. *Ibid.*, 261.

3. James Wood, for example, complains that a Franzen essay is "so autobiographically infected that his argument quickly sicken[s] into subjectivity" ("Abhorring a Vaccum," *New Republic*, 225.16 [2001], 32), while Ben Marcus examines Franzen's tendency to make universal claims based on his own experience in "Why Experimental Fiction Threatens to Destroy Publishing Jonathan Franzen, and Life as We Know It," *Harper's*, 311.1865 (2005).

4. John Kuehl and Steven Moore, eds., *In Recognition of William Gaddis* (Syracuse: Syracuse UP, 1984), ix.

5. Christopher Knight, *Hints and Guesses: William Gaddis's Fiction of Longing* (Madison: University of Wisconsin Press, 1997), 16. Indeed, Gaddis's use of data in his novels has often been linked to information theory. See Tom LeClair's essay on *J R* in *The Art of Excess* (1989), and John Johnston's study of the same novel in *Information Multiplicity* (1998).

6. Jean-François Lyotard, *The Postmodern Condition: A Report on Knowledge*, trans. Geoff Bennington and Brian Massumi (Manchester, UK: Manchester University Press, 1984), 41.

7. See, for example, Michael André Bernstein's essay "Making Modernist Masterpieces."

8. I explore, in some detail, Gaddis's approach to the encyclopedia in "The Collapse of Everything: William Gaddis and the Encyclopedic Novel," *Paper Empire: William Gaddis and the World System*, eds. Joseph Tabbi and Rone Shavers (Tuscaloosa: University of Alabama Press, 2007).

9. In the light of Franzen's critique of Gaddis's supposed elitism, it is ironic that the fourteenth edition of the *Encyclopaedia Britannica* — the edition that Gaddis, himself, used as a compositional tool — actually marked a significant break in the history of the *Britannica* as the editors sought to produce an encyclopedia "for the *many* instead of a book for the *few*." Herman Kogan, *The Great EB: The Story of Encyclopaedia Britannica* (Chicago: University of Chicago Press, 1958), 221.

10. William Gaddis, *The Recognitions* (New York: Penguin, 1993), 420.

11. *Ibid.*, 442.

12. *Ibid.*, 442.

13. Ralph Waldo Emerson, "Circles," *Selections from Ralph Waldo Emerson*, ed. Stephen Whicher (Boston: Houghton Mifflin, 1960), 111.

14. Because Franzen's ire seems to be particularly directed toward the length and scale of Gaddis's novels, I omit his short works from this brief discussion.

15. William Gaddis, *J R* (New York: Penguin, 1975), 518.

16. William Gaddis, *A Frolic of His Own* (New York: Poseiden, 1994), 309.

17. *Ibid.*, 122–23.

18. *Ibid.*, 341.

19. *Ibid.*, 56.

20. *Ibid.*, 16, 17.

21. *Ibid.*, 33.

22. The etymology of *encyclopedia* (which is believed to derive from a misreading of Quintilian, Pliny, and Galen) suggests the circle of learning encompassing both the arts and sciences. *The Oxford English Dictionary*, 2nd ed., vol. 5 of 20 vols. (Oxford: Clarendon, 1989), 219.

23. Gaddis, *Frolic*, 289.

24. *Ibid.*, 434.

25. *Ibid.*, 565.

26. See Rick Moody, ed., "William Gaddis: A Portfolio," *Conjunctions* 41 (2003): 372–415; and Steven Moore, ed., "Gaddis in Fiction" < http://www.williamgaddis.org/infiction/index.shtml>.

27. David Mitchell, *Ghostwritten* (New York: Random House, 1999), 201.

28. *Ibid.*, 213.

29. *Ibid.*, 232.

30. Gaddis, *Recognitions*, 221.

31. In an essay introducing Powers's fiction, Joseph Dewey, for example, described Powers as "among the most promising voices to emerge in the post–Pynchon generation" ("Dwelling in Possibility: The Fiction of Richard Powers," *The Hollins Critic* 38.2 [1996], 3). Tom LeClair makes the strongest case for Pynchon as Powers's precursor in his perceptive essay, "The Prodigious Fiction of Richard Powers, William Vollmann, and David Foster Wallace," *Critique*, 38.3 (1996): 12–37.

32. Unpublished interview with the author, 23 August 2005.

33. Richard Powers, *Three Farmers on Their Way to A Dance* (New York: Perennial, 2001), 207.

34. Richard Powers, *The Gold Bug Variations* (New York: William Morrow, 1991), 301.

35. Richard Powers, *Plowing the Dark* (New York: Farrar, Straus and Giroux, 2000), 207.

36. *Ibid.*, 45, 216. Joseph Tabbi, Introduction, xii.

37. Richard Powers, "Two Geeks on Their Way to Byzantium," interview by Harry Blume, *Atlantic Unbound* (July 20, 2000), available at http://www.theatlantic.com/unbound/interviews/ba2000–06–28.htm, par. 9.

38. Powers, *Three Farmers*, 46.

39. *Ibid.*, 38.

40. *Ibid.*, 13.

41. *Ibid.*, 205–6.

42. *Ibid.*, 209.

43. David Foster Wallace, *A Supposedly Fun Thing I'll Never Do Again* (Boston: Little, Brown, 1997), 66.

44. See Steven Moore, "The First Draft of *Infinite Jest*," available at http://www.geocities.com/athens/acropolis/8175/ij_first.htm, accessed 17 January 2009.

45. David Foster Wallace, *Infinite Jest* (Boston: Little, Brown, 1996), 322.

46. *Ibid.*, 508 ff. It is worth noting that this catalogue of blue things is presumably a parody of the exhaustive list that William Gass employs at the beginning of *On Being Blue* (1976).

47. I discuss Hal's engagement with data in my *David Foster Wallace's Infinite Jest: A Reader's Guide* (New York: Continuum, 2003), and some of the discussion, here, incorporates fragments from my earlier book.

48. Wallace, *Infinite Jest*, 507.
49. *Ibid.*, 841.
50. *Ibid.*, 641.
51. *Ibid.*, 642.
52. *Ibid.*, 379.
53. *Ibid.*, 910.
54. Franzen, "Mr. Difficult," 248.
55. Jonathan Franzen, *The Corrections* (New York: Farrar, Straus and Giroux, 2001), 431.
56. Chip's complaint that "without money he was hardly a man" (105) recalls Pivner's "a man does feel castrated in New York without money" (150–51).
57. Franzen, *The Corrections*, 265.
58. *Ibid.*, 537.
59. Gaddis, *Frolic*, 557.
60. Wallace, *Infinite Jest*, 1077 n366.
61. Oddly enough, however, some critics have mistakenly suggested that the novel is about the near future, rather than the recent past. Daniel Grassian, for example, lists the novel as one of several fictions that "envision a futuristic America" in *Hybrid Fictions* (Jefferson, NC: McFarland, 2003), 143.

62. Franzen has clearly taken great care over the accuracy of the novel's chronology, but he does make the odd error, such as when he dates the "morning of the day before Halloween" as a Monday (71). In fact, in 1984, Halloween occurred on a Wednesday.

63. Jonathan Franzen, *The Twenty-Seventh City* (New York: Farrar, Straus and Giroux, 1988), 5.

64. Jonathan Franzen, qtd. in Clarence E. Olson, "Don't Judge By Cover: Author Likes Hometown," *St. Louis Post-Dispatch*, 28 August 1988: 5.

65. These papers appeared in *Physics of the Earth and Planetary Interiors* between 1983 and 1988.

66. Jonathan Franzen, "How We Came to Be No Where," *Granta* 56 (1996): 112–123.

67. Andy's experiment with "gibberellic acid" (116) is expanded upon as one of Chip's anecdotes early in *The Corrections* (35).

Bibliography

Abádi-Nagy, Zoltán. "The Art of Fiction: An Interview with William Gaddis." *Paris Review* 105 (Winter 1987): 79–80.
Abrams, M.H. *The Mirror and the Lamp: Romantic Theory and the Critical Tradition.* Oxford: Oxford University Press, 1953.
Adams, Henry. *The Education of Henry Adams.* New York: Penguin, 1995.
Agamben, Giorgio. *Homo Sacer: Sovereign Power and Bare Life.* Trans. Daniel Heller-Roazen. Stanford: Stanford University Press, 1998.
———. *Remnants of Auschwitz: The Witness and the Archive.* Trans. Daniel Heller-Roazen. New York: Zone, 1999.
Alberti, Leon Battista. *On Painting.* Trans. John R. Spencer. New Haven: Yale University Press, 1970.
Alberts, Crystal. "Valuable Dregs: William Gaddis, the Life of an Artist." In Tabbi and Shavers 231–55.
Arendt, Hannah. *The Origins of Totalitarianism.* New York: Harcourt Brace Jovanovich, 1973.
Aristotle. *Politics.* Trans. T.A. Sinclair and Trevor J. Saunders. New York: Penguin, 1981.
Atkins, Christine. "Paul Muldoon." New York Writers Institute's *Writers Online*, http://www.albany.edu/writers-inst/webpages4/archives/olv2n2.html. Accessed 24 January 2009.
Auden, W.H. *Collected Poems.* New York: Vintage, 1991.
———. *Lectures on Shakespeare.* Ed. Arthur Kirsch. Princeton: Princeton University Press, 2000.
Barrie, J.M. *Peter Pan.* New York: Bantam, 1985.
Barthes, Roland. "The Death of the Author." *Image/Music/Text.* Ed. and trans. Stephen Heath. New York: Hill and Wang, 1977.
Barzun, Jacques. *The Use and Abuse of Art.* Princeton: Princeton University Press, 1974.
Battersby, Eileen. "The Elusive Interviewee." *The Irish Times*. 30 June 1994: 9, literary supplement.
Bazin, Andre. "Ontology of the Photographic Image." *Film Theory and Criticism: Introductory Readings.* Trans. Hugh Gray and eds. Leo Braudy and Marshall Cohen. 5th ed. New York: Oxford University Press, 1999.
Benjamin, Walter. *Illuminations.* Trans. Harry Zohn and ed. Hannah Arendt. New York: Shocken, 1968.
Benstock, Bernard. "On William Gaddis: In Recognition of James Joyce." *Wisconsin Studies in Contemporary Literature* 6, no.1 (1965), 177–189.
Bernstein, Michael André. "Making Modernist Masterpieces." *Modernism/Modernity* 5, no. 3 (1998): 1–17.
Bible, King James Version.
Birkerts, Sven. "Introduction." *Agapē Agape.* New York: Penguin, 2002.
Brown, Nicholas. "Cognitive Map, Aesthetic Object, or National Allegory?" *Carpenter's Gothic.*" In Tabbi and Shavers 151–60.
Buettner, Stewart. *American Art Theory, 1945–1970.* Ann Arbor: UMI Research Press, 1981.
Burn, Stephen. "The Collapse of Everything: William Gaddis and the Encyclopedic Novel." In Tabbi and Shavers 46–62.
———. *David Foster Wallace's Infinite Jest: A Reader's Guide.* New York: Continuum, 2003.
Bursey, Jeff, and Anne Furlong. "Cognitive Gothic: Relevance Theory, Iteration, and Style." In Tabbi and Shavers 118–33.
Bush, Douglas. *English Literature in the Early Seventeenth Century.* London: Oxford University Press, 1945.
Bush, George W. "No Child Left Behind" speech. 26 July 2007. Available at http://www.ed.gov/news/speeches/2007/07/07262007.html. Accessed 24 January 2009.
Carrington, Philip. *The Early Christian Church: Volume I, The First Christian Century.* 2 vols. London: Cambridge University Press, 1957.

Carter, Paul. *The Road to Botany Bay: An Exploration of Landscape and History.* New York: Knopf, 1988.

Coleridge, Samuel Taylor. *Biographia Literaria.* London: J.M. Dent & Sons, 1975.

Comnes, Gregory. *The Ethics of Indeterminacy in the Novels of William Gaddis.* Gainesville: University Press of Florida, 1994.

Coneybeare, F.C. *Myth, Magic, and Morals: A Study of Christian Origins.* London: Watts, 1909.

Conley, Tim. "William Gaddis Calling: Telephonic Satire and the Disconnection of Authority." *Studies in the Novel* 35, no. 4 (2003): 526–42.

Conrad, Joseph. "Preface." *The Nigger of The Narcissus.* London: Dent & Sons, 1945.

Contino, Paul J. "This Writer's Life: Irony & Faith in the Work of Tobias Wolff." *Commonweal* 21 October 2005: 18–24.

Cunningham, Don Rodger. "Cabala to Entropy: Existentialist Attitudes and the Gnostic Vision in William Gaddis's '*The Recognitions*' and Julio Cortazar's '*Rayuela.*'" Unpublished doctoral dissertation, University of Indiana, 1980.

———. "When You See Yourself: Gnostic Motifs and Their Transformation in '*The Recognitions.*'" *Soundings — An Interdisciplinary Journal* 71, no. 4 (1988): 619–637.

De Man, Paul. *Blindness and Insight: Essays in the Rhetoric of Composition.* Minneapolis: University of Minnesota Press, 1983.

Derrida, Jacques. "By Force of Mourning." Trans. Pascale-Anne Brault and Michael Naas. *Critical Inquiry* 22, no. 2 (1996): 171–192.

———. *Writing and Difference.* Trans. Alan Bass. Chicago: University of Chicago Press, 1978.

Dewey, Joseph. "Dwelling in Possibility: The Fiction of Richard Powers." *Hollins Critic* 33, no. 2 (1996): 2-16.

———. *In a Dark Time: The Apocalyptic Temper in the American Novel of the Nuclear Age.* West Lafayette, IN: Purdue University Press, 1990.

Donoghue, Denis. *Speaking of Beauty.* New Haven: Yale University Press, 2003.

Drabble, Margaret, ed. *The Oxford Companion to English Literature*, 5th ed. Oxford: Oxford University Press, 1985.

Eco, Umberto. *Travels in Hyperreality.* New York: Harvest, 1990.

Eliot, T.S. *After Strange Gods.* New York: Harcourt, Brace, 1934.

———. *The Four Quartets.* New York: Harcourt Brace Jovanovich, 1943.

———. *The Letters of T. S. Eliot, Vol. 1: 1898–1922.* Ed. Valerie Eliot. New York: Harcourt Brace Jovanovich, 1988.

———. *Selected Essays, 1917–1932.* London: Faber and Faber, 1932.

———. *Selected Prose.* Ed. and introd. Frank Kermode. San Diego: Harcourt Brace Jovanovich, 1975.

———. *The Varieties of Metaphysical Poetry.* Ed. and introd. Ronald Schuchard. New York: Harcourt Brace, 1993.

Emerson, Ralph Waldo. "Circles." *Selections from Ralph Waldo Emerson.* Ed. and introd. Stephen E. Whicher. Boston: Houghton Mifflin, 1960.

———. *Selected Essays.* New York: Penguin, 1982.

Ertel, Emmanuelle. "Interview de William Gaddis." *Profils américains* 6 (1994): 9–18.

Félix, Brigitte. *William Gaddis: L'alchimie de l'écriture.* Paris: Éditions Belin, 1997.

Foucault, Michel. "What Is an Author?" *The Foucault Reader.* Ed. Paul Rabinow. New York: Pantheon, 1984, 101–120.

Fowles, John. *The Journals of John Fowles*, vol. 2. New York: Vintage, 2007.

Franzen, Jonathan. *The Corrections.* New York: Farrar, 2001.

———. "How He Came to Be Nowhere." *Granta* 56 (1996): 112–23.

———. *How to Be Alone.* Rev. ed. New York: Picador-Farrar, 2003.

———. "Mr. Difficult: William Gaddis and the Problem of Hard-to-Read Books." *The New Yorker*, September 30, 2002.

———. "Perchance to Dream: In the Age of Images a Reason to Write Novels." *Harper's* April 1996: 35–54.

———. *The Twenty-Seventh City.* New York: Farrar, 1988.

Frost, Robert. "Education by Poetry." *Frost: Collected Poems, Prose, & Plays.* New York: Library of America, 1995.

Gadamer, Hans-Georg. *Dialogue and Dialects: Eight Hermeneutical Studies on Plato.* Trans. and introd. P. Christopher Smith. New Haven: Yale University Press, 1980.

———. *Heidegger's Ways.* Trans. John W. Stanlet and introd. Dennis J. Schmidt. Albany: State University of New York Press, 1994.

Gaddis, William. *Agapē Agape.* New York: Viking, 2002.

———. *Carpenter's Gothic.* New York: Viking, 1985.

———. "Erewhon and the Contract with America." In *The Rush for Second Place*, 80–87.

———."First Notes for a Television Program on Forgery." Keith Botsford Papers, Beinecke Library, Yale University, New Haven, CT.

———. *A Frolic of His Own.* New York: Scribner, 1995.

_____. *J R*. New York: Penguin, 1975.
_____. "The New York State Writers Institute Tapes." Ed. Christopher J. Knight. *Contemporary Literature* 42.4 (2001): 667–93.
_____. "Old Foes with New Faces." In *The Rush for Second Place*, 88–108.
_____. *The Recognitions*. New York: Penguin, 1993.
_____. *The Rush for Second Place: Essays and Occasional Writings*. Ed. Joseph Tabbi. New York: Penguin, 2002.
_____. William Gaddis Papers. Harry Ransom Center, University of Texas, Austin.
_____. William Gaddis Papers. Washington University Special Collections Library, St. Louis, MO.
Garber, Marjorie. *Vested Interests: Cross-Dressing and Cultural Anxiety*. New York: Routledge, 1992.
Gass, William H. *Finding a Form*. Ithaca: Cornell University Press, 1997.
_____. *Habitations of the Word*. New York: Simon and Schuster, 1985.
Gifford, Barry, and Lawrence Lee. *Jack's Book: An Oral Biography of Jack Kerouac*. New York: St. Martin's, 1978.
Goethe, Johann Wolfgang. *Faust*. Trans. Walter Kaufmann. New York: Anchor, 1961.
Gordon, Lyndall. *T. S. Eliot: An Imperfect Life*. New York: W.W. Norton, 1998.
Grant, Michael. *Saint Paul*. New York: Charles Scribner's Sons, 1976.
Grassian, Daniel. *Hybrid Fictions: American Literature and Generation X*. Jefferson, NC: McFarland, 2003.
Graves, Robert. *The White Goddess: A Historical Grammar of Poetic Myth*. New York: Octagon, 1972.
Green, Jack. *Fire the Bastards!* Ed. and introd. Steven Moore. Normal, IL: Dalkey Archive, 1992.
Grove, Lloyd. "Gaddis and the Cosmic Babble." Interview with William Gaddis. *Washington Post*, 23 August 1985: B10.
Guilbaut, Serge. *How New York Stole the Idea of Modern Art: Abstract Expressionism, Freedom, and the Cold War*. Chicago: University of Chicago Press, 1983.
Gunn, Giles. *The Culture of Criticism and the Criticism of Culture*. Oxford: Oxford University Press, 1987.
Habermas, Jürgen. "On the Relation Between the Secular Liberal State and Religion." *The Frankfurt School on Religion: Key Writings by the Major Thinkers*. Ed. Eduardo Mendieta. New York: Routledge, 2005, 339–348.
Hartman, Geoffrey. *Minor Prophecies: The Literary Essay in the Culture Wars*. Cambridge: Harvard University Press, 1991.

Hassan, Ihab. *The Postmodern Turn*. Columbus: Ohio State University Press, 1987.
Hemingway, Ernest. *A Farewell to Arms*. New York: Scribner, 2003.
Holt, John. *How Children Fail*. New York: Pitman, 1964.
Huizinga, Johan. *Herfsttij der Middeleeuwen: Studie over Levens- en Gedachtevormen der Veertiende en Vijftiende Eeuw in Frankrijk en de Nederlanden*. Amsterdam: Olympos, 2006.
Husserl, Edmund. *The Crisis of European Sciences and Transcendental Phenomenology: An Introduction to Phenomenological Philosophy*. Trans. David Carr. Evanston: Northwestern University Press, 1970.
Ingendaay, Paul. "Agent der Veränderung. Ein Gespräch mit William Gaddis." *Rowohlt Literatur Magazin* 39 (1997), 64–92.
_____. "Interview with William Gaddis." Trans. John Soutter. www.williamgaddis.org/nonfiction/intingendaay1995.doc. 11 November 2006.
James, Henry. *The Bostonians*. New York: Penguin, 1984.
James, Montague Rhodes. *The Apocryphal New Testament: Being the Apocryphal Gospels, Acts, Epistles, and Apocalypses*. Corrected ed. Oxford: Oxford Clarendon Press, 1953.
James, William. *A Pluralistic Universe: Hibbert Lectures at Manchester College on the Present Situation in Philosophy* (1909). Lincoln: University of Nebraska Press, 1996.
_____. *Pragmatism and Other Writings*. Ed. Giles Gunn. Harmondsworth, UK: Penguin, 2000.
_____. *The Varieties of Religious Experience*. New York: Penguin, 1982.
Jameson, Fredric. *Postmodernism or the Cultural Logic of Late Capitalism*. Durham: Duke University Press, 1991.
Johnston, John. *Carnival of Repetition: Gaddis's* The Recognitions *and Postmodern Theory*. Philadelphia: University of Pennsylvania Press, 1990.
_____. *Information Multiplicity: American Fiction in the Age of Media Saturation*. Baltimore: Johns Hopkins University Press, 1998.
Josipovici, Gabriel. *The Singer on the Shore: Essays 1991–2004*. Manchester, UK: Carcanet, 2006.
Joyce, James. *A Portrait of the Artist as a Young Man*. Oxford: Oxford University Press, 2000.
Kenner, Hugh. *The Counterfeiters: A Historical Comedy*. Bloomington: Indiana University Press, 1968.
Kermode, Frank. *The Sense of an Ending*. New York: Oxford University Press, 1967.

Kerouac, Jack. *The Subterraneans.* New York: Grove, 1958.

Kierkegaard, Søren. *The Sickness Unto Death: A Christian Psychological Exposition for Upbuilding and Awakening.* Ed. and trans. Howard V. Hong and Edna H. Hong. Princeton: Princeton University Press, 1983.

Knight, Christopher. "Flemish Art and Wyatt's Quest for Redemption in William Gaddis's *The Recognitions.*" In Kuehl and Moore 58–69.

_____. *Hints and Guesses: William Gaddis's Fiction of Longing.* Madison: University of Wisconsin Press, 1997.

_____. "William Gaddis's Parthian Shot: Social Criticism in the Posthumous *Agapē Agape* and *The Rush for Second Place.*" *Critique: Studies in Contemporary Fiction* 49, no. 2 (2008): 205–220.

Koening, David. "'Splinters from the Yew Tree': A Critical Study of William Gaddis' *The Recognitions.*" Unpublished doctoral dissertation, New York University, 1971.

_____. "The Writing of *The Recognitions.*" In Kuehl and Moore, 20–31.

Kogan, Herman. *The Great EB: The Story of the Encyclopædia Britannica.* Chicago: University of Chicago Press, 1958.

Kuehl, John, and Steven Moore. "An Interview with William Gaddis." *Review of Contemporary Fiction* 2, no. 2 (1982): 4–6.

_____, and _____, eds. *In Recognition of William Gaddis.* Syracuse: Syracuse University Press, 1984.

LeClair, Thomas. *The Art of Excess. Mastery in Contemporary American Fiction.* Chicago: University of Illinois Press, 1989.

_____. "An Interview with William Gaddis, circa 1980." In Tabbi and Shavers 17–27.

_____. "The Prodigious Fiction of Richard Powers, William Vollmann, and David Foster Wallace." *Critique* 38, no. 3 (1996): 12–37.

Lévy, Sophie, ed. *A Transatlantic Avant-Garde: American Artists in Paris 1918–1939.* Berkeley: University of California Press, 2003.

Lewis, Wyndam. *Tarr.* New York: Alfred A. Knopf, 1918.

Lin, Yu-Chin. *Justice, History and Language in James Joyce's "Finnegans Wake."* Lewiston, NY: Edwin Mellen, 2002.

Logan, Marie-Rose, and Tomasz Mirkowicz. "Interview with William Gaddis." *Literatura na Swiece* (Warsaw) no. 1: 150 (1984): 178–89.

Lyotard, Jean-François. *The Postmodern Condition: A Report on Knowledge.* Trans. Geoff Bennington and Brian Massumi. Foreword Fredric Jameson. Theory and History of Lit. 10. Manchester, UK: Manchester University Press, 1984.

Marcus, Ben. "Why Experimental Fiction Threatens to Destroy Publishing, Jonathan Franzen, and Life as We Know It." *Harper's Magazine* October 2005: 39–52.

Marx, Karl, and Frederick Engels. *The German Ideology.* Ed. C.J. Arthur. New York: International, 1970.

McGrath, Charles. "Word Freak." *New York Times Magazine* 19 November 2006: 60–65.

McHugh, Roland. *Annotations to "Finnegans Wake."* Baltimore: John Hopkins University Press, 1991.

Melville, Herman. *The Confidence-Man: His Masquerade.* New York: Norton, 2006.

_____. *Moby-Dick.* Eds. Harrison Hayford and Hershel Parker. New York: W.W. Norton, 1967.

Mencken, H.L. *The American Language.* New York: Knopf, 1947.

Miller, J. Hillis. *Topographies.* Stanford: Stanford University Press, 1995.

Mink, Janis. *Marcel Duchamp, 1887–1968: Art as Anti-Art.* Köln: Taschen, 2000.

Mitchell, David. *Ghostwritten.* 1999. New York: Vintage-Random, 2001.

Moody, Rick, ed. "William Gaddis: A Portfolio." *Conjunctions* 41 (2003): 372–415.

Moore, Steven. "The First Draft of *Infinite Jest.*" *The Howling Fantods.* 11 May 2003. Available at http://www.thehowlingfantods.com/ij_first.htm. Accessed 8 November 2004.

_____. *The Gaddis Annotations Project.* http://www.williamgaddis.org.

_____. "The Prodigious Fiction of Richard Powers, William Vollmann, and David Foster Wallace." *Critique* 38, no. 3 (1996): 12–37.

_____. *A Reader's Guide to The Recognitions.* Lincoln: Nebraska University Press, 1982.

_____. *William Gaddis.* New York: Twayne, 1989.

Morrissey, Ted. "Recognizing a Masterpiece: William Gaddis's Reinterpretation of Flemish Art." http://www.williamgaddis.org/criticalinterpessays/morrisseyrecsart.shtml. Accessed 17 September 2009.

Murdoch, Iris. *Metaphysics as a Guide to Morals.* New York: Allen Lane, 1993.

Nancy, Jean-Luc. *Being Singular Plural.* Trans. Richard D. Richardson and Anne E. O'Byrne. Stanford, CA: Stanford University Press, 2000.

_____. *The Inoperative Community.* Trans. Peter Connor, et al. Minneapolis: University of Minnesota Press, 1991.

Nietzsche, Friedrich. *The Twilight of the Idols and The Anti-Christ: or How to Philosophize with a Hammer.* Ed. Michael Tanner. Trans. R.J. Hollingdale. New York: Penguin, 1990.

_____. *The Will to Power.* Trans. Walter Kaufmann and R. J. Hollingdale. New York: Vintage, 1968.

Nuttall, A. D. *Shakespeare the Thinker*. New Haven: Yale University Press, 2007.
Olson, Clarence E. "Don't Judge By Cover: Author Likes Hometown." *St. Louis Post-Dispatch* 28 Aug. 1988: 5.
Orwell, George. *1984*. New York: Signet Classic, 1977.
Ovid. *The Metamorphoses*. Trans. Horace Gregory. New York: Viking, 1958.
Ozick, Cynthia. "William Gaddis and the Scion of Darkness." *What Henry James Knew*. London: Vintage, 1994, 218–225.
Palmer, Philip Mason, and Robert Pattison More. *The Sources of the Faust Tradition: From Simon Magus to Lessing*. New York: Oxford University Press, 1936.
Panofsky, Erwin. *Perspective as Symbolic Form*. Trans. Christopher S. Wood. New York: Zone, 1991.
——. "Style and Medium in the Motion Pictures." *Critique* 1, no. 3 (1947): 5–28.
Peukert, Helmut. "Enlightenment and Theology as Unfinished Projects." *The Frankfurt School on Religion: Key Writings by the Major Thinkers*. Ed. Eduardo Mendieta. New York: Routledge, 2005, 351–370.
Pinker, Steven. *The Blank Slate: The Modern Denial of Human Nature*. New York: Penguin, 2003.
Plato. *The Republic*. Trans. Benjamin Jowett. Cleveland: Fine Editions, 1946.
Pollock, Jackson. "Interview with William Wright, 'My Painting.'" 1950. Rpt. *Jackson Pollock: Interviews, Articles, Reviews*. New York: MoMA, 1999.
Pope, Alexander. "Essay on Man." *Essay on Man and Other Poems*. Ed. Stanley Applebaum. Mineola, NY: Dover, 1994.
Posner, Richard. *Law and Literature*. Cambridge: Harvard University Press, 1998.
Powers, Richard. *Galatea 2.2*. New York: HarperCollins, 1996.
——. *The Gold Bug Variations*. New York: Morrow, 1991.
——. *Plowing the Dark*. New York: Farrar, 2000.
——. *Three Farmers on Their Way to a Dance*. New York: Beech Tree-Morrow, 1985.
——. "Two Geeks on Their Way to Byzantium: A Conversation with Richard Powers." With Harvey Blume. *Atlantic Unbound*. 28 June 2000. 16 Sept. 2003. http://www.theatlantic.com/unbound/interviews/ba2000-06-28.htm. Accessed 15 September 2009.
Pynchon, Thomas. *The Crying of Lot 49*. 1966. Rpt. New York: Perennial Classics, 1999.
——. *V.* 1963. Rpt. London: Vintage, 2000.
Raban, Jonathan. "At Home in Babel." *New York Review of Books*, 17 February 1994. 3–4, 6.

Ricoeur, Paul. *Figuring the Sacred: Religion, Narrative, and Imagination*. Ed. Mark I. Wallace. Trans. David Pellauer. Minneapolis: Fortress, 1995.
Rothstein, Edward. "Classical Music Imperiled: Can You Hear the Shrug?" *The New York Times*, national ed. 2 July 2007: B1+.
Rousseau, Jean-Jacques. *Emile, or On Education*. Trans. Allan Bloom. New York: Basic, 1979.
Rufinus, Presbyter of Aquileia, trans. *Recognitions of Clement, The Ante-Nicine Fathers: Translations of The Writings of the Fathers Down to A.D. 325*, Vol. 8. Eds. Rev. Alexander Roberts and James Donaldson. Grand Rapids: Wm. B. Eerdmans, 1989.
Russell, Allison. *Crossing Boundaries: Postmodern Travel Literature*. New York: Palgrave, 2000.
Safer, Elaine B. *The Contemporary American Comic Epic: The Novels of Barth, Pynchon, Gaddis and Kesey*. Detroit: Wayne State University Press, 1989.
Salemi, Joseph. "To Soar in Atonement: Art as Expiation in Gaddis's *The Recognitions*." In Kuehl and Moore 46–57.
Sawyer, Tom. "False Gold to Forge: The Forger Behind Wyatt Gwyon." *Review of Contemporary Fiction* 2, no. 2 (1982): 50–4.
Schopenhauer, Arthur. "Transcendental Speculations on Apparent Deliberateness in the Fate of the Individual." *Parerga and Paralipomena: Short Philosophical Essays*. Trans. E.F.J. Payne. Oxford: Clarendon Press, 1974.
Schryer, Stephen. "The Aesthetics of First- and Second-Order Cybernetics in William Gaddis's *J R*." In Tabbi and Shavers 75–89.
Schuchard, Ronald. *Eliot's Dark Angel: Intersections of Life and Art*. Oxford: Oxford University Press, 1999.
Shklovsky, Viktor. *Theory of Prose*. Trans. Benjamin Sher. Normal, IL: Dalkey Archive, 1991.
Shranks, Andrew. *Faith in Honesty: The Essential Nature of Theology*. Aldershot, UK: Ashgate, 2005.
Smith, Thomas, Rev. "Introductory Notice to the Recognitions of Clement." *The Ante-Nicine Fathers: Translations of The Writings of the Fathers Down to A.D. 325*, Vol. 8. Eds. Rev. Alexander Roberts and James Donaldson. Grand Rapids: Wm. B. Eerdmans, 1989.
Solnit, Rebecca. "The Silence of the Lambswool Cardigans." *Storming the Gates of Paradise: Landscapes for Politics*. Berkeley: University of California Press, 2007.
Spencer, Nicholas. *After Utopia: The Rise of Critical Space in Twentieth-Century Ameri-*

can Fiction. Lincoln: University of Nebraska Press, 2006.

———. "Critical Mimesis: *J R*'s Transition to Postmodernity." In Tabbi and Shavers 137–50.

Spengler, Oswald. *The Decline of The West*, Vol. I: *Form and Actuality*. Trans. Charles Francis Atkinson. New York: Alfred A. Knopf, 2000.

———. *The Decline of The West*, Vol. II: *Perspectives of World History*. Trans. Charles Francis Atkinson. New York: Alfred A. Knopf, 2000.

Spinoza. *Ethics*. Trans. G.H.R. Parkinson. Oxford: Oxford University Press, 2000.

Stark, John. "William Gaddis: Just Recognition." *The Hollins Critic* xiv, no. 2 (1977): 1–12.

Steiner, George. *Real Presences: Is There Anything in What We Say?* London: Faber and Faber, 1989.

Stevens, Wallace. *Letters of Wallace Stevens*. Ed. Holly Stevens. Foreword Richard Howard. Berkeley: University of California Press, 1996.

Stonehill, Brian. "Plagiarizing *The Recognitions*." *The Self-Conscious Novel: Artifice in Fiction from Joyce to Pynchon*. Philadelphia: University of Pennsylvania Press, 1988, 114–140.

Tabbi, Joseph. "Afterword." *Agapē Agape*. New York: Penguin, 2002.

———. "Introduction." *The Rush for Second Place: Essays and Occasional Writings*. By William Gaddis. Ed. Joseph Tabbi. New York: Penguin, 2002, vii–xxi.

———. "Introduction." In Tabbi and Shavers 1–14.

———. "The Technology of Quotation: William Gaddis's *J R* and Contemporary Media," *Mosaic* 28, no. 4 (1995), 144–64.

———, and Rone Shavers, eds. *Paper Empire: William Gaddis and the World System*. Tuscaloosa: University of Alabama Press, 2007.

Tanner, Tony. *City of Words: American Fiction 1950–1970*. New York: Harper & Row, 1971.

———. *Thomas Pynchon*. Contemporary Writers. London: Methuen, 1982.

Thielemans, Johan. "Art as Redemption of Trash: Bast and Friends in Gaddis' *J R*." In Kuehl and Moore 135–46.

Thompson, E.P. *Witness Against the Beast*. New York: New, 1993.

Twain, Mark. *The Adventures of Huckleberry Finn*. London: Penguin, 2003.

Vaihinger, Hans. *The Philosophy of 'As if': A System of the Theoretical, Practical and Religious Fictions of Mankind*. Trans. C.K. Ogden. New York: Barnes and Noble, 1966.

Vanwesenbeeck, Birger. "Art and Community in William Gaddis's *The Recognitions*." *Mosaic* 42, no. 3 (2009): 141–56.

Wadlington, Warwick. *The Confidence Game in American Literature*. Princeton: Princeton University Press, 1975.

Walker, Christopher. Review of *A Frolic of His Own*, by William Gaddis. *The Observer*, 27 February 1994, 18.

Wallace, David Foster. *Infinite Jest*. 1996. London: Abacus, 1997.

———. *Infinite Jest*. Boston: Little, Brown, 1996.

———. *A Supposedly Fun Thing I'll Never Do Again*. Boston: Little, Brown, 1997.

Weber, Max. *The Protestant Ethic and the Spirit of Capitalism*. Trans. Talcott Parsons. New York: Charles Scribner's Sons, 1958.

Weisenburger, Steven. *Fables of Subversion: Satire and the American Novel, 1930–1980*. Athens: University of Georgia Press, 1995.

Werner, Craig Hansen. *Paradoxical Resolutions: American Fiction Since James Joyce*. Urbana: University of Illinois Press, 1982.

Whitehead, Colson. *John Henry Days*. New York: Doubleday, 2001.

Wiener, Norbert. *The Human Use of Human Beings: Cybernetics and Society*. 1954. Rpt. New York: Da Capo, 1988.

Williams, Raymond. *The Long Revolution*. New York: Columbia University Press, 1961.

Wilson, A.N. *Paul: The Mind of the Apostle*. New York: W.W. Norton, 1997.

Wittgenstein, Ludwig. *Philosophical Investigations*. Trans. G.E.M. Anscombe. Oxford: Blackwell, 2001.

Wolfe, Peter. *A Vision of His Own: The Mind and Art of William Gaddis*. Cranbury, NJ: Associated University Presses, 1997.

Wolfe, Tom. *The Painted Word*. New York: Farrar, Straus and Giroux, 1975.

Wolff, Tobias. *Old School*. New York: Alfred A. Knopf, 2004.

Wood, James. "Abhorring a Vacuum." Review of *The Corrections*, by Jonathan Franzen. *New Republic* 15 October 2001, 32–6, 40.

Wutz, Michael. "Writing from between the Gaps: *Agapē Agape* and Twentieth-Century Media Culture." In Tabbi and Shavers 185–210.

About the Contributors

Crystal Alberts is an assistant professor of English at the University of North Dakota. Her latest publications include "Valuable Dregs: William Gaddis, the Life of an Artist" and "Three Early Stories by William Gaddis." She also has an article in the forthcoming *The Salt Companion to Diane Glancy*.

Stephen J. Burn is an assistant professor of English at Northern Michigan University. He is the author of *David Foster Wallace's Infinite Jest: A Reader's Guide*. He is working on a book on the writings of Jonathan Franzen and has co-edited a collection devoted to Richard Powers.

Tim Conley is an associate professor of English and comparative literature at Brock University. He is the author of *Joyces Mistakes: Problems of Intention, Irony, and Interpretation* and a collection of short fiction, *Whatever Happens*, and is co-author (with Stephen Cain) of *The Encyclopedia of Fictional and Fantastic Languages*. His essays have appeared in such journals as *Comparative Literature, James Joyce Quarterly, Studies in the Novel, Papers on Language and Literature*, and *Soundings*.

Joseph Conway completed his dissertation on the subject of counterfeiting and confidence men in nineteenth- and twentieth-century American literature at Washington University in Saint Louis. In his spare time, he is a playwright.

Mathieu Duplay is a professor of literature at Université Charles-de-Gaulle-Lille 3. He is the author of *Carpenter's Gothic; William Gaddis: le scandale de l'écriture* and co-editor of *Nouveaux passages transatlantiques*.

William H. Gass is the David May Distinguished Professor Emeritus in the Humanities at Washington University in Saint Louis. He is an author, philosopher, translator and critic who has been awarded the National Book Critics Circle award for criticism three times. His numerous publications include *Finding a Form, Habitations of the Word, In the Heart of the Heart of the Country*, and *On Being Blue*.

Christopher J. Knight is a professor of English at the University of Montana and is the author of *The Patient Particulars: American Modernism and the Technique of Originality, Hints and Guesses: William Gaddis's Fiction of Longing,* and *Uncommon Readers: Denis Donoghue, Frank Kermode, George Steiner and the Tradition of the Common Reader.*

Christopher Leise is an assistant professor of English at Whitman College. He has articles forthcoming on Thomas Pynchon in *Pynchon Notes* and Marilynne Robinson in *Studies in the Novel*, and he is co-editing a collection of essays on Pynchon's *Against the Day* with Jeffrey Severs.

Lisa Siraganian is an assistant professor of English at Southern Methodist University, where she specializes in twentieth-century literature. Her recent publications include "Telling a Horror Story, Conscientiously: Representing the Armenian Genocide in Atom Egoyan's Films" and "Out of Air: Theorizing the Art Object in Gertrude Stein and Wyndham Lewis." She is completing a book titled *Breathing Freely: The Object of Art and the Subject of Politics in American Modernism.*

John Soutter is a professor of English at the University of Business and International Studies in Geneva. He is an active translator and contributor to scholarship on William Gaddis.

Birger Vanwesenbeeck is an assistant professor at SUNY Fredonia. He has forthcoming articles on Thomas Pynchon and William Gaddis in *Pynchon Notes* and *Mosaic*.

Index

Abádi-Nagy, Zoltán 171, 178, 181, 182, 183, 184, 185, 186, 187, 193; *see also* "The Art of Fiction: An Interview with William Gaddis"
Abd-er-Rahman 16, 173
Abrams, M.H. 75, 179, 193
Abstract Expressionism 43, 102, 108–111, 182, 195
Ackerley, J.R. 171
Adams, Henry 58, 59, 177, 193
Adversus Haereses 86
Afar Triangle 145
Afghanistan 149
Africa 2, 6–7, 9, 14–17, 19–20, 31, 91, 123, 143–159, 171, 188
After Strange Gods 59, 178, 194
Agamben, Giorgio 146–147, 150–151, 189, 193; *see also Homo Sacer: Sovereign Power and Bare Life*
agapē 5, 67, 95, 99
Agapē Agape 5, 36, 39–40, 42, 47, 53, 56, 64, 67, 87–88, 91–100, 126, 151, 164, 171, 175, 177, 179, 181, 182, 187, 189, 193, 194, 196, 198
"Agent of Change: A Conversation with William Gaddis" 184; *see also* Ingendaay, Paul
Aïda 78
Alberti, Leon Battista 81, 180, 193
Alberts, Crystal 3, 171, 175, 181, 184, 193
Algeciras (Spain) 15, 16, 17, 173
Algeria 15, 17
Algiers (Algeria) 15
Ambriere, Francis 173
American Art Theory, 1945–1970 183, 193; *see also* Buettner, Stewart
American Jurisprudence 181
The American Language 30, 174, 196; *see also* Mencken, H.L.
The Anatomy of Criticism 87; *see also* Frye, Northrop
Andre, Carl 102
Angola 149
Ansen, Alan 11
The Anti-Christ 121, 185; *see also* Nietzsche, Friedrich
The Apocryphal New Testament: Being the Apocryphal Gospels, Acts, Epistles, and Apocalypses 185, 195
apophaticism 4, 51–68
aporia 4, 35–50, 175
Arendt, Hannah 150–151, 157–158, 180, 189, 193
Argus 77, 81
Aristotle 147, 151, 189, 193; *see also* Politics
Arkansas 30
art 2, 4, 5–6, 7, 10, 11, 12, 18, 19, 24, 35–50, 51–52, 55, 57, 66, 69–70, 80, 82, 85, 89–99, 101–114, 125, 127, 132, 135, 141–142, 165, 175, 176, 179, 180, 182, 183, 183
The Art of Excess: Mastery in Contemporary American Fiction 190; *see also* LeClair, Tom
"The Art of Fiction: An Interview with William Gaddis" 171, 178, 183, 185, 186, 189, 193; *see also* Abádi-Nagy, Zoltán
artist 5, 6, 9, 10, 11, 18, 19, 35–50, 51–52, 54, 56, 64, 65, 66, 80, 88–90, 92, 97–99, 101–114, 125, 127, 135, 167, 173, 178, 182, 183
Atkins, Christine 177, 193
Atwood, Margaret 150
Auden, W.H. 51, 176, 193
Auschwitz 157
Austen, Jane 190
Australopithecus afarensis 145
Austria 95

Baal-zebub 78
Babbitt, Irving 57
Bach, Johann Sebastian 34, 54, 56–57, 121, 125, 134–136
Bacon, Francis 179
Baedeker (travel guides) 13, 14
Baghdad (Iraq) 83
Bakhtin, Mikhail 12, 71, 73
Barrie, J. M. 140, 142, 188, 193; *see also* Peter Pan
Barthes, Roland 12, 78, 81, 180, 193
Barzun, Jacques 177, 193; *see also The Use and Abuse of Art*
Battersby, Eileen 174, 177, 181, 193
Baudrillard, Jean 87, 172
Bazin, André 82, 85, 180; *see also* "Ontology of the Photographic Image"

201

Index

Beardsley, Monroe 92
Beat Generation 12, 101
"Bed" 112; *see also* Rauschenberg, Robert
Beelzeboul 78
Behmenists 33
Being Singular Plural 98, 182, 196; *see also* Nancy, Jean-Luc
Belgium 173
Belloc, Hilaire 54
Bellow, Saul 96
Benjamin, Walter 70, 82, 83, 85, 92, 106, 126, 142, 180, 193
Benstock, Bernard 171, 181, 184, 193
Bernstein, Michael André 190, 193
Bible 31, 54, 64–65, 121, 153, 178, 185, 193
Biographia Literaria 53, 177, 194; *see also* Coleridge, Samuel Taylor
biopolitics 143–159
Birkerts, Sven 40, 42, 43, 175, 176, 193
Biskra (Algeria) 15, 17
The Blank Slate: The Modern Denial of Human Nature 187, 197; *see also* Pinker, Steven
Blindness and Insight: Essays in the Rhetoric of Composition 181, 194; *see also* de Man, Paul
Bloch, Ernst 178; *see also The Principle of Hope*
Bloom, Allan 186, 187
Blue's Les Guide France 173; *see also* Francis Ambriere
Blume, Harvey 164, 190, 198; *see also* "Two Geeks on Their Way to Byzantium"
Boccaccio, Giovanni 24, 61; *see also Decameron*
Bogart, Humphrey 83
Bombay (India) 168
Booth, John Wilkes 123
Borges, Jorge 80
Bosch, Hieronymus 85
Boston 16, 59, 164
The Bostonians 59, 178, 195
Bous Saâda (Algeria) 15
Brentwood (Missouri) 168
Breton, André 108
Bride Stripped Bear by Her Bachelors, Even 183; *see also* Duchamp, Marcel
Brooks, Cleanth 179
The Brothers Karamazov 84; *see also* Dostoyevsky, Fyodor
Brown, Nicholas 187, 193
Bruckner, Anton 53
Buddha 78
Buettner, Stewart 183, 193; *see also American Art Theory, 1945–1970*
Burgos (Spain) 15, 16
Burn, Stephen 7, 181, 193
Bursey, Jeff 141, 188, 193; *see also* Furlong, Anne
Burundi 189
Bush, Douglas 174, 193; *see also English Literature in the Early Seventeenth Century*
Bush, George W. 126, 131, 187, 188, 193
"By Force of Mourning" 194; *see also* Derrida, Jacques
Byron, Lord 9

Cage, John 102
Calder, Alexander 108
Cape Ann (Massachusetts) 18, 59
Carnegie, Dale 84; *see also How to Win Friends and Influence People*
Carnival of Repetition: William Gaddis's "The Recognitions" and Postmodern Theory 12, 71, 171, 172, 179, 184, 195; *see also* Johnston, John
Carpenter's Gothic 2, 4, 6–7, 27–34, 38, 57, 63, 91, 96, 115, 121–125, 130, 140, 143–159, 174, 177, 181, 186–187, 188–189, 193
Carrington, Philip 185, 193
Carter, Paul 25, 174, 194; *see also The Road to Botany Bay: An Exploration of Landscape and History*
Casbah (Algiers) 15
Central America 9, 13, 14, 171
Cervantes 180
Chaos Bound: Orderly Disorder in Contemporary Literature and Society 175; *see also* Hayles, N. Katherine
Chomsky, Noam 129
Christ *see* Jesus Christ
Christianity 2, 4, 5, 6, 19, 32, 43, 47, 55, 57, 60–62, 65–67, 70, 86–100, 116–125, 149–150, 153, 176, 181, 182; *see also* Jesus Christ
City of Words: American Fiction 1950–1970 185, 198; *see also* Tanner, Tony
Clementine Recognitions 86, 117–119, 181
Cleveland 122
The Closing of the American Mind 187; *see also* Bloom, Allan
Coleridge, Samuel Taylor 53, 63, 67, 88, 177, 194; *see also Biographia Literaria*
Comnes, Gregory 59, 72–74, 172, 177, 179, 180, 182, 186, 194
Conceptual Art 111
Coneybeare, F. C. 185, 194; *see also Myth, Magic, and Morals: A Study of Christian Origins*
The Confidence Game in American Literature 185, 198; *see also* Wadlington, Warwick
The Confidence Man 86, 118, 180, 196; *see also* Melville, Herman
Conley, Tim 6, 187, 194
Conrad, Joseph 54, 177, 182, 186, 194; *see also Heart of Darkness; The Nigger of Narcissus*
Constantine 86
Conte, Joseph 175, 194
The Contemporary American Comic Epic: The Novels of Barth, Pynchon, Gaddis, and Kesey 185, 197; *see also* Safer, Elaine B.
Contino, Paul J. 176

Index

Cooper, Gary 83
Coover, Robert 190
Córdoba (Spain) 16
The Corrections 167–168, 191, 194; *see also* Franzen, Jonathan
The Counterfeiters: A Historical Comedy 185, 196; *see also* Kenner, Hugh
Crane, Stephen 59
The Crisis of European Sciences and Transcendental Phenomenology: An Introduction to Phenomenological Philosophy 95, 181, 195; *see also* Husserl, Edmund
Crossing Boundaries: Postmodern Travels in Literature 12–14, 172, 197; *see also* Russell, Allison
The Crying of Lot 49 93, 176, 197; *see also* Pynchon, Thomas
Cubism 108
The Culture of Criticism and the Criticism of Culture 177, 195; *see also* Gunn, Giles
Cunningham, Don Rodger 185, 194
cybernetics 37–41, 87, 132, 175; *see also* Wiener, Norbert

Dachau 150
Dadaism 108
Dali, Salvador 109
Dara, Evan 169
Darwin, Charles 29, 31, 144, 148, 165
David Foster Wallace's Infinite Jest: A Reader's Guide 191
Davis, Stuart 108
The Day After 149
Decameron 61–62
The Decline of the West 118, 185, 198
de Kooning, Willem 111–112
Deleuze, Gilles 71, 73, 87
DeLillo, Don 2, 88, 111, 186, 190
de Man, Paul 93–94, 96, 181, 182, 194
Demuth, Charles 108
Derrida, Jacques 3, 66, 87, 98, 178, 182, 194
Descartes, René 166
Detroit 122, 165
Dewey, Joseph 186, 190, 194
Dialogue and Dialectic: Eight Hermeneutical Studies on Plato 178; *see also* Gadamer, Hans-Georg
Dickens, Charles 190
Dickinson, Emily 59
Diggers 33
Diptera 77, 81–82
The Divinity School Address 60; *see also* Emerson, Ralph Waldo
Djelfa (Algeria) 17
Doctor Faustus 114; *see also* Mann, Thomas
Donoghue, Denis 178, 194
Dos Passos, John 59
Dostoyevsky, Fyodor 90; *see also The Brothers Karamozov*
Dresden 83

"The Dry Salvages" 18–19; *see also* Eliot, T.S.; *The Four Quartets*
Duchamp, Marcel 6, 109, 183

The Early Christian Church: Volume I The First Christian Century 185, 193; *see also* Carrington, Phillip
Earthworks 102–103, 111
Ebonites 118
Edinburgh 168
education 6, 30, 92, 127–132, 136, 140–142, 187
"Education by Poetry" 176, 194; *see also* Frost, Robert
The Education of Henry Adams 177, 193; *see also* Adams, Henry
Edwards, Jonathan 27
Egypt 60, 70, 78, 82
El Escorial (monastery) 14–17, 20–22, 25
Eliot, T. S. 3, 4, 18–19, 25, 52–53, 57–61, 67, 73, 77–79, 81, 85, 92, 174, 177, 178, 179, 180, 182, 194; *see also* "The Dry Salvages"; *The Four Quartets*; "The Little Gidding"; "The Metaphysical Poets"; *The Waste Land*
Eliot's Dark Angel: Intersections of Life and Art 179, 197; *see also* Schuchard, Ronald
El Salvador 149
Emerson, Ralph Waldo 4, 59–60, 67, 162, 177, 190, 194; *see also* "Circles"; "The Divinity School Address"
Emile 6, 132, 134, 142, 186, 187, 188, 197; *see also* Rousseau, Jean-Jacques
Encino 28
Encyclopedia Britannica 161–162, 190
Engels, Friedrich 185, 196; *see also* Marx, Karl
England 4, 173
English Literature in the Early Seventeenth Century 174, 193; *see also* Bush, Douglas
Enlightenment 79, 125
"Enlightenment and Theology as Unfinished Projects" 186, 197; *see also* Peukert, Helmut
Enron 1, 2
Enron: The Smartest Guys in the Room 2, 171
entropy 4, 35–50, 53, 56, 118, 132, 175
Epicureanism 79
Erasmus 27
Ertel, Emmanuelle 194
eschatology 88–90, 100
"Essay on Man" 77–78, 180, 197; *see also* Pope, Alexander
The Ethics of Indeterminacy in the Novels of William Gaddis 73, 172, 177, 179, 182, 186, 194; *see also* Comnes, Gregory
Eucharist 5, 23, 73, 97–99
Expressionism *see* Abstract Expressionism

Fables of Subversion: Satire and the American Novel, 1930–1980 183, 186, 198; *see also* Weisenburger, Steven

Falwell, Reverend Jerry 116
A Farewell to Arms 74–75, 179, 195; *see also* Hemingway, Ernest
Faulkner, William 149
Faust 86, 89–90, 114, 117–118, 180, 181, 185, 195, 197; *see also* Doctor Faustus; Goethe, Johann Wolfgang; Mann, Thomas
Félix, Brigitte 139, 141, 188, 194; *see also William Gaddis: L'alchimie de l'écriture*
Fes (Morocco) 15, 16
Fifth Monarchists 33
Figuring the Sacred: Religion, Narrative, and Imagination 177, 197; *see also* Ricoeur, Paul
Finding a Form 10, 171, 173, 195; *see also* Gass, William H.
"Fire and Ice" 90; *see also* Frost, Robert
Fire the Bastards! 181, 195; *see also* Green, Jack
Fish, Stanley 2
Flanders (Flemish) 5, 70, 80, 89, 105, 108, 110, 112
Flaubert, Gustave 3, 19, 95
Florence 69
Flynn, Errol 83
Ford, Gerald 136, 137, 188
Form and Actuality see *The Decline of the West*
Foucault, Michel 147, 194
The Four Quartets 18, 58, 78, 174, 177, 194; *see also* "The Dry Salvages"; Eliot, T.S.; "Little Gidding"
Fowles, John 35, 36, 194
France 15, 173, 189; *see also* Hendaye; Paris
Franzen, Jonathan 5, 7, 69, 70–71, 91, 160–161, 163–170, 179, 180, 189, 190, 191, 194; *see also The Corrections*; *How to Be Alone*; "Mr. Difficult"; *The Twenty-Seventh City*
French New Wave 82
Freud, Sigmund 72–73, 93
A Frolic of His Own 2, 35–38, 39, 41–47, 50, 91–92, 102–103, 111, 132, 140, 155, 162–163, 167, 171, 175, 176, 180, 181, 183, 184, 186, 187, 190, 191, 194
Frost, Robert 4, 51, 90, 176, 194; *see also* "Education by Poetry"; "Fire and Ice"
Frye, Northrop 87, 179; *see also The Anatomy of Criticism*
Furlong, Anne 141, 188, 193; *see also* Bursey, Jeff

Gadamer, Hans-George 66, 178, 179, 194; *see also Dialogue and Dialectic: Eight Hermeneutical Studies on Plato*
Gaddis, Sarah 10
Galen 190
Galleria degli Uffizi (Florence) 69
Garber, Marjorie 140, 188, 195
Gass, William H. 4, 10, 67, 171, 173, 179, 181, 182, 185, 186, 189, 191, 195
General Motors 90

The German Ideology 185, 196; *see also* Engels, Friedrich; Marx, Karl
Germany 11, 108, 114
Ghostwritten 163–164, 190, 196; *see also* Mitchell, David
Gibbs, Josiah Willard 38
Gibraltar 15–17
Gifford, Barry 101, 182, 195
Gnosticism 86, 117
Goebbels, Joseph 150
Goethe, Johann Wolfgang 89–90, 114, 181, 195; *see also* Faust
The Gold Bug Variations 164, 190, 197; *see also* Powers, Richard
Golgotha 124
Gordon, Lyndall 177, 195
Gorky, Arshile 6, 109
Granada (Spain) 15–16, 20
Grant, Michael 185, 195; *see also Saint Paul*
Grassian, Daniel 191, 195
Graves, Robert 72, 117, 185, 195
The Great Gatsby 90
Great Rift 145, 148
Greeley, Reverend Andrew M. 61
Green, Jack 181, 195; *see also Fire the Bastards!*
Greenberg, Clement 112
Greenwich Village 11, 15, 17, 89, 101, 104, 111
Gregory Rift 144
Grove, Lloyd 59, 177, 195
Guadalupe (Spain) 15, 21–22, 174
Guardians of the Secret 109
Guggenheim, Peggy 109
Guilbaut, Serge 108–109, 182, 183, 195
Gulf of Aqaba 145
Gulf of Suez 145
Gunn, Giles 55, 177, 178, 185, 195

Habermas, Jürgen 186, 196
Habitations of the Word 179, 195; *see also* Gass, William H.
Habyarimana, Juvenal 189
Hamlet 52; *see also* Shakespeare, William
The Handmaid's Tale 149; *see also* Atwood, Margaret
Hanoi 83
Hartman, Geoffrey 177, 195; *see also Minor Prophecies: The Literary Essay in the Culture Wars*
Harvard University 14, 59, 92, 168
Hassan, Ihab 177, 195; *see also The Postmodern Turn*
Hawthorne, Nathaniel 59
Hayles, N. Katherine 175; *see also Chaos Bound: Orderly Disorder in Contemporary Literature and Science*
Heart of Darkness 91; *see also* Conrad, Joseph; *The Nigger of Narcissus*
Heidegger, Martin 67, 179, 182
Heidegger's Ways 179, 194; *see also* Gadamer, Hans-Georg

Hemingway, Ernest 5, 9, 19, 74–83, 85, 179, 184, 195; *see also A Farewell to Arms*; *In Our Time*
Hendaye (France) 15, 173
Henner, Jean-Jacques 105
Herfsttij der Mideleeuwen: Studie over Levens- en Gedachtevormen der Veertiende en Vijftiende Eeuw in Frankrijk en de Nederlanden 181, 195; *see also* Huizinga, Johan
Hinduism 3
Hints and Guesses: William Gaddis's Fiction of Longing 161, 173, 184, 186, 187, 190, 196; *see also* Knight, Christopher J.
Hiroshima 19, 83, 157
Hofstadter, Richard 42
Holland, J.G. 160
Holt, John 129–130, 135–136, 187, 195; *see also How Children Fail*
Homo Ludens 93; *see also* Huizinga, Johan
Homo Sacer: Sovereign Power and Bare Life 147–149, 189; *see also* Agamben, Giorgio
Horn of Africa 145
How Children Fail 129, 135, 187, 195
"How Does the State Imagine? The Willing Suspension of Disbelief" 189
How New York Stole the Idea of Modern Art: Abstract Expressionism, Freedom, and the Cold War 182, 195; *see also* Guilbaut, Serge
How to Be Alone 160, 189, 194; *see also* Franzen, Jonathan
How to Win Friends and Influence People 94; *see also* Carnegie, Dale
Huckleberry Finn 90, 128, 198
Huizinga, Johan 89, 92–93, 126, 181, 182, 195
The Human Use of Human Beings: Cybernetics and Society 38, 175, 198; *see also* Wiener, Norbert
Hume, David 61, 76, 185
Husserl, Edmund 94–97, 181, 182, 195; *see also The Crisis of European Sciences and Transcendental Phenomenology: An Introduction to Phenomenological Philosophy*
Hutu 189
Hyde Park 31
Hypatia 61, 63

The Idea of a Christian Society 60; *see also* Eliot, T.S.
Illuminations 180, 193; *see also* Benjamin, Walter
Image/Music/Text 180, 193; *see also* Barthes, Roland
Impressionism 102, 104–105, 111
In a Dark Time: The Apocalyptic Temper in the American Novel of the Nuclear Age 186, 194; *see also* Dewey, Joseph
In Recognition of William Gaddis 161, 171, 184, 186, 190, 196; *see also* Kuehl, John; Moore, Steven
India 168

Infinite Jest 165–167, 191, 198; *see also* Wallace, David Foster
Ingendaay, Paul 184, 185, 195
The Inoperative Community 182, 196; *see also* Nancy, Jean-Luc
Introduction to Metaphysics 182; *see also* Husserl, Edmund
Io 78
Irenaeus 86
Irun (Spain) 15
Isis 78
Italy 32, 61, 172, 173

J R 1–2, 6, 30, 36–39, 41–43, 48–50, 54–57, 90, 92, 96, 102, 120–121, 125, 126–142, 143, 162, 164, 171, 176, 177, 181, 183, 186, 187, 188, 190, 195
Jack's Book: An Oral Biography of Jack Kerouac 182, 195; *see also* Gifford, Barry; Lee, Lawrence
Jackson Pollock: Interviews, Articles, Reviews 183, 197; *see also* Pollock, Jackson
James, Henry 59–60, 174, 177, 195; *see also The Bostonians*
James, Montague Rhodes 185, 195
James, William 42, 47, 54, 60, 185, 195; *see also Pragmatism and Other Writings*; *The Varieties of Religious Experience*
Jameson, Fredric 195
Jarry, Alfred 165
Jeffers, Robinson 149
Jesus Christ 4, 6, 16, 35, 66, 70, 97–98, 116–125, 134, 139; *see also* Christianity
John the Baptist 117
Johns, Jasper 112
Johnston, John 2, 12, 14, 17, 25, 71–73, 111, 171, 172, 173, 179, 180, 184, 190, 195
Josipovici, Gabriel 178, 195
Jove 78
Joyce, James 87, 91, 114, 127, 171, 181, 184, 187, 195; *see also A Portrait of the Artist as a Young Man*
Judaism 32, 65, 95, 122
Jung, Carl 63–64, 72–73, 109–110

Kafka, Franz 54
Kant, Immanuel 76, 93
Karl, Frederick 10
Keats, John 58
Keith Botsford Papers (Yale) 180, 194
Kenner, Hugh 185, 195
Kermode, Frank 88, 90, 181, 195; *see also The Sense of an Ending*
Kerouac, Jack 101–102, 182, 196; *see also The Subterraneans*
Kierkegaard, Søren 65–67, 179, 196
Kigali 189
Kingsley, Charles 61
Kline, Franz 111
Knight, Christopher J. 4–5, 129, 137, 139, 161, 173, 177, 184, 186, 187, 188, 190, 195, 196

Koening, David 196
Kogan, Herman 190, 196
Kraus, Karl 30–31
Kristeva, Julia 71, 73
Kuehl, John 161, 171, 184, 186, 190, 196

Lake Rudolf 144, 148
Leaves of Grass 99
Lebed, Jonathan 171
LeClair, Thomas 58, 67, 177, 179, 181, 186, 187, 190, 196
Lectures on Shakespeare 176, 193; see also Auden, W.H.
Lee, Lawrence 101, 182, 195
Léger, Fernand 108–109, 183
Letters from the Earth 62; see also Twain, Mark
Letters of Wallace Stevens 179, 198; see also Stevens, Wallace
Levellers 33
Lévy, Sophie 183, 196; see also *A Transatlantic Avant-Garde: American Artists in Paris 1918–1939*
Lewis, Wyndham 6, 107, 196
Libya 15
Lin, Yu-Chin 196
Linnaeus 81
"Literature and Crisis" 96
Lithuania 167
"Little Gidding" 77–78, 180; see also *The Four Quartets*
Logan, Marie-Rose 58, 177, 196
The Long Revolution 9, 10, 18, 171, 173, 198; see also Williams, Raymond
Lyotard, Jean-François 161, 190, 196

Madoff, Bernie 1
Madrid (Spain) 15–17, 20–21, 23
Málaga (Spain) 16
Male and Female 109
Mallarmé, Stéphane 98
Mandeville, Bernard 127
Mann, Thomas 114; see also *Doctor Faustus*
Marcel Duchamp, 1887–1968, Art as Anti-Art 183, 196; see also Mink, Janis
Marcus, Ben 190, 196
Marx, Groucho 66, 116
Marx, Karl 98, 176, 185, 196; see also Engels, Friedrich; *The German Ideology*
Marxism 32, 123
Masai 144, 154
M*A*S*H 166
Massapequa (New York) 15
The Masterpiece 114; see also Zola, Emile
Matta, Robert 109
Matters of Life and Death 52; see also Wolff, Tobias
McHugh, Roland 196
McGrath, Charles 177, 196
Mecca 32
Mekong Delta 122; see also Vietnam

Melville, Herman 59–60, 86, 88, 90–91, 93, 118, 180, 185, 196; see also *The Confidence Man*; *Moby Dick*
Memling, Hans 104, 108, 110
Mencken, H.L. 30, 174, 196; see also *The American Language*
Mephistopheles 89
Mercury 78
The Metamorphoses 77–78, 180, 197; see also Ovid
"The Metaphysical Poets" 53; see also Eliot, T.S.
Metaphysics as a Guide to Morals 65, 178, 196; see also Murdoch, Iris
Methodists 33
Metropolitan Museum of Art 109, 112, 183
Mexico 9
Michelangelo 97, 99
Miller, Arthur 172
Miller, J. Hillis 196
Milton, John 51
The Mimic Men 34; see also Naipaul, V.S.
Minimalism 102, 111
Mink, Janis 183, 196; see also *Marcel Duchamp, 1887–1968, Art as Anti-Art*
Minor Prophecies: The Literary Essay in the Culture Wars 177, 195; see also Harman, Geoffrey
Mirkowicz, Tomasz 58, 177, 196; see also Logan, Marie-Rose
The Mirror and the Lamp: Romantic Theory and the Critical Tradition 179, 193; see also Abrams, M.H.
Mr. Difficult 7, 69–70, 160, 167, 179, 189–190, 191, 194; see also Franzen, Jonathan
Mitchell, David 163–164, 183, 190, 196; see also *Ghostwritten*
The Moan of the Tiber 35–36
Moby Dick 91, 93, 118, 185, 196; see also Melville, Herman
MoMA see Museum of Modern Art
Mona Lisa 39
Mondrian, Piet 108, 109, 183
Montaigne, Michel de 78
Montmartre (France) 108
Moore, Steven 161, 171, 184, 186, 190, 196
Morales, Eulalio Abril 172
More, Robert Pattison 185, 197; see also Palmer, Philip Mason; *The Sources of the Faust Tradition: From Simon Magus to Lessing*
Morocco 15–16, 173
Morris, Robert 102
Morrissey, Ted 179, 196
Mozart, Wolfgang Amadeus 53, 55, 130
Muggleton, Ludowick 33
Muggletonians 33
Muldoon, Paul 52
Mulisch, Harry 90
Munich (Germany) 168

Murdoch, Iris 65, 178, 196
Museum of Modern Art (MoMA) 109–110, 183
Myth, Magic, and Morals: A Study of Christian Origins 185, 194; *see also* Coneybeare, F.C.

Nabokov, Vladimir 30
Nadel, Arthur G. 1
Nagasaki 19
Naipaul, V.S. 34; *see also The Mimic Men*
Nalut (Libya) 15, 17
Nancy, Jean-Luc 98–99, 182, 196; *see also Being Singular Plural; The Inoperative Community*
Napoleon Bonaparte 71
Napper, John 10, 15, 171, 173
Napper, Pauline 173
New Criticism 10, 92
New York City 1, 2, 11, 15, 17, 35, 53, 69, 59–60, 83, 84, 102, 108–110, 112, 163, 171, 173, 181, 183, 191
Newton, Isaac 179
Nicaragua 149
Nietzsche, Friedrich 12, 19, 88, 92, 115, 118, 121–123, 124, 179, 184, 185, 186, 196; *see also The Anti-Christ*
The Nigger of The Narcissus 54, 177, 182, 186, 194
1984 168, 181, 197; *see also* Orwell, George
Nuttall, A. D. 51, 176, 197

Okinawa 163
"Old Foes with New Faces" 61, 63–64, 66, 99, 116, 178, 181, 185, 186, 195
Old School 51, 176, 198; *see also* Wolff, Tobias
Olson, Clarence E. 191, 197
On Painting 81, 180, 193; *see also* Alberti, Leon Battista
"On the Relation Between the Secular Liberal State and Religion" 186, 195; *see also* Habermas, Jürgen
"On William Gaddis: In Recognition of James Joyce" 171, 181, 184, 193; *see also* Benstock, Benard
"Ontology of the Photographic Image" 82, 180, 193; *see also* Bazin, André
Oppenheimer, Dr. J. Robert 174
The Origins of Totalitarianism 189, 193; *see also* Arendt, Hannah
Ortega y Gasset, José 182
Orwell, George 181, 197; *see also 1984*
Ovid 77–79, 81, 180, 197; *see also The Metamorphoses*
The Oxford Companion to English Literature 178, 194
Oxford English Dictionary 166, 175, 190
Ozick, Cynthia 186, 197

The Painted Word 111–112, 184, 198; *see also* Wolfe, Tom

Palmer, Philip Mason 185, 197; *see also* More, Robert Pattison; *The Sources of the Faust Tradition: From Simon Magus to Lessing*
Pan 78
Panofsky, Erwin 80–82, 85, 180, *see also* "Perspective as Symbolic Form"; "Style and Medium in the Motion Picture"
Paper Empire: William Gaddis and the World System 58, 172, 175, 177, 181, 182, 186, 187, 188, 190, 198; *see also* Shavers, Rone; Tabbi, Joseph
Paris (France) 11, 13, 14, 15, 89, 105, 108, 110, 114, 168, 173
Pascal, Blaise 96
Paul (Apostle) 6, 31, 115–125, 153, 178
Paul: The Mind of the Apostle 185, 198; *see also* Wilson, A.N.
Péguy, Charles 165
"Perspective as Symbolic Form" 80, 180, 197
Perspectives of World History see The Decline of the West
Peter Pan (book) 140, 142, 188, 193; *see also* Barrie, J.M.
Peukert, Helmut 186, 197
Phelps, Guy Fitch 36, 174
Philosophical Investigations 154, 189, 198; *see also* Wittgenstein, Ludwig
The Philosophy of "As If": A System of the Theoretical, Practical and Religious Fictions of Mankind 6, 115, 185, 198; *see also* Vaihinger, Hans
Physics of the Earth and Planetary Interiors 191; *see also* Franzen, Jonathan
Picasso, Pablo 108, 110
The Picture of Dorian Gray 103–104, 183; *see also* Wilde, Oscar
Pierre 91; *see also* Melville, Herman
Pincher Martin 87
Pinker, Steven 129, 187, 197
Plato 12, 66, 73, 84–85, 92, 97, 116–117, 128, 175, 176, 187, 197
Pliny 190
Plowing the Dark 164, 190, 197; *see also* Powers, Richard
Politics 189, 193; *see also* Aristotle
Pollock, Jackson 6, 102, 109–110, 112, 183, 197
Pope, Alexander 77–79, 81, 179, 180, 197; *see also* "Essay on Man"
Portinari, Tommaso 69–70
Portinari Alterpiece 69–70
A Portrait of the Artist as a Young Man 114, 127, 184, 187, 195; *see also* Joyce, James
Posner, Richard 183, 197
The Postmodern Condition: A Report on Knowledge 190, 196; *see also* Lyotard, Jean-François
The Postmodern Turn 177, 195; *see also* Hassan, Ihab
Powers, Richard 6, 7, 164–166, 169, 190, 197; *see also Galatea 2.2; The Gold Bug Varia-*

tions; *Plowing the Dark*; *Three Farmers on Their Way to a Dance*
Pragmatism 42, 90
Pragmatism and Other Writings 185, 195; *see also* James, William
Prester John 162
The Principle of Hope 178; *see also* Bloch, Ernst
The Protestant Ethic and the Spirit of Capitalism 185, 198; *see also* Weber, Max
Proust, Marcel 190
Pseudo-Clementines see *Clementine Recognitions*
Pynchon, Thomas 45, 88, 93, 111, 164, 176, 190, 197; *see also The Crying of Lot 49*
Pythagoras 97

Quakers 33
Quintilian 190

Raban, Jonathan 176, 197
Rabelais 27
Ransom, John Crowe 179
Rauschenberg, Robert 102, 111
Ray, Man 108
A Reader's Guide to The Recognitions 171, 173, 174, 178, 179, 185, 196
Reaganomics 131
Real Presences: Is There Anything in What We Say? 56, 177, 198; *see also* Steiner, George
The Recognitions 2, 3, 4, 5, 6, 9–26, 35–36, 42, 45, 47, 50, 54–55, 57–58, 66–68, 69–85, 86–90, 92, 95, 98–100, 101–114, 115–119, 125, 127, 130, 143, 161–162, 164, 167, 171–185, 190, 195
Reed, Rebecca 36
Reeve, John 33
Rembrandt 110
Remembrance of Things Past 190; *see also* Proust, Marcel
Remnants of Auschwitz: The Witness and the Archive 189, 193; *see also* Agamben, Giorgio
The Republic 128, 184, 187, 197; *see also* Plato
Retiro Park 16
Return to Sorrento 35
Richards, I.A. 58, 92
Ricoeur, Paul 62–64, 176, 178, 197
The Road to Botany Bay: An Exploration of Landscape and History 25, 174, 194; *see also* Carter, Paul
Robins, John 33
Rockefeller, Nelson 109
Rogers, Will 30
Rome (Italy) 14, 117
Rosenberg, Harold 112
Rothstein, Edward 56–57, 177, 197
Rousseau, Jean-Jacques 6, 98, 126–142, 186, 187, 188, 197
Rubens, Paul 110
Rufinus, Presbyter of Aquileia 197
The Rush for Second Place (book) 40, 51, 90, 175, 176, 177, 178, 181, 185, 187, 188, 189, 194, 195
"The Rush for Second Place" (essay) 127, 136, 185
Russell, Allison 12–14, 18, 25, 172, 197
Rwanda 189

Sacré Coeur 13
Safer, Elaine B. 185, 197; *see also The Contemporary American Comic Epic: The Novels of Barth, Pynchon, Gaddis, and Kesey*
St. Augustine 63, 116
St. Clement of Rome 117
St. John of the Cross 78
St. Louis (Missouri) 59, 86, 88, 168, 181, 185
Saint Paul (book) 185, 195; *see also* Grant, Michael
Saint Paul (person) *see* Paul (Apostle)
Saint Peter 117
St. Vincent Millay, Edna 20
Salemi, Joseph 183, 197
San Francisco 163
Saramago, José 90
Sawyer, Tom 197
Schlegel, Friedrich von 98
Schling, Max 111
Schmitt, Carl 146–147
Schopenhauer, Arthur 197
Schrenker, Marcus 1
Schryer, Stephen 37–38, 45, 175, 197
Schuchard, Ronald 177, 179, 197; *see also Eliot's Dark Angel: Intersections of Life and Art*
"The Second Coming" 162; *see also* Yeats, W.B.
Segovia (Spain) 17
The Self-Conscious Novel: Artifice in Fiction from Joyce to Pynchon 179, 198; *see also* Stonehill, Brian
The Sense of an Ending 88; *see also* Kermode, Frank
Serra, Richard 102, 183; *see also* "Tilted Arc"
Seville (Spain) 15, 20, 25, 172, 181
Sfax (Tunisia) 15, 17
The Shadow of the Pope 174; *see also* Williams, Michael
Shakespeare, William 29, 51–52, 177; *see also* Hamlet
Shavers, Rone 2, 172, 175, 177, 181, 186, 187, 188, 190, 193, 196, 197, 198; *see also Paper Empire: William Gaddis and the World System*
Shklovsky, Viktor 76–78, 82, 85, 180, 197; *see also Theory of Prose*
Shranks, Andrew 178, 198; *see also Faith in Honesty: The Essential Nature of Theology*
The Sickness Unto Death: A Christian Psychological Exposition for Upbuilding and Awakening 179, 196; *see also* Kierkegaard, Søren
Sidi-Bel-Abbés 15, 17

Index

Sierra de Guadarrama 16–17
Simon Magus 86, 117–118
Sinai Pennisula 145
The Singer on the Shore: Essays 1991–2004 178, 195; *see also* Josipovici, Gabriel
Six Months in a Convent 36; *see also* Reed, Rebecca
Skinner, B.F. 129, 187
Smith, Adam 132
Smith, Rev. Thomas 197
Smith, Zadie 169
Soby, James Thrall 101, 104, 182
The Social Contract 187; *see also* Rousseau, Jean-Jacques
Socrates 66
Solnit, Rebecca 188, 197
Some Like It Hot 134
The Sources of the Faust Tradition: From Simon Magus to Lessing 185, 197; *see also* More, Robert Pattison; Palmer, Philip Mason
Soviet Union 149, 5
Spain 3, 9–26, 171, 173
Speaking of Beauty 178, 194; *see also* Donoghue, Denis
Spencer, Nicholas 129, 135, 180, 187, 188, 197
Spengler, Oswald 118, 185, 198; *see also The Decline of the West*
Spinoza 198
Stark, John 185, 198
Steichen, Edward 108
Stein, Gertrude 102–103
Steinberg, Leo 112
Steiner, George 56, 177, 198
Stendhal 178
Sterne, Laurence 180
Stevens, Wallace 67, 179
Stonehill, Brian 179, 198; *see also The Self-Conscious Novel: Artifice in Fiction from Joyce to Pynchon*
Storming the Gates of Paradise: Landscapes for Politics 188, 197; *see also* Solnit, Rebecca
Strong Motion 168; *see also* Franzen, Jonathan
"Style and Medium in the Motion Pictures" 82, 180, 197
The Subterraneans 101–102, 182, 196; *see also* Kerouac, Jack
A Supposedly Fun Thing I'll Never Do Again 191, 198; *see also* Wallace, David Foster
Surrealism 102, 104–105, 108–111
Switzerland 173
Syrinx 78

Tabbi, Joseph 2, 40, 41, 58–59, 90, 164, 172, 175, 176, 177, 178, 181, 185, 186, 187, 188, 190, 193, 196, 197, 198; *see also Paper Empire: William Gaddis and the World System*
Tangier 15, 16
Tanner, Tony 185, 198; *see also City of Words: American Fiction 1950–1970*
Tany, Thomas 33
Tarr 107; *see also* Lewis, Wyndham
Tennessee 27, 31
Tennyson, Lord Alfred 57
Tertullian 63, 88
Theory of Prose 76, 180, 197; *see also* Shklovsky, Viktor
Thielemans, Johan 186, 198
Thompson, E.P. 168, 174, 198
Thoreau, Henry David 13–14, 59; *see also Walden*
Three Farmers on Their Way to a Dance 164–165, 190, 197; *see also* Powers, Richard
"Tilted Arc" 102, 183; *see also* Serra, Richard
Timebends: A Life 172; *see also* Miller, Arthur
Tolstoy, Leo 94
A Transatlantic Avant-Garde: American Artists in Paris 1918–1939 183, 196; *see also* Lévy, Sophie
"Trickle Up Economics: J R Goes to Washington" 131
Tudor-Pole, David 15
Tunisia 15
Twain, Mark 62–63, 128, 198
The Twenty-Seventh City 168, 191, 194; *see also* Franzen, Jonathan
"Two Geeks on Their Way to Byzantium" 190, 197; *see also* Powers, Richard
Tyrol 21

Uganda 142, 158
Ulysses 87, 184; *see also* Joyce, James
The Use and Abuse of Art 177, 193; *see also* Barzun, Jacques

Vaihinger, Hans 6, 115–116, 118, 185, 198; *see also The Philosophy of "As If": A System of the Theoretical, Practical and Religious Fictions of Mankind*
van der Goes, Hugo 69–70, 85, 89
van Eyck, Jan 104
The Varieties of Metaphysical Poetry 177, 179, 194; *see also* Eliot, T.S.
The Varieties of Religious Experience 60, 178, 195; *see also* James, William
Verdi, Giuseppe 78; *see also* Aïda
Vested Interests: Cross-Dressing and Cultural Anxiety 188, 195; *see also* Garber, Marjorie
"The Vienna Lecture" 94–95; *see also* Husserl, Edmund
Vietcong 122
Vietnam 122, 136, 188
Virginia 46
A Vision of His Own: The Mind and Art of William Gaddis 71, 179, 186, 188, 198; *see also* Wolfe, Peter
Vogue 109, 183
Vollmann, William T. 169, 190, 196

Wadlington, Warwick 185, 198; *see also The Confidence Game in American Literature*
Wagner, Richard 49, 98

Walden 13–14; *see also* Thoreau, Henry David
Walker, Christopher 171, 180, 198
Wallace, David Foster 7, 111, 164–166, 169, 198; *see also Infinite Jest*; *A Supposedly Fun Thing I'll Never Do Again*
The Waning of the Middle Ages 89; *see also* Huizinga, Johan
Warhol, Andy 102
Warren, Robert Penn 67
Waugh, Evelyn 5, 58, 59
Weber, Max 118, 185, 186, 198; *see also The Protestant Ethic and the Spirit of Capitalism*
Weisenburger, Steven 107, 183, 186, 198; *see also Fables of Subversion: Satire and the American Novel, 1930–1980*
Werner, Craig Hansen 184, 198; *see also Paradoxical Resolutions: American Fiction Since James Joyce*
What Henry James Knew 186, 197; *see also* Ozick, Cynthia
The White Goddess 72, 117–118, 185, 195; *see also* Graves, Robert
Whitehead, Alfred North 63, 64
Whitehead, Colson 6, 198; *see also John Henry Days*
Whitman, Walt 59, 99; *see also Leaves of Grass*
Wiener, Norbert 37–39, 45, 176, 198; *see also The Human Use of Human Beings: Cybernetics and Society*
Wilde, Oscar 103–104, 183; *see also The Picture of Dorian Gray*
The Will to Power 184, 196; *see also* Nietzsche, Friedrich
William Gaddis (book) 71, 187; *see also* Moore, Steven
"William Gaddis Calling: Telephonic Satire and the Disconnection of Authority" 187, 194; *see also* Conley, Tim
William Gaddis Papers: at Washington University in St. Louis 3, 7, 9–26, 171, 172, 173, 174, 180, 181, 182, 195; at the University of Texas, Austin 171, 173, 195; *see also* Keith Botsford Papers
Williams, Michael 174
Williams, Raymond 9, 10, 18–19, 171, 173, 174, 198; *see also The Long Revolution*
Williams, William Carlos 102–103
Wilson, A. N. 185, 198
Wimsatt, W.K. 92
Witness Against the Beast 174, 198; *see also* Thompson, E.P.
Wittgenstein, Ludwig 66, 154–156, 189, 198; *see also Philosophical Investigations*
Wolfe, Peter 71–73, 137, 179, 186, 188, 198
Wolfe, Tom 111–112, 184, 198
Wolff, Tobias 51, 176, 198
Wood, James 190, 198
Woodmere (New York) 11
"The Work of Art in the Age of Mechanical Reproduction" 70, 82, 180; *see also* Benjamin, Walter
World War I 75
World War II 9, 13–14, 20, 89, 95, 108, 157
Writing and Difference 178, 194; *see also* Derrida, Jacques
Wutz, Michael 99, 182, 198

Yale University 28
Yeats, William Butler 162

Zola, Émile 114

www.ingramcontent.com/pod-product-compliance
Lightning Source LLC
Chambersburg PA
CBHW032056300426
44116CB00007B/763